George Thomas Stokes

Ireland and the Anglo-Norman church

A history of Ireland and Irish Christianity from the Anglo-Norman

George Thomas Stokes

Ireland and the Anglo-Norman church
A history of Ireland and Irish Christianity from the Anglo-Norman

ISBN/EAN: 9783744723268

Printed in Europe, USA, Canada, Australia, Japan

Cover: Foto ©Lupo / pixelio.de

More available books at **www.hansebooks.com**

IRELAND

AND THE ANGLO-NORMAN CHURCH

A History of Ireland and Irish Christianity from the Anglo-Norman Conquest to the Dawn of the Reformation

BY THE
REV. G. T. STOKES, D.D.

Professor of Ecclesiastical History in the University of Dublin; Keeper of St. Sepulchre's Public Library, commonly called Archbishop Marsh's Library; and Vicar of All Saints', Blackrock

THIRD EDITION

London
HODDER AND STOUGHTON
27, PATERNOSTER ROW

MDCCCXCVII

PREFACE.

THE present volume, which I designate *Ireland and the Anglo-Norman Church*, is designed as a companion volume to a previous one which I entitled *Ireland and the Celtic Church*. The origin of the book which I now submit to the public was the same as the origin of the previous volume. They both embody the lectures, for the most part identically, and in some few places only substantially, the same as those which I delivered to my classes in Trinity College. The title which I have chosen for this volume, *Ireland and the Anglo-Norman Church*, expresses the object of my lectures, which was to sketch the history of Ireland as well as of Irish Christianity till the dawn of the Reformation. A very considerable portion of this volume will be found, therefore, to deal with the purely secular side of our annals, the story of the Anglo-Norman Conquest, and of the anarchy which ruined Ireland as the natural consequence of the strife and division which held sway in England. I have treated the ecclesiastical side of my subject in connection with the Anglo-Norman Church as I discussed the earlier history of Ireland in connection with the Celtic Church. I do not, indeed, believe that we can fix any hard and fast limit before which the Celtic Church system flourished, and after which the Anglo-Norman and Papal system prevailed. The process of change was a gradual one. The ecclesiastical revolution was effected by slow degrees, covering in its operations the whole of the eleventh and twelfth centuries. I have endeavoured, also, to prove in my concluding chapter, what might have been expected on *à priori* grounds, that the Celtic Church system did not expire at once, but left its marks deep printed on the manners and customs of the more Celtic portions of this country. Yet I consider the Anglo-Norman Church, with its canon law, its hierarchical and monastic organizations, the great force which shaped the religious life of Ireland during the ages which elapsed between the Anglo-Norman Conquest and the Reformation. If we contrast the Ireland of the tenth century, as pictured in the *Annals of the Four Masters*, with the Ireland of the thirteenth century, as depicted in the *Annals* of Pembridge and of Friar Clyn, we shall require no further proof that Ireland and the Irish Church were Anglicised in the meantime. *Congé d'élire* and Writ of restitution of temporalities, to take two instances alone, were terms never found in the Celtic Church; while they abound under the Anglo-Norman system.

The original shape of this work explains two points which will strike the critical reader, the repetitions and the omissions thereof. In the course of my lectures I had perpetually to refer to certain documents, like the *Liber Niger* or the *Repertorium Viride* of

Archbishop Alan, which can only be consulted in manuscript, and are little known. I. explained, with a frequency which may seem tiresome, what these and similar documents contain, and where they may be found. I might indeed have recast the whole shape of the lectures, and thus have avoided the repetitions, but second thoughts are sometimes in literature by no means the best thoughts. When a man writes with a young audience vividly before his mind, the salient points of a story are seized, the mere subsidiary details are avoided, and the historical picture is made clear because the canvas is not too much crowded with figures. This circumstance is, in fact, my defence against one line of criticism to which I have been subjected. My volume on *Ireland and the Celtic Church* has indeed received, for the most part, a very kind and generous treatment at the hands of reviewers. But some critics have found fault with its tone. It treated Irish history, in their opinion, in a style very different from the great masters thereof in the past, and discussed it in a very flippant spirit, as one stern censor put it. I must confess that I have suffered such critics and such criticism very gladly. There are some circles where obscurity is mistaken for profound thought, and pedantic dulness for surpassing learning. But then, if a member of such circles tried his methods upon a young university audience, his lecture-room would be a howling wilderness, and himself but the voice of one crying therein. I am paid by the University of Dublin to teach Ecclesiastical History. I hold that a professor is just like a preacher,—he should be a teacher and an interpreter; and if students avoid the professor's prelections, or a congregation flee from the preacher's sermons, as if his words carried the plague with them, then whatever else professor or preacher may be fitted for, he is not fitted for the office he has assumed.

I did not submit my former volume, I do not submit my present volume, as exhaustive histories of the periods with which they deal, but I do submit them as attempts to redeem Irish history from its traditional dulness, and to show that it is not the pathless waste which some regard it. In doing so I have made it my object to interpret to young and eager minds the results attained by the great investigators, living and dead, whose works I have so frequently quoted, and have, therefore, systematically striven to make my narrative as interesting as I possibly could, a task at times by no means an easy one.

The origin of this work accounts also for its many omissions. Everyone desires to know something about the Conquest of Ireland, the Wars of Bruce, the Statute of Kilkenny, and Poynings' Act. I have devoted my efforts to illustrate these and other leading features of my period. I could have filled lectures with the numberless incidents which occupied the intervals of Irish history, but I had to bring my book within a limit marked out by the publishers, and have therefore been compelled to omit even much which I delivered to my class. Another cause forced me in the same direction. It will strike the reader that I have treated the earlier portion of my period much more fully than the latter, and necessarily so. A vast quantity of new light has been shed upon Irish as well as English history by the publications of the Record Commissioners, and by the great Rolls Series. Every lecture almost, embodied in this volume, owes something to the *Calendars of Irish Documents*, edited by Mr. Sweetman. These calendars deal with the thirteenth century, but go no farther. The last volume, including the taxation of Pope Nicholas, comes down to the year 1307, and stops there; and now, as I understand, the publication of these Irish calendars has been completely suspended, while the English work goes on as before.

Until the production of these works is resumed, we cannot hope for any fresh light upon the troubled epochs of Irish history covered by the fourteenth and fifteenth centuries.[1]

In conclusion I have to acknowledge my renewed

---

[1] The story of Anglo-Norman dominion in Ireland will never be fully known till the Rolls Series embody the documents lying in MS. in Dublin, viz., the *Liber Niger* and the *Repertorium Viride* of Archbishop Alan, the *Crede Mihi*, the *Liber Niger*, and the *Liber Albus* of Christ Church. A sum of £3,000, I suppose, would print them all, yet the English Treasury and Record authorities have, on various petty pleas, withstood on this point the unanimous wish of the Irish representatives in Parliament of every type of politics. They are printing at present a volume of the Thomas-Court Registers, omitting the most valuable and interesting portion;

obligations to the many original investigators into the sources of Irish history. I have used them as far as I have known them, and have endeavoured in every case to acknowledge my debt. If I have ever omitted to do so, the omission has been due to a lapse of memory. I have had many testimonies as to the good results of my previous volume in stirring up an interest in Ireland's ancient history. I can only hope that the present work may be as fruitful, and tend in some small degree to a better understanding and a more kindly feeling among the various races, Norman, Saxon, Scandinavian, and Celtic, inhabiting England, Ireland, and Scotland.

GEORGE T. STOKES.

ALL SAINTS' VICARAGE, BLACKROCK,
  DUBLIN, *September 2nd*, 1889.

---

while they have declined Archbishop Alan's *Liber Niger* on the extraordinary plea that it is only a copy of original documents, and not the original documents themselves. Two reflections naturally suggest themselves in connection with such an objection. First, a copy of original documents, no longer existing, made in 1530, ought surely to be original enough for these times. Secondly, where in the world did the Editors of the Rolls Series get the originals of numberless documents they have already included in their series?

NOTE.

AT the suggestion of my friend the Rev. M. H. Close, I beg to warn the English reader that the Irish " c " is always pronounced hard. Lough Cé, for instance, should be pronounced as if Ke or Key, Cencora as if Kenkora; and also that Columba and Columcille denote one and the same person.—G. T. S.

CONTENTS.

LECTURE I.

LAST YEARS OF IRELAND'S INDEPENDENCE.

PAGE

Sources of Irish history during this period—Decay of the O'Briens—Rise of the O'Neills—Of the O'Conors—Cruelty of the princes—Misery of the people—Treaty at Athlone—State of Irish politics in 1150—And civilisation—Tiernan O'Rourke and Dermot MacMurrough—Extent of Leinster—Danish Kingdom of Dublin—Dermot's Library and the *Book of Leinster*—Dermot and Dervorgil—Dermot's expulsion and escape to England . . . . 1—23

LECTURE II.

THE HISTORIAN OF THE CONQUEST.

Giraldus Cambrensis and the Welsh Church—Morice Regan and his Poem—Anglo-Norman MSS. at Dublin—Sweetman's *Calendars*—Giraldus, his birth—The Fitz-Gerald family—Its origin—Nesta and her story—Education of Giraldus—Archdeacon of Brecknock—Office of archdeacons—"Can an archdeacon be saved?"—State of Welsh Church in the twelfth century—Comparison with the Celtic Church in Ireland and Brittany—Marriage of Welsh clergy—Hereditary benefices—Lay and fighting abbots in Wales—Portionist benefices—Archidiaconal visitations in Wales in twelfth century—Giraldus excommunicates the Bishop of St. Asaph—Election to St. David's and appeal to Rome—English kings and Welsh Church—The Cistercians—Pope Adrian's Bull and Henry II. . . . . 24—47

LECTURE III.

DERMOT'S INTRIGUES AND FOREIGN PREPARATIONS.

PAGE

King Dermot MacMurrough and Bristol—Irish priest and preacher in Wales—Welsh princes in Ireland—Story of Earl Harold and the Dublin princes—Rise and progress of the Hardings of Bristol—Peerage of Berkeley—Robert Harding, Reeve of Bristol—Builds St. Augustine's—Befriends King Dermot—Introduces him to Henry II.—Dermot's treaties with Strongbow and the Fitz-Geralds—His return to Ireland, A.D. 1168—Social life in Ireland, A.D. 1170—Arrival of the Fitz-Geralds at Bannow . . . . 48—70

LECTURE IV.

THE INVASION OF THE GERALDINES.

Authorities for the Geraldine invasion—Landing at Bannow—Junction with Dermot's forces—Attack on Wexford—Baronies of Forth and Bargy—Inhabitants and dialect—Military orations among the ancient Irish—Description and extent of Ossory—The Fitz-Patricks, its princes—Invasion of Ossory—Battle of Carrickshock—Of Slieve Margy—Character of Dermot—His treachery towards his Welsh allies—His letter to Strongbow . . 71—94

LECTURE V.

THE INVASION OF STRONGBOW.

Strongbow, his history and family—His expedition to Ireland—Sends Raymond le Gros in advance—Battle of Bag and Bun promontory—Lepers and leprosy in Ireland—Norman cruelty—Strongbow's arrival and capture of Waterford—Marriage of Eva—March to Dublin—The city's size and appearance—Walls—Capture, September 1170—Death of King Dermot—Roderic O'Conor attacks the capital—Battle of Finglas—Last Danish invasion—The Gillemoholmocks . . . . . . 95—120

LECTURE VI.

HENRY II. AND ANGLO-NORMAN CONQUEST.

PAGE

Henry II.—Character of his reign—Bishop Stubbs and Professor Freeman on—Jealous of Strongbow's progress in Ireland—Edict against aiding him—Preparations for Irish invasion—Henry sails to Waterford—Wright's geographical errors—Arrival at Dublin—Palace and hospitality there—Results of his residence—On princes—On people—Irish dysentery—Finglas and vindictive tempers of Irish saints—Organization of the Church—Synod of Cashel—And of the law—Ranulf de Glanville—Statute of Henry Fitz-Empress . . . 121—149

LECTURE VII.

NORMAN ORGANIZATION OF IRELAND.

Office of Lord-Lieutenant—Origin of—First occupants of—Justiciary, office of—Relation to Chief Justice of King's Bench—Ireland and Egypt—Hugh de Lacy—Palatinates—Durham—Chester Parliament and Welsh Home Rule—Hugh de Lacy's career in Ireland—Marriage with Rose O'Conor—Want of continuous Irish policy—Murder of De Lacy—Strongbow as Justiciary—His death. . . . . 150—175

LECTURE VIII.

ST. LAURENCE O'TOOLE AND THE CATHEDRAL CHURCH OF THE HOLY TRINITY.

Anglo-Norman and Celtic Church in Ireland—Synod of Kells—St. Laurence O'Toole—Birth—Education—Abbot of Glendalough—Archbishop—Foundation of All Saints' Priory—Charter—*Repertorium Viride*—Archbishop Alan—St. Laurence and the Anglo-Normans—Attends Lateran Council—And royal council at Windsor—Council of Cashel—Royal supremacy—Charter of Laurence to Cathedral of Holy Trinity—Earliest clergy list of Dublin—Christ Church in twelfth century . . . 176—199

LECTURE IX.

JOHN COMYN AND THE ANGLO-NORMAN ARCHBISHOPS OF DUBLIN.

PAGE

English Church in middle ages—Royal supremacy—Episcopal laxity—Wimund, Bishop of Man, story of—St. Laurence last Celtic Archbishop of Dublin—Mediæval prelates all English—Archbishop Comyn—Early life as a lawyer—Consecration by the Pope—Bull of Lucius III. to See of Dublin—Controversy between Armagh and Dublin—Comyn as a courtier—Synod of Dublin, rules of—Addition of Glendalough to Dublin—John Comyn makes St. Patrick's a collegiate church—Erects St. Sepulchre's Palace—Manor and liberty thereof—Archiepiscopal prebend of Cualaun . . . . 200—226

LECTURE X.

AN EPISCOPAL VICEROY AND THE BEGINNING OF ANGLO-NORMAN ANARCHY.

Reign of King John and ecclesiastical troubles—Character of his reign—Failure of feudalism in Ireland—Grant of Ulster to John de Courcy—Quarrels with the family of De Lacy—Troubles from the De Burghs—History of William de Burgh—Visit of King John in 1210—John de Gray, Bishop of Norwich—As Viceroy—And Castle builder—Lough Ree and Randon Castle—Results of the Bishop's rule . . . . 227—250

LECTURE XI.

ARCHBISHOP HENRY OF LONDON AND ST. PATRICK'S CATHEDRAL.

Election of second Anglo-Norman Archbishop—Career as an archdeacon, a lawyer, and a judge—Course of promotion—English record system—His sporting tastes — Episcopal hunting — Last Bishop of Glendalough — Scorch-Villein — Deanery of Penkridge — Titles of

Dublin prelates—Lateran Council—Synod of Dublin—Archbishop Henry makes St. Patrick's a cathedral—Monastic chapters—Secular canons—Lambeth and Canterbury—Christ Church and St. Patrick's . 251—274

LECTURE XII.

THE WARS OF MEATH AND OF KILDARE, OR THE IRISH TROUBLES OF HENRY III.

Palatine jurisdictions in Ireland—Quarrels between Anglo-Norman nobles—Between De Lacy of Meath and De Courcy of Ulster—Arrest of De Courcy—Rebellion of De Lacy—And exile—War of Meath—William Marshall junior—English weakness—Siege of Trim—Crannogs—Intermarriage of Anglo-Norman, Welsh, and Celtic princes—History of Marshall family—Of William Marshall senior—Of his sons William and Richard—Plot against Richard—Henry III. and War of Kildare—Battle of the Curragh—Death of Richard Marshall, and extinction of the family of Eva . . . 275—306

LECTURE XIII.

TWO CENTURIES OF ANARCHY.

Limits of this volume—Specimens of Celtic and Anglo-Norman annals—Dismal character of Irish history in the fourteenth and fifteenth centuries—Irish anarchy and English wars—Henry III. and English supremacy—Ecclesiastical taxation—Development of English and of Irish parliaments—Sir John Wogan as Viceroy—Legislation of first Irish parliament—Committee of one—Useful modern precedent . . . . . . 307—321

LECTURE XIV.

THE WARS OF BRUCE AND OF THE ROSES.

Sir John Wogan and Edward I.—Scotch war—Irish correspondence—And promises—Invasion of Ireland by Edward Bruce—Complaint of Celtic princes to Pope John XXII.—Defeat and death of Bruce—Social disorganization of Ireland—Irish princes and Brehon law—Land question—Tanistry—Reign of Edward III.—French war and Ireland—Wickliffe—Franciscans in Ireland—Primate Richard Fitz-Ralph—Armagh primates—Black death in Ireland—Duke of Clarence and Statute of Kilkenny—Wars of the Roses—Butlers and Geraldines—Poynings' Act . . . . 322—342

LECTURE XV.

THE CELTIC CHURCH IN ANGLO-NORMAN TIMES.

Division of Irish Church—One part Celtic, the other Anglo-Norman—Church dedications—St. Nicholas of Myra—Columban order in Ulster—Derry—Iona—Fall of Iona—Celtic monasteries in the West—Contrast between Celtic and Anglo-Norman monasteries—The Celtic tonsure—Easter—The Culdees—Bishop Reeves upon—Celtic clergy in York Cathedral in A.D. 936—Culdees, hereditary officials—Survival at Armagh to the present time—Celtic literature in middle ages—Coarbs, or Corbes, and Herenachs—*Primate Colton's Visitation*—Marriage of an Abbot of Derry—Hostile Celtic monasteries—Episcopal battle at Clonmacnois in 1444—The last of the Irish chiefs—The "Episcopal Thirds"—The family of MacFirbis—Survival of ancient Celtic scholastic system—Spirit of the Anglo-Norman Church—Controversies—Persecution—Earliest Irish heretics—Foundation of Dublin University—Hostility of Anglo-Norman Church in middle ages towards Celtic clergy—Decree of Leo X. against the Celts—Utility of the study of Irish Church history . . . . 343—380

LECTURE I.

IRELAND AND THE LAST YEARS OF INDEPENDENCE.

I PROPOSE to give in this course of lectures a sketch of the history of Ireland and Irish Christianity from the conquest of Ireland by the Anglo-Normans down to the Reformation. In doing so I shall pursue the same course as I adopted in my previous volume dealing with the Celtic Church, and instead of treating my subject in the strict chronological order, I intend to select great personages of light and leading, or great central epochs, round whom I shall group the onward march of events.

The conquest of Ireland by Henry II. and by Strongbow is such a great epoch; much talked of, widely celebrated, but almost entirely unknown. It will be my object to withdraw that event from the region of mythical shadows into the clear light of historic day, using for that purpose the numerous contemporaneous documents, partly printed, partly still in manuscript, which our libraries possess. In order, however, to the full and perfect understanding of the conquest, we must previously realise to ourselves the state of Ireland during the last years of her national independence. To that work I shall devote the present chapter.

Whence, then, it may be asked, do we gain our information concerning the events of that period? The reply is easy. The various annalists—contemporaneous or else gaining their knowledge from contemporary documents, the *Book of Leinster*, the *Annals* of Clonmacnois, of Lough Cé, of Ulster, and of the Four Masters, together with the *Chronicon Scotorum*—furnish abundant information from the Celtic side, while the works of Giraldus Cambrensis and a curious Anglo-Norman poem, the substance of which is attributed to Morice Regan, secretary or chief domestic to Dermot MacMurrough, will supply us with vivid living traditions of the times from an opposite standpoint.[1] Let me endeavour to give you a picture of the social, political, and ecclesiastical life of Ireland as we find it in the first half of the twelfth century.

---

[1] All these works are now, or will shortly be, accessible to the general reader with one exception. A few words of explanation may, however, be useful. The *Book of Leinster*, otherwise called the *Book of Glendalough*, is one of the most important Celtic MSS. in existence. It dates from the twelfth century. The portion which now remains consists of one hundred and seventy-seven loose leaves of vellum in the library of Trinity College, Dublin, and of eleven leaves in the hands of the Franciscans of the Irish province. See Mr. Gilbert's *National MSS. of Ireland*, Nos. liii—lv. A transcript of it in folio, with introduction, analysis, and index by Professor Atkinson, was published in 1880 by the Royal Irish Academy. The MS. probably formed a part of King Dermot MacMurrough's library. The *Annals of Clonmacnois* exist only in an English translation made in the year 1627, three MS. copies of which have come down to us, one in the library of Trinity College, Dublin, another in the British Museum, and a third in Sir Thomas Phillips' library; see O'Curry's *Lectures on Irish MS. Materials*, p. 130 (Dublin: 1861). The *Annals of Lough Cé* have been published in two volumes by Mr. Hennessy in the Rolls Series. They are described by Mr. O'Curry in his *Lectures*, ed. 1861, p. 93. They were the annals of the MacDermot clan, and were composed at their residence, situated on an island in Rockingham demesne, the seat of the late

The eleventh century commenced with the battle of Clontarf, followed and marked by the predominance of the O'Brians in Ireland, a family which finds a living representative to this day in the Barons Inchiquin of the county Clare. The eleventh century opened with the splendid achievements of Brian Boru; the century closed with the decay and downfall of the O'Brian family, scarcely one of whom displayed any traces of the genius manifested in their great ancestor. So passed the eleventh century. The twelfth century was marked by the dominance of two families; on the one hand, by the restoration and revival of the O'Neills of the north, and on the other by the sudden rise to fame and fortune of the O'Conors of Connaught, dynasties whose bitter strife and restless ambition led finally to the Anglo-Norman conquest. To the development of this story —a very tangled and a very bloody skein, by the way— we must now bend our best attention. In the year 1083 Donnall O'Loughlin, a descendant of Niall of

---

Colonel King-Harman, M.P. The *Annals of Ulster* are now in process of publication, the first volume having appeared in 1887 under the direction of Mr. Hennessy and at the expense of the Royal Irish Academy. They were composed towards the close of the fifteenth century. Mr. Hennessy considers the *Annals* of Ulster and of Lough Cé superior in honesty and accuracy to those of the Four Masters. O'Curry describes them at length in his fourth Lecture. The *Chronicon Scotorum* is an ancient volume of annals composed in the Abbey of Clonmacnois prior to the Norman invasion of 1172. It has been published in the Rolls Series, under the editorship of Mr. Hennessy. The *Annals of the Four Masters* form a compilation out of the ancient annals known in their time by, Michael O'Clery and three other monks of the Franciscan monastery of Donegal. This great work was composed between the years 1632 and 1636. It was printed in seven volumes under the direction of Dr. John O'Donovan, and at the expense of Mr. Smith, a Dublin publisher, in 1851. The *Annals of the Four Masters* are fully described in Mr. O'Curry's seventh Lecture, and in Dr. O'Donovan's learned preface.

the Nine Hostages,[1] and an ancestor of the Ulster
O'Neills of Queen Elizabeth's time, became chieftain of
a comparatively insignificant tribe of northern Ireland.
He was an ambitious, a vigorous, and a brave ruler.
He reigned for forty years; and long reigns had one
great advantage in those times of anarchy—they were
continuous in policy and in design. Donnall O'Loughlin
rapidly developed and increased his power, smote down
his enemies on every side, and by the time of his death,
which happened at Derry on February 9th, 1121, he
had reigned for twenty-seven years as supreme king
over all Ireland, and thirty-eight years over his own
principality. The eulogy of the Four Masters upon
him, as recorded under that date, will give a fair
specimen of the very high-flown language in use among
the ancient Irish chroniclers, since he is there described
as "the most distinguished of the Irish for personal
form, family, sense, prowess, prosperity and happiness,
and for bestowing of jewels and food upon the mighty
and the needy."[2] Twenty years afterwards, or thereabouts, another king of the same family arose named
Murtogh O'Loughlin, who reigned, from 1140 to 1166,
with a vigour which gained for him the same position
as supreme king. But as it is now, so was it then.
Ulster and Connaught are now violently opposed to

---

[1] The descendants of Niall of the Nine Hostages (A.D. 400)
divided themselves into two great branches; first the southern
O'Neills, represented by the Kings of Meath, the Melaghlins;
secondly the northern O'Neills, called O'Loughlins. Niall of
the Nine Hostages is in the female line still represented in
the peerage by Lord O'Neill, of Shane Castle, county Antrim
(see Keating's *Hist. of Ireland*, ed. O'Mahony, pp. 719, 723).

[2] The same kind of language was used among the Welsh
about their favourite princes and warriors. See the Welsh
Chronicle, A.D. 1137, about Gruffyth ap Rees, Prince of
South Wales.

each other as regards some of the keenest human interests; Ulster and Connaught were just as bitterly opposed seven hundred years ago.

The county Roscommon is one vast plain, noted to the present day as the richest feeding-ground for oxen. The county is devoid of mountains save on its eastern and north-eastern boundary, where the Curlew range affords some fine scenery. A district which extends from Roscommon to Elphin, and from Strokestown to Castlerea, was ruled about the year 1100 by a family named O'Conor, many representatives of whom still exist there in every rank of life; the direct descendants indeed of these chieftains having often represented the county, and being widely known as The O'Conor Don. Now mark the progress of events. In 1106 the O'Brians of Clare still exercised a shadow of their ancient supremacy; for ancient name, and fame, and allegiance do not easily die out in Ireland. As supreme kings, they made Torlogh O'Conor ruler of the Roscommon principality, which, in his hands, developed into a kingdom, dominating the O'Brians themselves, his ancient patrons; and finally, upon the death of Murtogh O'Loughlin, attaining supreme authority over all Ireland under Roderic O'Conor,—only to yield it up, however, five or six years afterwards, to the Normans and Henry II. The history of Ireland from 1100 to 1170 turns round these two houses and their struggles, the O'Loughlins of Ulster, the northern O'Neills, descended from Niall of the Nine Hostages, representing the ancient kings; and the O'Conors, an important but still upstart race of usurpers striving to wrest the sceptre from hands consecrated by time and the nation's reverence. I will not weary you with an attempt to depict the varying fortunes of the contest. These you can read for yourselves, if so inclined, in the monotonous pages of the Four Masters, or of the *Annals* of Ulster or of Lough Cé. The O'Conors on the one side, the O'Loughlins on the other, strove to attain their purposes by perpetual raids and plundering forays upon their neighbours round about, sweeping away their cattle, burning their corn, plundering their houses. It is scarcely possible to imagine how any kind of prosperity could have dawned upon this unhappy country amid the scenes depicted by the Four Masters, or by any other of the numerous annalists. The kings themselves lived pretty secure. O'Conor at Croghan, in Roscommon; the O'Brians at Cencora, near Killaloe; the O'Loughlins at Aileach, near Derry, lived safe and secure behind their entrenchments,—massive earthworks which to this day excite the curiosity of the traveller, and, down to Queen Elizabeth's day, gave quite sufficient employment to the gunpowder and the ordnance of a more advanced civilization.[2] But the unfortunate peasantry must have lived in daily terror of their lives, and in a state of

---

[1] See Hennessy's edition in the Rolls Series.

[2] Fynes Morison thus describes one of these forts in the county Antrim, still used in the reign of Queen Elizabeth:— "The fort of Innisloughlan is seated in the midst of a peat bog, and is no way accessible but through thick woods very hardly passable. It has about it two deep ditches, both compassed with strong palisades, a very high and thick rampart of earth and timber, and well flanked with bulwarks" (*History of Ireland*, ii. 190). See also an extract from Petrie's unpublished essay on the military architecture of Ireland, in Petrie's Life, by W Stokes, M.D., p. 221. The crannogs, or fortified islands, continued in use among the Celts from the earliest times down to the end of the seventeenth century. See *Irish Archæological Miscellany*, p. 233, for an instance of their use in A.D. 1448—49. The English used the same kind of fortifications till the arrival of the Normans. See G. T. Clark's *Mediæval Military Architecture*, vol. i., ch. ii., p. 30 (London: 1884), where the following description is given of

insecurity utterly fatal to all improvement. Within these entrenchments, strengthened by formidable palisades of sharpened piles and stakes, the kings maintained a certain barbarous extravagance. Thus the *Annals of Ulster* tell us that in 1107 Cencora, the residence of the O'Brians at Killaloe, was burned, when there was consumed "seventy tons of drink called mead and of old ale."[1] But their mode of life proved destructive to the morals of the kings themselves. They lost all sense of religion and its obligations amid their ambitious projects. In my previous lectures on the history of Ireland from St. Patrick to the Norman Conquest, I showed how a knowledge of Byzantine art and literature penetrated to this country.[2] With Byzantine accomplishments, however, there came Byzantine vices as well. Truth and mercy disappeared from Byzantine morals. Faithlessness and cruelty marked each successive dynasty which held the throne of the Eastern empire, and defiled the sacred precincts of the Holy Eastern Church itself. So it was, and even worse in Ireland. Cruelty and falsehood were peculiar to no race of princes, but displayed themselves equally in the

---

Anglo-Saxon fortified residences of earth and timber :—" In viewing one of these moated mounds we have only to imagine a central timber house on the top of the mound, built of half trunks of trees, set upright between two waling pieces at the top and bottom, like the old church at Greensted, with a close paling around it, along the edge of the table top, perhaps a second line at its base, and a third along the outer edge of the ditch, and others not so strong upon the edges of the outer courts, with bridges of planks across the ditches and huts of 'wattle and dab,' or of timber, within the enclosures, and we shall have a very fair idea of a fortified dwelling of a thane or franklin in England from the eighth or ninth century down to the date of the Norman conquest."

[1] Cf. *Annals of Lough Cé*, ed. Hennessy, in Rolls Series, vol. i., p. 97.

[2] See *Ireland and the Celtic Church*, chaps. ix., xi., xii.

O'Loughlins, the O'Conors, and the O'Brians, as well as in the inferior chiefs, who showed themselves apt pupils of their betters. Let us take a few specimens which will illustrate more vividly than any description of mine the social life of Ireland during the last years of independence. The light they cast is a very lurid one indeed. Thus, to take the charge of cruelty first. Blinding, quite after the Byzantine fashion, was the ordinary fate reserved for dangerous captives, yea, and even for the members of the princely families who became obnoxious to the reigning sovereigns. The Empress Irene, about the year 800, blinded her own son when he threatened to become dangerous to her supreme power. King Torlogh O'Conor in 1136 blinded his own son Hugh when he was becoming dangerous. Five years later we read that Dermot MacMurrough, of whom we shall have much more anon, blinded Murtogh MacGillamocholmog, chief of Fercullen, a district near our own city of Dublin, together with twenty of his chief men.[1] While, again, in 1153 we hear of Melaghlin or Molloy, King of Meath, blinding his cousin Conor Melaghlin, and of Dermot MacMurrough, ever the

---

[1] The clan MacGillamocholmog inhabited the country through which the Dodder flows (see O'Donovan's note, *Ann. Four Masters*, A.D. 1044). In ancient Dublin there was a street called after their name (see Gilbert's *History of Dublin*, t. i., p. 233). The princes and chiefs of this family often appear in Anglo-Norman documents (see Gilbert's *Chartularies of St. Mary's Abbey*, Rolls Series, preface, p. xxiv; *Ann. Four Masters*, A.D. 1044, O'Donovan's edition). The *Rotuli Chartarum* (ed. T. D. Hardy, 1837, p. 173) gives the details of their property as it existed in the days of Henry II. They had fifteen carucates of land in the valley of Dublin, and some houses in the city itself. A charter of Luke, Archbishop of Dublin A.D. 1241, printed in the *Chartæ, Privilegia*, p. 24, published by the Irish Record Office, shows that the clan had property near the town of Rathcoole, in the county Dublin.

prince of evil-doers and of cruelty, blinding O'More, prince of Leix, in the Queen's County, and then with savage irony releasing the wretched man from the fetters in which he was bound. Scarcely a princely house throughout Ireland was there where some blind warrior lived not, occupying the corner of the hearth, and helping by the tale of his own wrongs and the speaking evidence of his sightless and mangled eyeballs to deepen that tribal hatred which was fast ruining Ireland. Permit me here to give you a word of warning. As a historian I must strive to be impartial. Specially as a historian of the Church, I am pledged to be fair and truth-telling. In this chair I know no politics, and hope to pander to no prejudices. Here, therefore, I am bound to tell you that cruelty of this wanton and hopeless kind was not limited to Ireland. It found a place among the more cultured and civilized Normans as well; and Mr. Freeman's pages or the *Chronicle of North Wales* will show how Henry II. treated his Welsh hostages in just the same fashion, rooting out their eyes, and parading them thus tortured round the walls of Caerleon when the brave townsmen refused to surrender at his summons. While again we learn that the Scotch Celts were possessed by the same bloodthirsty spirit, as we are told by the *Annals of Clonmacnois*, under date of 1098, that Donnell MacDonnogh, King of Scotland, was blinded in both his eyes by his own brother.[1]

Cruelty was not the only princely vice then prevalent. Treachery was closely allied with it. Let me give an illustration. In 1140 the ancient town of Athlone was just as important a military post as it

---

[1] Cf. *Ann. Four Masters*, ed. O'Donovan, A.D. 1100.

is to-day. The ancient Castle, still guarded jealously and fortified in modern fashion; the frowning batteries with guns all looking towards Connaught, speak clearly of the invasions expected from that quarter. Seven hundred years ago a Celtic dun of earth rose on the very same spot where now stands the Castle raised on the ancient site by King John's ecclesiastico-warrior architect John, Bishop of Norwich.[1] The Castle of Athlone has ever guarded the pass of the Shannon, and has seen many a hard fight for its possession, down to the last great struggle when De Ginkle defeated St. Ruth and destroyed the hopes of the Stuarts. In the early twelfth century it was just the same save that the attacks on the Celtic dun were infinitely more numerous, while the bridge which then connected the opposite shores of Meath and Connaught was a much more fragile structure than the long narrow rambling Elizabethan structure on which the famous struggle of July 1691 took place.[2] To Athlone in 1140 resorted Torlogh O'Conor, King of Connaught, to meet Melaghlin, King of Meath, whose kingdom bordered his own. O'Conor was in a penitent mood, it may have been; though the penitence and the religion were but short-lived. Gelasius, Primate of Armagh, had just made

---

[1] Athlone Castle, in Celtic times, was called the Bo-dun or Cow-Castle, or fort of the O'Conors. Bo-dun is the origin of the word bawn, which so often occurs in ancient Irish grants of property. A bawn was a fortified yard where cattle were secured. See Mr. Hennessy's edition of the *Annals of Lough Cé*, p. 207, cf. p. 245.

[2] This ancient and historic bridge was only removed forty-five years ago. Some Elizabethan monuments which stood upon it are now preserved in the cellars of the Royal Irish Academy. See two interesting pamphlets by the late Rev. J. S. Joly, Rector of Athlone, entitled *The Bridge of Athlone* and *Our Church Bell*.

his first visitation of Connaught, and succeeded at last in establishing the primatial jurisdiction of Armagh, hitherto jealously rejected, as involving the ecclesiastical supremacy of what to Connaught men was a foreign city and kingdom. Roman influence and ideas were steadily though slowly triumphing over ancient Celtic jealousies. "The churches of Connaught," we are told by the Four Masters, "were adjusted to the jurisdiction of Gelasius by Torlogh O'Conor and the chieftains of Connaught; and Patrick's successor and his clergy left a blessing on the king and his chieftains."

Under the influence of the mission thus held by the Primate himself, O'Conor invited Murrough Melaghlin of Meath to a conference at Athlone, which was duly held. The high contracting parties took mutual oaths, made mutual armistices, the bridge of Athlone was broken down (in token of peace, because only used for war), and they parted in apparent love and friendship. But the old Adam was too strong in O'Conor. The King of Meath doubtless withdrew his troops and tribesmen, trusting to the lately sworn oaths, and the flocks of Meath were grazing in peace. But then we read as the very next entry by the Four Masters: "Another wicker bridge was made by Torlogh across Athlone, and he devastated the west of Meath." So little binding force had oaths for him! The same Torlogh O'Conor three years later seized his own son, Rory O'Conor, and kept him a prisoner after he had solemnly sworn to keep the peace towards him, and the same year he captured the person and lands of Murrough, King of Meath, though the Primate of Armagh himself and the most venerated relics of Ireland, the staff of Jesus, the altar and shrine of

St. Kieran of Clonmacnois, the bells[1] of St. Fechin and of St. Kevin of Glendalough, had been solemnly invoked as witnesses and guarantees that peace should be preserved between Connaught and Meath. No oaths could bind O'Conor, and yet so little were this falsehood and cruelty regarded as blemishes, that when he died the annalists exhausted all the resources of their high-flown language in celebrating his panegyric. Thus they call this faithless, perjured, bloody tyrant "the flood of the glory and splendour of Ireland, the Augustus of the West of Europe, a man full of charity and mercy, hospitality and chivalry." Public opinion must have been in a low estate indeed when the religious teachers of the time—for they alone were the writers of history—could use such language about such a man. And yet he was not one whit worse than his neighbours. He merely acted towards the Melaghlins of Meath or the O'Neills of the north as they acted towards him.

It was a sad time, when every man's hand was against his neighbour, and when for the poor peaceable, industrious man there was neither light nor hope nor security.

To enable you to grasp the course of events which led up to the English conquest, you must understand the state of Irish politics about 1150. The northern O'Neills, princes of Tyrone, were the nominal kings of Ireland. O'Conor was seeking, but in vain, to deprive them of that very precarious and shadowy dignity. The kingdom of Meath and Tara—anciently and by right the supreme monarchy—was a kind of debatable

---

[1] About sacred bells and their profanation, see O'Donovan's note on *Ann. Four Masters*, A.D. 1044.

land between the two rivals. Just as Alsace and Lorraine and the Rhenish provinces have been in the past, and are destined still to be in the future, the battle-field between France and Germany, so Meath was at this time the perpetual battle-field between the kings of the north and of the west. Two individuals come now upon the scene whose deeds and quarrels contributed even more than those of the supreme kings to the making of Irish history.[1] Tiernan O'Rourke was Prince of Breifny, a district—to use modern phraseology—covering the counties of Leitrim and Cavan; or perhaps, to put it more exactly still, the dioceses of Kilmore and Ardagh, for the diocesan jurisdictions coincide more

---

[1] People sometimes think of these Irish princes, the Mac-Murroughs, O'Brians, O'Conors, and their fellows, as if they were simple savages, with no better culture or education than Red Indian chiefs. They were very cruel and very savage according to our ideas, but not more so than the English kings and nobles or the Welsh princes of their time. Dermot Mac-Murrough issued charters in regular form, and in the Latin language. In Mr. Gilbert's *Facsimiles of National MSS.* there will be found a charter issued by Dermot MacMurrough for the foundation of a Benedictine monastery at Duisk, now Graigenemanagh, in the county Kilkenny. In the same valuable publication there is contained the foundation charter of Holy Cross Abbey, issued by King Donnall O'Brian, of North Munster, in 1168. In fact the Irish annalists present the blackest side of their country's story; because, imbued with the spirit of their times, they thought nothing worth telling unless it dealt somehow with fighting, plunder, or murder. A series of Newgate Calendars would not give the truest picture of English life in the last century. We get scarcely a glimpse of social organisation or of material improvement from any of these sources. Yet there must have been skill, taste, and wealth when structures like Mellifont, Holy Cross, Cong Abbey, Cormac's Chapel at Cashel, and the Nun's Church with its exquisite carvings and mouldings at Clonmacnois, could be erected by Irish princes and ecclesiastics prior to the arrival of the Normans. These Irish princes erected castles after the model of the Anglo-Normans, as at Tuam, where Roderic O'Connor built a castle with strong central keep, courtyard

accurately than any other with the ancient tribal divisions of this country.[1] Dermot MacMurrough was Prince of Lagenia, or Leinster, a district embracing the modern Leinster less by the diocese of Meath on the north, which comprehends the ancient kingdom of Meath and the diocese of Ossory proper on the west, which corresponds to the kingdom of Ossory.[2] It is important that you should understand these local distinctions if you wish to follow aright the course of political development. Leinster and Dermot's kingdom, roughly speaking, embraced the country from Dublin and Naas on the north, to Wexford and Waterford on the south, touching in both directions on the bounds of Danish dominion. This Danish power, indeed, is a

---

fortified with outlying towers connected by curtain walls and protected by a deep fosse. See for a description of it a paper by Petrie in the *Dublin Penny Journal*, vol. i., pp. 99—147; Petrie's Life, by W. Stokes, M.D., p. 212 (cf. p. 282), for a disquisition on the excellence of the goldsmith's art at the court of King Torlogh O'Conor, at Roscommon, in the year 1123. The charters and other legal documents contained in the *Book of Kells* (see *Irish Archæological Miscellany*, pp. 137-49) prove the presence of the goldsmith's art, for instance, at Kells, together with the existence and legal transfer of individual property in that town about the year 1100. They show, too, that rent was paid in Ireland about the year A.D. 1000. Kells, it may noted, is one of the few places in the United Kingdom where traces of the old communal system of land-holding still survive. See Seebohm's *English Village Community*, p. 227 (London: 1883).

[1] Reeves' *Diocese of Dublin and Glendalough*; Graves on the tribes of ancient Ossory in the *Kilk. Archæological Journal*; *Three Fragments of Irish Annals*, ed. T. O'Donovan, LL.D. (Irish Arch. Soc.), pp. 8, 86; *Irish Archæological Miscellany*, p. 289.

[2] The kingdom of Leinster, broadly speaking, covered the south-eastern part of Ireland, from Dublin and the line of the Liffey and Barrow to Wexford and the Irish Sea. Its princes resided sometimes at Naas, or at the Hill of Allen, near Kildare, and in the twelfth century at Ferns, near which rises Mount Leinster, one of the finest mountains in Ireland.

most important fact, and has a special bearing on the course of our narrative; upon it, therefore, I must bestow a brief notice before I describe the quarrels of O'Rourke and of MacMurrough, which led up to the Conquest, in which the Danish population played no small part. The history of the Danes in Ireland has suffered under a grievous misapprehension. The Danes, as I explained in a previous course of lectures, were defeated by Brian Boru at Clontarf, but were not expelled from Ireland. Their supremacy was destroyed, but not their existence. Christianity, too, came to the relief of the Celtic Irish, and the conversion of the Danes rendered them more peaceable neighbours than they had previously been. Still, they did not sink into and coalesce with the mass of the Celtic population. Independent communities of Danes existed all round Ireland, and along the eastern coast of Scotland. The Scottish isles were ruled by Danish earls, whose fleets were ever ready to succour their Irish brethren,[1] or ally themselves for pay with the O'Neills of Ulster. Larne, Carlingford, Dublin, Wexford, Waterford, and Limerick were free Danish settlements during the twelfth century. Dublin was ruled by a family named Turkil,[2] or MacTurkil, which continued to occupy a high position both in Church and State during the thirteenth century. The Danes,

---

[1] Cf. *Annals of Four Masters*, A.D. 1142. In the years 1101, 1102, Magnus, King of Denmark, invaded Ireland with the help of the Manxmen, and fought a battle near Dublin. On that occasion the daughter of O'Brien, King of Munster, married the son of Magnus.

[2] See *Four Masters*, A.D. 1146, where MacTurkil is described as chief steward, or mayor, of Dublin. Gilbert's *Chartularies of St. Mary's Abbey*, in Rolls Series, t. i., p. 83, gives much information about this distinguished Danish family. Henry II. gave a portion of their estates to St. Mary's Abbey, Dublin. The family and name were known in England too (see Freeman's Appendix, *Norman Conquest*, iv., 780, on the Turkils

too, like the Anglo-Normans of later times, imbibed the same love for civil broils which marked the Celts of the period. The Danes of Dublin warred, for instance, upon the Danes of Waterford in 1137, and again in 1140 (cf. *Four Masters*), and defeated their countrymen, —a most dangerous kind of victory for themselves. The Irish chieftains were doubtless very glad to see such powerful and warlike neighbours destroying each other, specially when the Dublin Danes could muster two hundred ships.

Such was the position of Danish affairs. Let us now return to MacMurrough and O'Rourke and the native Irish. MacMurrough, King of Leinster, was a thorough villain. Providence sometimes works with very vile instruments, but never with a viler instrument than Dermot, King of Leinster, was. Yet with all his violence he was an energetic and an able man. Dermot's personal appearance is described by Giraldus (see *Ann. Four Masters*, A.D. 1172). His name indeed is, for most of us, but a shadow, and his personality has long since faded into that land of myth and fable which is, in scriptural phrase, "a land of darkness as darkness itself, and where the light is as darkness." Let us then strive to make it a reality; and for this we have abundant materials. This College, for instance, of our own, now the College of the Holy and Undivided Trinity, of Queen Elizabeth's foundation, is in its first origin a monument of one of Dermot MacMurrough's transient seasons of repentance. The Corporation of Dublin, again, possesses a Baldoyle estate of considerable value,

---

of Warwick, and the *Chronicle* of Joceline de Brakelonda, Camden Society's Series, p. 153). The name Turkil was not extinct so late as the last century. A brother of the celebrated Rev. Philip Skelton married, when Vicar of Newry about 1720, a Miss Turkil.

whose origin goes back to the same monarch. We have a charter, too, with his signature, witnessed by St. Laurence O'Toole,[1] setting forth an endowment granted by him about 1160 to the Abbey of Duisk, in Kilkenny. But we can go still further, and recover the books Dermot read, the education he received, the manner of men with whom he conversed. Let us see how this comes to pass. The *Book of Leinster* is a great collection of documents. Photius, a learned Greek patriarch, published in the ninth century some volumes of extracts accumulated during the course of a studious life, which he denominated a Bibliotheca, or a Library. The *Book of Leinster* is a similar bibliotheca or library of documents, written from time to time during the eleventh and twelfth centuries, many of them having been composed some time about 1120 or 1130, by the tutor to whom Dermot MacMurrough's education was entrusted. The *Book of Leinster* remained for more than seven centuries unedited,—till six years ago, when it was published in *facsimile*, and thoroughly analysed by our own Professor Atkinson, at the joint expense of this University and of the Royal Irish Academy.[2] Any of you can now consult it in our various libraries, and there you will find a volume which lay in the library and which exercised the attention of Dermot's early days. The careless or unsympathetic inquirer might easily be repelled from it. It is full of mythical stories. It goes

---

[1] Cf. Gilbert's *Facsimiles of Irish National MSS.*, No. LXII., and on the same page the charter of Holy Cross from Donnall O'Brian.

[2] A history and analysis of the *Book of Leinster* will be found in O'Curry's *MS. Materials for Irish History*, p. 186 (Dublin: 1861), and in the letterpress attached to Mr. Gilbert's *Facsimiles*, No. LIII. See also note on p. 2 above.

back to the Flood and before it, tracing the history of Ireland's various invasions thousands of years before the Christian era. But mingled with such legends there are scraps of genuine history which illumine the tangled and darksome past of Irish life.

There is another aspect, however, from which such literary efforts should be viewed. Egypt has been of late years rendering up its buried literary treasures, and among them we have found, not history alone, but legends, novels, poems, which are valuable as illustrations of the social life and literary influences which formed the national habits and character. Everyone nowadays recognises the vast influence exercised over men and women by the tales and poems poured by nurses into the ears of innocent childhood. The British Museum carefully collects and catalogues even the sixpenny children's books which come teeming from the press, on this special ground, that they will show future ages the social and literary influences which shaped our minds. And so, too, this *Book of Leinster* is most valuable, not alone for the true history which it contains, nor for the genuine annals which it embodies, but most of all as setting forth the social life, the habits, customs, the poetry and literary influences, amid which Dermot MacMurrough and men like him were cradled and trained. Read Professor Atkinson's analysis, and then you will cease to wonder at the civil strife of the twelfth century. Yea, rather, you will wonder how there could ever have been an hour's peace—not to speak of a year's—between tribes whose earliest notions must have been of war and mutual hate. One poem, for instance (p. 27), celebrates the story of the renowned King Conor MacNessa and his hospitality. He was a prudent man, too, and knew his guests right well; so before dinner, as each guest entered, the king secured his arms and piled them up in a strong chamber, lest they should run amuck at one another for some rough expression. And then, to show the nature of the guests, the poem celebrates one who from the time he took spear in hand wounded or killed every day some man of Connaught, and never slept comfortably unless the body of a Connaught man formed his pillow. The contents of the *Book of Leinster* will at once explain the career of Dermot and his brother chieftains. They were simply such as their education had made them. The *Book of Leinster* was written for the one purpose of exalting Leinster, and depreciating Connaught and Munster and everything connected with these provinces. One poet (p. 23) says, "If I had seven heads I could not tell all the prowess of the Leinster men even in a month, without seven tongues in each separate head"; and then, recalling the achievements of various battles, at the end of every tragedy adds, "'Twas the Leinster men killed them." This brief account of the *Book of Leinster* will prove, at any rate, that Dermot MacMurrough's character can be tested by a modern rule. Examine a man's library, and you can generally fairly gauge his habits and character. Examine the *Book of Leinster*, and you will not be surprised that Dermot MacMurrough's career was stained by bloodshed, vice, and falsehood.

MacMurrough belonged to a family which, for several generations, had reigned over Leinster,[1] and which still finds a lineal representative in that of the Kavanaghs

---

[1] Dermot MacMurrough was descended from a prince named Diarmaid, son of Mael-na-mbo, who succeeded to the principality of Leinster in the first half of the eleventh century. See

of the county Carlow. He was born about 1100, and was educated by Hugh MacGriffin, afterwards Abbot of Terryglass, in the county Tipperary. He ascended the throne of Leinster about 1135, and signalised the very year of his accession, according to the *Annals of Clonmacnois*, by attacking the city of Kildare, sanctified by the memory of St. Brigid, killing one hundred and seventy of the townsmen and of the members of the convent, and crowning his wickedness by taking the Abbess—the successor of St. Brigid—out of her cell, and compelling her to marry one of his courtiers. Henceforth his career was one continuous tale of violence. A lady, too, enters upon the scene. Tiernan O'Rourke, of Breifny, and Dermot MacMurrough had originally been suitors for the daughter of the King of Meath, Dervorgil by name.[1] O'Rourke succeeded in marrying her, though the lady favoured Dermot MacMurrough. Dermot, however, had his revenge. A man that would force the Abbess of Kildare to marry, a lady vested with even episcopal rights and authority, would not scruple to plot against another man's domestic felicity, and carry off another man's wife. So in 1152, when both parties had arrived at the mature age of forty at least, the princess Dervorgil and Dermot MacMurrough established a mutual correspondence; the lady signified, by trusty messenger, to Dermot where her husband had placed her during

---

Annals of the Four Masters, A.D. 1052, O'Donovan's edition, where the editor traces the succession of princes, and descent of the families of MacMurrough, Kavanagh, and Kinsellagh.

[1] Dervorgil was a common name in those times. See *Ann. Four Masters*, A.D. 1080 and the Index Nominum. The mother of John Balliol, King of Scotland, was so called. She was princess and heiress of Galloway. See *Stubbs, Const. Hist.*, i., 557.

one of his numerous predatory excursions. Thither MacMurrough marched, carried her off with all her cattle, and brought her to his own residence, at the town of Ferns, in the county Wexford.[1] This was too extreme an action even for that wild time, when marriage ties sat very lightly indeed upon Irish princes. O'Rourke appealed to Torlogh O'Conor, King of Connaught, his great ally, who assembled an army, marched against Dermot, defeated him, and restored Dervorgil to her rightful lord.[2] This laid the foundation of perpetual strife between O'Rourke and MacMurrough. Year after year the O'Neills of the north were summoned to Dermot's aid, while the O'Conors assisted O'Rourke; till at last a decisive crisis came, decisive for Ireland, for MacMurrough, and for England, too, embodying all the elements of violence, cruelty, and falsehood concerning which I have spoken. Mortogh O'Loghlin, of the northern O'Neills, was then supreme King of Ireland. He had sworn before the Primate of Armagh, upon the most solemn of Irish relics,—the staff of Jesus, given to St. Patrick by our Lord Himself,—to keep the peace with a number of chieftains whose names I will not attempt to repeat. As soon as he got them into his power he blinded one who is described as "the pillar of

---

[1] *Ann. Four Masters*, 1167. Dervorgil built the Nun's Church at Clonmacnois, the ruins of which are still visible. See O'Donovan's note *sub. an.* 1167. Morice Regan tells the story of Dervorgil's abduction with an evident relish. A successful achievement of that kind was clearly a thing to be proud of. The whole story reminds one of the scenes of the last century so vigorously depicted in Froude's *English in Ireland*.
[2] Dervorgil died at Mellifont, A.D. 1193, aged eighty-five. See note (c) *Ann. Four Masters* on that year, and 1152 and 1153 in same.

the prowess and hospitality of the Irish," and killed the others. This roused a number of the surrounding princes, who attacked Mortogh, utterly defeated his forces, and killed the sovereign himself, whom, notwithstanding his perjury and cruelty, the Four Masters describe as "the Monarch of all Ireland, the chief lamp of the valour, chivalry, hospitality, and prowess of the West of the world; a man who had never been defeated in battle till that time, and who had gained many battles." His defeat had many and far-reaching results. The O'Conors had always kept their eyes fixed on the supreme monarchy as the object of their highest ambition. And now this was their opportunity, when their rival was dead, and his country torn with civil strife. Rory O'Conor, son of the vigorous, though cruel and false, Torlogh, was now the monarch of Connaught. He assembled an army, marched to Dublin, purchased the alliance of the Danes, received the allegiance of the rebel tribes of the North, and then, turning upon Dermot MacMurrough, who alone held out, despatched against Dermot his ancient and deadly foe, Tiernan O'Rourke, burning with the remembrance of ten thousand injuries, public and private.

Dermot was now abandoned on every side. The Psalmist's words came true at last with Dermot as with many another: "Evil shall hunt the violent man to overthrow him." Dermot's cruelties had alienated his own tribesmen even, who forsook him on every side. O'Rourke easily defeated the few who remained faithful, seized Dermot's house at Ferns, and drove him forth an exile to seek aid from Henry II. of England. The *Book of Leinster* enables us to fix the

---

[1] See the events of this period briefly and vigorously told by the Four Masters, A.D. 1166.

very day of his defeat and exile. Upon the margin of folio 200 one of Dermot's scribes has written, under the date August 1st, 1166, "Oh Mary, it is a great deed that is done in Erin this day, the Kalends of August. Diarmid, son of Donnchadh MacMurchadha, King of Leinster and the Danes, was banished by the men of Ireland over the sea eastward. Uch! Uch! Uch! O Lord, what shall I do?"—despairing words of a courtier which yet are of deepest interest. They prove that bad as Dermot was there were some who loved him. They have a prophetic ring, too, about them, though the seer knew not of what he prophesied. It was a great thing that was then done, big with consequences for Ireland, and for England too, consequences which have not yet been completely developed. To trace the immediate results thereof and to describe the invasion of Ireland will supply ample materials for several lectures, and will show that our present difficulties fling their roots back into a very distant past.

LECTURE II.

THE HISTORIAN OF THE CONQUEST.

IN my last lecture I narrated the events which led up to the expulsion of Dermot MacMurrough and his exile to England. History repeats itself. It was just eleven hundred years since a defeated and exiled Irish prince sought, according to Tacitus, the help of Agricola, and strove to induce the Roman conqueror of Anglesea and Wales to attempt still farther conquests in Ireland.[1] And so again in 1166 we find an Irish prince, defeated in domestic strife, flying away for safety and for succour to foreign conquerors, who again stand upon the same Welsh shores. Before, however, I proceed to deal with the story of the conquest of Ireland and the fortunes of Dermot's later days, let me endeavour to make you realise the personage, the character, and the surroundings of the historian of the conquest; a subject which will incidentally raise many questions of deepest interest to the ecclesiastical historian of the Celtic Church in Wales and Ireland alike.

Giraldus Cambrensis is our great classical authority for the history of the Norman conquest of Ireland. We have several other authorities, indeed, some of them most important and trustworthy. Let us first

---

[1] See *Ireland and the Celtic Church*, pp. 14, 15.

briefly notice the latter, and then return to the subject of Giraldus Cambrensis. We have, for instance, the so-called Anglo-Norman poem of Morice Regan.[1] Morice Regan was the horse-boy, as the Celts called him,—the valet, private secretary, peculiar personal attendant, as we should call him,—of Dermot Mac-Murrough; and to him is certainly due much of the matter of the poem which now passes under his name. But the text of the poem as we have it was the work of another. This is manifest from the poem itself, which often refers to the traditions and stories of "the ancient folk," as well as to the words of Morice Regan, which are expressly distinguished from those of the ancient folk. The accuracy and truth of the

---

[1] This poem is taken from a MS. in the library of Lambeth Palace, written upon vellum in a fourteenth-century hand. It once belonged to Sir George Carew, who made an analysis which is printed by W. Harris in *Hibernica*, pp. 1-21 (Dublin: 1757). It was again published by Thomas Wright and Fr. Michel (London: T. Pickering, 1837). Both these editions are, however, most unsatisfactory. Such an original work as this would seem to be a most fitting one for publication in the Rolls Series, but somehow or other it is almost impossible to induce the authorities who have control of that undertaking to publish any of the great Anglo-Norman documents dealing with the history of the conquest of Ireland. There is a large number of MSS. dealing with this topic, such as the *Crede Mihi*, the *Register* or *Liber Niger* of Archbishop Alan, the *Liber Albus* and *Liber Niger* of Christ Church, the *Register* and *Chartularies* of St. Thomas's Abbey, containing public instruments of surpassing value and interest, which are in vain offered to them. Yet, as the *Academy* of July 14th, 1888, p. 19, points out, they have published among their last volumes the *Chronicle of Robert of Brunne*, which "is only a history in the sense that it is a translation of the old legends first collected by Geoffrey of Monmouth." The only use the reviewer can see in it is, that it will "give a lift by the way to the students of English words and syntax." And yet the reply lately made to a proposition to print the *Crede Mihi*, a work in the possession of the See of Dublin, and composed in the thirteenth century,

poem is amply proved, however, by the independent evidence of Giraldus Cambrensis, with which it remarkably agrees. Then again a series of documents dealing with the events of the Conquest was published in 1875 in the first volume of the calendar of documents relating to Ireland, edited by Mr. H. S. Sweetman, under the direction of the Master of the Rolls. This is an authority of first-rate importance, as it furnishes abstracts of all the original State papers preserved in London concerning the Conquest. They begin

---

was, that it was not an original, but a copy merely of still older documents. As I shall often have to quote these MSS. I may once for all describe them. The *Crede Mihi* is a MS. in possession of the See of Dublin, containing charters, bulls, etc., of the twelfth and thirteenth centuries. According to Ussher it was compiled about A.D. 1275. A poor transcript is in Trinity College Library. The *Liber Niger* of Archbishop Alan, A.D. 1530, is a register compiled by that learned prelate and friend of Wolsey out of ancient documents in possession of the Archbishop of Dublin at that time. The original is still in the custody of his successor. A fine transcript is in Marsh's Library, presented in the last century by the heirs of Archbishop Bulkely; an inferior one is in Trinity College Library. The *Repertorium Viride* is a full description of his diocese made by Alan about 1530. The original seems to be lost, though the Record Commissioners, *Report*, A.D. 1810—1815, pp. 307, 442, expressly state that it then existed in Christ Church Cathedral. Defective copies are in Trinity College and in Marsh's Library. The *Liber Albus* and *Liber Niger* of Christ Church are registers belonging to that Cathedral containing vast numbers of mediæval documents. The *Liber Niger* is fully analysed in the Record Commissioners' *Report*, just quoted, p. 308. The documents connected with St. Thomas's Abbey will shortly appear in the Rolls Series under the editorship of Mr. Gilbert, in whose letterpress attached to his *Facsimiles Nat. MSS.* several of the others are also described. In the *Report* of the Irish Deputy Keeper of the Records (Dr. La Touche) for 1888 there appears an exhaustive and valuable abstract of the Christ Church documents handed over to his custody.ABlica La Touche gives an account of 467 documents, the earliest being a grant by Strongbow to one of the family of Turkil, the Danish prince of Dublin.

in 1170 with the Pipe Roll accounts, and give us the details of all the preparations for the invasion. They show us how the army was raised, how the provisions were purchased, how the ships were secured, and how the various counties and cities,—Norfolk, Suffolk, Lancaster, Devon, Southampton, London, Berks,—all contributed of their substance and of their men to the great undertaking. It is evident from the survey there put before us that Henry II. when he came to Ireland came determined to make a thorough, a secure, and a lasting conquest. And then we have the narrative of Giraldus Cambrensis, contained in the *Topographia* and *Expugnatio Hiberniæ*.[1] To understand them we must first of all understand the man who wrote them, for his history presents us with many interesting details, throwing a strangely lurid light upon the ecclesiastical and political aspect of the second half of the twelfth century. To the story of Giraldus let us now apply ourselves. It will afford us abundant matter for this lecture.

Giraldus Cambrensis was born in 1147, and received the name Cambrensis from his native country Cambria, or Wales. He was a Welshman pure and simple on his mother's side, and his writings are full of details showing the similarity of the Welsh to the Irish Church of that date. Giraldus belonged to a family which furnished almost all the leading personages who

---

[1] The works of Giraldus Cambrensis are contained in the Rolls Series in seven volumes. This is the best edition. A convenient, though defective, edition for English readers of the *Topographia, Expugnatio*, the *Welsh Itinerary*, and the *Description of Wales* will be found in Bohn's "Antiquarian Library." The editor (Mr. Wright) makes several curious mistakes about Irish geography. At the same time he gives correctly and conveniently the sense of Giraldus' narrative.

figure among the earliest conquerors of Ireland, whose descendants occupy to this day a high position amongst us. His very name shows this. He was Giraldus, or Gerald, and he was nephew to Maurice Fitz-Gerald, the ancestor of all the Fitz-Geralds of Ireland, and he was connected by blood with Meyler Fitz-Henry and Robert Fitz-Henry and Robert Fitz-Stephen; while, again, he was the son of William de Barri, and the name Barry is still well known amongst us. Hereby, however, hangs a tale. A lady occupies, as I have shown, a very important place in the events which led up, on this side the Channel, to the exile of Dermot. A lady occupied a very important position, too, amid the events which led a number of Welsh chieftains to espouse Dermot's side in the Irish civil war. Henry I. of England, son of William the Conqueror, was no strait-laced moralist, and among his favourites, Nesta, granddaughter of Rhys ap Tudor, a prince of South Wales, held a distinguished position. By her Henry I. had a son, Henry, father of Meyler Fitz-Henry and Robert Fitz-Henry. These grandchildren of Henry I. by his Welsh mistress occupy no small place in the story of Irish conquest. After a while Henry I. grew tired of Nesta, and she then married Giraldus of Windsor, Constable of Pembroke, by whom she had three sons, William Fitz-Gerald, Maurice Fitz-Gerald, and David Fitz-Gerald, Bishop of St. David's. She had also a daughter named Angareth, who married an Anglo-Norman chief named William de Barri, whose son was Giraldus, doubtless so called after his grandfather Gerald of Windsor. You will see afterwards that this Fitz-Gerald family and its connexions and ramifications furnished the first conquerors who sought Ireland's shores long before—four years, at least—Henry II.

came here. Their achievements and success roused his envy and his ire,—and very justly so, from the king's point of view. These Fitz-Geralds were, in his eyes, a dangerous lot. They were all closely connected with the princes of South Wales, and descended on the female side from Nesta. The husbands indeed were Normans, but Celtic women have had in every age a wonderful power of assimilating their husbands to themselves. The descendants of the first Anglo-Norman settlers in Wexford were the fiercest rebels in 1798; the descendants of the Cromwellian settlers in Tipperary, intermarrying with the Celts, are the stoutest land and national leaguers of to-day. The Fitz-Geralds and the De Barris of the twelfth century showed themselves no less amenable to the same subtle influence. The husbands forgot their own Norman race and their father's house, and were inclined to champion the cause of Welsh independence as symbolised by and embodied in the person of the Welsh princes, with whom they were allied by blood.[1] To this subject we must hereafter return. It will suffice now to indicate the close connection between Giraldus Cambrensis and the leading families of the earliest Anglo-Irish colony, as opening various channels for special information, and lending peculiar authority to the narrative of the Welsh archdeacon. Let us now return to the story of Giraldus himself. He was born and brought up at his father's house of Maenor Pyrr (now Manorbeer), a small village on the sea coast between Tenby and Pembroke, where the remains of a large castle, with the sepulchral effigy of a brother of our author, still testify to the ancient importance of

---

[1] See Stubbs, *Constitutional History*, i., 554.

his family.[1] He was educated for the Church, and the extent of his classical acquirements, his frequent quotations from Terence, Virgil, Horace, Ovid, Juvenal, Cicero, and Seneca show that classical studies were, amid all their warfare, as carefully maintained in the fastnesses of Wales as amid the wilds and morasses of Ireland. It is amusing to notice the astonishment of Mr. Brewer, the latest biographer of Giraldus, as he records the evidences of his attainments.[2] "The wonder is," Brewer says, "that in a country so indubitably barbarous and uncivilized, any Welshman could be found at that time capable of giving even elementary instruction." Mr. Brewer knew nothing of the hedge school system of Ireland, as depicted by Carleton, which perpetuated to our own age the *al fresco* scholastic life of St. Columba studying under a tree at Clonard, and could not understand classical attainments unless associated with a substantial college and comfortable commons, accompanied by sound beer and good wine.[3] He concludes, therefore, that Giraldus

---

[1] A description of it is inserted in the *Welsh Itinerary* (Bohn's edition), bk. i., chap. xii., where the notes of Sir R. C. Hoare give much additional information. In this chapter Giraldus describes the original castle of Pembroke as built by Gerald of Windsor, "a slender fortress of stakes and turf," showing that the Normans at first used the same primitive kind of castles as the Irish and the Welsh. See G. T. Clark's *Mediæval Military Architecture*, t. i., ch. ii.

[2] Cf. Girald. Camb. *opp*. (Rolls ed.), t. i., pref., pp. xii, xiii.

[3] I have described the ancient Irish school system in my previous volume, *Ireland and the Celtic Church*, pp. 229, 230. That system continued to flourish all through the ages of Anglo-Norman dominion, and only died out—if it is even yet dead—under the influence of the present national system of education. In Primate Marsh's Library I lately found an astronomical treatise of the fourteenth century. It is written on vellum, and evidently belonged to one of the ancient Irish schools. It is an Irish translation from a Latin original, and is profusely interspersed with diagrams.

must have been instructed by the chaplains of his uncle, the Norman bishop, who then ruled the See of St. David's. These chaplains seem certainly to have exercised a healthy influence upon him. Giraldus early manifested a devout tendency, and was therefore dedicated to the priestly office, a profession in which his courtly influence would be of much use. He fell, however, into the common tendency of all boys, and became idle. The chaplains, observing this, roused him to exertion by declining to him, the one, *durus, durior, durissimus,* and the other, *stultus, stultior, stultissimus.* The rebuke had the desired effect, and never needed repetition. He studied hard, and then repaired to Paris, the favourite school for Western Europe, where he flung himself into the study of civil and canon law.[1] He returned to England about the year 1172, and in 1175 was created Archdeacon of Brecknock, an office which in those times brought with it so many duties and temptations that it was a popular problem for casuists to solve, "whether an archdeacon could possibly be saved."[2] Giraldus Cambrensis himself, how-

---

[1] See the article on "Universities" in the last edition of the *Encyclopædia Britannica* for an account of the University of Paris.

[2] Cf. John of Salisbury, *Ep*. clxvi. *opp*. ed. Giles, i., 260, and Girald., *opp*., t. vii. (Rolls Series), pref., p. lxxxvi. This tradition seems to have come over to Ireland with the Normans, and to have been perpetuated, as the following story proves. In the early part of this century there was an Archdeacon of Meath named De Lacy. He was a mighty hunter in days when the Irish clerical standard was not very high. He got a bad fall one day when trying a very stiff hedge, and was lying senseless beside his horse when some farmers rode up with whom he was very popular on account of his hunting propensity. "There you lie," cried one of them, thinking him dead, "There you lie, Archdaycon De Lacy, and if ever an Archdaycon gets to heaven, you will have a good chance of being found there."

ever, had no doubts on the topic; he thought very highly of his own office, and magnified it, but thought rather slightingly of the episcopal office, after which, however, he earnestly craved. He even gave utterance to very presbyterian notions on this subject. He knew of Jerome's opinion on the essential equality of bishops and presbyters, and the origin of the episcopal office.[1] He knew the spiritual danger of an archdeacon's office, but he thought the episcopal still more dangerous than the archidiaconal function, for in one of his works[2] he gravely discusses the question, "What, then, are all bishops to be damned?"—replying, "God forbid! for were not Nicholas, Martin, Germanus, Basil, and Thomas à Becket bishops?" Yet he thinks it more difficult for a bishop to attain salvation than a common man, asking, "Where now can we find episcopal love and temperance like that of St. Nicholas, or sackcloth and ashes, water and parched corn used by bishops, as Basil and Germanus used them?"

Giraldus was made Archdeacon of Brecknock in 1175, and immediately set himself to reform the Welsh Church. He came back from Paris burning with zeal for Church discipline. He knew the shortcomings of the Welsh Church, and heartily desired to remove them. His uncle was still Bishop of St. David's, and what was his horror to find that one of his uncle's archdeacons was a married man. Giraldus urged his suspension, and the bishop yielded, rewarding his vigorous and reforming nephew with the vacant archdeaconry. Giraldus' office gave him every opportunity of becoming intimately acquainted with the state of the Welsh Church, of which he has left us

---

[1] See his Epistle to Peter de Leia, Bishop of St. David's, in *opp.* i., 221 (Rolls Series).
[2] *De Invect.*, VI., 27; *opp.*, t. i., p. 191 (Rolls Series).

in his various works a complete picture. That picture proves that it was in all respects practically identical with the Irish.[1] Its clergy and its bishops were often married men. Anchorites were scattered in every direction, some of them living attached to churches, as at St. Doulough's.[2] The monks, who might be supposed to be bound to celibacy, disregarded their vows;[3] the clergy lived secular lives, joined in secular pursuits, and handed their livings from father to son just as the Primates of Armagh did for two hundred years prior to St. Malachy's time. Giraldus tells some anecdotes illustrating the tenacity with which the Welsh Celts clung to the marriage of the clergy and their hereditary claims upon Church livings.[4] In fact, I do not think

---

[1] Giraldus Cambrensis in his writings notices several points in which the Irish and Welsh ecclesiastical customs were identical. Thus, in the *Welsh Itinerary*, lib. i., cap. i., he mentions the staff of St. Cyric, just like the staff of Jesus long preserved at Armagh (cf. *Topograph.*, iii., 33, 34); the horn of St. Patrick, used alike in Wales and Ireland (*Topograph.*, iii., 34); the use of saints' bells (*Itinerary*, i., 1); the presence of Culdees (*Itinerary*, ii., 6, 7); the vindictive character of Welsh and Irish saints (*Itinerary*, ii., 7); the abuses of fosterage (*Description of Wales*, ii., 4). All the documents here referred to are printed in Bohn's edition of Giraldus' works.

[2] See Girald. Camb. *opp.* (Rolls Series), i., 89, 90; ii., 246. Cf. *Ireland and Celtic Church*, pp. 175-83.

[3] See Girald. Camb. *opp.* (Rolls Series), i., 89, 90.

[4] The following extract from the *Description of Wales*, ii., 6, will prove this:—"Their churches have almost as many parsons and sharers as there are principal men in the parish. The sons, after the decease of their fathers, succeed to the ecclesiastical benefices, not by election, but by hereditary right, possessing and polluting the sanctuary of God. And if a prelate should by chance presume to appoint or institute any other person, the people would certainly revenge the injury upon the institutor and the instituted. With respect to those two excesses of incest and succession which took root formerly in Armorica, and are not yet eradicated, Ildebert, Bishop of Le Mans, in one of his Epistles says 'that he was present with a British priest at a council summoned with a view of

you could possibly find more interesting sketches of Church life in the twelfth century than the writings of Giraldus afford if they were but translated out of his rude Latin.

Let me give you a specimen or two. He wrote a treatise, *De Rebus a se Gestis*, which is most amusing from the intense vanity of the man, and yet is full of touches letting us into the very inner life of the time. As soon as he was made archdeacon he commenced a round of visitation. New brooms always sweep clean. There was a distant corner of the diocese where he had heard rumours of strange doings.[1] In one church a knight was said to share with his brother, the priest, the alms and oblations of the faithful.[2] This abuse the new

---

putting an end to the enormities of this nation.' Hence it appears that these vices have for a long time prevailed both in Brittany and in Britain." Monastic vows seem to have sat loosely on the Celts, as Giraldus mentions an abbot who had eighteen children, *opp.* (Rolls Series), iv., 90; cf. iii. 214, and also Palgrave's *Rotuli Curiæ Regis*, Introd., sec. xvii. In the same chapter of the *Description of Wales* he notices another pre-nuptial custom which even still conduces to immorality, not only in Wales, but in various parts of Northern England. The practice of bundling, as it is called, is evidently a relic of barbaric times.

[1] Girald. Camb., *De Rebus*, i., 5. Cf. *opp.* (Rolls Series), t. i., Introd., p. xxii., and p. 30.

[2] He notices (*Welsh Itinerary*, ii. 4) a church in Wales which, like many others in Wales and Ireland, had a lay abbot or steward, who usurped the larger share of the endowment, paying the clergy some small portion thereof. These lay abbots were evidently the same as the Irish Corbes and Herenachs, officials who continued to flourish in Ireland till the reign of Charles I. at least. See Ussher's treatise on *The Original of Corbes, Herenaches, and Termon Lands, opp.* (Elrington's ed.), xi. 434-45. Giraldus tells us in the same chapter the following story, which helps to explain the frequent and bloody contests between rival churches and monasteries in Ireland and Wales. "It happened that in the reign of King Stephen, who succeeded Henry I., a knight born in Armorican Britain having travelled through many parts of the

archdeacon put down, not without threats of personal violence on the knight's part. In another direction, remote from his residence, he heard of a church where there were no less than seven participators or portionists in one parish, all doubtless connected by blood.[1] They sent a deputation to him, claiming exemption from his visitation. Then they threatened him; finally when he with his retinue approached the parish, the clergy attacked the bold archdeacon with lances, spears, and arrows. The archdeacon retired defeated for the moment, but sent off at once to a neighbouring chief to whom he was related by blood, Cadwallan, son of Madoc, demanding assistance, which was quickly granted. The threat of force was, however, quite sufficient for the warlike parsons, and they submitted to the archdeacon's jurisdiction.

A more amusing story still tells how Giraldus

---

world, came by chance to Llanpadarn. On a certain feast day, whilst both clergy and laity were waiting for the arrival of the abbot to celebrate mass, he perceived a body of young men, armed according to the custom of their country, approaching towards the church; and on enquiring which of them was the abbot, they pointed out to him a man walking foremost, with a long spear in his hand. Gazing on him with amazement, he asked if the abbot had not another habit or a different staff from that which he now carried before him. On their answering 'No,' he replied, 'I have seen indeed and heard this day a wonderful novelty!' And from that hour he returned and finished his labours and researches."

[1] The term portionist was often used in mediæval times. It was applied to two or three persons joint rectors of a parish. Portionists still exist in the Church of England. The celebrated Archdeacon Townson, for instance, was portionist rector of Malpas, in Cheshire; see the Memoir by Churton prefixed to his *Works*, t. i., p. xix. Malpas was a portionary parish in the time of Henry VIII.; see *Valor Ecclesiasticus*, t. v., p. 212. An unpleasant case concerning a grave irregularity in the celebration of Holy Communion lately before the Ecclesiastical Courts in England involved a portionist rector.

defeated the Bishop of St. Asaph, when he endeavoured to make a raid on the churches of St. David's (*De Reb. Gest.*, i., 6; cf. Brewer's preface, t. i., p. xxii). The archdeacon had just got home from the perilous expedition of which I have just told you, and had been three or four days in repose, when the rural dean of the same district came in a panic, announcing that the Bishop of St. Asaph had declared his intention to visit, consecrate, and celebrate mass the very next Sunday in the church of Keri, which lay on the extreme boundary of the diocese of St. David's, but had always been reckoned part of it. The archdeacon at once roused himself, despatched messengers to his brethren and kinsmen, asking them to come the next morning, Saturday, to his assistance with horses, arms, and provisions, as the bishop was advancing with an armed party also. The archdeacon was the younger and more active man, and so proceeding by forced marches he anticipated the bishop, and got on Sunday morning before the church door. After the usual Welsh style, there were two incumbents. They disliked Giraldus and favoured the bishop, so they fled to the bishop and hid the keys of the church. After some delay they were found, when Giraldus vested himself with all speed, rang the bells, and proceeded to celebrate mass. In the midst of the service word was brought that the bishop was approaching. Giraldus calmly concluded the service, and then proceeded to meet the intruder. He tells us that he knew the man right well, and his character, for he had studied with him at Paris. Leaving a party, therefore, to hold the church and ring the bells at a given signal, he advanced in his vestments to meet the bishop at the churchyard gate, demanding what brought him there. The bishop produced an ancient book which asserted that the church of Keri belonged to St. Asaph. The archdeacon told him he might write or read anything he pleased in his book, but challenged him to produce any authentic charter giving the parish to the diocese of St. Asaph. "I will excommunicate thee," said the bishop, waxing wrathful. "And I will excommunicate thee," replied the bold archdeacon. "You are only an archdeacon," said the bishop, "and an archdeacon cannot excommunicate a bishop." "If you are a bishop," replied Giraldus, "you are not my bishop, and I have as good a right to excommunicate thee as thou me." Hereupon the bishop slipped off his horse, clapped on his mitre, seized his pastoral staff, and began to read the dread sentence. Giraldus had, however, anticipated all this, so while the prelate was making preparations, Giraldus advanced at the head of his own procession of priests and deacons duly vested, and began his counter-sentence of excommunication in a still louder voice than the bishop's, and then signalling to the church tower, caused the bells to ring out as was usually done when the act of excommunication was complete. Boldness carried the day, as it always does with the populace. The bells were too much for the bishop; the dread signal quite upset him and his followers. They turned tail and fled, followed by a howling mob, who pursued them with stones, mud, and execrations, till the bishop fell into the hands of a party of the archdeacon's clergy, who were advancing to support him armed with bows and spears. The amusing story ends with telling us how, the same Sunday evening, they all, the intruding bishop and the victorious archdeacon included, became fast friends over the archdeacon's good dinner and his very best wine *peroptimo potu.*

A notable event in the life of Giraldus—in fact, the turning-point and crisis of his life—was his contest about the see of St. David's. He was, as I have noted, very presbyterian in his notions about presbyters and bishops, yet he was very desirous to be a bishop, and spent a long life vainly seeking for an office he pretended to despise. Upon the death of his uncle, David Fitz-Gerald, in May 1176, the Chapter of St. David's elected Giraldus bishop in room of the defunct. There was a difficulty, however. Since the reign of Henry I., the English kings had so thoroughly established their suzerainty over Wales, that though the princes were still nominally independent, yet the bishops were all chosen and admitted by the king's authority, and consecrated at Canterbury.[1] St. David's had been the Metropolitan See of Wales, and Giraldus was intensely desirous to revive its former glories and its ancient claims.

But Henry II. knew Giraldus too well. He distrusted the whole tribe of the Fitz-Geralds. They united Norman skill and courage to Celtic blood and pretensions. They had already tried, as I shall more fully show in a subsequent chapter, to establish what would have been an independent colony in Ireland;

---

[1] Cf. Stubbs, *Constitutional History*, t. i., chap. xiii., p. 554, where he writes concerning the Welsh princes :—" The fact that their bishops received their consecration at Canterbury, and were, from the reign of Henry I., elected and admitted under the authority of the kings of England, is sufficient to prove that anything like real sovereignty was lost to the so-called kings of Wales." It was just the same in Ireland, as we shall hereafter show. The kings of Connaught and the other Irish princes were acknowledged by Henry II. as princes. But the Archbishop of Tuam and the other bishops were all appointed by Henry. He had no intention of allowing such important officials to fall under local influence and patronage.

but he had stopped that. One Fitz-Gerald had been troublesome enough at St. David's, but matters would wax still worse if a much more active and a younger member of the same faction were elevated to the vacant See. The Welsh had already endeavoured to restore St. David's to its old position, but the king was inexorable. They offered him money, but it was of no avail. So long as life lasted, Henry declared he would never raise up a head for rebellion in Wales by giving the Welsh a Metropolitan. The sudden vacancy gave the Chapter a chance of choosing a man who would be a Metropolitan in fact if not in name, and so they chose Giraldus. It was now, however, the established custom that, before an episcopal election, the king should be apprised of the vacancy, and a *congé d'élire* issued.[1] The present practice, in fact, of the English Church goes back to these early Norman times. Roman Catholic controversialists sometimes taunt that Church with the secular and Erastian character of English episcopal appointments. The reply is easy and crushing. There is not one of the forms and ceremonies observed in our modern episcopal elections which does not come down from the Mediæval Church. A glance into the patent rolls preserved in the Record Office, as edited by Sir T. D. Hardy, will show that every form now in use in the English Establishment—royal assent, mode of election, restitution of temporalities, homage—has continued the same since the days of Thomas à Becket. The Chapter of St. David's did not wait for the royal

---

[1] The issue of a *congé d'élire* was most rigidly insisted upon by the early English kings. See Dr. La Touche's *Report* for 1888 on Irish Public Records, p. 64, No. 155, for an instance of this in A.D. 1299; cf. No. 164.

permission, but chose Giraldus and two others (the most unfit they could find) to submit to the king, in order to force him to select the Fitz-Gerald whom they desired. Henry II. waxed outrageous when he heard of their presumption. As Mr. Brewer puts it in his preface to the Works of Giraldus, "He snorted out his wrath as none but he and Henry VIII. knew how. He swore he would banish every one who had taken any part in these matters. Not a Welshman of them all should escape him. 'As they have allowed me no part in this election, I'll take care they have no part in this promotion,' he exclaimed in a tone of savage banter which seldom forsook him in his irritable moments." He annulled the whole election, and made choice of Peter de Leia, an Augustinian monk, to succeed David Fitz-Gerald. This made a final and irretrievable breach between Giraldus and the king. The archdeacon may conceal it for a time, but on every possible occasion he lets us see how he hated Henry II. and all his supporters. He declaims against Anglican tyranny and the type of bishops whom the Normans were forcing on Wales. He denounces a practice from which both Ireland and Wales have suffered deeply, which began in Norman times, and has scarcely yet ceased. Norman bishops were intruded into Welsh dioceses, which they abandoned to neglect, or visited as seldom as possible, concentrating all their energies upon efforts to obtain translations to English Sees.[1]

---

[1] It is amusing to notice how the same policy is still pursued in the Colonies, where English bishops are despatched to every vacant post, to the neglect of the resident clergy. These colonial bishops from England are, of course, just like the ancient Welsh bishops, ever on the look-out for an English translation, or a comfortable English living.

Mere worldly policy was the impelling motive of the Norman kings. They sent Norman bishops to Wales, not as spiritual pastors, but as secular policemen, to watch the princes and make early report of their intention to burst into rebellion; and they thus laid, seven centuries ago, the foundations of those religious feuds and distractions which have alienated the masses of the Welsh people from the communion ot their ancient Church.

The latter portion of the life of Giraldus was divided between two great purposes. He appealed to Rome against Henry II. concerning the bishopric of St. David's. Again and again did he resort thither. Four times did he travel to Rome and back between 1199 and 1203,—a fair allowance even for a modern traveller, with all the advantages of the steamer and railway. A clergyman of those days apparently thought much less of a trip to Italy than we do now, notwithstanding all the perils of the way which then had to be encountered. And the narrative of Giraldus shows them to have been numerous enough. But the perils of land and sea were not the worst. When Giraldus got to Rome he found the perils of the city no less dangerous. Royal influence was against him, and the Roman court has never cared over-much for quarrels with English kings. In fact, I believe that Irish Roman Catholics complain bitterly that English influence, even though hostile to the Pope from a religious point of view, is much more potent in papal court circles than that of the more faithful Irish, and that an English nobleman is a much more acceptable personage to a Roman cardinal than a bishop from Connaught or Munster. Intrigue, too, abounded on every side; while, withal, the charges, fees, and bribery absolutely necessary, drained poor

Giraldus completely dry. And after all he failed. Once or twice the episcopal prize seemed almost within his grasp, the Pope seemed ready to decide in his favour; yet he failed, and had to live and die Archdeacon of Brecknock.

The other object to which he devoted his life was the attainment of literary fame. He wrote widely, and he wrote well. The man who wishes to get a realistic picture of the state of mediæval Christianity will do well to study the numerous and portly volumes which Giraldus fills in the Rolls Series. That study will possibly disillusionise some of you who may be tempted to think of the "ages of faith," as sometimes they are called, as a time of halcyon peace and holiness. The picture drawn by our historian is of the saddest character. The priesthood were often careless and immoral, the bishops worldly, the people coarse and barbarous, the monks, even the order which St. Bernard had reformed, selfish, sensual, avaricious. Let me give you a specimen of Giraldus' description. He specially hated the Cistercians, the order to which Mary's Abbey and Mellifont, among ourselves, belonged. He piles up tale after tale against them. Cistercians—English, Welsh, Irish—are all equally his abomination.[1] He tells us how the Cistercians of St. Mary's Abbey (whose beautiful Chapter House still exists, just off Capel Street, as perfect as the first day it was finished,—reduced, alas! however, to the low estate of a guano store) persuaded all the people of Dublin to join their order on the death of St. Laurence O'Toole, pretending that it was the only

---

[1] See his *Itinerary through Wales*, lib. i., cap. 3, or pp. 359-64 in Bohn's edition, where many amusing stories to the disadvantage of the Cistercians will be found.

way of salvation remaining to them.[1] He pictures them as the great evictors of the Middle Ages. They certainly were some of the greatest farmers of those times. They cut down forests, reclaimed bogs, drained morasses, and now, wherever a Cistercian monastery stood, you will find—as at Fountains—good land, fine trees, and beautiful scenery.

But if they farmed well, they were sweeping in their clearances, merciless in their evictions. And they allowed no obstacles to stand in their way. They were hampered neither by scruples nor by land Acts. Giraldus compares them to William Rufus forming the New Forest, and tells us how a parish priest in his time went mad through their action.[2] He went away for a single night, leaving his church, village, and parish in peace. He came back the next day to find no trace of either church or village, his parish a howling waste, and all annexed to a neighbouring Cistercian farm. The monks had made a clean sweep of everything in one day, and the poor incumbent lost his head, convinced the world had come to an end. Giraldus doubted even their faith in Christ, and tells us of a biting joke of Walter Mapes, Archdeacon of Oxford, who, when he heard that a number of them had become Jews, rejoined that it was a pity they had not first tried Christianity.[3] Giraldus is best known as a literary character by his works on Ireland, his *Topographia* and his *Expugnatio*, which are to this day authorities of primary importance concerning the social state of Ireland, and the actual facts of its

---

[1] Cf. Girald. Camb. *opp*. (Rolls Series), t. iv., p. 178.
[2] *Speculum Ecclesiæ*, *opp*. t. iv., 135-37 (Rolls Series).
[3] Cf. Brewer's preface to the fourth volume of the Works of Giraldus Cambrensis in Rolls Series, p. xli, for an amusing story illustrating the hatred which existed between Mapes and the Cistercians.

conquest, from 1166 and onwards. He had every advantage qualifying him for his task. He was related by close ties to all the first invaders. He made frequent visits to Ireland to consult them. On one occasion he took a sudden determination to fly to Rome without royal leave. Before he did so he sailed across to Dublin in the course of one day to consult Meyler the justiciary, and the rest of the Fitz-Gerald clan, as to his course of action.[1] He was sent officially to Ireland with Prince John, then a youth, to be his guide, philosopher, and friend,—a somewhat difficult office rightly to discharge in that particular instance. He had access—free, abundant access—to official documents at home and in Rome, and as the result he has bequeathed to us two valuable works. One is called the *Topography of Ireland*. It is a kind of handbook of Irish wonders and curiosities, real or reputed. It is divided, after the scholastic fashion, into three Distinctions: the first treating of the natural history of Ireland; the second of its wonders and miracles; and the third, of the inhabitants of Ireland. It was originally published about the year 1186, but Giraldus republished it at different times, making constant additions. He was very proud of it, too. He presented a copy to the Archbishop of Canterbury, and tells us the worthy prelate could never grow weary of hearing it. He went off to Oxford,—then rising into note as a place of learning,—and read it publicly, on three successive days, to the doctors, students, and the populace, securing a favourable audience by liberally feasting all his hearers. This work is well worth reading, embodying, as it does, the remarks of a very keen observer, though a very vain man. The other

---

[1] Cf. Girald. Camb. *opp.*, i., 122 (Rolls Series).

work of Giraldus dealing with this island is the *Conquest of Ireland*, which gives a history of the English invasion, beginning with the intrigue of Dermot MacMurrough and Dervorgil, and reaching down to Prince John's expedition to Ireland in the year 1185. In his history of the Conquest, we have in fact the narrative of the first twenty years of English, or rather Norman, rule in Ireland. From that narrative I shall hereafter draw very largely; I shall only now call your attention to one statement in it which has excited no small controversy. In the sixth chapter of the second book of the *Conquest*, he publishes the bull of Pope Adrian granted to Henry II. in 1155, making over Ireland to that prince, in order that, as it proceeds, "King Henry might labour to extend the borders of the Church, teach the truths of the Christian faith to a rude and unlettered people, and root out the weeds of wickedness from the field of the Lord." This bull and the statements of Giraldus have excited a warm controversy among Roman Catholics. In the pages of the *Dublin Review*, some short time ago, the opposing views were very vigorously debated. One party boldly gets rid of the difficulty by asserting the bull to be a forgery, relying upon the fact that no copy of the bull has been found, or now exists in the Vatican archives. They do not like to admit that the Norman invader had papal sanction for his action. I am perfectly unprejudiced in this matter, but I am bound, as a historian, to hold that the case of the opponents of the bull is very weak. Suppose Adrian did not issue this bull, and that Giraldus and all the historians of the period conspired to foist a forgery on the public. Still they are in no better case. Pope after pope, legate after legate, even during Henry II.'s reign, solemnly proclaimed the papal sanction of the Norman conquest. Alexander III. confirmed Henry's action. The papal legate Vivianus renewed the confirmation at a public synod in 1177. Numerous bulls extant with ourselves in Alan's *Register*, the *Crede Mihi*, the *Liber Albus* and *Liber Niger* of Christ Church, and in the documents published by the Vatican itself some twenty years ago, proclaim the same thing.[1] Objectors argue, indeed, that the document is not now to be found in the Vatican, but the reply is absolutely crushing. Neither, according to Theiner, is any document dealing with Ireland to be found there earlier than 1215,—which will prove that no bull about Ireland was issued prior to that year; and if so, what becomes of the papal claims to have ruled Ireland long before the English came at all? Such arguments are suicidal. The truth is that we still possess many bulls issued by popes about Ireland all through the reigns of Henry II. and John, the originals of which have been lost from the Vatican. Ussher's *Sylloge* will show you bulls issued to Laurence O'Toole; Mason's *History of St. Patrick*, the work called *Chartæ Privilegia et Immunitate*, published by the Irish Record Office, embody others unknown to the present Vatican Archives. The lapse of time, war, rebellion, carelessness, plunder, all these combine to reduce the number of documents in any ancient repository, and they will amply account for the loss of the Vatican copy of Adrian's bull.

---

[1] Cf. *Vetera Monumenta Hibernorum et Scotorum*, by A. Theiner (Rome: printed at the Vatican press, 1864). On p. 2 of that volume will be found the letters of Pope Honorius III., the fourth of which, dated January 17th, 1217, is headed "Archiepiscopo Dublinensi, ut rebelles Hibernos ad obedientiam Regis Angliæ redire compellat;" while on the previous page there are notices of several letters from Innocent III., specially Nos. 136 and 137, which are equally strong

Lastly, Giraldus had abundant means to satisfy himself as to the authenticity of the document. He lived for years at Rome, he had continual access to the papal registers, which he carefully investigated, and it will require something more than *à priori* presumptions to convince us that a document publicly proclaimed, boasted of, confirmed within twenty years of its original grant, was a carefully-planned swindle. Men when they thus argue forget the standpoint from which Giraldus must have viewed Ireland. To an enthusiastic Irishman now it may seem the centre of the universe, and the Normans a set of robbers whose one desire was to get possession of it. To Giraldus and the men of his time, Ireland must have seemed a barbarous out-of-the-way island,—a very desirable possession indeed for the Geraldine clique, one too from which they would gladly have excluded the Anglo-Norman king, but even in their sight a spot much inferior in value to Poitou or Normandy, or the smallest continental fief. Giraldus had no conceivable motive for forging this bull in favour of a king he hated, and who had mortally injured him. We therefore conclude that though our historian may have been vain, foolish, credulous, yet a liar he was not in telling us that the foundation of Norman and English dominion over Ireland was laid deep and fast in the grant of Pope Adrian IV. To the facts of the first Anglo-Norman invasion as narrated by Giraldus Cambrensis we must now turn our attention.

LECTURE III.

DERMOT'S INTRIGUES AND FOREIGN PREPARATIONS.

IN my first lecture I traced the blood-stained and villainous career of Dermot MacMurrough till he fled to England seeking relief and armed assistance. He escaped first of all to Bristol, from some such port as Arklow or Wicklow, landing doubtless somewhere about St. David's Head, as that was the nearest point to Ireland, and a favourite spot for travellers to land,— answering, in a degree, to our modern Holyhead. An Irishman wandering along the road which led through Haverfordwest towards Bristol was no unusual sight at St. David's in the days of the twelfth century. North Wales now sees most of the Irish people; South Wales was then their great resort. The physical features of the coast, the navigation of the times, and the distribution of population, accounted for this. South Wales is, at the narrowest point, only some forty-five miles from Ireland. A favourable breeze would bring a boat across in five or six hours. Holyhead, on the other hand, is sixty-four and Carnarvon some seventy-five miles from Dublin. Bristol was then, too, a great city, and a leading commercial emporium. North Wales had no centres of population and of trade to induce a traveller to wend his way thither, while many an Irishman found his way to South Wales. Giraldus Cambrensis, whose life and work I sketched in my last chapter, tells us many a story illustrating the active commerce which existed from earliest times between Ireland and Wales. Some of them are mythical, and all are very amusing. An early Irish saint is said to have ridden his horse over the sea from Wales to Ireland, and to have imported bees with him, which previously were unknown in our flowery island. Giraldus relates many a tale to the disadvantage of our countrymen of his own age. If a scoundrel or an impostor is to be produced on the stage of history, if he is not a Cistercian monk he is sure to be an Irishman, priest or layman.[2] Thus in the *Speculum Ecclesiæ*[3] he tells a story which casts a vivid light upon the state of the Welsh Church. An Irish presbyter passed over to Wales. He married a Welshwoman, by whom he had a son, who became a monk. The Irish priest was not satisfied with one Welsh wife. He had a second (the first being still alive), by whom he had another son, who also became a monk. The Irish priest, notwithstanding his moral laxity, was a fine preacher, and captured the hearts of his Welsh audiences—Welshmen being to this day great lovers of sermons—by his flowery eloquence. His sermons were not, however, like those of which a modern Irish pulpit orator boasted, saying that he never knew before he began what he was going to preach about.

---

[1] See the articles "Domhnog" and "Molagga" in the *Dictionary of Christian Biography;* Girald. Camb. *opp.* (Rolls Series), iii., 394, 396; Rev. R. Walsh's *Fingal and its Churches*, p. 35 (Dublin: 1888).

[2] It is one of the numerous inconsistencies of Giraldus that, while he used the Celtic race, Welsh and Irish alike, for his own purposes, he never wearies of sneering at them and exposing their many weak points.

[3] *Opp.*, t. iv., p. 161-67.

4

This Irish priest, if not strict in morals, was careful in preparation for the pulpit. He wrote out his sermons at full length, committed them to memory, and then carefully preserved the manuscripts. Hereby hangs our tale. The son of the first wife was an ambitious character, embracing within himself, as Giraldus puts it, the vices of both races, the Welsh and the Irish. He was a born intriguer too. He intrigued as a monk against his abbot, deprived him and caused himself to be substituted in his room. He intrigued as an abbot against his brother abbots, gaining rule ever over a richer convent, till at last he fixed his eyes on the episcopal office itself. With this end in view he became a sycophant of the ruling prince of Wales, flattered him, and even descended to the vile methods of denying his own birth and asserting, contrary to the testimony of his brother, and of his mother, that he was an illegitimate member of the prince's family. Like many a bad man he succeeded, however; the prince yielded to the claims of kindred,—as the Celts ever have done, even if the kinship be not the most creditable,—and nominated him to the vacant bishopric, when he capped his audacity and his wickedness by preaching his father's old sermons, thus gaining the reputation of a magnificent and devoted pulpit orator. We can scarcely wonder that the worthy archdeacon's verdict is —*Mira igitur hominis impudentia*. Wondrous was the man's audacity.

I wish to impress this fact upon you strongly. When Dermot sought Wales he sought no unknown or foreign land. He sought a country with which communication constant and helpful had been kept up for centuries, and specially for the previous century and a half.[1]

---

[1] The communication between South Wales and Ireland

Dermot's forefathers and his Danish allies had been much more closely involved in the history of the Norman conquest of England and the tragic struggles of Edward the Confessor, of Harold, and of William the Conqueror than is usually believed. Mark how this came about. The kingdom of Leinster was always bounded by, and even at times embraced, the great Danish settlements of Dublin, Waterford, and Wexford.[1] These places formed harbours of refuge

---

has always been very constant, and was specially so in the eleventh and twelfth centuries. From South Wales Christianity in all probability passed over to Ireland. The earliest traditions of the Irish Church represent St. Finnian of Clonard as spending thirty years at Menevia under St. David (cf. *Dict. Christ. Biog.*, ii., 518). Dr. Petrie was so struck with the Christian antiquities of Wales that he expressed himself thus to Lord Adare in a letter dated 24th October, 1849: "I suspect you got Christianity in South Wales long before we got it in Ireland, and also that we are indebted to you for it" (cf. Petrie's *Life*, by W. Stokes, M.D., p. 365). The works of Giraldus offer many proofs of the frequent intercourse between Wales and Ireland. Marriages were frequent between the chiefs and their families. Ireland was the favourite refuge of Welsh princes obnoxious to English sovereigns (cf. *Brut y Tywysogion*, in Rolls Series, p. 53, where we find, in 1087, a Prince Rhys retreating into Ireland. Cf. for other similar cases, p. 61, A.D. 1096; p. 63, A.D. 1097). Irish fleets were often hired to intervene in Welsh quarrels, as in A.D. 1143. See *l.c.*, pp. 165, 167; cf. p. 41, where we have an account of the North-men of Dublin capturing Griffith, son of Llywelyn, a prince of South Wales. Giraldus Cambrensis, *Welsh Itinerary*, p. 350 (Bohn's ed.), mentions a Gruffydh, son of Rhys ap Theodor, prince of South Wales, about 1113. This man was for years concealed in Ireland from the power of Henry I. Giraldus in the same *Itinerary* mentions many points of practice and organisation wherein the Welsh and Irish Churches were identical, as in the matter of crosiers, bells, torques, trumpets, the Culdee order, lay abbots, hereditary benefices, and reverence for St. Patrick (see *Brut y Tywysogion*, p. 43, and notes on pp. 33, 34 above).

[1] These places were in the twelfth century considerable trading towns. They were certainly as large and important as Bristol. There were mints at Dublin, Waterford, and

where fugitive English rebels found safety and succour. Every student of English history knows the story of Harold, son of Earl Godwine, the brave antagonist of William the Conqueror, who fell when leading the English against the Norman invaders at the Battle of Hastings. A few years earlier, when Norman influence was paving the way for the conquest of 1066, and throwing its toils and nets round the feeble Edward the Confessor, Earl Godwine and his sons were found to bar the road. In 1051 they were exiled therefore. Godwine, the father, was driven to Flanders; Harold and his brothers fled to Bristol, secured a ship lying there at anchor, and sailed to Dublin.[1] The great-grandfather of this very Dermot, King of Leinster, concerning whom our tale runs, received them and furnished them with troops for an invasion of England.[2] That, mark you, was just a hundred and ten years

---

Limerick long prior to the English invasion, and even prior to the year 1000. See Simon's and Lindsay's works on Irish coinage. From the Pipe Roll accounts for the year 1172 we learn that there were large wine merchants in Waterford. In that year £40 was paid to local merchants for wine for the king's use when he landed. Multiply that by twenty, to represent the changed value of money, and I think you would find it difficult to get £800 worth of claret in Waterford to-day.

[1] The Danish kings of Dublin seemed to have known and imitated the coinage of Edward the Confessor. In Lindsay's *Coinage of Ireland*, pp. 14, 15, is a description of coins belonging to Ifars III. and to Ecmargach, kings of the Dublin Danes from 1050 to 1064, on which the type both of obverse and reverse is exactly that of the Confessor. On p. 17 of the same volume there will be found an account of the coinage of Askel MacTorquil, Prince of Dublin, from 1159. He became feudatory to Dermot MacMurrough. If the inferior princes produced such neat coinage as therein described, the superior princes, their lords, must have been something more than mere barbarians.

[2] See O'Donovan's genealogy of Dermot MacMurrough in the *Annals of Four Masters*, A.D. 1052.

before Dermot's exile. Sixteen years later—that is, in 1068—the same process was repeated. Harold was dead indeed, but his sons kept up the hereditary hostility to the Normans. William's hand was then heavy upon England, and he narrowly watched the west and southwest of the country,—Devon and Somerset,—where Harold's influence was specially strong, owing to his vast estates in these counties.[1] In 1068 Devonshire, Somerset, and Cornwall were in fact completely independent of the Conqueror, and as yet had never owned his sway. In the spring of that year Harold's mother and Harold's three sons were assembled at Exeter, which raised the standard of revolt against the Norman invader. The attempt was, however, all in vain. William crossed from Normandy, marched to the west, and after a severe struggle, captured Exeter. Harold's mother and her grandsons succeeded in making their escape, and the young men fled in panic flight to Dublin, where King Dermot and the Ostmen of our city again received them, furnished them with assistance, and in fifty-two vessels sailed to attack Bristol.[2] The Bristol men did not love the Normans, but they had still less love for wild Irish kerns and plundering Irish Danes. So they rose up, fought valiantly, and repelled their attack. The leader of the English on that occasion was a notable person. His name was Eadmoth. He had been Master of the Horse to Harold, and had been faithful to his house in days gone by. He was a prudent man, however, and wise in his generation.

---

[1] Freeman, iv. 140-58.
[2] The authorities about this alliance of Harold and his sons with King Dermot are Freeman's *Norman Conquest*, ii., pp. 153-55, 315-19, 387, 596-98; iv. 158-65, 224; App. S. and DD. ;—Seyer's *Memorials of Bristol*, t. i., ch. iv.

He watched with a keen glance the course of politics. He saw in what direction the tide of success was tending. He allowed no vain sentiment to blind his eyes to stern facts; and he changed sides, therefore, just at the very nick of time, and was consequently one of the few west country Englishmen admitted to favour and permitted to retain their estates by the victorious conqueror. A successful renegade is, however, always the most bitter against the party he has left, as we oftentimes still see. No one can ever hate a hereditary foe with the bitter feeling cherished by the injurer towards the injured; and Eadmoth naturally became the most vigorous opponent of the sons of Harold, whose father's bread he had for long time eaten. So vigorous, indeed, was Eadmoth's resistance that he was slain at the head of the Somerset peasantry rising in opposition to the Leinster men and Danes who, in the heedless license of invasion, were ravaging and plundering districts which otherwise would have been favourable to their cause. This was the last invasion of England from Ireland. Mark its date, for it is important. It took place in the June of 1069. The Bristol river then for the last time saw a fleet of hostile Irishmen sailing beneath the little chapel of the Irish saint, St. Brendan, which then crowned its heights.[1] But Bristol men and

---

[1] St. Brendan was called the Navigator, and was a favourite patron of sailors. He was connected equally with Wales and Ireland. He was the founder of Clonfert, in the county Galway. His *Acts*, published by Cardinal Moran in 1872, from the *Liber Kilkenniensis* in Primate Marsh's Library, Dublin, tell the story of his wanderings in the Western Ocean in search of Paradise. See the *Dict. Christ. Biog.*, t. i., p. 335, where Bishop Forbes makes a curious mistake in placing Clonfert in the county Longford, while it is actually far away in Galway. For a description of St. Brendan's chapel and hermitage at Bristol see Nicholls, and Taylor's

Leinster men and Dublin city formed connexions in these wars and intrigues which have a most important bearing on the story of the conquest of Ireland and the invasion of Strongbow. I must ask you to follow me a little into detail on this point. I shall try and make them as little burdensome as possible. I must ask you to remember, as the central figures, Dermot the elder, of 1066, and Eadmoth, at first Harold's follower and afterwards his foe and that of his family.

The descendants of Dermot MacMurrough and the descendants of Eadmoth retained the friendship originally cemented in the days of Harold's power. Dermot MacMurrough the younger, of Strongbow's time, was great grandson of Dermot of Harold's and William's time. Dermot was expelled from Ireland in August 1166. He was attended by Morice Regan, his secretary, valet, and personal attendant. That man, as I have already mentioned, wrote a most interesting account of the wanderings and efforts of his master, which has been worked up into the celebrated Anglo-Norman poem concerning the conquest of Ireland. In that poem we are told that Dermot sailed to Bristol with more than sixty ships.[1] Morice Regan is true to his native instinct. He cannot allow that his king and master fled in any low or ignominious manner. Even in flight the honour of the MacMurroughs must be maintained, and the fugitive prince represented as travelling with a convoy fitted for a triumphant conqueror; though in all probability he escaped in a

---

Bristol Past and Present, ii., 121. The chapel was thoroughly Irish in its dimensions, measuring only 27 feet by 16. An anchorite's cell was attached, as at St. Doulough's near Dublin, and at Fore, in county Westmeath. A cashel, or stone fortification, 120 feet in diameter, enclosed the whole.

[1] See *Anglo-Norman Poem*, ed. Wright, p. 12.

common fishing smack. With a favourable wind Dermot soon reached Bristol, and took up his lodgings at the house of Robert Harding at St. Austin's.

Now it is to this point I would specially direct your attention, as a most striking illustration of the historical accuracy of this ancient poem. Like all our ancient Irish chronicles, this Anglo-Norman poem, though based on the evidence of an eye-witness, has suffered depreciation at the hands of people who regard all Irish history as worthless lies; and yet the more critically it is investigated, the more closely it is compared with the testimony of contemporaneous annals, the more amply will its authority and accuracy be established. Just take this one point alone, for it is towards it I have been hitherto working up. "He took up his abode," says Morice Regan, "in the house of Robert Harding, at St. Austin's." No historian treating of this topic has, so far as I know, noticed that Robert Harding was a celebrated character of those times, famous in the Bristol annals, and intimately connected with Irish history as I have depicted it. It was not by chance King Dermot took up his residence with this man at St. Austin's, for their families had been connected, either as friends or foes, for more than a hundred years. Let me tell the story of Robert Harding, and you will easily see how this came about. This Harding was the grandson of Eadmoth, who had fought first beside Dermot's great-grandfather and then against Dermot's great-grandfather, and had been killed by him in one of the numerous struggles and wars connected with the Norman conquest. I have already told you how Harold's sons ravaged Bristol and Somerset and Devon, with the help of Dermot the elder, King of Leinster and of Dublin, about 1070.

They were defeated by Eadmoth, Harold's own most trusty follower, who had made his peace with William the Conqueror. Eadmoth had considerable estates in Somerset, but he was a wise man, and he saw that commerce was opening out new and wider fields for the attainment of wealth. He built therefore a house in Bristol,[1] engaged in trade, and was Reeve, or Mayor as we should say, of Bristol when he fell in 1068, repelling the attack of the Leinstermen. He had a son, Robert Harding, who followed his footsteps, continued to accumulate wealth, and also attained the office of Reeve of Bristol. This Robert Harding was, like his father, a prudent man. He came of a fighting race, but he did not care to imitate them. He thought, and thought rightly, that war was not a paying profession, and is therefore somewhat scornfully described by a chronicler of that age, William of Malmesbury, as shrewd and litigious, "more used to whet his tongue in suits of law than wield his weapons in war." Eadmoth's grandson was Robert Fitz, or son of, Harding. He maintained the traditions of his father and grandfather throughout a very long life. He was born in 1085. He died in 1170, and succeeded in founding a family which still continues to flourish among our highest nobility, and still cherishes among its names that of its original founder, this Bristol merchant, Robert Fitz-Harding. He married a wife named Eva, who, for aught we know, may have been an Irishwoman of King Dermot's own family, for Danish, and afterwards Anglo-Norman, princes and nobles often married the daughters of Irish chieftains.

---

[1] The Hardings lived in a great stone house, with an extensive garden attached, on the south side of Baldwin Street in Bristol. The foundations of it were discovered in 1823. See Nicholls and Taylor, *l.c.*, t. i., p. 58.

Robert Fitz-Harding became, in his turn, Reeve of Bristol, traded diligently, and added to his hereditary wealth. He purchased estates too; was, like his grandfather, a wise politician, noted the certain failure of King Stephen and his anarchical rule in the first half of the twelfth century, sided with Henry II., and when that prince came to the throne in 1154, our Bristol merchant was rewarded for the help he had rendered by the gift of the fief of Berkeley, previously held by one of Stephen's supporters. This was the origin of the present earldom of Berkeley, which holds its honours and traces its descent from this Bristol trader, and if you look into Sir Bernard Burke's *Peerage*, you will find his name of Fitz-Harding still perpetuated in that distinguished family.[1] Robert Harding imbibed in another respect the spirit of the age. The Norman conquest of England inaugurated an age of church-building. Bristol as yet possessed no great church. So the wealthy Reeve determined to rectify the omission, and in 1140 he founded the Church of St. Augustine, or St. Austin, dedicated to the Holy Trinity and commonly called Christ Church. In this fact I trace a proof of Robert Harding's connexion with Dublin thirty years before Dermot sought his protection. Ancient Dublin and ancient Bristol were like one another in one important point. They were each built on a hill, with an open space, or Carfax, on the top.[2] Christ Church Place in Dublin answers to the Carfax

---

[1] See *Berkeley MSS., Abstracts from Smyth's Lives of the Berkeleys*, ed. T. D. Fosbroke (London : 1821), and Seyer's *Memorials of Bristol*, t. i., chap. iv. G. T. Clark's *Mediæval Military Architecture*, t. i., p. 229-39, gives much interesting information about Berkeley Castle and the origin of that family.

[2] See *Historic Towns* ("Bristol"), ed. W. Hunt, p. 7: "On the summit of the hill four streets still meet, forming a Carfax

or square, which occupies the top of the Bristol hill. On one side of it to this day stands Robert Harding's Church of the Holy Trinity, afterwards changed, like our own Church of the Holy Trinity, from an Augustinian priory into a cathedral, when Bristol was made the seat of a bishopric under Henry VIII. Dublin is traditionally regarded as owing the foundation of St. Werburgh's Church to its Bristol connexion. Bristol seems to me to owe its cathedral of Christ Church to Robert Harding's trading expeditions to Dublin, where he saw a Cathedral Church of the Holy Trinity already a century old when he laid the foundations of his own pious erection.[1]

(*quatre voies*), and these divide the four ancient quarters of the town—the parishes of St. Mary-le-Port, Trinity or Christ Church, St. Ewen's, and All Saints."

[1] On this topic of Harding and Bristol Cathedral, see the *History of Bristol* by Nicholls and Taylor (Bristol: 1881); Ricart's *Kalendar* (Camden Soc.: 1872); Dugdale's *Monasticon*, vi., 363; Seyer's *Memorials of Bristol*, i., 462-80. Christ Church, Dublin, was originally a cathedral with secular canons attached. This was its earliest constitution under the Danish princes. The twelfth century was marked by the introduction of the reformed Augustinian order into England and Ireland. St. Laurence O'Toole made Christ Church, Dublin, an Augustinian establishment. Robert Harding erected Christ Church, Bristol, in connexi n with the same order. Christ Church, Dublin, was regarded as a cathedral prior to the Reformation; see the Calendar of Christ Church Deeds in the Appendix to the *Report* for 1888 of the Irish Deputy Keeper of the Records (Dr. La Touche), p. 42, No. 42. It is rather curious that the Roman Catholic Church has not maintained any Chapter corresponding to Christ Church, though she has maintained one corresponding to St. Patrick's. It is usually said that this has happened because the Cathedral Chapter, Dean, Canons, etc., was established by Henry VIII. These scruples did not always exist, however, as Dr. Latouche's *Report* shows. On p. 122 we have a bull of Pope Innocent X. calendared, ordering in 1644 the Roman Catholic Archbishop of Dublin to admit Patrick Chaell as Dean of Holy Trinity Church. King James II. also ousted the legal Dean and intruded a Roman Catholic.

Let us return to Harding's own career. Life had been intensely prosperous for our worthy citizen. He had accumulated wealth and honours, and had been spared to a green old age. Robert Harding and his wife determined that they would devote the remainder of their days to the monastic life; and so Harding entered his own Priory of the Holy Trinity as a Canon, while his wife founded the Magdalen convent, where she dwelt till her death in 1173. You can easily understand, therefore, why it was that Dermot sought refuge at St. Austin's with Robert Harding. He was an ancient friend, possibly allied by marriage. Harding's was a potent name in Bristol, and a still more potent influence with Henry II., the monarch whose cause he had championed in days of darkness, and with whom he might now fairly claim some influence. Dermot, then, displayed his usual prudence, when driven from Ireland, in resorting first of all to Bristol and lodging with Robert Harding at St. Austin's.[1]

Dermot did not tarry over-long at Bristol. He doubtless made use of Harding's purse, received letters from him, and then in the course of the autumn and winter of 1166-67 sought Henry, away in Southern France. Under other circumstances, Dermot's visit would have been most welcome to Henry II. The very first year of his reign had seen the conquest of this country mooted in the cabinet of that prince. About Michaelmas, 1155,[2] Henry held a council at

---

[1] It is interesting to note that in the earliest list of Dublin citizens occurs "John, son of Jordan, son of Harding." He may have been a son of one of Robert Harding's numerous sons by Eva, his wife. See "History of Bristol" in *Historic Towns* series, p. 25; and the list itself in Gilbert's *Municipal Documents* (Rolls Series), pp. 3-48; cf. the preface, pp. vii-x.

[2] See *Chronicles of Henry II.*, t. ii., p. xxxvii (pref.), Rolls Series.

Winchester, when he proposed to conquer Ireland and confer it as a fief on his youngest and favourite brother William. The project was then abandoned owing to the counsel of the Empress Matilda, who clearly saw that her son had quite enough on his hands, if order was to be restored in England after Stephen's anarchy, if the Welsh were to be restrained, and, above all, the continental dominions of the prince were to be protected from their numerous foes.[1] He laid aside the project for a time, indeed, but made provision for a future attempt by procuring from Pope Adrian IV. the famous bull by which Ireland was transferred to Norman dominion. And now the advent of King Dermot would have seemed the very opportunity he desired. Henry II. probably knew and had had dealings with King Dermot beforehand. In 1164 and 1165 the Welsh rose in rebellion against King Henry. He marched from Chester to crush the insurgents of North Wales, engaging a fleet of combined Danes and Leinstermen to attack them in the rear.[2] Henry sought Dermot's aid in 1164. Two

---

[1] Henry's task was a tremendous one. The restoration of order in England, the destruction of the robber castles which threatened the peace and security of the nation, the reform, or rather the creation, of a judicature, the expulsion of the roving armies of Flemish mercenaries which dominated the whole country, these alone would have been sufficient work for the ablest prince, and yet Henry had much more to do. The continental dominions of the English Crown were largely responsible for the gross neglect shown towards Ireland from the twelfth to the sixteenth centuries. All thought was centred on the Continent, none was left for Ireland. Just as in later times the interest of William III. in Holland and of the early Georges in Hanover prevented all attention to English and Irish difficulties.

[2] *Chronicles of Henry II.*, t. ii., pref., pp. xlii, lxviii. See *Brut y Tywysogion*, pp. 201-3 (Rolls Series). We learn from this Welsh chronicle, p. 61, that the Irish were leagued

years later Dermot seeks Henry's court with a similar petition on his side. But Henry had just then quite enough to do without interfering in Irish squabbles. The quarrel with Thomas à Becket was waxing fiercer and fiercer. The French king and Henry were locked in deadly conflict. His mother, too, hostile as ever to a further extension of the empire in a westerly direction, was still alive. Henry away in France would not trouble himself about Dermot's misfortune. And Dermot could get nothing but fair words and promises, and a few presents which the Pipe Roll of the twelfth of Henry II. notices as bestowed on certain Irishmen.[1] Henry, however, gave Dermot letters patent authorising him to employ assistance wherever he could find it. Dermot returned from France back to Robert Harding in the spring or summer of 1167, spent a month with him, and finally concluded an agreement with Richard, commonly called Strongbow, Earl of Striguil, son of Gilbert, Earl of Pembroke.

Richard Strongbow was one of those nobles who rose to great eminence and power under Stephen, when every man did whatsoever seemed right in his own eyes, and the only law which secured observance was the law of the sword. Henry II.'s strong arm struck down all such disturbers, and among the

with the Anglo-Normans—or the French, as this chronicle always calls them—against the Welsh as early as 1096.

[1] Cf. Girald. Camb., *Expugnatio*, lib. i., cap. ii.; Morice Regan, pp. 15-17; *Chronicles of Henry II.*, t. ii., p. lxxiv (Rolls Series). The Pipe Rolls of 12 Hen. II., as published by the Pipe Roll Society, t. ix., pp. 88, 117, have notices of several transactions with Irishmen in 1165—1166. There appears, for instance, a payment of £4 7s. 1d. to the Chancellor of the King of Ireland by the king's writ, but without any hint of the reason of it.

rest despoiled Strongbow of his father's title and estates, permitting him to reimburse his losses by establishing for himself a castle on the Welsh frontier. Strongbow was just the man for Dermot's purposes. Spendthrift, bankrupt in money and reputation, reckless, skilful, Dermot's was an enterprise which promised to retrieve his fortunes and make him a prince independent of Henry II., for Dermot promised to bestow on him his daughter and make him his successor in the kingdom of Leinster.[1] Dermot sought help in other quarters too. The neighbourhood of the Bristol Channel had been utilised by Henry II. as the Romans used the Danubian principalities a thousand years before. He had planted along the Welsh coast bands of military colonists. At his accession he found his kingdom overrun by Flemish mercenaries. He quietly transferred them to south-west Wales, and diverted their energies from wasting and plundering England to harrying and watching the ever-rebellious and revolting Welsh.[2] Among them, doubtless, Dermot found old soldiers of fortune anxious for battle and plunder as of yore. He passed over, therefore, into South Wales when he thought of returning to Ireland. He visited Rhys ap Gryffith, who welcomed him with

---

[1] Morice Regan's *Anglo-Norman Poem*, ed. F. Michel, pp. 17, 18 (cf. Wright's preface, pp. xii, xiii). G. T. Clark's *Mediæval Military Architecture*, t. i., pp. 111—15, gives many details about Strongbow's Welsh castles and those of his followers, many of whom became famous in the Irish invasion. These castles were often rude structures of earth and timber, like the Irish castles of the same period. Cf. Beaufort's essay on Irish Architecture in the *Transactions* of the Royal Irish Academy, t. xv., pp. 161-65, and note p. 30 above.

[2] The Flemish settlements in South Wales were begun, according to Holinshed, by William the Conqueror, and enlarged under Henry I. (cf. Giraldus Camb., *Welsh Itinerary*, lib i., cap. xi.).

genuine Celtic hospitality, releasing at his request a knight half Norman and half Welsh by descent, a certain Robert Fitz-Stephen, one of Nesta's many sons by her numerous husbands, and destined afterwards to play an important part in Irish history.[1] From the prince's court Dermot passed on to St. David's Head, then the favourite port of embarkation for Ireland. There he found the Geraldine faction in full sway. David Fitz-Gerald was Bishop of St. David's, and Maurice Fitz-Gerald, his brother, and Giraldus Cambrensis, his nephew, were hanging about the episcopal palace. The Fitz-Geralds in fact swarmed in the neighbourhood of St. David's, and did good service to their Norman suzerain, Henry II., in keeping the unruly Welsh in due subjection. Dermot purchased the whole faction by promising them the town of Wexford,—which he had never possessed, it being the property of the Danes. He exercised a kind of liberality oftentimes since imitated,—he was very liberal and generous in bestowing other people's property. Listen to the account of the transaction given by Giraldus Cambrensis, writing less than twenty years after the event: "Through the mediation, therefore, of David, Bishop of St. David's, and Maurice Fitz-Gerald, a contract was entered into that Dermot should grant to Robert and Maurice Fitz-Gerald the town of Wexford,—with two adjoining cantreds of land to be held in fee; in consideration whereof the said Maurice and Robert engaged to succour him in recovering his territories,

---

[1] These princes of South Wales were closely allied with the Irish princes, and, as I have already noted, often sought refuge among them when hard pressed by the Anglo-Normans. On the release of Fitz-Stephen at Dermot's intercession, see *Brut y Tywysogion* (Rolls Series), A.D. 1168, p. 207.

as soon as the winds were favourable and the first swallow appeared," that is, in spring.

The summer of 1167 and the winter and spring of 1168 passed away in these preparations. Dermot now became home-sick. As Giraldus puts it, "Snuffing from the Welsh coast the air of Ireland, he inhaled the scent of his beloved country." Two years, then, exactly, from the time of his exile he embarked at St. David's, on the 1st August, 1168; and sailing with an easterly wind, in a few hours arrived at Glasscarrig, a small village on the Wexford coast,[1] and secreted himself for the winter among his adherents in an Augustinian abbey, at his ancient family-seat of Ferns, where the ruins of an Anglo-Norman castle still mark the site of his primitive palace.[2] The interest in our tale now shifts from

---

[1] Glasscarrig is about twenty miles north-east of Wexford, and ten miles east of Ferns. The village has almost entirely disappeared. Glasscarrig must always have been a very dangerous landing-place save in fine summer weather. Courtown harbour, some five miles to the north, has only been made accessible to small vessels at great expense. I saw Glasscarrig and Courtown on a stormy day last October (1888), when no vessel could possibly approach the coast to land a passenger. A road still runs from it to Ferns. There are ruins of an abbey at Glasscarrig built into the walls of a cowhouse. Cf. Mr. Wakeman's report in *Ordnance Survey Correspondence* in Royal Irish Academy, County Wexford, *Letters*, t. i., p. 65.

[2] The village of Ferns is even still redolent of Dermot Mac-Murrough. The castle, called after him, is evidently an Anglo-Norman structure, built in the thirteenth century by some of Strongbow's heirs. It stands doubtless on the site of Dermot's Celtic Dun. Its plan was somewhat like that of Harlech castle in Wales. There was a central courtyard. At the four corners stood lofty drum towers connected by strong curtain walls. One of these towers remains perfect. In the second storey is a chapel with a beautifully groined roof, where the groining springs from consoles. See a description of this castle in *Ordnance Survey Correspondence*, in Royal Irish Academy, County Wexford, *Letters*, t. i., p. 77; *Extracts*, t. ii., p. 544. The view from this tower towards Mount Leinster, and the

England to Ireland, and centres in the county Wexford, a district which to this day, in its ruins, inhabitants, and even in its language, retains many traces of the Anglo-Norman invasion. The winter of 1168-69 passed as winters usually passed in Ireland in those times. The ancient Irish inverted the order of their descendants. The long nights are famous in the annals of modern Irish disturbances for many a sad tale of assassination and bloodshed. The long nights and the short days and the tempestuous weather in ancient times gave the inhabitants of this land their only season of peace. The circumstances of the case at once explain the reason why. The resources of civilisation have benefited and blessed mankind in a thousand ways, but they have also made crime easier and more terrible. Good roads, railways, telegraphs, have made life more convenient and enjoyable, but they have also served to help the criminal. If a party of moonlighters wish to attack a house twenty or

---

passes through which an invading foe from Meath or Ossory would come, is very fine and commanding. In the churchyard Dermot's grave is shown. It was once covered with a plain stone cross, of Celtic pattern. The upper portion has been broken off, removed, and utilised as a head-stone over another grave. This broken part is called Dermot's pillar. In the cathedral there lies a fine mediæval recumbent figure of St. Mogue, or Maedhog, the reputed founder of the See. See Bassett's *Wexford Directory*, p. 332. Dermot founded the Augustinian Abbey of Ferns in A.D. 1158, its deed of foundation being witnessed by St. Laurence O'Toole, then Abbot of Glendalough (see Archdall's *Monasticon Hibernicum*, p. 743). The ruins of this abbey still exist a couple of hundred yards east of the cathedral in the ancient episcopal demesne. It is evidently very ancient; the chapel is of the regular Celtic type, very small and square, while attached is a tower, square at the bottom and then becoming round after a few feet, together with the ruins of a cloister or hall of an English type. See *Ordnance Survey Correspondence* as above, Wexford, *Letters*, t. i., p. 215; *Extracts*, t. ii., p. 546.

thirty miles distant, a good road serves their purpose as well as that of the merchant or honest labourer. Seven hundred years ago the roads of Ireland ran in the main upon the same tracks as at present, but they were mere passes through forests and bogs which the September rains rendered impassable till the following spring opened them again. Some of these passes still remain in their primitive state. Would you see one of them, often used doubtless by Dermot and his men, go to the head of Glenmalure valley in Wicklow and traverse the pass which leads from that wild glen to the towns of Donard and Dunlavin. It is a magnificent walk over the shoulder of Lugnaquilla. It proceeds up by the Ess water-fall to the height of two thousand feet, and then descends beneath the beetling cliffs of the North Prison and beside the head waters of the Slaney into the vale of Imail. I have traversed it on a beautiful day at the end of a fine April, and yet it brought me well within the snow line, and was in parts almost as impassable as the Slough of Despond itself.[1] Such were all the roads of Ireland, and of Wales too, in those times. It is no wonder that winter was then Ireland's time of halcyon peace, when even such a noted fugitive as Dermot MacMurrough could lie hidden, safe and secure from the attacks of the injured O'Rourke of Breifny himself. With the spring of 1169 the work of invasion began. The first arrivals were Fitz-Geralds, headed by Robert Fitz-Stephen, whom Dermot had hired the previous summer. His small army seems to have been composed entirely of those Flemish military colonists whom, as I have already mentioned, Henry II. had

---

[1] This pass is pictured most accurately in Hall's *Picturesque Ireland*, vol. ii.

settled along the coast line of South Wales to keep the restless chiefs of that country in order. The *Annals of the Four Masters* speak in very contemptuous tone of the first invaders under date of 1169. Here is their entry: "The fleet of the Flemings came from England in the army of MacMurchadha, *i.e.* Diarmaid, to contest the Kingdom of Leinster for him; they were seventy heroes, dressed in coats of mail;" and then we are told the Irish princes "set nothing by them." Giraldus Cambrensis gives their numbers more exactly; as thirty knights of his own kindred and sixty others clothed in mail, and three hundred archers.[1] They sailed, according to tradition, in two vessels called respectively Bag and Bun, names which are now preserved in the designation of the promontory of Wexford where they first landed. That promontory lies on the eastern side of the peninsula, terminated by the famous Hook tower which intervenes between Waterford and Wexford harbours, and forms one side of Bannow Bay. The town of Bannow has often been called the Irish Herculaneum. A town existed there three centuries ago which now exists no longer, because it has been covered up by the drifting sands of that stormy coast, though the names of its streets still survive on the quit-rent rolls. Mark and observe one point however. The choice of Bannow Bay as their landing-place proves to demonstration, were demonstration needed, that the men of Bristol and the Welsh of St. David's had the most close and intimate acquaintance with the geography of the coast of Ireland. I do not think that any proof is necessary to show the active intercommunication between

---

[1] Girald. Camb., *Expug.* i., 3.

Wales and the east and south-east of Ireland at this period. The Welsh annals, as the *Brut y Tywysogion*, agree with the Irish in describing the frequent visits of Irish fleets to Wales, and of Welsh fleets to Ireland, with various purposes, peaceful or hostile, from A.D. 900 to 1200. Fitz-Stephen chose Bannow Bay because it was the only haven open to him for two great reasons, the one political, the other physical. He wished to form a junction with Dermot at Ferns: the only ports fitted for the purpose were Dublin, Wicklow, Arklow, Wexford, and Waterford, all of them at that time, as their very names indicate, in the power and jurisdiction of the Northmen, and hostile to Dermot. Bannow was the only port open to the invader, because too insignificant for Danish notice. Fitz-Stephen must have had accurate information as to the facts of Danish dominion when he made his selection. Physical reasons, too, determined him in his choice Wexford was shut against him. Waterford was hostile, as Strongbow a year or two later learned to his cost. Between Waterford and Wexford, Bannow was the only port permitting the approach of a troopship, even as small as those used in the twelfth century. The coast between Carnsore Point and Wexford Harbour on the one side, and the Tower of Hook at the entrance of Waterford Harbour on the other, is, perhaps, the most dangerous in the British Islands. Take up the sailing directions for the coast of Ireland, issued by the Admiralty in 1885, and study the portion relating to the coast of Wexford, and then you will see how wise, prudent, and practically experienced was Fitz-Stephen when he chose Bannow as his port of disembarkation. The Saltees, the Tuscar Rock, and dozens of other dangers line the whole coast, and have proved fatal to multitudes, notwithstanding all our modern improvements.[1] The Welsh sailors and pilots knew their business and proved their experience when they led Fitz-Stephen to the promontory of Bag and Bun Head.

I have now shown you how Dermot organized his revenge; I have brought the Fitz-Geralds to the shores of Ireland and introduced them to Bannow Bay. But—very fittingly, and quite in character with their mission—there is a grand controversy concerning the exact spot of Bannow Bay where they landed. Mr. and Mrs. S. C. Hall, in their *Picturesque Ireland*, took one side; the Kilkenny Archæological Society took the opposite side. The details of that discussion, if given in full, would only weary and confuse. A brief reference to them will introduce us to the next stage of the invasion, and also help us to realise the perilous circumstances of the first adventurers.

---

[1] For a description of this dangerous coast, with its numerous shoals and rocks, see *Sailing Directions for the Coast of Ireland*, part i., 1885, published by the Admiralty, pp. 66-87.

LECTURE IV.

THE INVASION OF THE GERALDINES.

POPULAR impressions are hard to dissipate. They grow with a nation's growth and strengthen with a nation's strength, till at last they become part and parcel of a nation's faith. Such a national delusion now comes before us. Henry II. gets the credit of planning the invasion of Ireland and of carrying out his purpose. To the popular mind his is the one dominant figure, seconded and supported indeed by Strongbow, but ordering and directing all by his commanding influence. Such is the popular view—a testimony doubtless to the force of Henry's character, but yet a notion founded upon a total misconception. The original invaders of Ireland were Welshmen, Flemish mercenaries, Norman-Welsh knights; they were anything at all but pure Normans, sent by royal authority and subject to royal rule. The first invaders, again, were private speculators, adventurers like the earliest settlers in India who founded the East India Company, or the earliest settlers in the regions of the North who founded the Hudson's Bay Company, or like those other Companies we have heard much of during the last few years, the Congo Company, or the Borneo Company. The first invaders were Fitz-Geralds, and belonged to the Geraldine clan. The next invaders were Strongbow and his allies. It was not till Henry II. became jealous of the progress and success of his lieges that he condescended to turn aside from the more exciting and notable field of European politics to the consideration of Irish affairs. This lecture will be devoted to the object of illustrating and explaining the action, character, and conduct of these first private invaders of Ireland; and will embrace the years 1169 and 1170, when the foundations of Norman dominion were laid by these adventurers. The poem of Morice Regan and the History of Giraldus Cambrensis, when compared together, enable us to follow almost day by day the warlike deeds of the earliest Anglo-, or perhaps I should more properly say, Cambro-Normans. I may indeed here repeat what I have already stated, that the more carefully you study this Anglo-Norman poem, the more thoroughly you will trust it.[1] It is evidently based on original documents. It fixes dates, Church festivals, mentions the precise periods during which the armies reposed, the roads they took, the rivers they crossed, and many other topographical details which have escaped the notice of the editor, Mr. Wright, who, being an Englishman, had none of that local knowledge which alone would have cleared up the difficulties of the narrative. And here let me note one extraordinary piece of editorial folly,—I was going to say, of Anglican wrongheadedness. It was bad enough to have Morice Regan's narrative edited and Giraldus Cambrensis translated by a man who, in his notes on Giraldus Cambrensis, identifies Kinsale, a town in Cork, with Kinselagh, an Irish tribe in Wexford;[2] but then, when the Government

---

[1] See for a description of it the note on p. 25.
[2] See Wright's edition of Giraldus Cambrensis (Bohn's Series), pp. 222, 224. I have given in a succeeding chapter another laughable instance of a similar mistake made by the editor of Roger Hoveden, in the same series. Three very similar names often occur in early Anglo-Irish history, which

were officially publishing an edition of the collected works of Giraldus Cambrensis, to hand over the editing and annotating of his *Topographia Hiberniæ* and of his *Expugnatio Hiberniæ* to another Englishman equally ignorant of Ireland, was one of those thoughtless, hopelessly stupid actions which help to explain the failure of English policy in this country. One can scarcely imagine how even officialism of the densest character could pass over Irish scholars like Bishop Reeves, Mr. Hennessy, Mr. James Graves, or Mr. Gilbert in favour of any Englishman, no matter how learned in textual criticism, where a history and a geography dealing with Ireland were concerned. What would be said of Irishmen, supposing they wanted Bede's *Ecclesiastical History of England* edited, if they committed the work to a resident in Donegal who had never seen England and was totally ignorant of the English tongue? Yet the exact parallel of this has been perpetrated in the publication of Giraldus Cambrensis' works in the Rolls Series. The mere scholarly work has been indeed admirably done. We have the best text presented to us, but we get no antiquarian, geographical, or historical assistance whatever, simply because the editor had none to give.

Let us return to the narrative of the invasion.

---

should, however, be carefully distinguished, viz., Kinsale, a town in Cork; Kinsellagh, a tribe and tribal division comprehending the county of Wexford, the barony of Shilelagh in Wicklow and Kavanagh's Country, in Carlow (see Grace's *Annals*, published by Irish Arch. Soc. A.D. 1842, p. 120); and Censale or Kennsalich (now Kinsaley, near St. Doulough's), a village and parish once the property of the Torkils, Danish princes of Dublin before the arrival of Strongbow (see Dr. La Touche's *Report on Irish Public Records* for 1888, p. 36). This property was transferred in 1174 to Christ Church Cathedral (cf. D'Alton's *History of the County Dublin*, p. 219).

Robert Fitz-Stephen, the knight whose freedom Dermot had won by his interest with Rhys, Prince of South Wales, arrived about May 1st, 1169, with three ships, and landed either at the promontory of Bag and Bun, where his name is still perpetuated on the ordnance map, or else at the town of Bannow across the bay.[1] With him came another descendant of Nesta, Fitz-Stephen's nephew, Meyler Fitz-Henry. Next day Maurice de Prendergast, of Haverfordwest, arrived from Milford Haven with ten knights and a considerable body of archers. They landed at the same point. It was a well-chosen spot for two reasons, as I have already briefly noticed. First, from a sailor's point of view, it was the only safe spot on the most dangerous coast of Ireland, the ports of Waterford and Wexford

---

[1] The Rev. James Graves contended strongly in favour of Bannow as the first landing-place of the invaders, in the *Kilkenny Archæological Journal* (1849-51), t. i., p. 189; cf. p. 194. The ruined church of St. Brendan at Bannow still exists. It is depicted in Hall's *Picturesque Ireland*, t. ii., p. 153, and mentioned in a deed now in Cambridge University Library, dated 1245. See *Kilk. Arch. Journal* (1854-55), t. iii., p. 219. This Cambridge deed is a curious document, showing that modern difficulties found their counterpart in ancient times. Hervey de Mountmaurice was Strongbow's uncle, and one of his companions in invasion. King Dermot gave him a large tract of land between Wexford and Bannow. Mountmaurice bestowed the lands upon Christ Church, Canterbury, and its monks, who, however, as absentee landlords, could get no rents. The Canterbury absentee monks leased them therefore to the resident monks of Tintern Abbey in 1245 at an annual rent of £4 6s. 8d. In 1318 the Tintern Abbey monks redeemed this rent by a payment of £100, —more than twenty years' purchase of the same. I should imagine the present landlords would be very glad to get the same rate of purchase for their interest. Tintern Abbey and all the leading points of interest in the district of Bannow and Bag-and-Bun are pictured in the second volume of the joint work of Mr. and Mrs. S. C. Hall, to which I have already referred. Mrs. Hall had special opportunities of knowing that neighbourhood, as she was a native of Bannow.

being unavailable. Secondly, from a military and
political point of view, it divided the enemy's forces, cut
off the Waterford Danes from those of Wexford, and
opened up a direct road to the north of the county
Wexford, where King Dermot was lying concealed.
Even to this day the nearest railway stations to Bannow
for Dublin and North Wexford are Ballywilliam and
New Ross, towns north of Wexford, and not Wexford
itself. The invaders spent some ten days in making
preparations, erecting temporary dwellings, the site of
Fitz-Stephen's house being still pointed out.[1] On the
11th of May[2] Dermot, then at Ferns, received a letter
from Fitz-Stephen announcing their arrival. He at once
despatched his favourite son Donall Kavanagh, following
next day with such small forces as he could muster.
The combined armies rested for a night at the coast,
and then proceeded to Wexford, some twenty-five miles
distant. Wexford, as the Danes called it, Lough
Carman, as the Celtic Irish did, had been from the
earliest date a leading Scandinavian settlement.[3] Its
inhabitants had united with their brethren of Dublin
and the Celtic Irish in resisting the tyranny of Dermot,
and they now unanimously determined to oppose him,
though aided by Welsh and Norman mercenaries. They

---

[1] See Bassett's *Wexford Directory*, p 270, and Hall, *l.c.*,
t. ii., p. 148.
[2] See O'Flaherty's *Ogygia*, pars. iii., xciv.
[3] Wexford presents down to the present day many features
manifesting the presence of the Scandinavian rovers, specially
in its topography. Thus we find Carnsore, Greenore, and
Raven Points along the sea coast. The castle was the citadel
of the town even in Danish times. It is now the Militia
barracks. The Danish rath was replaced by a Norman castle
erected on its site by Geoffrey de Marisco, after the embarkation of Henry II. at Wexford in the spring of 1172. See
Bassett's *Wexford Directory*, p. 67.

met in conflict outside the walls, but speedily retired within the gates, unable to resist the impulse of the mail-clad knights. Wexford was then much smaller than it is now, just as Danish Dublin was a very contracted spot. Even still the crowded and narrow streets in the centre of the town, where two vehicles can scarce pass, like those of our own city round Christ Church Cathedral, abundantly testify to the trust reposed in the protection of the Castle and the narrow circuit of its Danish fortifications, which were enlarged, or rather entirely superseded, in the fourteenth century by walls, large portions of which still remain.[1] Behind these fortifications the Danes fought boldly. The Normans advanced to the attack, but were repelled. Robert de Barry, one of the Fitz-Gerald clan, and elder brother of Giraldus Cambrensis himself, led the attack. He mounted the walls, and must have been sorely discomfited when he found that the Danish Irish did not fight according to the rules of war as known among English and Norman gentlemen. A Wexford man beholding the portly and glittering figure of the knight, magnificent with helmet, escutcheon, battle-axe, and shield, took deliberate aim with a stone, and delivering it with true Irish vigour and accuracy, hit the knight upon the side of his helmet with such force that he fell prostrate into the town ditch; a blow which must have been a fearful

---

[1] The present walls of Wexford were erected outside the Danish ramparts in the fourteenth century, probably in the war of Bruce in Ireland, when the Dublin walls were likewise extended. See Bassett, *l.c.*, pp. 67-9. It is a great pity that we have no really good county history of Wexford. It could only be produced by some local resident. But, alas! in Ireland the enthusiasm for fox-hunting swallows up all literary taste.

one, as his brother Giraldus assures us that sixteen years after,—that is, just when he was writing,—his brother's double teeth all fell out, and, still more marvellous to relate, that new ones grew in their place, though he must have been then a man of middle age. The ignominious fall of their leader so disheartened the allied Norman and Leinster men that they at once retired, having suffered the loss of eighteen men, while the townsmen had lost only three.[1] This was the first battle of Wexford fought against the Normans, and Robert de Barry was the first man-at-arms struck down and wounded in the Norman invasion of Ireland.[2]

The Normans now turned their attention to the harbour of Wexford; and the Danes, no match for them in the open field, were obliged to look on while they burned all the ships which lay there.[3] These may, indeed, have been for the most part fishing boats, but Giraldus gives us an incidental notice proving that

---

[1] Morice Regan's poem, lines 487-93, gives us the details of the assault on Wexford, supplementing the narrative of Giraldus thus—
> "La cité asailli à tute sa force
> Les autre pur garir lur cors
> Sa défendirent par defors.
> XVIII. i perdi de ces Engleis
> A icel saut li riche reis,
> E les traiters à icel feiz
> Ne perdirent de lur que treis."

The third chapter of the First Book of the *Expugnatio* of Giraldus may be compared with the whole passage from which I have just given an extract. This Anglo-Norman poem sadly needs re-editing. Dr. Atkinson, Professor of the Romance Languages in Dublin University, informs me that he has noted numberless errors in Wright's edition when compared with the MS. in Lambeth.

[2] Girald. Camb., *Expug.*, i., 4.

[3] The harbour of Wexford covers an enormous space. When the tide is full it looks like an inland sea. The town of Wexford is situated on a hill at one point of the harbour, but

Wexford commerce even then embraced a cross-channel trade; for the Normans having found there and seized an English ship just arrived from the coast of Britain with a cargo of corn and wine, a band of soldiers rowed out and seized it. The sailors slipped the anchors and made their escape. A strong westerly wind was blowing, which rapidly carried the captors out to sea, and it was only at great risk and after a long pull in their boats that the Norman soldiers regained their friends. The night brought repose to both parties, and gave the Wexford people time for consultation. They saw clearly enough that they were in a dangerous situation, and that, notwithstanding their temporary success, they were sure to be defeated in the long run. So, early in the morning, as the Normans advanced to the attack after duly hearing Mass, they were met by two bishops, who happened to be in the town, and by some of the leading citizens, with proposals of surrender, which were accepted; four of the principal townsmen being delivered as hostages, and a treaty of peace duly signed in the Abbey of Selsker, now a prominent ruin in Wexford.[1] The town and the two cantreds or baronies of Forth and Bargy adjoining the city were

---

it cannot have afforded any protection to ships lying in the harbour, exposed as it was to attack from an enemy encamped beside the town. See the description of Wexford harbour in the Admiralty *Sailing Directions for the Coast of Ireland*, Part I., p. 85 (London: 1885).

[1] Bassett's *Wexford Directory*, p. 71, has a long description of Selsker Abbey; cf. for a view of it Hall's *Picturesque Ireland*, t. ii., p. 173. Its origin is attributed to the Danes, and its restoration to the Roche family. An interesting tale hangs thereby. Sir A. Roche, of Artramount, fell in love with the beautiful daughter of one of the burgesses. His parents sent him to the Crusades to cure him of his affection. He returned after some years to claim his bride. He found, however, that she in despair had become a nun, where-

at once conferred by Dermot upon Fitz-Stephen and Maurice de Prendergast as a reward for their assistance, and it is a strange but yet a simple historical fact that these baronies are still inhabited by numerous descendants of these original Norman, Flemish, and Welsh settlers, transformed in many cases by the magic influence of Irish air into the most extreme opponents of the deeds and views of their warlike ancestors.[1]

I have bestowed more time and space on this narration of the capture of Wexford than I can spare for some other warlike achievements of the first invaders,

---

upon he vowed celibacy, restored this abbey, and became its prior. Its present name is, of course, only a corruption of St. Sepulchre; it being dedicated in honour of the Holy Sepulchre at Jerusalem, like the ancient palace of the Archbishops of Dublin, concerning which more hereafter. Archdall's *Monasticon*, p. 755, calls it the Priory of SS. Peter and Paul, of Selsker. A synod was held in this monastery in 1240, when canons were enacted which are now printed in Wilkins's *Concilia*, t. i., p. 681; cf. Ware's *Bishops of Ireland*, p. 440.

[1] On the baronies of Forth and Bargy, their inhabitants, dialect, customs, etc., see Hall, *l.c.*, t. ii., pp. 143-73; Bassett's *Wexford Directory*, p. 27; Martin Doyle's *Notes and Gleanings of the co. Wexford* (Dublin: 1868). The peculiar dialect of Forth and Bargy may be studied in Poole's *Dialect of Forth and Bargy*, edited by the Rev. W. Barnes, B.D. (the Dorsetshire poet), London, 1867; in a paper by General Vallancy, *Transactions* of Royal Irish Academy, t. ii.; in Fraser's *Statistical Survey of Wexford*, A.D. 1807; and in an essay by the late Dr. Russell, of Maynooth, in the first number of *Atlantis*, A.D. 1858, an extinct Dublin literary venture of that period. The works above quoted, together with Walter Harris's *Hibernica*, p. 21, and the papers on Bannow by Messrs. Graves and Tuomy in the *Kilkenny Arch. Journal* for 1849-51, t. i., pp. 187, 194, afford numerous proofs that the present inhabitants are direct descendants of the first Anglo-Norman settlers. Dr. O'Donovan, in a note on A.D. 1169 in the *Annals of Four Masters*, says: "The editor, when examining the baronies of Forth and Bargie for the Ordnance Survey, was particularly struck with the difference between the personal appearance of the inhabitants of these baronies

because I felt it necessary to make you realize how minute is our information concerning the movements of the earliest Norman invaders. We, in fact, know just as much about them as we know about the earliest achievements of William the Conqueror after the battle of Hastings, as a very cursory examination of Giraldus Cambrensis and of the Anglo-Norman poem so often quoted will amply prove.

Wexford was captured, and the strength of resistance to Dermot's sway in the south of Leinster was thus paralysed. Dermot and his allies, leaving a garrison in Wexford, forthwith marched to Ferns, in the north of the county, where Dermot's royal residence was situated. There they remained three weeks, healing the wounded, and recruiting their forces from the tribesmen, who, now that Dermot showed signs of success, flocked in crowds to his banners; for it is the simple fact that Ireland, then and ever since, has always been a land where nothing succeeds like success, and nothing fails so completely as failure. At the end of three weeks Dermot proposed to Robert Fitz-Stephen and Maurice de Prendergast to accompany him in an attack upon Gillpatrick, King of Ossory.[1] The

---

and those of O'Murphy's country, the northern baronies of the co. Wexford. The Kavanaghs and Murphys are tall and often meagre, while the Flemings, Codds, and other natives of the baronies of Forth and Bargie are generally short and stout."

[1] Morice Regan's poem is fuller and more accurate than Giraldus, in the details of the military movements after the capture of Wexford. Giraldus makes the combined army of Leinster and the Normans advance at once to the attack of Fitzpatrick, Prince of Ossory. This would have demanded a march across a hostile country to the site of New Ross, and then along the marshy course of the Nore and Barrow. Morice Regan, on the other hand, knowing the country and its roads, brings the allied forces along the valley of the Slaney

Anglo-Norman poem of Morice Regan and Giraldus Cambrensis pretend to give the speeches which were made on this and other occasions in the course of the invasion, but they are manifestly fancy orations, composed by the authors of these works and put into the mouths of the speakers. The most amusing instance of this convenient kind of oratory is the speech supposed to have been uttered by Roderic O'Conor, King of Connaught, when, in the course of this summer of 1169, he had assembled an army to attack Dermot and the Normans. He is represented by Giraldus (i. vii.) as addressing a very spirit-stirring oration to his troops of wild Connaughtmen, commencing in the following high-pitched strain: " Right noble and valiant defenders of your country and liberty, let us consider with what nations and for what causes we are now about to wage battle." He then proceeds to pour unbounded abuse on the head of King Dermot, with whom he unites the Anglo-Normans. " Himself an enemy, he has called in our greatest national enemy; a people who have long aimed at being lords over him as well as over all of us." He next enlarges upon the wickedness of the King of

---

by Enniscorthy to Ferns, a route which I followed last year on a tricycle. It is now the great coach road from Dublin to Wexford, and must have existed, though in a rude state, in Dermot's day; for the great roads of Ireland have always maintained the same lines. It is a beautiful road for a tricycle trip, passing through some of the finest Wexford and Wicklow scenery, along by the little known Blackstairs and Mount Leinster Range, varied by glimpses of the Slaney. Morice Regan's words are—

> " D'iloec s'en turne li Reis Dermod
> Vers Fernez, al einz qu'il pout
> Pour ses naffrez saner
> E pur ses barons sojorner.
> Treis semeines sojornout
> En la cité li Reis Dermod.

Leinster in provoking internal wars, but he does so in a style and language which would scarcely move a mob in Galway, Clare, or Tipperary nowadays, after all the efforts of the national system of education. " Mark, my countrymen, mark well how most states have been overthrown by civil discord. Julius Cæsar, after having twice shown his back to the Britons, returned the third time and subdued the country on the invitation of Androgius, who was a victim to his own thirst for revenge. This same Julius after having at length conquered the western parts of the world, ambitious of supreme power, did not hesitate to bring foreign nations to shed the blood of the Roman people in a worse than civil war." I am very much afraid that our Irish public men, or at least our Irish audiences and their literary taste, have so far degenerated that an appeal to the days of Julius Cæsar, or even to those of Brian Boru or Roderic O'Conor himself, would not tell half as well as a reference in one part of the country to Derry, Aughrim, and the Boyne, or in another quarter to the stirring times of '48, or an apt quotation from that historic ballad, "Who fears to speak of ninety-eight."

In treating of the history of the invasion, we may totally disregard the speeches put into the mouths of the principal actors by Giraldus Cambrensis or by Morice Regan, and fix our attention on their deeds alone as narrated by them. Dermot proposed first of all to invade Ossory with the help of the Normans. Ossory was at that period a leading kingdom of Ireland, though not one of the five principal divisions.[1] It bordered

---

[1] See *Journal* of the Kilkenny Archæological Society, t. i., pp. 230-57, for two articles by the Rev. J. Graves and Dr. O'Donovan, on Ossory and its tribes, where the boundaries of the kingdom of Ossory are described. On p. 249

upon Leinster. The kingdom of Leinster, the hereditary or family possession of Dermot MacMurrough, embraced the east of Ireland from Dublin to Wexford, extending westward to the county of Kilkenny and the Queen's County. The kingdom of Ossory is now represented by the diocese of Ossory, strictly so called, as you will find it defined in Lewis's *Topographical Dictionary;* for I must here repeat what I stated in a previous course of lectures, that the best idea of the ancient kingdoms and principalities of Ireland is to be derived from a study of the diocesan boundaries, which exactly correspond with, and have been derived from, these ancient secular divisions.[1] The kingdom of Ossory extended over the greater portion of Kilkenny and that portion of the Queen's County called the Barony of Upper Ossory. And now mark here an illustration of the tenacity of the Celtic race and of the mixed character of our Irish population in even the very highest ranks. The nobility of Ireland are to a large

---

O'Donovan quotes a verse from O'Heerin's topographical poem (edited by himself in 1862 for the Irish Archæological Society's series of antiquarian works) p. 95, defining its limits thus :—

"Mac-Gilla-Phadraig, of the Bregian fort,
The land of Ossory to him is due
From Bladma out to the sea."

That is, as he explains, from the summit of the Slieve Bloom Mountains in the Queen's County on the north, to the meeting of the Three Waters opposite Cheek Point, in the county Waterford, on the south. I shall usually spell the formidable Celtic name Mac-Gilla-Phadraig in the more modern form Gill.-Patrick. About Ossory and its extent a note by O'Donovan on A.D. 1175, in *Annals of the Four Masters*, and the authorities there quoted, should also be consulted.

[1] See Rev. J. Graves's paper on Ancient Ossory in the *Journal* of the Kilkenny Archæological Society, t. i., p. 231, where he states that the rural deaneries of Ossory correspond to the tribes, as the diocese to the kingdom of that name, adding a very remarkable illustration of his view.

extent English in their origin, even when that origin goes back to the twelfth century, as in the case of the Fitz-Geralds of Leinster and Munster. Yet many even of our nobility can trace themselves back to Celtic chieftains, and notably in the case now under consideration. The King of Ossory in 1169 was one Donnchadh Gillpatrick.[1] His family is now represented by the Fitzpatricks or Gillpatricks, who enjoy the title of Castletown Barons of Upper Ossory; and I saw some short time ago in the London *Times* a letter from the present holder of that title, in which he deprecated compulsory sale of Irish estates to the tenants on the express ground that his family had held the property he at present possesses for the last one thousand years, a period of uninterrupted ownership almost without parallel in these islands, save in the case of Church lands.[2] Dermot hated this Gillpatrick of Ossory, and with good reason, for only the very previous year he had blinded Dermot's son, "the royal heir of Leinster," as the Four Masters call him, and thus deprived the King of Leinster of all hope of perpetuating his kingdom in the male line, blindness being a fatal bar to a tribal election to sovereignty.[3] Against Donnchadh

---

[1] Donough Gillpatrick was the founder of Jerpoint Abbey, one of the finest monastic ruins in Ireland. See *Antiquities of Kilkenny*, by J. G. Robertson (Kilkenny: 1851), and Archdall's *Monasticon Hibernicum*, p. 355. The founder is said to have been buried there in 1185. His tomb is still pointed out adorned with some figures clothed in the dress of the twelfth or thirteenth century.

[2] The glebe lands of Kells, in the diocese of Meath, were Church property, certainly for more than eight hundred years (see Archdeacon Stopford's *Handbook of Ecclesiastical Law*, p. 50). They have been lately sold, though sentiment would have retained them.

[3] This prince's name was Enna MacMurchadha (see Four Masters, A.D. 1168, O'Donovan's edition). He seems to have

Gillpatrick, therefore, Dermot and the Normans directed the first blow. Dermot acted like a wise general as he was, and determined to crush the enemies nearest to him before they had time to summon the forces of Roderic O'Conor of Connaught and of O'Rourke of Breifny. He advanced, therefore, against Gillpatrick, about the beginning of June, 1169.

His task was no easy one. The King of Ossory had, as Dermot knew, made preparations to give him and his friends a warm reception. He had cut trenches across the roads, as still they do at evictions, planted them with palisades of timber and of thorn bushes, and manned them with five thousand men. Dermot's Leinster troops had in addition been demoralised by three defeats received at the hands of the Ossory men. Celtic troops and nations are specially subject to the spirit of depression. They fight splendidly while successful; they become abject cowards in the hour of defeat. They are deficient in solid staying power, —a trait of national character which we have seen strikingly illustrated in the case of the French in the last Franco-German war. Dermot's Ossory expedition as described by our authorities offers another example of this fatal weakness. The Leinster troops came to the spot where, three times over, Gillpatrick had

---

survived his mutilation for many years, and to have had children. His daughter Dervorgil married Donnall Gillamocholmog, prince of the tribe which inhabited the Dodder Valley and the glens leading thence into the Dublin Mountains. Enna's name appears as a witness to a grant made by Dervorgil to St. Mary's Abbey about 1190. See Gilbert's *Chartularies of St. Mary's Abbey*, t. i., p. 32 (Rolls Series). Cf. another grant in the same volume, p. 35, by which another chief of the same clan bestowed the wild, picturesque valley of Glencullen on the same monastery in 1230. Donnall Kavanagh, Dermot's favourite son, was not legitimate even according to the very loose matrimonial laws then prevalent among the Celtic princes.

defeated them. A panic seized them, and they fled in a moment, disappearing into the depths of the forest which then and long after covered the districts of Idrone, Slieve-Margy, and the Queen's County.[1] His Norman allies were but of little avail to Dermot under such circumstances. Heavy armed and mail-clad knights on horseback, cross-bowmen on foot, were formidable to the light-armed and unarmoured Irish in plains and in the open country. But they were worse than useless when marching along a narrow forest footpath, where they had to proceed in single file and in straggling order. Then was the Celtic opportunity; and often indeed, in the history of this country, have the native Irish used it to avenge themselves upon their adversaries. Why, even down to our own times, with all our improvements in the art of destruction, the Irish peasantry have succeeded in defeating English forces under similar circumstances. Half a century ago the last deadly victory was thus gained by Irish peasants, armed with pitchforks and scythes, over British forces. The men of this generation know nothing of the Battle of Carrickshock, when a large body of police, horse and foot, was annihilated in the very same neighbourhood as Dermot MacMurrough was now invading. It was the terrible time of the tithe agitation, the latter part of the year 1831, when a body of police were enticed into a wooded defile in the county Kilkenny, and almost completely destroyed, unable to use their weapons of precision against an unseen foe. At the battle of Carnew, in the rebellion of 1798, Sir Watkin Wynn's

---

[1] See on this forest the *Journal* of the Kilkenny Archæological Society for 1856, t. i., N.S., p. 238, where an interesting article will be found on " The Woods of Ancient Leinster," by H. F. Hore, Esq.

regiment of cavalry, called the Ancient Britons, was annihilated under similar circumstances. In 1599 the fiery Essex was obliged to retire from an expedition made into the King's County, because the woods of Durrow were so entrenched, plashed, and defended that the roads were impassable. A few years earlier he was taught, by bitter experience, the dangers of such an attempt from the losses he sustained when passing through the woods of Tipperary, where so many knights fell that the spot was afterwards called the Pass of Plumes. So it was with the Norman adventurers on the occasion of this invasion of Ossory. Had they been troops trained in continental warfare they would doubtless have all perished. But fortunately for themselves they had been exercised in the very similar warfare waged among the Welsh woods and morasses. They were half Celts too, and they knew right well how to deal with the Irish under their existing circumstances. The time of the year, the leafy month of June, added to the Norman difficulties. There was a proverb current long ago in Ireland which explains this statement. "The Irish will never be tamed," so ran the saying, "whilst the leaves are on the trees"—implying that the best season for carrying on war against the natives was after the fall of the leaf, as they found shelter for themselves, and food for their horses and cattle, in and under the leafy boughs of the forest. Behold now a practical example of the somewhat abstract principles I have been laying down. Dermot and the Normans ravaged Ossory after the usual fashion, burned houses, destroyed the growing crops, swept off the cattle. They were returning laden with plunder, when the Ossory men fell upon them. They had come to the spot—a dangerous defile it was—where the Leinster men had been so often defeated. A cry was raised that the Ossory men were upon them. Dermot's native soldiers at once fled, while the Normans, expecting immediate attack, pushed on to firm and clear ground as rapidly as possible.[1]

Maurice de Prendergast showed himself a thorough general at this crisis. He never for a moment lost his head. He summoned Robert Smith, the chief of the archers, to his side,—the poem demonstrates its authenticity by such minute details,—placed him in ambush, so as to take the Irish in the rear, and then marched

---

[1] All the details of this expedition, as stated in Morice Regan's poem, between lines 600 and 815, are lifelike and geographically accurate. The combined forces of Dermot and the Normans marched from Ferns, crossed the Slaney, penetrated the defiles of Mount Leinster, marched over the plains of Carlow to the River Barrow, and then entered Ossory, either by the road which then, as now, crossed the Slieve Margy range, by Leighlin Bridge and Old Leighlin, where the Black Castle of Leighlin Bridge shows the military importance of the ford in those early days; or else by Clogrenan, a few miles to the north, where a castle still exists, erected by the Butlers in the fourteenth century to guard that ford. The battle was probably fought in the forest of Grenan, which then covered the northern and western slopes of Slieve Margy, some relics of which are still to be seen in the woods of Clogrenan demesne. The western slope of Slieve Margy, of mingled bogs, woods, and morasses, was eminently suited to Celtic warfare. The range is bounded on the west by a tempestuous mountain stream, locally called "the red and deceitful," Dinin,—giving a name to the entire district from its destructive ravages, which was hence called the Desert of the Dinin, or Fasach-dinin in Irish (see for a description of this natural fastness O'Donovan's paper on Ancient Ossory in the *Journal* of the Kilkenny Archæological Society, t. i., p. 230-36, where he notes that a Celtic tribe maintained its independence, in the desert on the banks of the Dinin, till the reign of Charles I., against all the efforts of the House of Ormond; with which may be compared p. 365 of the same volume, where he gives the legends of the Dinin). At Old Leighlin, near the cathedral, on the south, a pass still retains the name of the Bohreen of the

on, riding a white horse named Blanchard. Pretending flight, he successfully drew the Ossory forces on till he reached the open; but then turning, and raising the national Welsh war cry of "St. David for ever!" the mail-clad knights, Prendergast and Fitz-Stephen, Meyler and De Montmorenci, flung themselves on their opponents, while the archers emerging from their concealment attacked them from behind, with such terrible results that no less than two hundred and twenty human heads were, after the battle, laid at the feet of King Dermot Mac-Murrough.[1] I will not weary you with the narrative of

---

Saxons, from a battle once fought there between the English and Irish. The hill is pointed out where the English made their stand, but this site does not tally with Morice Regan's story (see the *Ordnance Survey Correspondence*, Carlow Letters, p. 224, in the Royal Irish Academy). King Dermot and Fitz-Stephen fought at some distance from Old Leighlin. The Normans wished to encamp after their victory, but the king refused, and did not feel safe till he got to Leighlin (Morice Regan's poem, lines 800-812), where he found shelter behind the earthworks and cashel of the Abbey of S. Laserian, whose site is now occupied by the thirteenth century Anglo-Norman cathedral. I may just note that this ancient but little known cathedral of Leighlin occupies a splendid position on a lofty hill. The view from its tower is magnificent; on the west Slieve Margy rises above it, while upon the east the horizon is bounded by the Mount Leinster range, the conical peak of which is 2,700 feet high.

[1] Giraldus Cambrensis tells a horrid story of King Dermot's conduct upon this occasion, *Expugnatio*, i., 4. "The victory being thus gained, about two hundred of the enemies' heads were collected and laid at the feet of Dermitius, who turning them over one by one, in order to recognise them, thrice lifted his hands to heaven in the excess of his joy, and with a loud voice returned thanks to God most High. Among them was the head of one he mortally hated above all the rest, and taking it up by the ears and hair, he tore the nostrils and lips with his teeth in a most savage and inhuman manner." See for a somewhat similar incident in the last century the history of Tiger Roche, as told by the late Right Hon. J. E. Walsh, Master of the Rolls in Ireland, in his *Ireland Sixty Years Ago*, p. 122 (Dublin: 1847).

the various raids made during this summer of 1169 by the allied forces. They ravaged Ossory a second time, and expelled its prince. They plundered Offaly, or the modern county of Kildare. They turned in the opposite direction, penetrated the recesses of the vale of Imail, crossed the Wicklow range by the pass along by the Ess waterfall into Glenmalure, and seized the sacred city of Glendalough, the capital of the O'Tooles, working as much mischief as they possibly could, according to the custom of the times.

Roderic O'Conor, King of Connaught, became alarmed at the progress made by Dermot during these early summer months. He assembled his forces and allies and marched across the island to attack Dermot in his ancestral castle at Ferns. It was now Dermot's turn to retire. He entrenched himself in the usual Celtic fashion,—not yet extinct, as we learn by the proceedings at modern eviction scenes. His followers felled trees, cut up and barricaded the roads, such as they were; while Fitz-Stephen, using his Norman military science, taught them how "to break up the surface of the level ground by digging deep holes and trenches, cutting secret and narrow passages through the thickets for the purposes of egress and ingress;" and with such success that Roderic found the position of the allies utterly inaccessible. The Connaught king then tried negotiations and bribery; dealing with each party separately. To Fitz-Stephen he represented the odious character of Dermot, offering him liberal presents if he would abandon such an unworthy service and return to his own country. To Dermot he represented the dangerous character of the foreigners to all Irish parties alike, offering him the undisputed sovereignty of Leinster if he would join with him in exterminating the mercenary foe. Dermot's guile came to his help as usual. He made a secret treaty, promising to dismiss his allies and to import no more of them, while by a public agreement Roderic confirmed him in the kingdom of Leinster, stipulating merely that Dermot should give hostages and do homage to himself as supreme king. Roderic's opposition was thus for a time disposed of, though Dermot had not the slightest intention of fulfilling the conditions of the treaty.

Success, however, told with its usual effects on the character of Dermot. That character as well as his bodily appearance have been painted for us by Giraldus in a few vigorous strokes in the sixth chapter of the first book of his *History of the Conquest*. Dermitius, says the chronicler, was tall in stature, and of large proportions. And being a great warrior and valiant in his nation, his voice had become hoarse by constantly shouting and raising his war-cry in battle. Bent more on inspiring fear than love, he oppressed his nobles, though he advanced the lowly. A tyrant to his own people, he was hated by strangers; his hand was against every man, and every man's hand against him. Prosperity made a man like that haughty, insolent, and overbearing. He began to attribute all his success to his own efforts and skill. He wished to kick away the Welsh and Norman ladder by which he had risen, and began to treat his allies with contempt. The quarrel proceeded in the course of the autumn to such lengths that Maurice Prendergast abandoned his service, and, taking his two hundred followers with him, marched towards Wexford to embark for home. Dermot anticipated his action, however, and gave orders that permission to embark at Wexford should be refused. Prendergast however, had his revenge. He was a soldier of fortune, and his arms were open to the highest and best bidder. He entered into negotiations with the defeated Prince of Ossory, joined him at Timolin, now St. Mullins, in the south of Carlow, and in union with the Ossory forces proceeded to ravage the surrounding lands. His secession proved a warning to the treacherous Dermot, while the gap in his forces was soon made good by the arrival at Wexford of Maurice Fitz-Gerald, who landed with ten knights, thirty horsemen, and one hundred archers. Matters stood in the following position at the close of 1169. Dermot had recovered his sway over his ancient kingdom. The citizens of Dublin even had made a league with him, which, however, they were determined to break as soon as they could. Fitz-Stephen had been put into possession of Wexford and the present baronies of Forth and Bargy, and had built himself a castle on the commanding pass of Carrig, two miles north of Wexford, where its ruins are in part still to be seen; while the Normans had divided into two sections, one part supporting Dermot and the other his opponent Gillpatrick. The quarrels of the colonists, England's fatal weakness in this country, had thus early begun. In future lectures we shall see how this original taint ever clung to their action and hindered their success. The winter of 1169-70 passed as Irish winters usually passed,—in eating and drinking, fighting among themselves, love-making, and working now and then. The spring saw the results. Gillpatrick of Ossory agreed no better with Maurice Prendergast than Dermot had done. The fault may not have been altogether on the Irish side. The Normans, mayhap, were inclined to take too much on themselves and rate their services at too high a value. In the spring of 1170 Prendergast abandoned Gillpatrick also, and marched towards Waterford, determined to abandon Ireland for ever. Gillpatrick tried the usual Irish device and attempted to entrap him at a wooded defile. At Kilkenny, where he spent a night, Prendergast learnèd their design, and proved himself their match in subtlety. He sent a message to Gillpatrick that he had changed his mind and would form a new alliance with him if he came to Kilkenny. The Ossory men at once dispersed and came to Kilkenny, only to find the bird flown, for Prendergast had marched to Waterford, where, after a row with the citizens arising out of some drunken squabble, he took ship and crossed to St. David's. Dermot, the Leinster king, on the other hand, learned a useful lesson from the secession of Prendergast. He moderated his tone, treated his Norman allies with more respect, and, aided by them, engaged in successful expeditions against Dublin, and even as far as Limerick. His hopes began to aspire even higher, and though he was now long past the allotted threescore years and ten, he began to cherish dreams of the supreme sovereignty over Ireland. He communicated his ambitious hopes to Fitz-Stephen and Fitz-Gerald, entreating them to invite over still larger bands of their countrymen to aid him in his efforts. For their encouragement he offered his eldest daughter in marriage to either of them, with right of succession to his kingdom. There was, however, a bar, which to the Normans, trained under the discipline of Roman canon law, seemed insuperable, though to Dermot himself, doubtless, their scruples seemed utterly unreasonable. These knights had already wives to whom they were bound in lawful wedlock. They advised, however, that he should despatch messengers to Earl Richard, usually called Strongbow, urging his immediate departure for Ireland. I shall conclude this lecture with reading for you this specimen of an Irish king's correspondence seven hundred years ago, as given by Giraldus Cambrensis: "Dermitius, son of Murchard Prince of Leinster, to Richard Earl of Striguil, son of Earl Gilbert, sends greeting." He begins his epistle in right classical style, and then adds a quotation from an epistle of Ovid—

"Tempora si numeres bene quæ numeramus egentes
Non venit ante suum nostra querela diem"—

which Mr. Wright thus turns into rhyme:

"Were you, like those who wait your aid, to count the weary days,
You would not wonder that I chide these lingering delays."

He then proceeds:—"We have watched the storks and swallows. The summer birds have come and are gone again with the southerly wind, but neither winds from the east or from the west have brought your much-desired and long-expected presence. Let your present activity make up for this delay, and prove by your deeds that you have not forgotten your engagements, but only deferred their performance. The whole of Leinster has been already recovered, and if you come in time with a strong force, the other four parts of the kingdom will be easily united to the fifth. You will add to the favour of your coming if it be speedy. It will turn out famous if it be not delayed, and the sooner, the better welcome. The wound in our regards which has been partly caused by neglect will be healed by your presence; for friendship is secured by good offices, and grows by benefits to greater strength." That letter decided Strongbow. He determined to proceed to Ireland, where his arrival opened a new phase in the scene of invasion.

LECTURE V.

THE INVASION OF STRONGBOW.

DISTANCE has a wondrous power of enchantment. It throws a halo of glory about persons and characters oftentimes very inglorious in themselves. It tones down the roughness, the harshness, the weakness, the unlovableness of scenes and individuals, so that men become rapturous over places and persons they detested when known, or would have detested had they been known. It lumps together and confuses enterprises and operations which were in fact separate and distinct in time, in motive, and in circumstance. The conquest of Ireland illustrates these principles. Time and distance confuses for the popular mind the various and distinct invasions which preceded the final conquest of Henry II. The Geraldines and Strongbow are regarded as merely leaders or chiefs of the royal army, while, as a matter of fact, the Geraldine invasion of 1169 and the invasion of Strongbow in 1170 were independent wars undertaken by chieftains of Welsh or Norman extraction in the hope of establishing feudal principalities which should be quite independent of the royal supremacy.

I have described the Geraldine invasion. The Fitz-Geralds felt, however, their own weakness. They held a respectable position, but did not belong to the great nobility of the twelfth century.[1] They were desirous, therefore, of securing the help and prestige which a great Norman noble could confer. These they sought at Strongbow's hands, and were therefore most desirous of his co-operation. Let me first tell you somewhat of Strongbow himself. His name of Strongbow is unknown to Giraldus Cambrensis, and is due simply to an interpolation in a late copy of his Irish history.[2] He is almost always called by Giraldus, Richard Count of Striguil, son of Count Gilbert. He drew his descent from exactly the same stock as the Conqueror, his direct ancestor two centuries earlier being a son of Richard the Fearless, Duke of Normandy. He belonged to the family of De Clare, a great Norman noble who came over with William the Conqueror, whose descendants have perpetuated their

---

[1] See *The Earls of Kildare*, A.D. 1057—1773, by the Marquis of Kildare, 2nd edition (Dublin: 1862). The origin of the Geraldines can best be traced in *Brut-y-Tywysogion*, or the *Chronicle of the Princes of Wales*, written by Caradog of Llancarvan and published in the Rolls Series (London: 1860), where Gerald of Windsor, the founder of the family, appears as steward to Ernulf, brother of Robert, Earl of Shrewsbury, about the year 1100 (see *l.c.*, p. 67). Gerald was sent by Ernulf in that same year to demand in marriage the daughter of Murtogh O'Brian, supreme King of Ireland. This Welsh Chronicle is a most important witness, showing the intimate knowledge of Ireland, its affairs and its princes, possessed by Normans and Welsh alike during the century prior to the conquest of 1172. The Four Masters do not mention the marriage of Ernulf and King Murtogh O'Brian's daughter. On a comparison, however, of the Welsh Chronicle, A.D. 1100, with the Four Masters, A.D. 1102, it would seem as if Magnus, King of Denmark, intervened, and secured the young lady for his own son Sitric, whom he made King of Man. The Irish brides sought by Norman nobles and Scandinavian princes cannot have been simple barbarians, as some would represent them (cf. note on p. 51 above).

[2] See Mr. Dimock's remarks on this point in the Rolls Edition of the works of Giraldus Cambrensis, t. v., p. 228.

name in the designation of a well-known western county of our island. Gilbert de Clare, his father, made extensive conquests in South Wales during the reigns of Henry I. and Stephen, and was created Earl of Pembroke by the latter monarch in the year 1138. He had the bad luck to espouse the losing side; and when King Henry II. came to the throne he deprived the De Clare family of their property.[1] His son, Count Richard, was living in poverty and idleness at his Castle of Striguil, about four miles from Chepstow, when King Dermot approached him with an offer of marriage to his daughter and of succession to his kingdom of Leinster. Richard Fitz-Gilbert was a soldier of fortune. He had nothing to do and nothing to live upon, save what he could win by his right arm and his broad sword, and was the fitter agent therefore to carry out the designs of Dermot MacMurrough.[2] At the conclusion of my last lecture I read for you the letter which Dermot despatched to Count Richard, requesting the fulfilment of the promises he had made two or three years earlier. Strongbow was nothing loath to respond to Dermot's invitation. King Henry II. was daily getting deeper and deeper in trouble at home and abroad, and Ireland seemed to offer the idle but ambitious soldier a field, secure from royal tyranny, where he could

---

[1] The De Clares lost the earldom at the same time, but an earldom conferred then a jurisdiction rather than a title. There were, in fact, no hereditary titles at that period.

[2] See a paper by the Rev. J. Graves in the *Journal* of the Kilkenny Archæological Society, t. i., p. 501, on a charter and seal of Richard, Earl of Pembroke, surnamed Strongbow, where the curious reader will find much information concerning the descent, arms, and achievements of Strongbow. The original charter, described by Mr. Graves, exists among the records of Kilkenny Castle. Cf. Dugdale's *Baronage*, pp. 206-209.

recoup his lost fortunes. He spent the winter of 1169-70 in preparation, encouraged by the reports he had received of the successes and victories of Fitz-Stephen and the Geraldines. He feared the royal jealousy, however; and so, notwithstanding the general license involved in the letters patent granted to King Dermot some two years before, he applied to the king for special permission to engage in the Irish expedition, or else for restoration to his confiscated family estates. Henry II. was in one respect very modern in his policy. He delighted to satisfy English malcontents in Irish bonds. When any persons were specially troublesome at home he preferred that they should be contented at the expense of Ireland rather than of England. He much preferred war and trouble on the western side of the Irish Sea to the presence of a powerful, a persistent, and a discontented noble upon the Welsh borders. Henry II. gave, therefore, a grudging assent to Strongbow's intended expedition, which the Earl forthwith proceeded to carry out. Strongbow despatched, about the 1st of May, 1170, an advance guard under the command of one of the Fitz-Gerald clan, Raymond le Gros, nephew of Fitz-Stephen, who had already taken an active part in the work of conquest.[1] Raymond landed probably where twelve months before his uncle had disembarked, on the Wexford coast, where he was at once attacked by the citizens of Waterford, helped by the chiefs of Decies, Ossory, and Idrone.[2] His

---

[1] Raymond was called Le Gros, or the Corpulent. He was the ancestor of the Graces, Barons of Courtstown. See *Memoirs of the Family of Grace*, by Sheffield Grace (London, 1823), pp. 1-10. And cf. below, p. 188.

[2] The Norman poem of Morice Regan describes the allies thus:—

'Del Deys Dovenald Osfelan
E de Odrono Orian

assailants were, for the most part, Danes, like the townsmen of Wexford. They remembered the fate of that city twelve months before, and attempted therefore to destroy the invaders before they came in overwhelming numbers. They marched from Waterford three thousand strong, crossed the Suir, and attacked Raymond and his followers, who numbered at first but ten men-at-arms and seventy archers. Hervey de Mountmaurice, to whom Dermot had granted the baronies of Forth and Bargy, with three knights and their followers, joined him upon his arrival; so that Raymond may have had a force of one hundred and fifty or two hundred men with which to resist the attack of the Waterford citizens.[1] He threw up some hasty fortifications on the point of Bag and Bun, where to this day the traces of earthworks attributed to Strongbow are to be seen,[2] and then marched out to meet the Waterford Danes, who, however, proved too many and vigorous for his little band. They were overwhelmed by the force of numbers,

---

E tuz les Yrreis de la cuntré
Le Chastel unt aviruné."

These words refer to Donald O'Phelan, chief of the Decies, a district in the west of the co. Waterford; and O'Ryan, chief of a tribe of that name in Carlow, not yet extinct. See O'Donovan's edition of O'Heerin's *Topographical Poem* in the Irish Archæological Series, A.D. 1862, pp. 75-101, and notes in the Appendix. The editor of Bohn's edition of Giraldus, p. 206, misled by the word Ophelan, brings Raymond's assailants from the barony of Offaly in Kildare, one hundred miles away, instead of from the immediate neighbourhood of Waterford, where they lived. Cf. Smith's *History of Waterford*, pp. 3-9, 45, 53, and the letters of J. O'Donovan, LL.D., in the *Ordnance Survey Correspondence*, Waterford Letters, pp. 180, 181, in the Roy. Ir. Acad.

[1] See, for interesting facts about Hervey de Mountmaurice, the *Journal* of the Kilkenny Archæological Society, t. iii. (1854-55), p. 217. Cf. note on p. 74 above.

[2] See Hall's *Picturesque Ireland*, t. ii., p. 148.

and fled to their fortifications, entering pell-mell, Danes and Normans all mixed up together. The fate of the English invasion hung in the balance a second time that May-day of 1170. Had the Danes of Waterford succeeded where the Danes of Wexford had failed, and had they crushed the advance guard of Strongbow, that chieftain would have been himself intimidated from farther advance, and the history of Ireland might have been radically different. The personal exertions of two men altered the whole complexion of affairs, and snatched victory from the Danes when it was now almost achieved.[1] These two men were Raymond le Gros himself and one of his companions, William Ferrand. Ferrand was a man of undaunted courage. That courage was nerved and intensified by the fact that he was seized of an incurable disease. Leprosy, the direst enemy of the Middle Ages, is now extinct in Ireland, but seven centuries ago it was a terrible, a destructive, and a dreaded pestilence. Mercer's Hospital, in our own city, stands upon the site of the Leper Hospital of Dublin. Leperstown, in the immediate neighbourhood of Stillorgan and Blackrock, still witnesses in its name to the prevalence of the disease, because its fields were then the endowment appropriated to the support of St. Stephen's Leper Hospital.[2] Waterford, again,

---

[1] The authorities for this battle and its results are Giraldus Cambrensis, *Conquest of Ireland*, bk. i., ch. xiii.—xv., pp. 206—211, Bohn's edition; and Morice Regan, ed. Wright, pp. 68—72, or Harris's *Hibernica*, p. 9.

[2] "Ecclesia de S^{to}. Stephano. Leprosi habent in proprios usus, qui habent Rectorem per institutionem Archiepiscopi ad presentationem Majoris et Comitatus Civitatis Dublinensis" (*Repertorium Viride*, A.D. 1530, pp. 3, 6, in Marsh's Library. Cf. Rev. W. G. Carroll's *Succession of the Clergy of St. Bride's*, pp. 7, 10 (Dublin: 1884). Mercer's Hospital in Stephen Street now stands on the site of this ancient leper hospital. Leperstown is called in the Irish language Ballinloure, or

possesses a hospital called to this day the Leper Hospital, dating its foundation back to those times when leprosy was a real and dreaded plague. William Ferrand was like Naaman, the captain of the host of the King of Syria. He was a mighty man of valour and a brave soldier, but he was a leper. Giraldus Cambrensis puts his case very briefly and neatly. "His body was weak, but his spirit was resolute; for, being diseased with leprosy, which threatened his life, he sought to anticipate the effects of disease by a premature though glorious death."[1] A desperate man, utterly careless of life, can do something even still, with all our progress in modern warfare, as the last Soudan war showed, where the headlong charges of Arab fanatics often threatened to overcome the resistance and neutralise the power of the breechloader and of the Gatling gun. But a desperate man, regardless of himself and only seeking a death which seemed to fly from him, could do much more in those times to retrieve the fortunes of his own party, and to bring defeat and dismay into the ranks of his opponents. Raymond himself was, however, their great support, and proved himself a worthy leader

---

Baile-au-lobhair, or the town of the lepers. There is another Leperstown in the parish of Killea, near Waterford. It formed the endowment of the Waterford Leper Hospital, which was built in a street (Stephen Street) of the same name, and organised in the same manner, with custos, wardens, etc., as the Dublin institution. They date probably from the same time, King John's reign.

[1] See *The Census of Ireland for the Year* 1851, pt. v., vol. i., p. 75, Report on Tables of Deaths, pp. 418—21, for much interesting information about leprosy in Ireland. This volume, compiled by Sir W. Wilde, deals specially with the history of Irish medicine and disease from the most ancient times. Cf. Smith's *History of Waterford*, p. 183; Reeves's *Antiqq. of Down and Connor*, pp. 218, 232. A full account of Irish Leper Hospitals, by Sir W. Wilde, will be found in *The Census of Ireland* 1851, part iii., Report on the Status of Disease, pp. 90, 91.

at this crisis of the Anglo-Norman invasion. The terrified Normans were hurrying within their entrenchments, and with them the Danes were simultaneously entering. There was neither time nor opportunity to raise the barricade. Raymond thereupon turned, opposed his immense and corpulent frame to the entire Danish host. In a narrow passage one man can face a vast multitude when only one or two can come on at a time. He cut down one after another as they advanced to meet him, and thus reaped the reward of his boldness. A chance circumstance, told us by the poem of Morice Regan, effectually seconded his efforts. The Normans had adopted the Napoleonic plan of making war support itself. They had swept off the cattle from the neighbouring lands, and penned them up within their own fortifications. When the battle waxed furious the cattle took to headlong flight, and, seeing the barricades fallen, rushed through the gap thus opened, sweeping the allied Irish before them. The effect was magical. The Waterford host and their allies became panic-stricken, faced about, and fled in turn, pursued by the victorious Normans, who killed five hundred, and flung vast numbers over the cliffs, which here rise precipitous over the sea. Thus ended the battle of Bag-and-Bun, little known by moderns, when English rule in Ireland well-nigh came to an untimely end, and that through the exertions, not of Celts, but of Danes. Had Raymond and Ferrand but faltered for an instant, the course of Irish history had been quite different. It is no wonder that Hanmer, an Elizabethan chronicler, has sung of the spot as—

"That Creek of Bag and Bun
Where Irelond was lost and won." [1]

---

[1] Hanmer was a prebendary of St. Canice's Cathedral. See *Journal* of the Kilkenny Archæological Society, 1849-51, t. i., p. 456.

The Normans were not content with their victory, but stained it by an atrocious act of cruelty, which proves conclusively that, bad as the native Celts were, as I have depicted them in my first lecture, their conquerors were no better. The Normans, indeed, never hesitated to imbrue their hands in blood if they could thus strike terror into the hearts of their opponents. William the Conqueror devastated England north of the Humber, and for one hundred miles utterly extirpated the Saxon inhabitants whom he failed to conquer or conciliate. On this occasion Norman invaders acted in exactly the same manner. They took as prisoners seventy of the principal citizens of Waterford. Raymond wished to spare them. Hervey de Mountmaurice, the settler of twelve months' experience, using all the influence of his local knowledge, addressed the assembled council, scoffed at Raymond's argument in behalf of mercy, urged the danger of timid courses, the advantages of boldness and terror, concluding his speech thus, in words worthy of Cromwell himself, and full of his spirit: "We must so employ our victory that the death of these men may strike terror into others, and that, taking warning from their example, a wild and rebellious people may beware of encountering us again. Of two things, we must make choice of one; we must either resolutely accomplish what we have undertaken, and, stifling all emotions of pity, utterly subjugate this rebellious nation by the strong hand and power of our arms, or, yielding to deeds of mercy as Raymond proposes, set sail homewards, and leave both the country and our patrimony to this miserable people;"[1] an oration

---

[1] Girald. Camb., *Expugnatio*, i., 14, 15 (p. 208 Bohn's ed.). The orations as given by Giraldus are of course fancy speeches, but they represent the popular Anglo-Norman feelings of the time.

bloodthirsty and heartless, which nevertheless appealed powerfully to the fears of a panic-stricken band surrounded by overwhelming numbers. They were, in fact, appalled at their position, and could not understand or appreciate the wiser counsels of Raymond their leader. They jumped at the advice of Mountmaurice, whom they considered the more experienced, and Giraldus tells us the result. " Hervey's opinions were approved by his comrades, and the wretched captives, as men condemned, had their limbs broken, were cast headlong into the sea, and were drowned." In Ireland as in England the Norman conqueror determined to rule by terror, not by love. From May to August of 1170 Raymond and Hervey Mountmaurice maintained themselves at Bag-and-Bun, shut in behind those entrenchments which can still there be seen. Why, you may ask, did not Dermot MacMurrough and the FitzGeralds come to the aid of their allies during all the long days of the early summer? The answer is simple,—they had quite enough to do to defend themselves; and besides, Raymond was effectually cut off from any assistance save from Wales and by sea. The King of Ossory and the Prince of Idrone and the Danes of Waterford were much nearer the scene of action than Dermot. They had the advantage of water communication. They could sail down the Suir, the Barrow, and the Nore to the port of Waterford, and there uniting their forces, they were able to cut off all communication between the Normans in the north of Wexford and their brethren in the south of the county. Even to this day it is very hard to get at Bag-and-Bun. With all our modern advances and improvements the townsmen of Waterford could still cut off most effectually an enemy at Bag-and-Bun from their allies at Ferns in the north of the same county. In fact, it is a curious circumstance illustrating my argument that while you can reach Ferns in two hours from Dublin, if you wish to visit the spot where Ireland was lost and won, which is in the same county as Ferns, your shortest way will be to go to Waterford by train, sleep a night there, take an early steamer to Duncannon Fort, and then travel by car some six or seven miles to the historic spot where Norman and Celt and Dane were contending for the mastery of our green island.[1]

Dermot could not help Raymond and his little band, but help was coming from another quarter. Earl Richard, commonly called Strongbow, was doubtless kept informed of their perilous position. A day's sail— a few hours' sail in fact, even in those times—would carry a ship from Bannow Bay to Milford Haven. The Earl was hampered, however, by the direst of foes, and that was poverty. He had no money, and could only pay in promises. He had to beat up followers in every direction. He marched from Chepstow, where his patrimonial castle of Striguil lay; directed his course along the coast road which then, as now, ran along the shores of the Bristol Channel; marched through Cardiff, Swansea, and Carmarthen, alluring to his banner the numerous soldiers of fortune, descendants of the Flemish military settlers, along the sea coast. At last he completed his armaments, and embarking at Milford Haven with two hundred men-at-arms and other troops to the number of a thousand, landed at Crook, in Waterford Harbour, on August

---

[1] The nearest points by railway to Bag-and-Bun are: Wexford, about twenty-five miles; New Ross, about eighteen; and Waterford, about fifteen. Last summer I enjoyed a trip round that district on a tricycle, and found excellent roads and good accommodation.

23rd, 1170, the eve of St. Bartholomew's Day.[1] He employed the feast day in devotions, doubtless, and preparations, united his forces to those of Raymond, and at once marched, on August 25th, to the assault of Waterford, which they took after a hard fight. A relic and memento of that struggle remains in Waterford, where Reginald's Tower, as it is called in the History of Giraldus Cambrensis, and as it is still called, can yet be seen, a genuine specimen of the warlike and constructive art of the Danish settler who led the way in resistance to the invasion of their Norman cousins. In this tower were taken the leading men of the city, Reginald the Danish king, or chief magistrate of Waterford, the two Sitrics (a well-known Danish name), and Melaghlin O'Phelan, Prince of the Decies, a district of country near Waterford which now gives a title to an Irish nobleman.[2] Waterford being captured, and a competent army, a pledge of future victory, assembled, Earl Richard claimed the fulfilment of

---

[1] Here I may give another specimen of how English translators of documents concerning Ireland do their work. Hoveden was an annalist of King Henry's time. He gives us much valuable information about the Irish expeditions which I am describing. He tells us that Henry disembarked at Crook and marched thence to Waterford. The Rev. James Graves, in the Kilkenny Archæological Society's *Journal* for 1856, vol. iv., p. 386, has identified the spot. Hoveden has been translated in Bohn's Series, and the translator in a note on the name gravely suggests that Crook is a mistake of Hoveden's for Cork. Hoveden, t. ii., p. 29 (Rolls Series), describes Croch, or Crook, as distant from the city of Waterford " per octo milliaria." Surely a glance at a map would have shown the English editor that Cork was more than eight miles from Waterford.

[2] See Girald. Cambrensis, *Expugnatio*, i., 16; Morice Regan, ed. Wright, pp. 72, 73. Giraldus tells us that when Strongbow and his followers were in despair owing to the vigorous resistance of the Waterford citizens, Raymond le Gros espied a cagework house built on the outside of the walls. He cut

Dermot's promise, and was at once married to the Princess Eva, perhaps in a church raised on the spot where the present cathedral of the Holy Trinity exists in the city of Waterford, this dedication to the Holy Trinity being a favourite one, as in Dublin, Cork, and Bristol, wherever the Scandinavian element prevailed.[1] Strongbow and Dermot, leaving a garrison to hold the port of Waterford and keep open their communications with Wales and Bristol, marched thence direct to Ferns, where Dermot always maintained his headquarters. Dermot, though a very old man, was still a thorough general. Strongbow, too, had the eye and energy of a conqueror. Both of them fixed their gaze on Dublin as the central objective point of all their efforts. Their opponents, too, had come to the same conclusion. The Danes of Dublin had a long list of injuries to avenge, and a long list of unforgiven and unforgotten injuries inflicted by them on Dermot and his ancestors to stir them up to desperate resistance. Dermot's enemies O'Conor and O'Rourke, and every subordinate chieftain, recognised our Danish city as the fittest spot for resistance, and the Danish colonists there as their great support and backbone. Their bravery was undoubted, their right arms were strong, and their fleets, numerous and well-appointed, could keep open the sea, bringing allies and provisions to their help. To Dublin, then, assembled all the enemies of Dermot, where, for the first time since

---

the post supporting it, and the house tumbled down, bringing the wall with it. This breach afforded an entrance to the besiegers. These cage work houses survived in Dublin in a few instances till the present century. See Harris's *Dublin*, ch. iv.

[1] The marriage of Strongbow and Eva now forms one of the series of illustrations of national history adorning the walls of the Houses of Parliament at Westminster.

Brian Boru's heroic age, there occurred the most thoroughly national movement and the truest national union. All Ireland and the Danes were combined against Dermot and the Normans.[1]

Let us now strive to realize what this Danish city of ours was like just then. We have materials enough for doing so if two conditions were fulfilled. First, if these materials were printed; but the English Government and Treasury will print nothing for us unless forced to do so, while they will print anything for England and Scotland. Printing for the vast majority of us is the first necessary condition to render a manuscript useful. And you need not be ashamed to confess this. Mr. Freeman is a great historian. He was called upon to complete the edition of Giraldus Cambrensis published in the Rolls Series, upon the death of the original editors; and in a note he honestly informs us that he belongs to that large class to whom a manuscript is useless till it has been committed to the printing press.[2] The other condition necessary to realize the state of Dublin in A.D. 1170 is that we should have somewhat of the eye and imagination of an archæologist, and be able to reconstruct a concrete and living past out of very dead and dry and dusty details. Ecclesiastical annals furnish us with the richest materials for such reconstruction. The Archbishop of Dublin possesses in the *Crede Mihi* a manuscript dealing with this diocese, composed about 1275, in large part from much older materials. He also possesses the original of the *Liber Niger*, or *Register*, of Archbishop Alan, drawn up in 1530 out of very ancient documents, while as for the bulls and charters dating

---

[1] Morice Regan, ed. Wright, p. 75; Giraldus Cambrensis, *Expugnatio*, i., 17.
[2] Girald. Camb., *opp.*, t. vii. (Rolls Series), Pref., p. ciii.

from the last half of the twelfth century, in Mr. Gilbert's works, in the *Book of Christ Church Obits*, in the *Register of All Hallows*, in the *Chartæ, Privilegia et Immunitates*, they are almost innumerable. Dublin was, as I have already noticed, like old Bristol of that date. It was a busy trading community crowded together round the top of a hill where four ways met and four churches found a site. They were much the same, too, in point of dedication. Each city had an Augustinian monastery dedicated to the Holy Trinity,—the Dublin one being the earlier, however; each had a St. Werburgh's near the monastery; each had a St. Audoen's similarly related to the Cathedral. Four ways crossed one another in each case. From St. Audoen's to Dublin Castle is a straight line. From St. Patrick's through St. Nicholas Street and Wine Tavern Street you can still walk direct to the quays. The city was then much the same as it remained, so far as appearance and area were concerned, down to the seventeenth century, when Speed published his map in 1610.

Let me give you an idea of the extent of the city walls. The wall started from the Castle, ran down to the river near the present Essex Bridge, then along the river till Wine Tavern Street and Merchants' Quay were reached. Thence it took a southerly direction, included St. Audoen's Church, and skirted the base of the hill on which Christ Church was built, crossing depressions which are well and clearly marked to this day in St. Nicholas Street and St. Werburgh's Street, and finally joining the castle again in the neighbourhood of Ship Street.[1] The city of Dublin as it was to be seen

---

[1] The original wall of Dublin, as built by the Danes, did not run so far west as Bridge Street, but ran across Wine Tavern Street and by St. Audoen's Arch, where one of the original Danish

when Roderic O'Conor joined the Danes there to resist Dermot and the Normans, was simply a town clustering thick round Christ Church Place and Hill. There were numerous gates,—at the Castle, at Werburgh's Street, at Nicholas Street, and the Newgate at the Cornmarket. Outside the walls were pleasant gardens watered by the clear limpid waters of the Poddle flowing straight down from the Dublin Mountains. Away among these gardens lay a Celtic village, which clustered round the Celtic churches of St. Bride's, St. Kevin's, and St. Patrick's, not yet a cathedral. Beyond these, and extending over the present Stephen's Green and Baggotrath, and all that neighbourhood, was a wood where the citizens went forth duly armed to hunt the hare, the fox, and even the wolf, following sylvan lanes which originally marked out the site of the busy streets which are now George Street, then called St. George's Lane, and Camden Street. While, again, when the Dublin trader wished to take the sea air he could ramble along a country road, which in the course of half a mile took him to the distant Convent of All Saints and the Nunnery of St. Mary's, which stood, surrounded by trees, on the site of the modern Grafton Street and Molesworth Street, in fields to the present day called in legal phraseology the Mynchin fields. From this sketch you

---

gates of Dublin still exists. The wall was extended to Bridge Street at the time of Bruce's invasion of Ireland. Considerable portions of the old city wall still exist. The boundary wall of Mr. Price's china and delft warehouse in St. Nicholas Street is composed of the ancient city fortifications. The base of one of the towers of Newgate can still be seen built into a house opposite Messrs. Webbs' in the Cornmarket. For many of these details I am indebted to my friend Mr. Edward Evans, the diligent archæologist, of 40, Cornmarket. Harris's *History of Dublin*, chap. iii., has a good account of the walls written a century and a half ago; cf. Gilbert's *Dublin, passim*.

can understand the advantages and disadvantages of the position held by the united forces of Danes and Celts, as against the allied armies of Dermot and Strongbow. The Irish and Danes held a strong position. But the Normans and Dermot had also this advantage, that the primeval forest flourished close up to the city, and thus offered opportunity for those surprises in which lightly armed and lightly equipped Irish forces especially delighted.

So far as to the city and position to be assaulted. And now for the expedition itself. Morice Regan gives us the dates far more accurately than Cambrensis does. Waterford was taken on August 24th; Dublin was assaulted on September 21st, St. Matthew's Day. Strongbow knew the secret of modern warfare,—that rapidity of action is essential to success. It was now September of 1170, and within the next twelve months Dublin was to sustain three distinct assaults and sieges. The first was this original one of September 1170; the second took place about Whitsuntide of 1171; and the third took place later still, in the summer or autumn of the same year. The first assault was made by the Normans. It was successful, and wrested Dublin from the Danes. The other two assaults were made by the Danes and Irish to recover the lost city, and they utterly failed. Strongbow and his Normans never once relaxed the grasp which they had laid upon what their instincts told them was the very centre and heart of national resistance. Let me now explain briefly how Dublin was lost by the Danes and won by the Normans. Dermot was becoming very old, and felt the day of his death approaching. He was anxious, too, to pay off old scores before his final departure. Sixty or seventy years before, the Dublin

Danes had murdered his father sitting unsuspecting in a house, and cast his body into a pit, burying it not even with the burial of an ass,—which the Jewish prophet thought the lowest depth of degradation,—but burying it with the burial of a dog, for they flung a dog into the same grave and covered up all together. He hated them too because they were commercial and prosperous, and knew how to defend their prosperity with a vigorous right hand. So he organised an expedition against the Danes, who had combined with Roderic O'Conor of Connaught. Dermot showed all his ancient skill in this last expedition. His enemies not only held the city, but had also thoroughly surrounded it in the direction from which Dermot and his Norman allies were expected. The Connaughtmen occupied Clondalkin and the woods of that neighbourhood lying west of Dublin. They dug ditches across the roads and paths which led then as now towards Naas and Blessington and Carlow, round the western base of the Dublin Mountains. The Dublin Mountains themselves they neglected. They esteemed them and their bogs quite a sufficient defence against the march of the heavy-armed and steel-clad Normans. And I do not wonder. There is now a good military road across the Feather-bed and Killakee and Sally-gap Mountains, which intervene between Dublin and Glendalough, and drainage has done much to lessen the bogs; but even to this day, if you quit the road for five minutes, the most active and athletic undergraduate, marching with no heavier luggage than a tooth-brush and a clean collar, will soon find himself making desperate jumps to save himself from pits of bottomless mud. Dermot proposed, however, the bold course, and Strongbow adopted it. He knew how impossible it would be to force his way through plashed woods and along roads uprooted and barricaded. He proposed instead to follow the way he knew well, advancing by the great Wicklow Road connecting the sacred city of Glendalough with Dublin, and thus to take the enemy in the rear. Dermot's plan was thoroughly successful. Morice Regan gives us the details of the expedition.[1] The first division of the army, led by Miles de Cogan, consisted of seven hundred Anglo-Normans. With this division marched Donall Kavanagh, Dermot's favourite son, acting as guide. Next came Raymond le Gros with eight hundred Englishmen, followed by Strongbow with one thousand and Dermot with three thousand Irish soldiers, while behind all these followed the main body of the Leinster Celtic forces. They marched straight for Dublin, and called a halt somewhere in the neighbourhood of the modern Rathmines, hiding behind the woods which then covered the whole district;[2] while the advanced guards under De Cogan and Raymond moved close to the walls. Dermot and Strongbow sent a message by Morice Regan to Turkil, the Danish prince, demanding the surrender of the city and of thirty hostages. St. Laurence O'Toole urged the peaceful surrender of the city. He lived at this time beside his cathedral of the Holy Trinity. We can fix the very site of his palace.

---

[1] See *Anglo-Norman Poem*, ll. 1570—1700, and Wright's Preface, p. xxxviii.

[2] A memorial of this forest is still preserved in the name Cullenswood applied to so many streets and avenues. The prebendal stall appropriated to the Archbishops in St. Patrick's is called Cualaun from this wood. In the Latin of Archbishop Alan it is Colonia. See *Liber Niger Alani* and the *Repertorium Viride* in Marsh's Library, and a paper on the Manor of St. Sepulchre, by J. Mills, Esq., of the Dublin Record Office, in the *Journal* of the Royal Archæological and Historical Society for Ireland, A.D. 1889.

It occupied the ground on St. Michael's Hill now covered by the Synod House.[1] But military impatience anticipated the delays of negotiation. Cogan and Raymond encamped in the valley where St. Patrick's now stands, saw their opportunity, rushed in through the gates, and gained possession of the city before even their own friends knew an attack had begun. Turkil and the Danes seem to have been stricken with a panic, or else, seeing the desperate position of affairs, rushed to the shore, seized their ships, and sailed off to the Isle of Man and Scotland. Thus Dublin was conquered September 21st, 1170. I repeat the date because it was most important and most fateful for the history of Ireland. Strongbow at once proceeded to organise his dominion there. Communication by sea was needful for his safety, and that was now amply secured. He placed therefore in the Castle a strong garrison under De Cogan and Raymond, appointed magistrates, issued charters, made laws, and then retired to Ferns for the winter, to bide the time when he should succeed to the kingdom of his father-in-law.[2] He had not long to wait. Dermot died in the course of the winter or spring of 1170-71, which saw the murder of Thomas à Becket. Giraldus indeed fixes the exact date as the Calends or first of May. The manuscript *Annals* of Dudley Loftus in Marsh's Library make it the Nones or 7th of May. The Four Masters record under the year 1171 his death with national bitterness.

---

[1] See the *Repertorium Viride*, p. 1, in Marsh's Library, where we find St. Michael's Church described thus: "Unde infra mœnia urbis ecclesia ista parochialis a primævia fundatione capellae extitit infra pallatium S^{ti}. Laurentii."

[2] Strongbow issued charters before Henry II. arrived in 1171. Two such charters to St. Mary's Abbey, Dublin, are contained in Gilbert's *Chartularies of St. Mary's*, t. i., pp. 78, 83.

"Diarmaid MacMurchadha, King of Leinster, by whom a trembling sod was made of all Ireland, after having brought over the Saxons, after having done extensive injuries to the Irish, after plundering and burning many churches at Kells, Clonard, etc., died before the end of a year of an insufferable and unknown disease, for he became putrid while living, through the miracle of God, of Colum-Cille, of Finnian, and of the other saints of Ireland, whose churches he had profaned and burned some time before; and he died at Ferns without making a will, without penance, without the body of Christ, and without unction as his evil deeds deserved."

Strongbow now succeeded to the kingdom of Leinster according to treaty, though, according to Irish law and usage, he should have been elected by the tribes of his kingdom.[1] He set himself at once to the work of organising the principality upon feudal principles, appointing officials—seneschal, constable, chancellor, as they were known in England. Strongbow was not, however, left long in peaceable possession. As soon as Dermot's death was known throughout Ireland, the native chiefs raised an insurrection, or rather we should perhaps say organised another national movement to repel, once and for all, the intruding foreigners. Roderic O'Conor, as supreme king, assembled an army sixty thousand strong, towards which the leading princes of Ireland contributed their share. They all moved towards Dublin. Dunleavy of Ulster encamped at Clontarf, O'Brian of Munster at Kilmainham, Murtogh O'Kinsalagh, from Wexford, at Dalkey, while Gothred,

---

[1] See Richey's *Short History of the Irish People*, 2nd edition, pp. 48-50, upon Irish regal elections and the custom of Tanistry.

the Danish prince of Man, and other roving Northmen, assisted by blockading the port of Dublin and cutting off its supplies by sea. The infant colony was once again in mortal peril. Strongbow recognised the greatness of the danger imminent over his enterprise. He marched from Ferns, flung himself into the threatened city, and summoned his scattered adherents from every quarter. Among others, he sent for succour to Robert FitzStephen, the first invader, who commanded at Carrig, the fort which dominated and secured Wexford.[1] FitzStephen despatched to Strongbow's assistance thirty-six men-at-arms, which so weakened his garrison that the men of Wexford forced him to surrender, massacred the common soldiers, retaining FitzStephen himself and a few of his chief men in prison on Beg-Erin, an island which then existed in Wexford Harbour, though it has disappeared of late years as an island, owing to the reclamations of slob lands which have been carried out. The siege of Dublin lasted for some two months, till at last provisions began to run very scarce. The Earl called a council, and laid before them the state of affairs. He proposed to send an embassy to King Roderic O'Conor, offering terms of peace, and promising to hold Leinster from him as the superior lord thereof. St. Laurence O'Toole, the Archbishop of Dublin, was the ambassador selected for this purpose, but he returned with a message so hostile that the council determined upon immediate attack. They resolved to conquer or perish in the

---

[1] See Girald. Cambrensis, *Expug. Hib.*, i., 11, 25; Morice Regan in Harris's *Hibernica*, p. 11. This ancient fort of Carrig is pictured in Hall's *Picturesque Ireland*. It still exists, occupying a very formidable position a couple of miles north of Wexford.

attempt. The siege of Dublin seems to have been conducted by the Irish kings in a very leisurely fashion. The various princes had their different encampments; they and their soldiers were enjoying themselves thoroughly, and seem to have been utterly careless of all the ordinary precautions of warfare, such as sentries, guards, and outposts. Boldness, as usual, carried the day. The total available fighting force possessed by Strongbow consisted of some six hundred men, which, for the purpose of attack, he divided into three companies. Myles de Cogan led the van with two hundred, followed by Raymond le Gros with two hundred more, while Strongbow himself brought up the rear with the same number. The bold attempt was crowned with complete success. The Normans marched first against Dunleavy and the Ulster contingent, who were encamped at Finglas. The enemy were careless and secure. "In the name of God," said Cogan, as he approached the rude encampment of huts made of turf and sods and wattles, "let us this day try our valour upon these savages or die like men;" and then, suiting the action to his words, and raising the Welsh national war-cry, "St. David for ever!" rushed headlong among the astonished Celts, carrying death and destruction wherever he went. The battle was short but decisive. Panic fear seized the Irish, they dispersed in every direction, communicated their fears to their allies in the other encampments, who likewise dispersed, and the siege of Dublin was terminated; while, as if to show the cause of their careless security, Morice Regan tells us that in the camp of the Ulster men "a store of baggage was gotten, and such quantities of corn, meal, and pork, as was sufficient to victual the city for a whole year." A fulness of bread had wrought havoc with the mental and moral calibre of the Irish, as with that of the men of Sodom of old.[1]

After this battle Strongbow went southwards to Wexford, leaving Myles de Cogan to hold the fortress of Dublin. He wished to chastise the men of Wexford for their rebellion, and he desired above all to watch King Henry's movements, for that sovereign was becoming increasingly hostile and suspicious of Strongbow's intentions. During his southern progress Dublin was again assailed by a fresh danger. Hasculf MacTurkil, the former prince of Dublin, allying himself with various branches of the northern rovers, and specially with a body of Norwegians under a noted leader, John le Dene, sailed back to Dublin. Cogan was, however, again successful. He made a compact with a chief who ruled the country south and west of Dublin, called Gillamocholmog.[2] Cogan simply stipulated that he should remain neutral during the fight, watching the progress of the fray, and then should fall upon the defeated party. We can trace all the details of the fight in Morice Regan's

---

[1] Morice Regan's Norman poem, l. 1,916, p. 92 in Wright's edition, or p. 12 in Harris's *Hibernica*.

[2] I have already said something about this clan and its possessions. See more about them in Gilbert's *Chartularies of St. Mary's Abbey*, i., 31-7. This prince was probably Donald Gillamocholmog, who married Dervorgil, a granddaughter of Dermot MacMurrough. This Donald appears as a witness to King Dermot's charter to All Saints' Priory, Dublin, granting the lands of Baldoyle, now owned by the Corporation of Dublin, who hold in direct succession from the said priory, which is now Trinity College. See *Registrum Prioratus Omnium Sanctorum, juxta Dublin.*, ed. by Rev. R. Butler (Dublin: 1845), in the Irish Archæological Series, p. 50. St. Michael's Lane, near the Synod House, in Dublin, was formerly called after this clan. See W. Harris's *Hibernica*, p. 15, and note on p. 8 of this work.

poem. The battle was fought on the strand of Dublin, which then intervened between the modern Cork Hill and the site of Trinity College, while Gillamocholmog looked on from the wooded heights which then occupied Stephen's Green and its neighbourhood. The Danes, leaving their ships, marched boldly to the attack of the eastern gate, which stood at the foot of Cork Hill. Myles de Cogan had not a large army, but he utilised his ground. He ordered his brother, Richard de Cogan, to take three hundred of his cavalry, and, issuing out of the southern gates in St. Werburgh's and St. Nicholas' streets, to fall upon the rear of the Northmen when the fray waxed fiercest.[2] Success again smiled upon Anglo-Norman skill and courage. To any persons who know the ground, and the many passages corresponding to ancient rural lanes which lead from the south of the old Danish city round to the former strand of the Liffey, now represented by College Green, Dame Street, and the adjacent streets, the plan of the battle and the wisdom of Cogan is self-evident. The assailants were utterly defeated. Myles de Cogan himself slew John le Dene after performing prodigies of valour. Hasculf MacTurkil was taken

---

[1] See pp. 107-19 in Wright's edition, or pp. 14-16 in Harris's *Hibernica*.

[2] St. Werburgh's and St. Nicholas' gates are even still marked by depressions in the streets called by these names. They are connected by lanes which once led the traveller by paths just outside the walls. Morice Regan calls the eastern gate, St. Mary's Gate, La Porte Seint-Marie, or Dame's Gate,—that is, Our Lady's Gate, the name by which it was known till its demolition in the last century. Ware and Harris both tell us that an image of the Blessed Virgin occupied a position over it till the Reformation; and Harris says the pediment of the statue remained in his own time. The stones of the gateway now form the pedestal of King William's statue on College Green.

prisoner, and without further ceremony beheaded, on account of an insolent speech made to the victor; while the remnant, escaping from the pursuit of Gillemo-holmock, who, true to his promise, fell upon the defeated party, escaped to their ships. Strongbow was thus successful enough in Ireland; yet he was exceedingly uneasy, and his Celtic foes seem to have been aware of the cause of his uneasiness. He feared the hostility of Henry II., who had already cut off all supplies from England. The Wexford men had even made it a pretext for resistance to Strongbow, that he was a rebel against his own liege sovereign. The Earl felt it necessary, therefore, to cross to England and propitiate King Henry, whose army was now assembling in the west for the invasion of Ireland. The first adventurers had, in fact, done their work. They had prepared the ground, and borne the burden and heat of the earlier day. The dominating personage of King Henry II. now appears on the scene, to reap the full fruits of the harvest.

LECTURE VI.

HENRY II. AND ANGLO-NORMAN CONQUEST.

THE reign of Henry II. was a very remarkable epoch in English history. Two of our greatest, I should perhaps say rather our two greatest living historians, Bishop Stubbs and Professor Freeman, warm into enthusiasm in describing the great work which Henry II. did for England. He introduced order where anarchy reigned. He reduced to submission a proud and oppressive nobility. He laid the foundations of that marvellous system of law which now, through its extension to the United States and to our Colonies, dominates some of the most populous and prosperous States in the world.

His history was a very chequered one. If you wish to study it,—and it has a very direct bearing on our own local Irish history,—you should read the fifth volume of Mr. Freeman's *Norman Conquest*, embracing the period from 1068 to 1265, or the last chapters of Bishop Stubbs' first volume of his *Constitutional History*. Freeman divides Henry's reign into three periods. First the period when he was busied with the restoration of order in England after Stephen's anarchy. This covered from 1155—1165. Secondly, the period of his disputes with Thomas à Becket, from 1165—1170. Thirdly, the period of his domestic and civil wars, the period of unhappiness, disaster, and failure, extending from 1170—1189. The most famous of these three periods is that of his quarrel with Thomas à Becket, terminating with the murder of that prelate at Christmas 1170. During that winter of 1170, Strongbow was holding Dublin, and fortifying himself there against the threatened attacks of Irish Celts combined with those Scandinavians whose invasions were yet a real danger, dreaded even by the now powerful civilized and united England. The murder of Thomas à Becket was at once regarded by Henry II. in its true light. With a politician's insight he saw it to be much worse than a crime. It was a gross blunder. He applied at once to Rome for absolution from all share in the guilt. The Pope despatched a formal legation to inquire into the circumstances. Henry II. determined to keep out of the way, so as to avoid all unpleasant or inconvenient questions. He crossed from France to England in August 1171, and thence proceeded to Ireland in the course of the same autumn. This is Bishop Stubbs' account of King Henry's actions. It seems to me, however, very imperfect. The murder of Thomas à Becket and its consequences would seem from it the only impelling motive to the conquest of Ireland. Original documents printed since Dr. Stubbs wrote his *Constitutional History* reveal the fact that Henry was moved by quite other and perhaps more powerful motives as well. Let us strive to realize them.

Henry II. had put down the power of the rebel barons who threatened, under King Stephen, to establish jurisdictions rival to that of the Crown. Count Richard, whom we call Strongbow, and his father had been typical leaders among the rebel barons. Henry II. had watched them narrowly, had lessened their powers, circumscribed their jurisdiction, banished them when he could to the Welsh borders to wear themselves out in warfare with the bold and hardy Celts. But now he saw a fresh danger growing up. Count Richard Fitz-Gilbert, availing himself of the king's letters patent authorising King Dermot MacMurrough to get assistance whenever he could, had allied himself with the Irish prince, had become the recognised heir of his kingdom, and threatened to set up an independent kingdom within forty miles of England, where Norman skill would be united to Celtic wit and bravery,—a dangerous combination, of which Henry II. had already got quite enough in the intrigues of the Fitz-Gerald and other factions of the Welsh borders. The record of Strongbow's successes during the autumn of 1170 did not please him. He issued orders from France, that no one should attempt to proceed to Ireland without his special permission. This act was no arbitrary one. It was quite in accordance with our modern notions. The Foreign Enlistment Act still prohibits any attempts to enlist forces for warfare with any state or kingdom at peace with our own; and King Henry only acted in accordance with the spirit of British legislation when he prohibited any succour or armed assistance proceeding to Strongbow. Giraldus tells us the story very pithily in the nineteenth chapter of his first book. "Reports having been spread abroad of these events, which were much exaggerated, and the Earl having made himself master, not only of Leinster, but of other territories to which he had no just claims in right of his wife, the King of England made a proclamation that in future no ship sailing from any part of his dominions should carry anything to Ireland, and that all his subjects who had been at any time conveyed there should return before the ensuing Easter (that is, the Easter of 1171), on pain of forfeiting all their lands and being banished from the kingdom for ever." This proclamation was issued in the autumn or early winter of 1170. The Earl received intelligence of it, and at once despatched Raymond le Gros to Aquitaine as an ambassador to the king, deprecating his wrath, pleading his own letters patent as his authority for invading Ireland, and offering to hold all his lands and conquests in the country as fiefs dependent upon Henry and subject to his supreme authority. All this occurred, according to Giraldus, in the winter of 1170-71; say between the months of October and March of that period.

Now behold an interesting illustration of the accuracy of Giraldus, and a most striking illustration of the utility, in a historical point of view, of those very dry-as-dust investigations which have been proceeding for the last fifty years in the great record repositories of England. Take up a book with a very long unwieldy title, the *Calendar of Documents relating to Ireland preserved in Her Majesty's Public Record Office, London*. It will give some idea of the vast store of manuscript materials touching upon Irish affairs preserved in London, when I tell you that this volume consists of nearly six hundred pages, that it contains more than 3,200 abstracts of distinct documents, for the most part extending to four or five lines merely, and yet it only covers a period of eighty years, from 1171—1251. The first eighty-four of the abstracts deal with the reign of Henry II. and the actions and deeds of the conquest, and there in the very beginning we find a notice of this proclamation against aiding or assisting Strongbow, mentioned by Cambrensis. In the fourth abstract we have a notice from the Pipe Roll accounts of 1170 to the following effect:—" Robert

Fitz-Bernard, Sheriff of Devonshire, renders his account of 6s. out of the land of Geoffrey Cophin, who went into Ireland against the King's command; paid into the Treasury and he is quit." Again, abstract No. 24, under date 1171-72, tells us: "The Sheriffs of Bucks and Bedfordshire render their account of 12s. out of the land in Edingrava of Peter Morell, who went into Ireland against the King's command; paid into the Treasury and they are quit." And there are others telling the same tale, showing that while the king's proclamation was no dead letter, it was also violated by many an adventurous spirit who flocked to the standard of Strongbow, leaving his landed property in England to pay the penalty.

Henry II. returned to England from France in the summer of 1171. Dr. Stubbs thinks a desire to keep out of the way of the Papal legates sent to investigate the circumstances of Becket's murder sufficiently accounts for Henry's expedition to Ireland. I think, on the other hand, that the king had quite distinct and far deeper and wiser motives for his action. He feared Strongbow. He was a vigorous man, of the same blood and family as himself. He was one of those barons who had bearded Stephen and Henry himself in his earlier days, rendering England a howling wilderness through their exactions and oppressions. Strongbow now threatened to set up a new and independent state right under his nose, just forty miles across from St. David's Head; and Henry determined to crush Strongbow before he became too strong. Ireland in Celtic hands and ruled by Celtic princes ever at war amongst themselves was one thing, and might be despised; Ireland in hands half Norman and half Welsh, hostile to English rule and to the descendants of the Conqueror, and offering a refuge for every rebel and opponent, was quite another thing, and must be reckoned with. Henry II. was a great prince, and he went about all his work systematically and thoroughly. He planned the invasion of Ireland, or rather his attack upon his rebellious lieges, and his conquest of Strongbow very carefully. We can trace the rise, the progress, and the development of the expedition in the entries of the Calendar to which I have just referred. He first conceived the notion as soon as he heard the news of Strongbow's departure for Ireland. He at once saw that the matter was becoming serious. The Fitz-Geralds and their expedition he did not mind. But now that the heir of the great titles of De Clare and Pembroke, a man of his own kith and kin, had taken the matter up, he felt that he must attend to it. He issued orders to collect an army to invade Ireland in the summer or autumn of 1170. We can trace every single step of the process, and read the particulars and details of the armaments, provisions, and ships, with well-nigh as much fulness as if we were studying the last Egyptian expedition.

Henry II. had invented a new process for raising an army, or, to use modern language, he had perfected a new scheme of military mobilisation. Let me explain. Hitherto the Norman kings raised an army when they wanted one by calling upon the barons and knights, who held their properties by military tenures, to come and discharge their duties. The knights and barons came to the assembly attended by a number of men-at-arms and inferior soldiers in proportion to the extent of land held by them. Henry II. substituted a tax called scutage for the personal service thus rendered. This arrangement suited both parties: the barons and knights got rid of a troublesome duty; the king became independent of unwilling subjects. It was a dangerous exchange, however, for the barons, since they thus put into the hands of the king the means of raising a mercenary army dependent solely upon himself, which he could use to crush opposition or revolt on their part. The strength of the Crown became in fact the weakness and destruction of the nobility. This scutage was first collected in 1156. It was repeated in 1159 and 1161, and in 1170 was again imposed for the purpose of the Irish invasion.[1] The sheriffs of the different counties were directed to purchase provisions, arms, accoutrements, and forward them to Bristol, whither the army was directed to assemble.

The details of the purchases made by the sheriffs will be found in this Calendar.[2] The very first entry, dated about October or November, 1170, shows that no part of England, even the most distant, was exempt from contributing to this Irish expedition, which was a great national movement, in which the whole nation took part, and for which the whole nation was responsible. The earliest entry, dated 1170-71, tells how Norfolk and Suffolk contributed their share, through Bartholomew de Glanville,[3] Wimar the chaplain, and William Bardul, who render their account for three hundred and twenty hogs sent to the army of Ireland, which cost £26 16s. 5d.,

---

[1] See Madox, *Hist. of the Exchequer*, ch. xv.; Stubbs, *Const. Hist.*, i., 582; and Thorold Rogers, *Six Cent. of Work and Wages*, Introd., p. xxix.
[2] Pipe 17, Henry II., Roll 1.
[3] Bartholomew was brother of the famous justiciary and legal writer, Ranulf de Glanville, whom we shall meet later on as Sheriff of Norfolk. Bartholomew was associated with Wimar, one of the king's chaplains. The royal chaplains discharged a large part of the executive work of the royal court.

not quite 2s. per hog; for making bridges, hurdles, and other ship's apparel, £6 5s. 5d.; and for six handmills with their appendages 14s. 4d., all ordered by the king's writ. I have selected this entry because it is the first, and because it shows how widespread throughout England were the preparations for the king's invasion. But there are other entries far more interesting. We can trace the various kinds of food used, and the prices paid for them. Dorset and Somerset supply wheat, beans, cheese. Hogs appear in vast numbers,—bacon and pork evidently were the favourite food with the soldiers of those times.[1] Lancaster and Carlisle supply wooden towers for attacking towns and castles. The spade and the pickaxe were as important in the middle ages as they are in modern warfare. Gloucester, therefore, from its contiguity to the great iron districts, furnishes two thousand pickaxes, one thousand spades, one thousand shovels, sixty thousand nails, and iron for two thousand spades. Stafford sends one hundred and forty axes, one hundred and forty spades, and seven thousand nails. The See of Winchester, in keeping with its ecclesiastical character, supplies more peaceful articles. Thus we read that Richard, Archdeacon of Poitiers, rendered his account for one thousand pounds of wax sent into Ireland, 12s. 10d.; five hundred and sixty-nine pounds of almonds sent to the king in that country, £5 18s. 7d.; twenty-five ells of red scarlet cloth for the king's use, £6 17s. 6d.; and twenty-six ells of green, £3 13s. 8d.; ten pairs of boots, 15s. The medical supply and the doctor were not forgotten, and thus we read that the same See of Winchester supplied Joseph the doctor, who was probably a monk, with

---

[1] See note on p. 140.

spices and electuaries to the extent of £10 7s. 0d.,—a very respectable allowance considering the value of money. The whole series of entries, covering some eight or nine closely-printed pages, are most interesting reading from every point of view. Considering them in a military light, they show us how mediæval armies were equipped; while from a social and political point of view, they give us a glimpse into the inner life, the manners, habits, employments, the whole organisation of the age, displaying at the same time an authentic record of prices more than seven centuries ago.

After six months and more of such elaborate preparations, King Henry left France, landed at Portsmouth August 3rd, 1171, and then marched to the neighbourhood of St. David's, collecting a fleet of some four hundred vessels to the port of Milford.[1] Strongbow, who was on the opposite coast of Wexford, was kept fully informed of these preparations. He despatched messenger after messenger to appease Henry's wrath, and at last, taking ship, met the king near Gloucester, where he made his submission, promising to put him in peaceable possession of Dublin and of all the fortresses and seaports of the kingdom, holding his other conquests as fiefs dependent on the feudal supremacy of the crown of England. Strongbow thus surrendered his dream of establishing

---

[1] The Welsh chronicle *Brut-y-Tywysogion* (Rolls Series) p. 213, gives very minute details of King Henry's progress. He arrived at Pembroke about September 20th, having been expected on September 8th. He dined with David Fitz-Gerald, Bishop of St. David's, on Saturday, September 29th; attempted to sail for Ireland on October 14th, but was driven back by the west winds which prevailed all that autumn, making the season very wet and destructive to the crops; "for it was a misty season, and then scarcely any ripe corn could be had in any part of Wales."

an independent principality across the Irish Sea, and King Henry got rid of a very pressing danger.

After some considerable delay the king set sail for Waterford on October 16th, 1171, having sent his seneschal William Fitz-Aldelm and some other members of his household to make preparations for his arrival. His landing-place was on the western shore of Waterford Harbour, between the towns of Dunmore and Passage. The exact spot where the first English king landed in Ireland has been made the subject of an elaborate memoir by the late Rev. James Graves in the *Journal* of the Kilkenny Archæological Society for 1856-7, p. 385. From it I quote the following passage, marked by all that local knowledge combined with wide historical reading which make Mr. Graves's communications models of their kind. Mr. Graves says: "When Henry's fleet entered the Waterford Harbour, their first care would be to look for a safe anchorage. This the Waters of Passage afforded them. The navigation of the Suir was probably unknown to the seamen, or the king would have proceeded higher up the river. At all events, we know that he landed at Crook, just below Passage, and marched thence some seven miles to Waterford. At present, except at the top of a very high spring-tide, it would be difficult to land forces under Crook; but we may well suppose that the tidal currents which have, within the memory of man, filled up the boat-docks at Passage (a little higher up), may during the six centuries which have elapsed since Henry's debarkation have materially added to the shoal which extends from the shore of Crook to a considerable distance into the harbour."[1] Mr. Graves then

---

[1] Mr. Graves, in the same paper, *Journal* of the Kilkenny Archæological Society, t. i., N.S. (1856-57), p. 386, gives the

notes an extraordinary instance of the crass blunders perpetrated by men who undertake to edit chronicles and histories dealing with Irish matters, though themselves utterly devoid of all knowledge of either Irish history or Irish geography. I have already in a previous lecture given you an instance of this in Mr. Wright's edition of Giraldus Cambrensis. He transports Kinsale from the county Cork, and moves it by the magic witchery of his pen fifty or sixty miles east, placing it in the county Wexford.[1] Mr. Graves exposes another blunder equally gross and stupid. Hoveden was a historian and chronicler of Henry II.'s time to whom we owe many valuable details. His Chronicle has now been splendidly edited in the Master of the Rolls Series by that eminent historian Dr. Stubbs, the present Bishop of Oxford. Thirty-five years ago a

---

following interesting sketch of the exact spot designated by Hoveden :—" A glance at any good map of Ireland, but more especially at those models of all good surveys, the Ordnance Maps of the district, will indicate the position of the parish of Crook, on the western shore of the noble harbour of Waterford, below and close to the secure anchorage of Passage, where Queen Victoria lay-to in her splendid steam yacht for a night, on the occasion of her first visit to Ireland. A low sandy beach, with clay cliffs, intermixed here and there with slaty rocks, forms its sea boundary; from this the land swells upward gradually to a considerable height. On this slope, now mapped out with a formal network of enclosures and very bare of trees, about half a mile from the beach and in the centre of some fine pasture lands, stand the remains of the preceptory and parish church of Crook. The Templars seem to have formed an early settlement here, as Crook is mentioned in the most ancient lists of their establishments in Ireland." According to Hoveden, *Chronica*, t. ii., p. 29 (Rolls Series), the king arrived at Crook " at three o'clock in the afternoon, with 400 great ships laden with warriors, horses, arms, and food." When the king jumped on shore a white hare leaped out of the bushes, and, being caught, was offered to the king as a token of victory.

[1] See the note on Kinsellagh or Hy-Kinsellagh on p. 72.

translation of Hoveden was published in Bohn's Library, the copious and convenient source of many a crib dear to schoolboys and even to undergraduates. In that Chronicle Hoveden, a contemporaneous writer, tells us accurately enough that Henry II. landed at Crook and marched thence to Waterford. This was too tempting a chance for an editor who knew nothing of Ireland. He concluded *à priori* that there could not possibly be such a place as Crook. He had heard, however, of such a place as Cork, and knew that it was somewhere in the south of Ireland. He therefore gravely suggests that Hoveden mistook Crook for Cork, and concludes that the king and his army landed at Cork and marched thence to Waterford in the course of a morning promenade,—a journey which they could not possibly achieve, even now, in the course of a day, with all the resources of railway communication at their command.[1]

King Henry landed at Crook on the eve of St. Luke's Day, October 18th, 1171, with four hundred ships, containing five hundred men-at-arms, a large body of horsemen and archers, and vast stores of arms and provisions. Indeed, a glance through the sheriff's returns—and they are imperfect—will show you how vast must have been the stores brought with the king on this occasion. He stayed at Waterford fifteen days, till the feast of All Saints' Day had been celebrated. A record of his stay in Waterford can still be traced in the Pipe Roll accounts. I have already referred to it, but it will bear repetition, as it makes the far-off life of the twelfth century so very real and vivid for us. We there find the following account brought forward by the sheriffs of Dorset and Somerset. At the risk of wearying you with these details, and with a desire to stir you up to

---

[1] Cf. p. 72 and note, and p. 106 and note.

consult these original documents for yourselves, I will quote this return in full. It vividly illustrates the principles I have been laying down. "Alured de Lincoln, Sheriff of Dorset, renders his account: for 400 seams [1] of wheat sent into Ireland, 40*l.*; 300 seams of oats, 15*l.*; 100 seams of beans, 100*s.*; 60 axes by the King's writ; pay for seamen of six ships at Bristol which carried supplies from many counties into Ireland, 16*l.* 13*s.* 9*d.*; canvas granaries and other ship's apparel, 7*l.* 10*s.* 10*d.*; 4 horses sent into Ireland, 8*l.*; ropes and cables to raise the houses of Reginald de Winton, 66*s.* 8*d.*, all by the King's writ; payments to Philip Palmer of Bristol for wine, 14*l.* 10*s.*;" after which comes the item which refers to Waterford and King Henry's stay there:—"To Bernard le Coliere for wine bought at Waterford, 27*l.* and 20*d.*" Then follow a number of entries which show that the Ireland of 1171 was very like the Ireland of 1889. Englishmen may abuse us on some points, but they have ever admired our horses; and so we read: "To Pagan de Ria for the

---

[1] "The horse load, seam or sum of 100 pounds, by which so many saleable articles were measured or weighed, was a rude contrivance suited to miserable roads, over which no wheels could make their way, and has been always adopted in mountainous districts. Within fifty years, in the recollection of the editor, great part of the coal that came out of the Forest of Dean to the town of Ross was brought in this way down the sides of that elevated land, on mules and asses or small horses."—Webb's Illustrations of Swinfield's *Household Roll*, in Camden Society's Series, 1855, p. cxvi., note. The inhabitants of Dublin are well accustomed to the sight of the same primitive mode of communication. The natives of the Dublin Mountains still bring turf and other produce of their farms for sale in the city, laden on horses and asses in creels or wicker baskets, like those in use in the twelfth century. The same custom prevails in the mountains of Sligo and generally throughout the west; so near are we still in Ireland to the Middle Ages.

passage of 100 horses from Ireland into England, 50s.; to Thomas Fitz-Chnictwine, Robert de Welles, and Lambert Teste, each 40s. for 80 horses, and to Waleran de Scaldebec 25s. for 50 horses."[1] I presume from these notices that they referred merely to the cost of transporting the horses from Ireland to England. We are not told what the king paid for them in Ireland. I imagine he received them as presents from the various chiefs who made their submission to him.

For you will observe this, King Henry II. did receive, either personally or by deputy, the submission of all the Irish princes,—even that of Roderic O'Conor, King of Connaught,—with only one exception. That exception, the one Irish prince who stood out and refused submission and homage to the Norman, was the O'Neill of Ulster. More remarkable still is the fact that King Henry attained his purpose, and became feudal lord and king of Ireland, without firing a single shot in anger, or spilling, so far as we know, a single drop of Irish or Norman blood. All the fighting had been done already for him by the Fitz-Geralds and by Strongbow. The Irish princes saw clearly that if the small, ill-appointed, and ill-equipped bands of private adventurers could defeat their armies though allied with the Danes, they had no chance whatsoever against an army numbering ten thousand men at least, equipped with all the resources of England and France, and supported by the largest fleet the Irish Sea had ever seen. They simply yielded to the inevitable, and flocked to pay homage to the Norman Conqueror.

King Henry remained for a fortnight in Waterford, and then marched to Dublin, where he arrived about the feast of St. Martin, November 11th. There a palace

---

[1] See Sweetman's *Calendar*, t. i., p. 4, No. 28. Cf. Pipe Accounts, 18 Henry II., Roll 6.

had been erected for him after the manner of the country. The chiefs and nobles were determined to give King Henry a hearty reception; probably they were glad to get a king celebrated for legal knowledge and vigorous rule in exchange for the plundering and fighting adventurers who for two years and more had been ravaging the whole country. The kings and nobles of the land, we are therefore told, built a royal palace of beautiful earth roofed with wattles, nigh the church of St. Andrew, outside the walls of Dublin.[1] We can determine the very spot where Henry II. spent the Christmas of 1171. St. Andrew's Church now occupies the top of the hill where the Danes of those times held their thingmote.[2] But it was erected there only two hundred years ago, when the hill was cut down by the barbarians of those times, who had no eye for either antiquities or for scenery, and the soil carted away to raise Nassau Street to its present height above

---

[1] Such a palace of earth and wattles may seem to us very unworthy the dignity of a king like Henry II. But then we are very apt to imagine that the Norman kings of England enjoyed a much higher degree of civilisation and domestic comfort than actually was the case. Mr. G. T. Clark, in his *Mediæval Military Architecture*, t. i., cap. iii.-viii., has shown that numbers of the castles, royal and noble, of that age were constructed of wood. The wattled roof can yet be found in use in the more backward parts of Ireland. The Irish have ever been famous for their wattle-work, which will bear great weights. They used it for centring their arches; evident proofs of this can be seen in many an Irish ruin. They still use wattle-work for bridges in bogs, and for the carriage of turf. Every Irish boy, whether of Celtic race or not, can still in country parts make a crib of wattles for catching birds in frosty weather.

[2] See my *Ireland and the Celtic Church*, p. 280. There was a lawsuit between the Crown and the rector of St. Andrew's in the time of Charles I., concerning the restoration of this church, which was then used as the Castle stable. See Gilbert's *History of Dublin*, ii., 258-262, t. iii., App. II. The present Castle stables occupy the site of Henry's temporary palace.

the College Park. Then St. Andrew's Church was moved from its ancient site, now occupied by the shop numbered 10, Dame Street. It was, in fact, one of a cluster of small churches (St. Martin's and St. Michael le Pole) which stood amid trees and gardens along the banks of the Poddle. In that palace King Henry II. received the homage of most of the princes of Ireland, the kings of Meath, of Cork, of Limerick, of Ossory, of O'Rourke of Breifny; and there he confirmed them in their lands and possessions, entertaining them at the same time with a magnificence and profusion of which they had hitherto no idea.[1] We are specially told that he taught them to eat cranes, a food which before this they had loathed. This probably was not the only foreign taste they acquired. The royal hospitality

---

[1] The Irish kings were all acknowledged as such by Henry II., substituting however Strongbow in the kingdom of Leinster instead of or in succession to the MacMurroughs, and Hugh de Lacy in that of Meath instead of the Melaghlins, or rather, perhaps, carving the palatinate of Meath out of the kingdom of that name, and leaving the remainder of it to the Melaghlins. The Anglo-Norman suzerain acknowledged the Irish princes as his feudatories, placing them in the same position as the princes of Wales and the king of Scotland. A glance at Rymer's *Fœdera* (London: 1816), t. i., pars. i., pp. 31, 45, 101, 116, 123, to take but a few instances, will amply prove this. Several of these Irish princes were acknowledged as such down to the reign of Elizabeth. Henry II. took the title of Lord of Ireland, which continued to be the legal title of the English sovereigns till the reign of Henry VIII. Upon the feudal distinction between the titles Dominus and Rex, see *Rotuli Curiæ Regis*, ed. Sir F. Palgrave, A.D. 1835, Introd., pp. lxxxvi.—xcvii. The following extract from p. xcvii. sums up his argument:—"What was intended by the style of *Dominus Angliæ?* This title appears to indicate the right to the superiority over the soil when distinguished from the chieftainship of the people. The king might be admitted as *Dominus Angliæ* before he was acknowledged as *Rex Anglorum;* and this distinction was consistently maintained. John was *Lord* of Ireland, but he did not claim to be *King* of the Irish. Edward wrote himself *Lord* of Scotland and

was doubtless well intended, but it laid the foundation of still more profuse and extravagant tastes in the breasts of these Irish princes, and thus prepared the way for their financial ruin and collapse.[1]

The king remained in Dublin until the 1st of March, 1172, a four months' residence, during which he devoted his whole attention to the organisation of Ireland in Anglo-Norman fashion. His stay in Dublin covered exactly the period now counted the Castle season, and it was doubtless one of the most excited and crowded seasons that Dublin has ever seen. Every class in Irish society thronged to Dublin for that first royal visit. The princes came there, and when an Irish prince came he was attended by as large an army of retainers as he possibly could raise, partly from motives of ostenta-

---

acknowledged Balliol to be *King* of the Scots." Cf. Professor Richey's remarks on this subject in his *Short History of the Irish People*, 2nd edition, ed. R. R. Kane, LL.D., p. 155.

[1] Giraldus Cambrensis, *Conquest of Ireland*, i., 32 (Bohn's edition, p. 231):—" The feast of Christmas drawing near, very many of the princes of the land repaired to Dublin to visit the king's court, and were much astonished at the sumptuousness of his entertainments and the splendour of his household; and having places assigned them at the tables in the hall, by the king's command, they learned to eat cranes which were served up, a food they before loathed." Hoveden the chronicler describes the palace he occupied, and tells us the length of his residence in Dublin, which was from St. Martin's Day (November 11th) to Ash Wednesday. See *Chronica Rogeri de Hoveden*, t. ii., p. 32 (Rolls Series). The magnificent hospitality displayed by Henry II. can best be understood by a study of the preparations made for the visits of Prince John in 1184, and, when king, in 1210. In 1184 we find that Prince John brought a bakehouse and kitchen with him. The sheriff of Gloucester was allowed £9 5s. to procure requisites for them (see Sweetman's *Calendar of Documents*, t. i., p. 11). Cf. Swinfield's *Household Roll*, t. ii., p. liii., and Lacroix's *Manners of the Middle Ages*, p. 154, for a description of the kitchen arrangements of the period. The crane was then esteemed a French delicacy (Lacroix, *l.c.*, p. 130).

tion, but much more from those of prudence and wise discretion, for Heaven alone could tell what battles he might have to fight before he returned home. We get glimpses here and there in the English and Irish annalists and historians into the social life of Dublin during those four eventful months. Prices were affected by the sudden influx of strangers from all parts. "In the time of the king's stay in Dublin all kinds of victuals were at excessive rates," is Morice Regan's concise reflection upon the high prices which the momentary demand and a defective supply had caused. The winter too was exceptionally tempestuous, following upon an autumn which had been exceptionally wet. The Dublin winters are and always have been specially mild. I have often known persons who left London in December and January covered with thick fog, surprised, when they arrived on the shores of Dublin Bay, to find us revelling in a sunshine worthy an Italian sky. I am writing these words in the month of January, and it was only two days ago that, as I walked by the seaside, I saw a lady sitting on the rocks reading a book. It is in the earlier spring months that Dublin experiences real winter weather, under ordinary circumstances. But in 1172 the usual order was reversed. Tempests so raged during the whole four months of the king's stay—Christmas night itself was marked by a terrific thunderstorm, felt over the whole of Western Europe—that the superstitious saw clear evidences in them of Heaven's wrath declared against an impious sovereign who had outraged God and His anointed servants.[1] Plague and sickness, too, added

---

[1] Concerning the thunderstorm of Christmas night, see *Radulf. de Diceto*, t. i., p. 350 (Rolls Series), where it is described as "generale subitum et horribile."

their horrors,—and no wonder, as we can now see without resorting to any supernatural explanations.

The Irish princes who thronged to Henry's court from every quarter brought with them large hosts of retainers. They easily encamped after the Irish fashion in huts of turf and branches, spreading themselves over the meadows, fields, and strand which extended on every side of the Dublin of that day. I have often mentioned that Dublin in 1172, and for hundreds of years after, was a very small place. It bore about the same proportion to Dublin of to-day that the city proper in London bears to the whole of that gigantic conglomerate which men now call London. Fields and gardens ran close up to the Castle in Dame Street, the last relic of which is now the garden of the Viceroys.[1] Woods intermingled with meadows covered St. Stephen's Green and Ranelagh and Cullenswood, the last name bearing witness to the ancient fact.[2] An immense strand or common called the Steyne stretched away towards Ringsend and the Bay. The wild Celtic soldiery squatted down on every vacant spot, specially along the highlands of St. Stephen's Green, then called Colonia or Cualan,[3] where wood and water were abundant. But we may be sure they never thought

---

[1] Helena Mocton in 1390 endowed St. Stephen's Church in Stephen Street, at the back of the Castle, with three acres of meadow land round the chapel, so that Grafton Street and William Street were then meadow land. See Carroll's *Succession of St. Bride's Clergy*, p. 8.

[2] See an interesting paper on the manor of St. Sepulchre in the *Journal* of the Royal Historical and Archæological Society of Ireland for 1889, by J. Mills, Esq., of the Irish Record Office. It is full of details of the state, social and agricultural, of the Dublin suburbs about this period.

[3] A name now represented by the prebend of Cullen in St. Patrick's Cathedral, always held by the Archbishop of Dublin, and still retained in Cullenswood Avenue.

of drainage or sanitary questions. They satisfied themselves from the brook which then ran from Stephen's Green to the sea, as it still runs in the sewers beneath Grafton Street. They used the Poddle, which then formed a large portion of Dublin's water-supply, all hideous though it now be with the filth of countless sewers, as it flows into the waters of the Liffey. The Irish peasant soldiers were as supremely contemptuous of sanitary considerations or the welfare of their neighbours as their descendants our rural peasantry are to this day. They used the bright brown mountain streams as we now use, when bound a-picnicing, the kindred streams of the Dublin Mountains, but they cared not how they defiled them for their friends and neighbours farther down the valley, who depended on them for one of the necessaries of life. It is no wonder then that disease and death spread far and wide among the Anglo-Norman hosts who were encamped round Henry's temporary palace on the banks of this very Poddle where it then formed the harbour of Dublin. We now hear daily complaints in the Press and in Parliament concerning the unsanitary state of the Royal barracks, and the typhoid fever which seems to have made that spot its chosen home. Seven centuries ago exactly, the same causes produced the same results on the English invaders; and thus we learn from an English historian of the period that "the eating of fresh meats[1] and the drinking of water,

---

[1] Bacon and corned pork were evidently the favourite food with the Anglo-Norman soldiers. In Sweetman's *Calendar of Documents relating to Ireland* 1171—1251, t. i., pp. 1-7, we have details of the provisions carried into Ireland from England. The only animal food mentioned consists of hogs numbering about three thousand,—Norfolk and Suffolk, for instance, supplying three hundred and twenty at an expense of

as well unaccustomed as unknown, afflicted with dysentery many of the king's army, who were suffering from want of bread."[1] A change of diet may have had something to say to the matter, the riotous living and free licence allowed, and the crowded state of Dublin, something more; but sure am I that the defective and impure water-supply had most of all to say to the dysentery and fever which smote terror into the hearts of king and people haunted with the dread of Divine wrath as embodied for them in the threatened Papal interdict.[2]

It is amusing to notice that even Giraldus Cambrensis fails to recognise the source whence the dysentery

---

£26 16s. 5d., or 1s. 8d. each, which was the highest price. York sent three hundred hogs at £20 15s., or 1s. 4d. each, which seems the lowest. The only notice of oxen which I remember is found in the *Annals* of Caradoc, alias *Brut-y-Tywysogion* (Rolls Series), A.D. 1170, where we learn that Rhys, prince of South Wales, brought Henry II. when on his road to Ireland a present of three hundred horses and four thousand oxen, a portion of which alone he seems to have accepted. I suppose the transport accommodation for cattle was insufficient. The price of pigs was in 1172 much the same as in Bishop Swinfield's time, A.D. 1290. See the *Roll of his Household Expenses*, edited by Rev. John Webb for Camden Society 1855, t. ii., p. xlviii., where we read of the episcopal banquets, "Swine's flesh was in great request, from the brawny boar and bacon hog down to the sucking pig and its trotters." Cf. Paul Lecroix, *Manners and Customs of the Middle Ages*, p. 118 (London: 1874). The reader curious about mediæval banquets and cookery should consult the whole passage from Swinfield's *Roll*, t. ii., pp. xl-liii, where the prices of provisions in the thirteenth century are given.

[1] *Radulfi de Diceto*, t. i., p. 350 (Rolls Series): "Recentium esus carnium et haustus aquæ, tam insolitus quam incognitus, plures de regis exercitu panis inedia laborantes fluxu ventris afflixit in Hibernia." R. de Diceto had specially good sources of information; he was a contemporary of these events, and Dean of St. Paul's.

[2] Sir W. Wilde in his able report on the Tables of Irish Deaths, Pestilences, Cosmical Phenomena, etc., in the *Census of Ireland* 1851, part v., t. i., p. 74, shows that dysentery was the

came, and can only ascribe it to the vindictive temper of the Irish saints, which follows them even to heaven, where they can gratify it to the full by pouring out plagues upon those who outrage their earthly sanctuaries. He tells a story in his *Topography of Ireland* (i., 54) which proves this. The city of Dublin being crowded with troops, King Henry encamped a detachment of archers at Finglas, a town and district belonging to the Archbishop of Dublin.[1] This step the king took probably as much from motives of prudence as of convenience, as Finglas commanded the northern road, and was therefore a convenient outpost to give timely notice of any attack upon the part of the northern tribes. This circumstance, thus incidentally recorded by Cambrensis, throws an interesting side-light upon the careful dispositions made by the king for the security of his person and court during his winter residence in Dublin. Finglas was noted for its ash and yew trees planted in the cemetery by abbots of fame and renown in days gone by. The rude English archers cared nothing, however, for the handiwork of ancient piety. They wanted fuel to cook their Christmas dinners. They tore down the trees, lighted their fires, cooked their food, eating and drinking doubtless far too much, and then were seized with the prevalent sickness, which was duly credited to the

---

disease which played such havoc in the army of Henry II. He notices under the years 1649 and 1689 that Cromwell's army at Wexford and Schonberg's army at Dundalk suffered in the same manner.

[1] A regular manor court was held at Finglas by the Archiepiscopal officials from A.D. 1200. See Gilbert's *Municipal Documents* (Rolls Series), preface, p. xxix, p. 371. Cf. *Liber Niger Alani* in Marsh's Library, and King John's charter to the Archbishops of Dublin in *Chartæ, Privilegia et Immunitates*, p. 8.

wrath of the holy St. Canice, through whose fervent piety the place had become celebrated.[1]

King Henry, however, was in no wise turned aside from his purpose. He steadily pursued his policy of organization during all these four months, devoting his attention to every department of Irish social life. He strove, for instance, to model the kings and their principalities after the feudal fashion, imparting to the princes some notions of personal magnificence and grandeur. He appeared before them, therefore, in scarlet robes, lined with green silk and trimmed with fur, while the sword with which he was girt was brilliant with gold and silver.[2] He treated them to lavish banquets, where rich wines and rare dishes, cheese from Gloucester, and unknown eastern fruits, like almonds, of which alone he brought five hundred-weight with him from England, astonished and tickled their fancy.[3] His array of officials—chancellor, cham-

---

[1] St. Canice, patron of Kilkenny, had been once a member of a monastery at Glasnevin. See Cainnech (3) in the *Dict. Christ. Biog.* It was a very serious offence in the eye of the canon law to interfere with or destroy trees in a churchyard. One of the Constitutions of Peckham, published at Reading in October 1279, treats of this point, *De crescentibus in sacris locis.* Cf. Wilkins' *Conc.*, ii., 140; *Household Roll of Bishop Swinfield*, t. ii., p. lxxiii, note (Camden Society, 1855).

[2] See Sweetman, *Cal. of Documents*, pp. 5, 6, Nos. 29 and 37.

[3] Lacroix, *Manners of the Middle Ages*, pp. 165-173, gives a good idea of the banquets and dishes then in vogue. On p. 170 two bills of fare will be found. One of them describes a banquet given to a bishop on a fast day about 1300. It proves that the resources of gastronomic science had discovered many ways to mitigate the severity of asceticism. It runs thus: "First, a quarter of a pint of Grenache was given to each guest on sitting down, then hot eschandes, roast apples with white sugar plums, roasted figs, sorrel, watercress, and rosemary. Soups, a rich soup composed of six trout, six tenches, white herrings, fresh water eels salted twenty-four

berlains, clerks of the closet—and their stately order must have impressed them with a sense of awe and a desire for imitation,[1] while he sent them all away delighted with the charters he issued, for which he had made ample preparation in the thousand pounds of wax which Richard, Archdeacon of Poitiers, had sent to the king as the contribution of the diocese of Winchester.[2]

King Henry organized the Church too, which seems sadly to have needed that process, notwithstanding the fitful exertions of the Pope during the previous half-century, aided by St. Malachy, St. Laurence O'Toole, and the Cistercians. The Irish prelates, headed by the primate Gelasius, flocked to the royal

---

hours, and three whiting soaked twelve hours; almonds, ginger, saffron, cinnamon powder, and sweetmeats. Salt water fish, soles, gurnets, congers, turbots, and salmon. Fresh water fish, pike with roe, carps from the Marne, breams. Side dishes, lampreys, orange apples, porpoise with sauce, mackerel, soles, bream, and shad with verjuice, rice and fried almonds upon them, sugar, and apples. Dessert, stewed fruit with white and vermilion sugar plums; figs, dates, grapes, and filberts. Hypocras, wines and spices." Almonds evidently were much used in the cookery of the twelfth and thirteenth centuries.

[1] Episcopal households had an enormous train of officials; how much larger must the royal following have been, see Swinfield's *Roll*, t. ii., pp. xxix-lviii. Cf. also Lacroix, *Manners and Customs of the Middle Ages*, passim.

[2] King John when he came to Ireland in 1210 brought for the same purpose no less than fifty-three dozen skins of parchment, which he obtained at Winchester. I have made no statement about dress or modes of living in this section, which may seem to some rather fanciful, without authority either from Henry's own visit or the visits of his son John. We know from various sources that Henry II. practised the usual Norman habits of personal neatness. In his hasty flight from the burning town of Le Mans in June 1189 he brought with him changes of linen, when even his own son saved nothing. See Bishop Stubbs' preface to Roger de Hoveden's *Chronicle*, t. ii., p. lxiv (Rolls Series).

levees. The Norman clergy who accompanied the king must have been astonished at the appearance presented by some of the bishops. The king had in his train Ralph, Abbot of Buildewas in Shropshire; Ralph, Archdeacon of Llandaff; and Nicholas, Dean of St. Julian's Church at Le Mans, one of the king's favourite chaplains.[1] Accustomed as these men were to stately monasteries, dignified prelates, and courtly living, they must have been astonished when they saw the Primate of Armagh, Gelasius, coming to visit the king attended by a white cow, whose milk was the only nourishment he partook.[2] Giraldus Cambrensis, though half a Welshman, and knowing well the failings of the Celtic clergy in Wales, cannot conceal his contempt for the Irish clergy of the period. He preached a sermon before them at Christ Church Cathedral, some fifteen years later than the king's visit, when Archbishop John Comyn was holding a synod of his province in the city of Dublin. There he told them some very plain truths, which he has embodied in his *Topography of Ireland*, bk. ii., chs. xxvii.-xxxii., where he describes the prelates, clergy, and monks of Ireland in the most unfavourable terms. The bishops were negligent of their pastoral

---

[1] Nicholas was one of the king's most trusty chaplains. He was dean of St. Julian's Church at Le Mans, King Henry's favourite residence, and was afterwards bishop of it. He was the king's deputy at the council of Cashel, and witnessed his treaty with Roderic O'Conor of Connaught, made at Windsor in 1175. He was a great traveller too, as we find him marrying Richard I. to Queen Berengaria in Cyprus in May 1191. See Roger de Hoveden (Rolls Series), t. ii., pp. 31, 85; t. iii., p. 110.

[2] See Colgan's *Acta SS. Hib.*, p. 772, for the life of Gelasius. He died March 27th, 1174. The poor Irish Primate must have been a strange sight to the Norman clergy, accustomed to episcopal pomp and luxury like that described in Swinfield's *Household Roll*, ed. by Rev. J. Webb (Camden Society, 1855), Abstracts and Illustrations, pp. xxviii-xl.

duties, dumb dogs never preaching the word of God; the clergy were coarse and sensual, fasting all day and drinking all night. It was no wonder, in his opinion, that the Irish people had not even the form of religion and honesty when their teachers were so utterly worthless. The view thus taken of the Irish clergy by the Welsh archdeacon in 1184 was doubtless practically the same as that entertained by the king's chaplains some twelve years earlier. The king had also an able assistant in his ecclesiastical operations in the Papal legate of that day, Christian, Bishop of Lismore. The local peculiarities and irregularities of the Irish bishops and clergy must have been just as abhorrent to Christian as to the chaplains, for the Lismore prelate was French by training at least, having been one of the original Cistercians sent by St. Bernard to introduce that order into Ireland some thirty years before. Acting under the guidance of these Norman divines, Henry II. assembled a synod at Cashel, under the presidency of Christian, where Ralph the abbot, Ralph the archdeacon, Nicholas the chaplain, and other clergy appeared, armed with the king's commission. At this synod eight canons were passed, enforcing the payment of tithes, regulating the mode of catechising and of baptism, establishing the Roman table of affinity in matrimonial matters, and finally decreeing uniformity of divine worship throughout England and Ireland, in these words, "That divine offices shall be henceforth celebrated in every part of Ireland according to the forms and usages of the Church of England."[1]

But King Henry did not limit his attention to princes and prelates alone during those four months of quiet

---

[1] See Wilkins' *Concilia*, t. i., p. 471.

and seclusion secured to him by the tempestuous west winds which cut off all communication with England. He devoted himself as well to the legal, municipal, and social organization of Ireland. Henry II. is celebrated as the founder of the English legal system. To him and his able assistants are due gaols, itinerant justices, assize courts, and all the main outlines of the system of law and order as at present established. Henry introduced precisely the same system into Ireland. He had by his side very capable advisers in Ralph the archdeacon and Nicholas the chaplain. Archdeacons were indeed in those times far more of lawyers than of clergymen, while as for Nicholas, he was so thoroughly learned in law that we find him acting, some seven years later, as an itinerant justice throughout the midland counties of England.[1] But he had a greater still. He had the greatest and earliest of English lawyers in the person of Ranulf de Glanville, whose name appears as one of the witnesses to the Charter of Dublin, issued at that city in 1171. Henry, aided by these men, established a Chief Justiciary as in England, an Exchequer Court, itinerant and forest justices, and then some twelve years later sent over, in 1184, the same great lawyer, Ranulf de Glanville, to consolidate the system which he had himself introduced.[2] The king did not

---

[1] See Dugdale's *Chronica Series Cancellariorum*, p. 3, in his *Origines Juridiciales*.

[2] Ranulf de Glanville accompanied Prince John. See Girald. Camb., *Conquest of Ireland*, ii., 31. The prefaces of Dr. Stubbs' edition of Roger de Hoveden, tt. i. and ii., have much about this great lawyer and statesman, whose handiwork lies at the basis of the Irish as well as of the English legal system. The signature of Ranulf de Glanville to the Dublin Charter of 1171 can be seen in *Chartæ, Privilegia et Immunitates*, published by the Irish Record Office, p. 1, or in Gilbert's *Municipal Documents*, p. 1 (Rolls Series).

limit himself to the organization of legal institutions alone; he introduced English law, and by the end of the century we have ample evidence that the whole body of English jurisprudence was at work in Ireland. But Henry's own experience showed him that special enactments were required by Irish needs. He was himself cut off by tempestuous winds from communication with England. What would happen to the Irish colony if a chief governor, in whose person centred the chief executive and judicial work, were to die during a similar season? He passed, therefore, in a great council an act called the statute of Henry Fitz-Empress, authorising the Anglo-Norman magnates resident in and near Dublin to elect a chief governor who should hold office till the king's pleasure was known.[1] He issued charters too in abundance. He granted to Dublin its earliest charter, which is still in force and preservation. He issued similar documents in favour of various noblemen, churches, and monasteries, confirming the grants made by Strongbow during his brief period of independence. Finally, he did not despise measures for the social and material improvement of the people, and thus we find in the accounts of the invasion an item of £78 18s. 6d., charged for garments bestowed upon one hundred and sixty-three cottagers who were in the king's service in Ireland. Henry II. had a great mind, which could embrace every topic, even such an insignificant one, as men then counted, as the temporal welfare of the poorest classes.

Such was the work of Henry's four months of seclu-

---

[1] This statute of Henry II. is recognised in an Irish Act passed in the second of Richard III., and printed in Lynch's *Prescriptive Baronies*, p. 63. Cf. Year Book 20 Henry VI., fol. 8. This Act was last put in force in 1787.

sion. I have had to piece my information together, and perhaps to some my sketch may seem fanciful, but yet I feel certain that the more the documents are studied, and facts, names, and statements compared together, so much the more will my views be confirmed. The king's stay in Ireland now drew to a close. As the days became longer he became impatient for news from England. He left Dublin, therefore, about Ash-Wednesday of 1172, and made his way to Wexford. The winds were, however, again contrary to his purpose.[1] March and April have ever been famous on the east coast of Ireland for their easterly winds, and the king was kept waiting for weeks, till at last, on Easter Monday morning, a sudden change took place. The west winds blew a favouring breeze, the king started in his swift-sailing galley at four o'clock in the morning, arriving at St. David's about twelve, just in time to hear mass said in the cathedral, after which with his usual impetuosity he pushed on to Haverfordwest Castle.

Thus ended the great Plantagenet's work in Ireland. He intended as soon as he had restored order to his affairs and settled with the Papal legates about the death of St. Thomas à Becket, to return and finish the work of Irish organization. But Providence ordered it otherwise. Henry II. never saw Ireland again, and the strong hand which laid the foundations of English prosperity never completed the work it had undertaken for the sister island.

---

[1] The east winds brought him, however, his first news of England and English affairs, though they kept him in Ireland. See Girald. Camb., *Conquest of Ireland*, bk. i., ch. xxxvi.

LECTURE VII.

NORMAN ORGANIZATION OF IRELAND.

HENRY II. left the shores of Ireland in April, 1172, after a six months' visit, proposing to return soon and finish his work. He reigned for seventeen years longer, but domestic treason, family discords and strife, the opposition of wife and children, effectually prevented the completion of his intentions. Henceforward he had quite enough to do to maintain his rights and power in England and France, while Ireland was left to its own devices. Upon his departure from Ireland he made various important arrangements. He established the various kings of Ireland as feudal princes, holding their dominions by feudal tenures in subjection to himself as the supreme suzerain, just as he himself held his Continental dominions in subjection to the King of France. He confirmed Strongbow in his principality of Leinster.[1] He found the Kingdom of Meath, the central principality of Ireland, a derelict possession. The Melaghlins had ruled it. O'Rourke of Breifny had deprived them of it, and usurped its

---

[1] The extent of Strongbow's principality is accurately given in Grace's *Annals* (Irish Archæological Series, A.D. 1842), ed. by Rev. R. Butler, p. 21, as extending over Wexford, Ossory, Carlow, and Kildare. That at least was the extent of territory possessed by William Marshall, Earl of Pembroke and Lord of Leinster, in virtue of his marriage with Strongbow's daughter by Eva.

authority. Henry determined to use it for the purpose
of establishing the feudal system in its perfection. He
conferred the greater portion of ancient Meath upon
Hugh de Lacy, and made it a palatinate similar to
those which already existed in England, and have not
even yet completely disappeared.[1] To this arrangement
I shall return after a little, but now pass on to notice
his other regulations. The fortresses which Strongbow
had conceded to him Henry determined to retain in his
own hands. He constituted Dublin the capital, and
entrusted it to Hugh de Lacy, Count Palatine of Meath,
assisted and watched by Fitz-Stephen and Maurice Fitz-
Gerald, together with a garrison of five or six hundred
men. Waterford was committed to Humphrey de
Bohun, Robert Fitz-Bernard, and Hugh de Gundeville,
with the same garrison, showing plainly that Waterford
was then just as important a town as Dublin; while
Wexford, the nearest port to England, was handed over
to William Fitz-Aldelm, Philip de Hastings, and Philip
de Braose, with two hundred men.[2] Around the leaders

---

[1] Henry II. gave a charter to Hugh de Lacy, which is printed
in the *Rotulorum Cancellariæ Hiberniæ Calendarium*,
published A.D. 1828, vol. i., pars. 1, 2 Henry V., No. 137.
The document recites that the king has inspected a charter
of Henry II. to H. de Lacy, by which he gave him the land of
Meath for the service of fifty knights, to be held of the king as
Murcard Humelachlin held it, and by way of increase he gave
him all the fees which he might gain about Dublin while he
was the king's bailiff; and that he and his heirs might have
the said land and all its liberties and franchises which the
king had there or might have. Granted at Wexford in presence of Count Richard, Will. de Braose, Reg. de Courtenay,
Hugh de Cressy, and several others. Cf. Gilbert's *Viceroys of
Ireland*, p. 487; Lynch's *Legal Institutions*, etc., p. 140.

[2] My authority for these statements is Giraldus Cambrensis,
Conquest of Ireland, i., 37 (p. 237, Bohn's ed.). My numbers
do not apparently agree with his. He, as I conceive, simply
mentions the number of knights or men-at-arms, taking no
notice of the foot soldiers, archers, etc., by whom they were

whose names are thus set forth, the fortunes of the Anglo-Norman colony long hung in the balance. We may now disregard Henry II. personally, and concentrate our attention upon the representatives to whom he entrusted the government of Ireland. Four of them stand out prominent in secular and religious matters alike. Their names are Count Richard, otherwise called Strongbow, Hugh de Lacy, Earl of Meath, John de Courcy, Earl of Ulster, and William Fitz-Aldelm, Earl of Connaught, and founder of the family of Clanricarde.

Henry II. before he quitted Ireland instituted an office which still continues in our midst, and that is the office of Lord Lieutenant, constituting Hugh de Lacy his representative under the title of Justiciarius Hiberniæ,[1]

---

accompanied, which I reckon at fifteen for each man-at-arms. Giraldus states that King Henry left forty men-at-arms to hold Dublin. But if the entire garrison contained merely forty men, it would simply have invited destruction. Henry II. brought with him four hundred men-at-arms in four hundred ships. Reckoning fifteen common soldiers to each man-at-arms, this would make the total of the army of invasion six thousand men, exclusive of those already in Ireland. The vast majority of the four hundred ships were doubtless mere coasting vessels or fishing smacks. Cf. Morice Regan's poem, ll. 2580—2595.

[1] Howard, in his *History of the Irish Exchequer*, p. 2, seems to think that the English laws and English judicial system were not introduced into Ireland till early in the thirteenth century, somewhat late in John's reign. Hoveden's *Annals*, t. ii., p. 34 (Rolls Series), state the contrary, specially when we consider the meaning of the term Justiciarius Hiberniæ as I have expounded it in my next note. Hoveden's words are, telling of King Henry's arrangements, "Sed antequam ab Hybernia recederet, dedit et carta sua confirmavit Hugoni de Laci, totam terram de Mida cum omnibus pertinentiis suis, tenendam in feodo et hæreditate, de ipso et hæredibus suis, per servitium centum militum; et tradidit ei in custodia civitatem Diveliniæ et constituit eum Justitiarium Hyberniæ." Sweetman's *Calendar of Documents relating to Ireland*, t. i., No. 87, shows that the office of Justiciary was an established one in Ireland in the early months of John's reign, August, 1199; while a much earlier document, the

a title which survives in that of Lord Justice of Ireland, a deputy or deputies chosen, as the case may be, to act instead of the Lord Lieutenant. Hugh de Lacy was the first to represent the Crown under the style of Justiciary of Ireland. Now this title plainly proves my contention that Henry II. intended to introduce the Norman feudal system as already known in

---

charter of St. Laurence O'Toole to Christ Church in A.D. 1178, is witnessed by Hugh de Lacy, Constable of Dublin (see *Chartæ, Privilegia et Immunitates*, p. 2; Gilbert's *Viceroys*, notes to ch. ii.; Lynch's *Legal Institutions, etc., of Ireland*, ch. iv.). Giraldus Camb., *opp.*, t. i., p. 65 (Rolls Series), treating of 1186, calls Bertrand de Verdun the Seneschal of Ireland; which fact shows that the Norman feudal system was then established in Dublin. Dudley Loftus, in his *MS. Annals of Ireland*, in Primate Marsh's Library, A.D. 1172, says that De Lacy represented Henry II. under the title of Lord Justice, but at first he was called Rector Dublinensis. Loftus, great grandson of Primate Adam Loftus, was an eminent scholar and antiquarian resident in Dublin all through the seventeenth century. His MSS., or at least such of them as remain in Marsh's Library, are well worth consulting for the history of Ireland, specially in the seventeenth century. Howard, *l.c.*, t. i., pref., p. 3, mentions that his mother, who was a descendant of Dudley Loftus, had four manuscript volumes of his filled with information about the wars and confiscations of the seventeenth century. They were regarded in his family circle as waste paper, and treated accordingly. Howard rescued one volume from destruction, using it in his History. Loftus was a great oriental scholar, a pupil of Ussher, and a friend of all the distinguished orientalists of his time. He was a lawyer, not a clergyman. In politics he was a regular vicar of Bray. Under Charles I. he was a royalist; under Cromwell a republican, and his minutes of the courts-martial held in Dublin under the Commonwealth are still in Marsh's Library. Under Charles II. a royalist again, he was Churchwarden of St. John's Church in 1661, Vice-Chancellor of the University, Judge of the Prerogative Court, and Vicar-General. Under James II. he was too old to make any more changes, so he remained quiet in his house on the Blind Quay in Dublin (now 17, Upper Exchange Street) all the troublous times of 1690, editing Syriac liturgies. A chequered and a changeful life forsooth!

England. The Justiciary of England was the English representative of the Norman kings when absent in their Continental dominions. The office was probably invented by William the Conqueror. The main object of his policy was to prevent the supreme administration falling into the hands of a hereditary noble, who would transfer his functions to his son, till at last, like the Mayors of the Palace in France, they might oust the legitimate occupants of the throne. Justiciaries exactly answered this purpose. They were temporary officials, their jurisdiction was limited, and when its occasion passed away its jurisdiction also terminated. Dr. Stubbs, in the eleventh chapter of his *Constitutional History*, has well explained the origin of this office, and shown the relation in which it stands to the great legal official now called Lord Chief Justice of England.

The Norman kings were very jealous of the hereditary nobility. Hence they generally entrusted this office of Justiciary to an ecclesiastic, and therefore it is that here in Ireland the Archbishops of Dublin were almost always the recipients of this high office down to the time of disestablishment, when it was last held by Archbishop Trench. A great ecclesiastic, by his office, was cut off from ambitious projects, while his office itself was merely a life peerage, and involved no danger or plots from hereditary successors.[1] The office of Justi-

---

[1] The office of Summus or Capitalis Justiciarius has been the subject of much learned investigation among legal and constitutional writers. Bishop Stubbs in the eleventh chapter of his History has thrown much light upon it. He has illustrated it from the field of Neapolitan, Sicilian, Aragonese, Norman, and Anglo-Norman history, but has overlooked the light which Anglo-Norman organization in Ireland can throw upon it. Selden, *Office of Chancellor*, p. 4; Dugdale's *Origines Juridiciales*, and his *Chronica Series Cancellariorum*; Madox, *Hist. of the Exchequer*, ch. ii.; Lord Campbell's *Lives*

ciary of Ireland was one offering special facilities for plots, stratagems, and wiles; and therefore it is that from the beginning, even during Henry II.'s reign, the holders were so frequently changed. It was in this respect like a very celebrated office under the Roman Empire. The government of Egypt occupied a unique position in the Imperial organization. The great cities of the Empire, Rome and Constantinople, depended upon Egypt for supplies of corn, and if these supplies were cut off, famine, rebellion, and revolution at once stared the emperor in the face. The governor of Egypt had the emperor at his mercy if he chose to rebel; while again, the resources of the country were so large, that he could find ample means to sustain himself in such action. A special arrangement was therefore devised for Egyptian administration. The other provinces of the Empire were assigned their rulers according to a certain fixed order. The consuls for each year had a recognized claim to succeed to vacant pro-consular governments as they fell vacant. But Egypt was an

---

of the Chief Justices, t. i., c. i.; Foss's *Judges of England*, t. i., afford much light on this point. The office of Summus Justiciarius Angliæ was the historical source whence was derived the modern office of Chief Justice of the King's or Queen's Bench. Originally the Justiciaries of England were executive and judicial officers. The judicial have now eclipsed the executive functions, but even still, as Selden points out (*Office of Chancellor*, p. 4; cf. Madox, p. 21), the Chief Justice of England may be called Viceroy, as he is also Chief Coroner of England. The last of the Norman Justiciaries was either Philip Basset, who died in 1271, or the great jurist Henry de Bracton. At any rate, the first Chief Justice of the King's Bench in our modern sense was Lord Chief Justice Bruce, A.D. 1268—1295. See Campbell's *l.c.*, t. i., pp. 59-69; Dugdale's *Orig. Jurid.*, p. 20. It is curious that no writer has referred to the illustration which the Norman organization might receive from the treatise of the Bollandists in their *Thesaurus Antiquitatis*, t. i., p. 421, on the Palatine Laws of Majorca.

exception to the rule, and its governors were always selected by the emperors from among their most trusty adherents, quite independent of any rule; and lest they should learn to entertain ambitious projects they were closely watched, and very frequently changed.[1] The Justiciaries of Ireland were very like the Augustal Prefects of Egypt. They were distant from the seat of Norman Government, which was often fixed away in the south of France. They had much in their power, and had copious resources behind them. Henry II. sent therefore his most trusty adherents to the post, and then, not satisfied with this precaution, he attached to their retinue spies who would watch them closely, and at once report any symptoms of revolt. Hugh de Lacy was the first Justiciary of Ireland, but he also held another position, by which Henry strove to bind him to his cause. De Lacy was constituted Count Palatine of Meath. By this grant, which the king made at Wexford, he conferred the kingdom of Meath upon De Lacy, and thus raised up a power to be a counterpoise to that of Strongbow, who held Leinster. This policy he further developed in various other parts of the country, constituting Ulster, Kilkenny, and Waterford Liberties or Palatinates, with feudal rulers of their own.

This point is so important, and has such an intimate bearing on the history of Ireland, that I must explain it at some length. You are all aware that the Duchy

---

[1] See about Egypt and the Augustal Prefects, Marquardt's *Römische Staatsverwaltung*, t. i., p. 284, in Marquardt and Mommsen's *Römische Alterthümer* (Leipzig: 1873); Mommsen's *Provinces of the Roman Empire*, t. ii., ch. xii. (Dickson's translation: London, 1886). Cf. also his *Staatsrecht*, ii., 963, with Tacit., *Hist.*, i., 11 ; and a treatise by Le Bas and Waddington, entitled *Fastes des Provinces Asiatiques* in their *Voy. Archéol.*, t. iii., p. 655, for the rules of promotion in the Roman Civil Service.

of Lancaster and the Duchy of Cornwall form even now peculiar jurisdictions, with special officials of their own. The Duchy of Lancaster is now indeed an appanage of the Crown. The Duchy of Cornwall belongs to the heir-apparent. Still there they are, peculiar and exempt jurisdictions in the heart of nineteenth century England, curious remnants and relics of a feudal system which has almost utterly passed away. Palatinates like these formerly existed over large portions of England,—ruled, however, not by the Crown or members of the Royal family, but by subjects.[1] Down to the year 1836 the Bishop of Durham was a Palatine prince within his diocese, which he ruled in temporal as well as spiritual matters.[2] The king's writ did not run within that diocese till countersigned by the bishop's official. The Palatine earldom of Chester had formerly its own courts, its own attorney-general, judges, and staff of officials, together with its own parliament. It was not till 1541 that the Palatinate of Chester was represented in the Parliament at Westminster; an interesting fact which may afford a historical basis for a demand for Welsh Home Rule in the not distant future. These Palatinates were a feudal device for ruling distant or disturbed parts of the empire. The king invested an earl with royal power, so that he could create peerages and confer titles, hold courts and execute justice,—reserving, however, to all parties aggrieved, the right of final appeal to the supreme royal authority. The Norman kings did not relish such

---

[1] On Palatinate earldoms see Stubbs, *Const. Hist.*, t. i., pp. 271 and 363, chs. ix. and xi.; Ormerod's *Cheshire*, t. i.; Selden's *Titles of Honour*, pp. 640, etc.; and *Irish Arch. Miscell.*, p. 26, in the series of the Irish Archæological Society.

[2] See 6 Will. IV., c. 19, for the transfer of the Durham jurisdiction.

jurisdictions overmuch. They had originated in Saxon times. They were used sparingly by the Normans, but only sparingly, because they conferred too much power upon subjects, and tempted them to rebellious courses. Henry II. found one in existence in Ireland. Leinster already owned Strongbow as its king. Henry compelled its surrender as a kingdom, and regranted it as a Palatine earldom ; and then, dreading the power and the ambition of Earl Strongbow, he found rivals for him, turning the ancient kingdom of Meath into a Palatine earldom for Hugh de Lacy, and erecting Ulster, comprising quite a fourth of the whole country, into a Palatinate for John de Courcy.[1] It may have been a wise policy, from one point of view, to erect these great feudal dignities. From another point of view we can see that it sowed the first seed of decay and weakness in the Anglo-Norman conquests. These great dignitaries had royal power, as I have said. They could and did create nobles. The De Lacys, Lords of Meath, created numerous baronies, some still existing, like those of Slane, Navan, Dunboyne, Killeen, Galtrim, Gormanstown, Delvin. The Lords of Leinster were the first to bestow a title on the Fitz-Geralds, on whom they conferred the Barony of Ophaley, a dignity still enjoyed by their descendants. But they also possessed the right to wage war one with another, summoning their dependent barons to their assistance. This arrangement effectually introduced

---

[1] Mr. Lynch, in his *Legal Institutions, etc., of Ireland*, p. 153, maintains that there were no Palatinate jurisdictions in Ireland. Dr. Richey, in his *History of the Irish People*, 2nd ed., p. 170, asserts the contrary. Not being a lawyer, I do not wish to mingle in this fray; but I notice that Lynch, p. 91, states, in opposition to his own view, that the Ormond Palatinate of Tipperary was abolished only in the second year of George I.

the most fatal and destructive discords among the colonists. The wars waged within the first fifty years between the De Lacys and the De Courcys and the De Burghs; above all the war of Kildare, waged in the earlier years of the thirteenth century, destroyed the power of the Anglo-Norman settlers, without any effort on the part of their opponents.

Now let me give you a sketch of Hugh de Lacy's career in Ireland.[1] It is typical of the lives led by the nobles of the Anglo-Norman colony, and sufficiently explains the failure of English policy in this country. Hugh de Lacy was descended from Walter de Lacy, one of the noblest associates of William the Conqueror, who conferred upon him large grants of English lands. The De Lacys adopted the usual plan in the twelfth century for extending their estates. They established themselves on the Welsh border, and strove to steal all the land they could from the native Celtic chieftains. They combined piety with plunder, after the manner of the times, and William de Lacy, in 1103, founded the Abbey of Lanthony, deep in the recesses of the Black Mountains of Brecknock and Monmouth, where an attempt has been made, and is even now being made, to restore the exercise and practice of the monastic life for men in the Church of England. The De Lacys gained the confidence of Henry II., and espoused his side in the contest with King Stephen. Hugh de Lacy accompanied him into Ireland, and was rewarded with

---

[1] About the family of De Lacy, his ancestors and descendants, see a long article in Dugdale's *Baronage*, pp. 95-106, and O'Donovan's note on A.D. 1186, in the *Annals of the Four Masters*, where O'Donovan tells a fact of which Dugdale knew nothing, that by Rose O'Conor, his second wife, Hugh de Lacy was the ancestor of Pierce Oge Lacy, a noted rebel in Queen Elizabeth's time.

the Viceroyalty of Ireland, and a magnificent grant of the ancient Irish kingdom of Meath, with all its former royal rights. The words of Henry's charter, granted at Wexford in 1172, and witnessed by Earl Richard (Strongbow) and William de Braose, a distinguished noble in subsequent Irish history, are very express. "Know ye that I have given and granted, and by this my present charter confirmed, to Hugh de Lacy, for his service the land of Meath, with all its appurtenances by the service of fifty knights, to him and to his heirs, to have and to hold from me and my heirs, as Murcardus O'Melaghlin, or any other before or after him better held the same." These words plainly conferred royal power upon De Lacy as legal successor to the dispossessed Melaghlin. The dominion thus given to De Lacy was a splendid one. It covered, broadly speaking, the present diocese of Meath and Clonmacnois, extending from the Shannon to the Liffey, and from the borders of the Queen's County and Tipperary to Monaghan, or all the great central plain of Ireland, celebrated to this day as the finest feeding-ground for cattle in the whole island.

Hugh de Lacy carried out the traditional policy of Dermot MacMurrough, who had introduced the Anglo-Normans. He retained the ancient hostility to O'Rourke, prince of Breifny. As the ally of the Leinstermen, De Lacy was necessarily the enemy of their bitterest foe. But farther still, O'Rourke had, amid the confusion of the times, taken possession of the kingdom of Meath, which Henry II. had now granted to Hugh de Lacy. This introduced a new element of strife into a combination of circumstances where such elements already abounded. Hugh de Lacy cleverly availed himself too of those tribal dissensions which have ever been the bane of Irish social life. O'Rourke had quarrelled with a member of his own family, Donnell O'Rourke, who fled for protection and revenge to Hugh de Lacy, now ruling at Dublin. De Lacy invited O'Rourke to a friendly conference at the Hill of Ward, near Athboy, where the Irish chieftain is said to have attempted the murder of the Justiciary. He was rescued, however, by the interference of Donnell O'Rourke, who had his revenge, for he slew the Prince of Breifny with his own hand, while De Lacy, to accentuate his triumph, had the body decapitated and gibbeted over the northern gate of Dublin Castle, as a warning to his countrymen coming from that direction.[1] He set to work vigorously building castles and erecting fortresses at Trim, at Kells, and at every other point of vantage.[2] He fell into a snare, however, which has often proved fatal to Englishmen. He fell in love with an Irishwoman, and married Rose the daughter of Roderic O'Conor, King of Connaught, without the leave and license first obtained of King Henry II.[3] King Henry resented this action, and feared that a Lord Deputy son-in-law to the King of Connaught would never prove loyal to an Anglo-Norman sovereign at Westminster. Hugh was dismissed from his office as Lord Justice in 1180, but restored in 1181, as he was found to be the only man who could rule Ireland.

---

[1] Cf. O'Donovan's notes on the *Annals of the Four Masters*, A.D. 1172.

[2] Giraldus Camb., *Conquest of Ireland*, ii., 19, attributes to De Lacy the building of the Black Castle, still existing at Leighlinbridge.

[3] This lady's case was anticipated by that of the princess O'Brian married, by Sitric, King of Man, son of Magnus, King of Denmark, in A.D. 1100, whom the Earl of Shrewsbury also sought in marriage as I have told in a note on p. 96.

The fatal weakness of the first forty years of English rule in this country was a very modern complaint. In reading that far-away story I have been often reminded of modern times. There was in ancient times a new lord lieutenant or lord justiciary on an average about once a year, and as the natural result there was an utter want of continuity in policy and of strength in purpose and in action. No man felt sure of his own tenure of office. No man dared to mark out and pursue a vigorous and independent line. A few words will illustrate what I mean. Let us take the seventeen years of King Henry II.'s reign which elapsed from the conquest to his death. During that period we had the following lords lieutenant ruling in Ireland. The first was Hugh de Lacy, from 1172-75. Then came Strongbow, from 1175 till his death in 1177. After him followed William Fitz-Aldelm, the original of the De Burghos or the Burkes, who ruled two years, and was dismissed in 1179; whereupon Hugh de Lacy was restored, only to be again dismissed in 1180, when the government was committed to two English officials: John, Constable of Cheshire, and the Bishop of Coventry.[1] That experiment, however, did not succeed, and De Lacy was appointed for the third

---

[1] In Sweetman's *Calendar of Documents*, p. 10, we have the following note of the expenses of these English officials: "A.D. 1180-81, Stafford.—Henry de Stratton renders his account: for defraying the passage of John, Constable of Chester, Richard de Peche, Geoffrey de Hay, and Wildo the clerk, sent as messengers into Ireland, £11 11s. 8d., by writ of Ranulf de Glanville; and for forty seams of wheat and twenty hogs which the king gave to Richard de Peche going to that country, 66s. 8d., by the king's writ [*Pipe, 27 Hen.* II., *Rot.* 8.]" The king evidently thought an official from Chester with Celtic experience among the Welsh might succeed where pure Norman officials failed. Cf. Giraldus Cambrensis, *Conquest of Ireland*, bk. ii., ch. xxi.

time in 1181, but only to be dismissed again in 1184, when Philip of Worcester was appointed. There had been already seven chief governors in twelve years of Norman rule. One would imagine I was lecturing about the closing years of the nineteenth century, and not upon the similar period of the twelfth.

But to make the parallel still more complete, we find that Henry II. then thought he would try the effect of a royal residence and a viceroy chosen from his own family. Prince John was, therefore, sent over as Lord of Ireland in 1185. He was only a boy, indeed, and he came over with a parcel of boys like himself, who insulted the natives, princes and people alike. They plucked the beards of the kings, pulled their noses, stuck pins in them, pulled about their best clothes, shut the doors on their heels as they left the royal presence, and treated men of lineage going back a thousand years as if they were wild savages, and in consequence sent princes away thoroughly hostile, who had come as friends to pay their respects to their feudal lord.[1] But John's short rule of eight months alienated more than the Irish princes. He brought a shoal of needy Norman courtiers with him, men who had known nothing of the work of conquest, but wished to enjoy

---

[1] The notices of John's expedition in the Pipe Roll Accounts prove that Prince John came to Ireland amply supplied for all purposes of pleasure. Thus we read in Sweetman's *Calendar of Documents*, pp. 11 and 12: "The Sheriff of Gloucester renders his account: paid to Robert Ruffus and other attendants of John, the king's son, to procure requisites for the bakehouse and kitchen of the king's son, £9 5s. 0d." And again: "Robert Fitz-Pagan renders his account: for a cheese bought for the use of John, the king's son, £10 19s. 4d.; hire of a ship to carry into Ireland Roger Rastel and other sportsmen, with their horses and dogs, 23s.; fittings for the chamber and kitchen of John, the king's son, £15 17s. 3d." The prince's journey must have been an

all its spoils. "Great talkers," as Cambrensis describes them, "boasters and swearers, very proud and contemners of all others, greedy of places, of honour, of profit, but backward in undertaking any hazardous and dangerous action, or performing any service that might deserve them."[1] These worthies despised the men who had borne the burden and heat of the day; treated them as mere provincials, only one degree better than the Celts whom the new comers had insulted. The old warriors knew nothing of Norman refinement or courtly life as these young sprigs had seen it developed within the previous ten years on the banks of the Thames, and were, therefore, pushed aside to make way for the prince's boon friends and companions. The first residence and rule of a royal prince in Ireland originated the most fatal of all the divisions which hindered the power of England in Ireland—the division, I mean, between the English by blood and the English by birth, or, to use modern expressions, between the English and the Anglo-Irish. Prince John's government was in every respect a disastrous one. It lasted but eight months, and yet it sowed seeds of mischief which have not yet fully matured. To John succeeded Earl de Courcy as Lord Justice, who after the usual two years' tenure of office

---

expensive one for his father. With these details of the expedition in 1184 there may be compared the expenses incurred when the same prince visited Ireland in 1210. John as king was much the same as John when prince. See p. 64, where we read: "To Robert de Ros, for play at Carlingford with Warin Fitz-Gerold, when the king was his partner, 37s. 4d. To the same, 20s. 4d when he played with Warin and the king was his partner." Cf. Lacroix's *Manners, etc., of the Middle Ages* for a full statement of the games and other customs of these times.

[1] Giraldus Cambrensis, ii., 35.

was dismissed, and followed by Hugh de Lacy the younger.[1] Now remember what my point was. I insisted that the fatal weakness of Norman policy in this country was its want of continuity. And how could there have been continuity of policy when no less than seventeen chief governors ruled in Dublin during the period of the first seventeen years of Norman power?

De Lacy was the most vigorous of them all, and the fittest for that rough work the times demanded. His personal appearance can even be realized, as Giraldus Cambrensis has left us a vigorously-drawn portrait of him. He was short in stature, ill-proportioned in shape; his neck short, his body hairy and very muscular; his complexion was dark, his eyes black and sunken; his nose was flat, while his face was decorated with a scar reaching from his right eye to his chin.[2] He was certainly no beauty in person; but he had all the qualities for such a chief ruler as Ireland then needed. He was firm, temperate, and indefatigable in the work of government and public business. He was wise and prudent in his view of Irish affairs and the remedies most needed by them. He put a stop to the wholesale evictions the Norman chiefs were indulging in. Like William the Conqueror in Northumberland, and Rufus in the New Forest, they thought the only plan to secure their conquests was by the extermination or exile of all the original inhabitants. De Lacy reinstated the exiled peasants upon their submission, and thus

---

[1] We can trace many of these changes of chief governors in the Pipe Roll Accounts. See for De Courcy's appointment Sweetman's *Calendar*, p. 13. His passage to Ireland cost £10 3s. 4d. The official journeys of the Lord Lieutenant are still very expensive things.

[2] Giraldus, *Conquest of Ireland*, ii., 20.

turned the barren wastes into pastures stocked with herds of cattle. He gained the confidence of the people by his mild administration and firm adherence to treaties, and then enforced a rigid submission to the laws, by which means we are assured that "where his predecessors had spread ruin and confusion, he restored order; and where they had sown toil and trouble, he reaped the happiest fruits."[1] He was great as an organiser. He planted castles in every direction, the remains of some of which still testify to the grandeur of his ideas. He built Kilkea Castle, still used by the Dukes of Leinster, and Black Castle, at Leighlin Bridge, on the banks of the Barrow, to command that famous pass between Ossory and Leinster. The ruins of that castle now excite the admiration of the few stray tourists who care to investigate the beauties of our own scenery; while if you will wander along the Boyne valley and through the fertile plains of Meath and Westmeath, you will find many an ancient ruin—some of them, like Trim Castle, still almost habitable—testifying to the vigour and genius with which De Lacy ruled, amid all the difficulties by which he was surrounded.[2]

---

[1] Giraldus, *Conquest of Ireland*, ii., 19.
[2] About Kilkea Castle see O'Donovan's notes on A.D. 1186 in the *Annals of the Four Masters*. Cf. Ryan's *Carlow*, p. 54, and the *Journal* of the Kilkenny Archæological Society (1854), iii. 123. Kilkea Castle will well repay inspection. It is about four miles from Athy, and is one of the finest mediæval castles now inhabited. Its narrow staircases and passages and deep embayed windows show how inconvenient these castles must have been, judged from our modern standpoint. I am sure De Lacy never could have built the castles attributed to him by Giraldus and others in the style and fashion now indicated by their ruins. He began the work with some rough fortifications; others completed them. See also Dean Butler's *Trim* and Wilde's *Beauties of the Boyne and Blackwater* for much information about De Lacy's buildings.

He organised the feudal society of which he was head in its various ranks. He was palatine prince of Meath, and as such claimed and possessed power to create peers of his own; and down to the present time there are peerages in existence, like that of Nugent, Marquess of Westmeath, and Plunkett, Baron of Dunsany, besides numerous extinct ones, which trace their first origin back to grants, not from the Crown, but from the De Lacys, Lords of the kingdom of Meath.

De Lacy's organizing genius did not forget another great influence. He recognised the power of the Church, and duly strove to propitiate it in his own behalf. He bestowed lavish endowments on the Norman monastery built just outside the gates of Dublin, dedicated in honour of the new and fashionable martyr St. Thomas à Becket. There he buried his first wife,[1] and there part of his own body was laid. He built Bective Abbey, whose magnificent ruins, overhanging the Boyne near Navan, still testify to the grand conceptions of mediæval architects, and there his body rested for a time. King Henry and Prince John bestowed lavish endowments on Mellifont Abbey, near the site of the Battle of the Boyne. De Lacy, in the charter conveying the royal grants, adds his own gift of two carucates of land in the county Meath, the very names and positions of which can still be traced.[2] His second marriage even, which caused his fall in royal favour, may have formed

---

[1] See *Chartæ, Privilegia et Immunitates*, p. 17, published by the Irish Record Office, where H. de Lacy the younger states, in a charter to St. Thomas's Abbey, Dublin, that his mother, Rosa de Munemna, rested in its cemetery.

[2] See *Irish Archæological Miscellany*, p. 159, in the Irish Archæological Society's series, where all the grants to Mellifont are identified from the Ordnance Maps. The names of the

part of the same masterly scheme of organization. He married Rose O'Conor, daughter of the King of Connaught, because he recognised more clearly than his countrymen that the Irish might be gained over to alliance and friendship with England more quickly by the methods of love and gentleness than by those of wrath and terror. And yet, with all his wisdom, Hugh de Lacy fell a victim to the outraged feelings and prejudices of the Celtic race. The story of his death is a sad and a striking one, for it involves all the elements which have ever since combined to produce similar deeds of blood.

In the year 1186 he was prosecuting with vehemence his plans for developing his dominion of Meath. Every corner of it was to be secured by castles. Durrow, in the south-west of his kingdom, was a famous spot from ancient times. There Columba founded one of his most famous Irish convents. The *Book of Durrow* to this day testifies, in Trinity College Library, to the skill and piety with which some of Columba's followers laboured at Durrow more than a thousand years ago. De Lacy did not, however, care one whit about ancient Celtic saints. He had a great regard for Cistercian Abbeys, and St. Thomas's Monastery in Dublin, and similar Anglo-Norman foundations.[1] But he had a profound contempt for the old Celtic saints like Columba and Kieran of Clonmacnois, and violated their sanctuaries, and appropriated their cemeteries with

---

townlands are the same in 1889 as they were in 1184. A carucate of land was the space one plough could cultivate in the course of a year.

[1] Cistercian Abbeys were often built by Norman nobles on the sites of ancient Celtic foundations. See Ulster *Journal of Archæology*, t. ii., p. 52.

the most cynical disregard for religious instincts.[1] He wished to build a castle at Durrow; he seized, therefore, a portion of the Abbey lands, and utilised it for this purpose. Another powerful motive in a Celtic breast came into play, and that was the land question. The country round Durrow belonged to a chief and family named Fox. This chieftain had been dispossessed by De Lacy, and was determined upon revenge. O'Caharny Fox sent a foster-brother or foster-son to work upon the castle, and to carry out his fell purpose. The man waited and watched till at last he saw his opportunity, on July 25th, 1186. De Lacy was headlong in all his operations, flinging himself personally into every work and taking his share in every task. He was using a pickaxe when the Irishman, seeing his body bent, sprang forward, and with one blow of his keen Irish axe deprived De Lacy of life and the English colony of its ablest leader.[2] The body of the murdered chieftain fell into the ditch or fosse of the castle, while the murderer, who was thin and active as a greyhound, escaped all pursuit, and, like many a similar offender since, was hailed as a champion of independence by his country-men.[3] De Lacy was murdered in July 1186. It is a

---

[1] Cf. the account given of De Lacy's death by the Four Masters, A.D. 1186, together with O'Donovan's notes and his letter on Durrow and De Lacy's death in the *Ordnance Survey Correspondence,* " King's County Letters," t. i., p. 147, dated Jan. 6th, 1838.

[2] See upon the use of the axe among the ancient Irish the *Archæological Miscellany* of the Irish Arch. Soc., p. 241. Cf. Dymmok's *Treatise of Ireland,* pp. 7, 57, in *Tracts relating to Ireland* (Irish Arch. Soc.: Dublin, 1843).

[3] The man that killed De Lacy was called O'Meyey, a family name not yet extinct in Westmeath. He escaped to the wood of Killclare, where he was met by Fox, the local chieftain who had incited him to the assassination, and by O'Breen, the chief of Brawney, the district round Athlone. The family of Fox is

curious circumstance that nearly seven centuries later, on exactly the same spot, another eminent English noble met with the same fate, arising out of somewhat similar reasons. In 1839 the Earl of Norbury was assassinated at Durrow after he had erected a castle on the site of De Lacy's. Religious motives too entered into the transaction. Norbury, like De Lacy, is said to have insulted Columcille. De Lacy appropriated his land; Lord Norbury prevented his tenantry burying their dead in the ancient Columban cemetery of Durrow.

Such was the life, such the achievements, and such the death of a typical Norman conqueror. He was vigorous, thorough, restless in activity, wise in council, prudent in action, indefatigable in business. He took the measure of the people he ruled, and succeeded so well, that in later ages his government was looked back to as those halcyon times when "the priest kept his church, the souldier his garrison, and the plow-man followed his plow," in peace.[1] A few Hugh de Lacys might have changed the fortunes of the English colony and of the Irish people.

Hugh de Lacy was the first Justiciary, Constable, Bailiff, and Lord-Deputy of Ireland. The second, Count Richard, or Earl Strongbow, was even a more famous man; but as I have already said a great deal about him, I shall now dismiss his history in a few

---

still represented among the landlords of the same district. In the *Parliamentary Gazetteer of Ireland* I find, under the head of Durrow, that the parish church was restored in the present century at the expense of Mrs. Fox. See O'Donovan's notes on the *Annals of the Four Masters*, A.D. 1186; his letter in the *Ordnance Survey Correspondence* already quoted, and a paper by him on the family of Fox in the *Irish Archæological Miscellany*, p. 184 (Dublin: 1846).

[1] Hanmer's *Chronicle*, p. 318, ed.

words. Hugh de Lacy was deposed from his post as Lord Justice in 1175. Henry II. had carried Strongbow over to France to assist him in his wars against his rebellious sons. He wished also to secure himself against Strongbow's suspected treason. He was now too powerful a subject to leave all unhampered and unrestrained with such a tempting prize as the kingdom of Ireland lying derelict within his grasp. Strongbow used his three years in Normandy to good purpose, proved his fidelity and his courage, and so gained upon the king that when De Lacy was dismissed Strongbow was sent over as Justiciary to represent the supreme power of England before the Irish clans. He ruled two years and then died. Yet of those two short years we have many memorials. He created peers, as King of Leinster, and thus pursued the feudal system of land conquest and settlement. Kilkenny Castle contains one of the greatest collections of historical documents existing in these kingdoms, gathered during the seven centuries in which the Butler family have played a leading part in our historic annals. At Kilkenny Castle we therefore find an original charter of Strongbow's. It is a precious curiosity, bringing us back to the earliest days of the Norman Conquest, and purports to convey to Adam de Hereford half the town of Aghaboe, and the half cantred of land adjoining in Ossory. This Adam of Hereford is one of the Norman knights mentioned by Morice Regan [1] as richly gifted by Strongbow, and then, to confirm Regan's accuracy, we find in Kilkenny Castle the very charter conveying Strongbow's gifts, with the original seal appended, containing figures of a knight on one side and a heavy-

---

[1] *Anglo-Norman Poem*, ed. Wright, 1. 4006.

armed footman on the other,—authentic pictures, that is, of the soldiery who conquered Ireland.[1]

Strongbow claimed all his rights as King of Leinster. He disposed of Church patronage as kings were wont. We have still a charter from Strongbow bestowing the Abbey of Glendalough upon a favourite of his. He built and endowed abbeys in honour of Norman saints,—evicting Celtic saints to make room for them. He bestowed endowments on Christ Church Cathedral,[2] and when he died in 1177 the Prior and Chapter of Christ Church buried him with all due honour and magnificence. St. Laurence O'Toole, the Archbishop, himself presided over the funeral rites, while the Chapter commemorated his memory in the most solemn manner, as among its chief benefactors; his ordinary obit being celebrated on April 20th, the day probably of his death, while his memory was still more solemnly celebrated every year, with bells ringing and lights burning, on the Sunday next after August 1st, the feast of St. Peter ad Vincula.[3]

The viceroyalty of Strongbow is said, by tradition, to have been marked by a great tragedy. He had a son by his first wife, and by him Strongbow was accompanied into Ireland. He was marching to relieve Fitz-Stephen when the Irish forces attacked the earl. His son supported him for a time, and then fled. The earl gained the day, and then ordered his son to be cut in two for his cowardice, burying him in Christ Church Cathedral,

---

[1] See *Journal* of Kilk. Arch. Society, t. i., p. 501—504.
[2] See Strongbow's charters in *Chartæ, Privilegia et Immunitates*, Dublin Record Office.
[3] See *Book of Obits* of Christ Church, pp. 21, 57, in Irish Archæological Series (Dublin: 1843). Girald. Camb., *Conquest of Ireland*, ii., 14, states that Strongbow died about June 1st. Cf. Gilbert's *History of Dublin*, t. i., pp. 102, 112.

where Hanmer states he set up the following Latin inscription :

> "Nate ingrate mihi pugnanti terga dedisti
> Non mihi, sed genti et regno quoque terga dedisti,"—

lines which the chronicler turns into English verse as follows :—

> "My son, unkind, didst flye the field, the father fighting hard ;
> Nor me, nor English birth didst weigh, nor kingdome didst regard."

Strongbow's career as Chief Governor of Ireland was not a lengthened one, as after a two years' rule he fell sick and died, leaving the English colony in a position of great peril. The ready wit of a woman brought them relief. Strongbow had married his sister Basilia to Raymond le Gros, one of the original adventurers. This Raymond was the ablest and most successful general of all the Fitz-Gerald faction. Strongbow died in the late spring or early summer of 1177. Raymond and the great body of the English troops were at that time engaged in suppressing a formidable rebellion at Limerick. Basilia was with her brother, Earl Strongbow, in Dublin. She knew right well how dangerous the position of the Normans, few in numbers, would be if their leader was known to be dead. So with all a woman's tact she concealed the earl's death, and despatched a letter by a special messenger to her husband summoning him to her side as the ablest Norman in the land. The letter was sufficiently enigmatical to puzzle any hostile person into whose hands it might fall. It ran as follows : "To Raymond, her well-beloved lord and husband, his Basilia wisheth health as to herself. Be it known to your sincere love that the great jaw-tooth which used to give me so much uneasiness has fallen out. Wherefore if you have any care or regard for me, or even for yourself, return with all speed."[1] A summons which the gallant Raymond obeyed at once, and thus saved the infant colony from serious peril.

I need not pursue the history of the Viceroys further, for they will often come before us in future lectures. But what a lesson the historical student gains from our brief survey! These earliest Viceroys and their masters formed the type and determined the course of English policy in this country. Just as David's polygamy introduced a fatal weakness into Judah's national history; just as Jeroboam's idolatry poisoned the sources of Israel's national life, so that from the sins of Jeroboam the son of Nebat king after king departed not; so the earliest history of our Irish Viceroys determined the course of future policy. Instability of purpose, want of continuity and of strength, intrigue and perpetual changes—these things constituted the weakness of Irish administration in the Plantagenet times, and led infallibly to Irish discontent and confusion. You may be sure of this, that confusion in a nation is like confusion in a schoolroom. If a school is confused, noisy, rebellious, it is the master's fault just as much as the children's. The children may be bold—and what children are not?—but the confusion results, not from the innate boldness of the pupils, but from the lack of force and determination in the teacher. Nations are simply big schools. Ireland has been an exceptionally troublesome one, but its troubles and confusion have arisen quite as much from the faults, the weakness, the vacillation, the want of continuous policy in its earliest rulers, as from the vices or defects of its inhabitants,

---

[1] Giraldus Cambrensis, *Conquest of Ireland*, ii., 14.

Celtic, Norman, or Saxon. Instability, weakness, want of will and purpose, must ever fail with nations, families, or individuals, for instability has marked upon its brow the stigma of the Divine judgment, and stands condemned in the records of Inspiration, which, reiterating and enforcing the lesson of this lecture, declares: "He that wavereth is like a wave of the sea driven with the wind and tossed. Let not that man think that he shall receive any thing of the Lord."

LECTURE VIII.

ST. LAURENCE O'TOOLE AND THE CATHEDRAL CHURCH OF THE HOLY TRINITY.

I HAVE spent a great deal of time over an exposition of the political and social state of Ireland during the period of Henry II. It was absolutely necessary to do so. The ecclesiastic pure and simple looks at all mundane affairs merely from his own narrow professional point of view; he regards wars and political changes and social revolutions as of no importance save so far as they touch upon and affect his own personal or caste interests. But we have not so learned ecclesiastical history, and our ideas of the Kingdom of God are not limited by the interests or designs of any special class whatsoever. We believe in Church and State as embodying a grand ideal. The Church affects the State and the State affects the Church. David prepared precious stones, and cedar-wood, and gold and silver in abundance; and Solomon built up a wondrous house, where neither axe nor hammer was heard; and that house in turn reacted upon Jerusalem and made it the city of the Great King, the centre of earthly interests unto all generations of His people. Church and State in Zion were united most closely, and no matter how statesmen may plot to divorce religion from daily life, the dearest of all human interests, the keenest of all human hopes, must assert itself and claim a voice in the disposition and government of human affairs. For this reason we have devoted the preceding lectures to the development of the Anglo-Norman State and its organisations as introduced into Ireland by the Anglo-Normans of the twelfth century. We now proceed to our more immediate subject—the introduction and development of the Anglo-Norman Church and the relations which existed between it and the ancient Celtic Church of this country.

I must ask you to start from the Synod of Kells in March 1152, when Cardinal John Paparo established the four archbishoprics of Ireland, turning Gregory, the last bishop, into the first Archbishop of Dublin. To him succeeded St. Laurence O'Toole in 1161. I have already given a very brief sketch of St. Laurence's life in a published lecture on the See of Dublin,[1] but must now go into his history a little more fully, as Archbishop Laurence forms the connecting link between the ancient Celtic, the Danish, and the Anglo-Norman Church of Dublin. All the previous bishops of Dublin had been Danish by birth, connexion, and consecration, but Laurence O'Toole was a Celt by birth; you can still see the tomb of his ancestor, or, at least, his connexion, in the Refert Church at Glendalough, where formerly was an inscription testifying to the death of King O'Toole in 1010. St. Laurence was not only a Celt, he was also brother-in-law of King Dermot himself, who, notwithstanding, is said to have

---

[1] See *Ireland and the Celtic Church*, p. 326. The authorities for the life of St. Laurence are Surii, *Vitæ SS.*, t. vi., pp. 331-39; Messingham's *Florilegium*, p. 379; a MS. Life in Marsh's Library classed v. 3, 4; and a convenient English version of his life, by the Rev. John O'Hanlon (Dublin: 1857).

treated him very cruelly in our saint's boyish days.[1] Laurence O'Toole was born at Castle Dermot in the co. Kildare about 1132. He was educated at Glendalough, —which was then no mean seminary, as a bi-lingual inscription in Greek and Irish, now preserved in St. Kevin's stone-roofed church, plainly proves.[2] He devoted his life to works of piety, charity, and learning, so that he was elected Abbot of Glendalough when only twenty-five years of age. There was at that time an Abbot and also a Bishop of Glendalough, quite distinct the one from the other; and the most curious point is this, the abbacy would seem to have been much richer in value and extent of estates than the bishopric. However, we shall come across this abbey somewhat later in our narrative, and have more to say about it.

Laurence O'Toole, after serving the office of abbot, was elevated in the year 1161 to the Archbishopric of Dublin, an election which was all the more popular perchance because King Dermot MacMurrough was bitterly hostile to St. Laurence. The new prelate took up his residence on Christ Church Hill, where his palace was situated on the site occupied by the present Synod House, and previously by the Church of St. Michael.[3] Now, it is worthy of careful

---

[1] O'Hanlon's *Life of Laurence O'Toole*, pp. 11-13, makes Laurence's sister, Mor O'Toole, wife of Dermot MacMurrough. See *Book of Leinster*, fol. 245, in the Royal Irish Academy; cf. O'Donovan's note on the *Annals of the Four Masters* A.D. 1164, where his genealogy is given.

[2] See a paper in the *Journal* of the Historical and Archæological Association of Ireland, A.D. 1883-4, by the Rev. James Graves, on this inscription.

[3] The site of St. Laurence's residence is fixed by the following quotation from the *Repertorium Viride* of Archbishop Alan, A.D. 1530, confirmed by Giraldus Cambrensis, writing more than three centuries earlier. Alan says: "Ecclesia de S^{to} Michaele. Ecclesia ista parochialis a primæva fundatione

notice that the See of Dublin seems at that time to have been limited territorially to the walls and suburbs of the city,[1] extending, perhaps, its sway over the Danish inhabitants of Dublin wherever they settled all along the coast. An episcopate of this kind, not territorial but rather personal in its jurisdiction, has not been and is not unknown. Even in pre-Christian times we find that the Jewish high priest at Jerusalem and the Sanhedrim exercised such a personal jurisdiction over the Jews scattered throughout the world.[2] The Roman Catholic Church has such bishops ruling the Uniat Greeks and their married priesthood scattered through the provinces of Southern Italy.[3] Our own bishops of Gibraltar and

---

capella extitit infra Palatium S^{ti} Laurentii." While we read in Giraldus Cambrensis' *Topography*, ii., 46, of a certain archer who confessed to having stolen money from the bishop's residence within the precincts of the Church of the Holy Trinity. The palace must have therefore adjoined the Cathedral. Cf. Ussher's Works, ed. Elrington, vi. 424.

[1] Ussher, in his *Religion of the Ancient Irish*, Works, ed. Elrington, iv. 326, expressly asserts this on the testimony of a letter from the Archbishop of Tuam to Pope Innocent III., A.D. 1216: "John Papiron, the legate of the Church of Rome, coming into Ireland, found that Dublin indeed had a bishop, but such a one as did exercise his episcopal office within the walls only," quoting as his authority the *Black Book* of Christ Church and the Archbishop's Register or *Liber Niger Alani*. Mr. Mills of the Irish Record Office, who has lately inspected the Archbishop's Records, informs me that the original *Liber Niger Alani* is now imperfect. The Archbishop has however a transcript of it when perfect. Another perfect copy exists in Marsh's Library, devoid, however, of Alan's own valuable marginal notes. It was made under Archbishop Bulkely in the reign of Charles II., and presented to Marsh's Library by his heirs.

[2] See *Codex Theodosianus*, ed. Gothofred., lib xvi., tit. viii.; t. vi., pars. i., p. 235 (Lips.: 1743). The imperial authorities strove, in the fifth century, to put an end to the forum domesticum exercised by the Jews among themselves, but failed. It was flourishing in London in the twelfth century. See Sweetman's *Calendar*, t. i., p. 8, No. 49.

[3] See Aldis and Arnold's *Catholic Dictionary*, art. "United Greeks."

Jerusalem exercise a similar authority, not over districts, but over individuals scattered through several countries. The Synod of Kells, confining its attention to the affairs of the Celtic Church, did not attempt to assign a territorial diocese to the See of Dublin, which was Danish and in communion with Canterbury, but simply adopted the arrangements then existing, creating the holder of the bishopric an archbishop.[1] The fact is that the bishopric of Glendalough seems to have been the one great territorial diocese of this district in the time of St. Laurence O'Toole. Bishop Reeves, in his memoir on the diocese of Dublin, has shown that in the twelfth century the diocese of Glendalough extended from the border of Meath to Wexford Harbour, and from Naas to Lambay, including, of course, the Danish settlements, like Baldoyle, Dalkey, and Wicklow, where the Dublin and Danish prelate naturally bore sway. But the jurisdiction exercised seems to have been of the loosest character. One bishop thought no more of intruding into the diocese of another than a modern dissenter thinks of intruding into the jurisdiction of the most orthodox prelate. Let us take an instance, closely connected with ourselves too. I have several times referred to the foundation of the Priory of All Saints, which preceded the modern Elizabethan foundation of Trinity College. Let me now give you a more detailed account of it, as it will illustrate episcopal affairs and Church life in the time of St. Laurence O'Toole. About the year 1165 Dermot MacMurrough made one of his numerous raids into the principality of Uriel, including the modern Louth, Armagh, and Monaghan. Having obtained considerable success and committed doubtless

---

[1] See Keating's *History of Ireland*, ed. O'Mahony, pp. 596-98.

some very gross crimes, he was seized with a fit of repentance, which induced him to found a convent for canons on the spot where this college stands, under the title of the Church, Priory, and Canons of All Hallows or All Saints. This church he endowed with an extensive estate at Baldoyle, conveying by his charter, which is still extant, not merely the lands of Baldoyle, but also the serfs or slaves resident upon them,—a very important statement in the charter, as it sheds much light on the social state of Ireland at that period, and proves that serfdom or slavery of the peasantry prevailed in Ireland, that was free, as well as in England, that was subject to the Norman yoke. As this charter given by Dermot MacMurrough proves his own scholarship and that of his scribes, and also illustrates our social state, I shall translate for you in full. Its title is : "Charter of Dermot, King of Leinster, of Baldoyle and its men, made to All Saints." It begins, curiously enough, with the exact title this college afterwards received and still enjoys. Could there have been anything more than a chance coincidence therein ? " In the name of the Holy and Undivided Trinity, Father, Son, and Holy Ghost. I, Dermot, King of the Leinster men, for the love of God and salvation of my soul, have given and delivered to my spiritual father and confessor Edan, Bishop of Louth, for the assistance of the canons of the Church of the daughter of Zola and their successors, a certain territory called Baldoyle, with its men ; to wit, Melisa Macfeilecan with his sons and grandsons, free and absolved from procuration and expeditions both of me and of all succeeding me in the government of Leinster and of Dublin in perpetual alms, with the lawful and ancient bounds and all things pertaining to the same vill. Further, I command and firmly order to all Leinster and

Dublin men present and future, that they quietly allow the said bishop and his canons and their successors serving in the said church, to have and to hold the said land for ever with all liberty, without any exaction of tithes, in peace and honour, as well and honourably as any other college of canons or monks in Ireland, and that they maintain and defend from all injury the said bishop and church with all its men, lands, and possessions." And then the charter is duly witnessed as follows (the names attached are of great interest):—"And in order that my donation may remain sure and firm to posterity I have signed it with my seal. Witnesses, Laurence, Archbishop of Dublin; Kinad, Bishop, and Edenignus, Abbot, of Glendalough; Enna, my son; Felanus Macfeolanus; D. MacGilla Colmoc; G. MacGunnar, and many others."[1]

I have given this charter thus at length for many reasons. It must be of special interest for ourselves to look back and see a document which dealt with the site of our own college long before any colleges existed in Oxford or Cambridge. It is of use to us from a historical point of view, because it compels us to recognise that before the English conquest there were estates, settled estates, and tenantry, and conveyances, and seals, and a legal phraseology much the same as a conveyancing lawyer of to-day would use, but couched in much better Latin than he could possibly muster if he were to try. But we learn something further still from this charter. We see

---

[1] See *Registrum Priorat. Omn. SS.*, pp. 50, 125, in the Irish Archæological series; cf. Ware's *Bishops*, ed. Harris, t. i. p. 180. Enna was the eldest son of Dermot, whom Fitz-Patrick of Ossory blinded. MacGilla Colmoc was Enna's son-in-law; cf. p. 118, note.

somewhat of the loose diocesan organisation then prevalent; for we have an estate conveyed to the Bishop of Louth[1] in Baldoyle, which probably, as a Danish settlement, was subject to St. Laurence as archbishop; and the same charter founds a college of canons on the strand next the river Liffey, making the same Bishop of Louth head of this college, and neither the Archbishop nor the Bishop of Glendalough utters a word of protest against such an intrusion, but rather sign the charter as assenting witnesses. The Celtic Archbishop St. Laurence and the Bishop of Glendalough were easy-going prelates, while King Dermot, on the other hand, was a very fierce and a very headstrong sovereign, who did not easily tolerate any interference with his will. Probably they looked at the matter in this light. The charter founded a new institution indeed, and made the Bishop of Louth head of it; but then they knew he would die, and a new prior would arise who would not be a bishop, and so they let the matter slide, after the fashion of easy-going Irish landlords with defaulting tenants of later ages.

But fifteen years passed away; the Celtic archbishop died and an Anglo-Norman bishop came in his stead, with his notions of canon law sharpened and developed in the University of Paris, and then matters soon changed. Archbishop John Comyn found a Celtic Bishop of Louth intruded into his diocese of Dublin and

---

[1] Edan was bishop, not of the county Louth, but of the monastery of Louth in the same district. Till disestablishment the parish of Louth was one of the richest in the Irish Church. See the Index to O'Donovan's edition of *The Four Masters* (under the word "Lughmhagh") for lists of the bishops, abbots, and anchorites connected with this monastery.

claiming rights of which the canon law knew nothing. He determined to crush the intruder and terminate utterly and at once such very Hibernian laxity. Archbishop Comyn had full power to do so. He came armed with complete papal authority. He came, too, the trusted friend and counsellor of King Henry II. and of King Richard. All the resources of the Anglo-Norman colony lay at his disposal, and poor Bishop Edan of Louth had no choice but to obey; and in the same *Register of All Saints* from which I have already quoted you can read his act of surrender of all independent claims and his consent to hold the priory in subjection to the Archbishop and his Cathedral Church of the Holy Trinity, duly executed in the year 1181. These two charters of 1166 and 1181 tell their own tale of Celtic freedom and Celtic laxity verging upon license; of Norman rule and law and strictness, very necessary for our nation, but easily gliding into harsh and unloving sternness and cruelty.

Let us now return to Laurence O'Toole and his life. The ten years of St. Laurence's life prior to the English invasion are practically blank. He was a great church-builder in Glendalough;[1] he doubtless continued to apply himself in the same direction in Dublin.

---

[1] Cf. "Vita S. Laurentii" in *Surii Vitæ SS.*, Nov. 14, t. vi., p. 334. The reading of this passage of Surius considerably modified Dr. Petrie's views with respect to the age of the ornamented architecture at St. Saviour's Church, Glendalough, as he originally stated it in his treatise on the *Ecclesiastical Architecture of Ireland*, p. 253, *Trans.* R. I. A., t. xx.; cf. Petrie's *Life*, by W. Stokes, M.D., p. 182, St. Laurence's restorations accounted for the phenomena which at first puzzled Petrie and led him to ascribe them to an earlier date: an interesting illustration, by the way, of how historical investigation serves to correct professional theories.

Christ Church, or, as it then was called, the Priory or Cathedral of the Holy Trinity, was developing itself apace. The old Irish order of canons held it hitherto. Like everything else pertaining to the Irish Church, it was a free and easy-going establishment. St. Laurence heard of the fame of the reformed Augustinian order of Aroasia in Flanders, which he introduced into Dublin, turning the old Irish canons into monks of this order: a process of reformation which the similar Cathedral or Convent of the Holy Trinity at Bristol underwent at the same time. St. Laurence doubtless encouraged the outburst of church-building which Dublin experienced just before the Norman invasion. When Strongbow and Henry II. came to Dublin they found it studded with churches. To this day the district round Christ Church Cathedral is thickly planted with churches, which were much more numerous when the now deserted churches of St. Nicholas, St. John's, St. Michael's, and St. Bride's were in full operation. But we must add to these many others which have since faded from memory, though flourishing in St. Laurence's time. The *Repertorium Viride*, to which I have several times referred, enables us to recover their names. This *Repertorium Viride* is a wonderfully full and interesting account of this diocese, drawn up by Archbishop Alan in the year 1530. That Archbishop deserves our grateful recollection. He was an Englishman, the confidential friend and agent of Wolsey at the Papal Court. He came here to carry out and assist the views of Wolsey and of Henry VIII. But he was not, like many an English Archbishop of Dublin before and since, who came here simply to make as much as he could out of the See, and never took one atom of interest either in the diocese, its records, or its antiquities. Archbishop Alan took the keenest, liveliest interest in the affairs of the ancient church which had raised him to high eminence, and it is owing to the manuscript narratives he compiled and transmitted to us—his *Register*, or *Liber Niger Alani*, as it is called, and his *Repertorium Viride*—that we now possess authentic Church history going back to the times of Laurence O'Toole. His *Repertorium Viride*, or *Green Repertory* (so called doubtless from the colour of the cover), used to be preserved in Christ Church Cathedral. But, like a great many other valuable documents which ought to be in our cathedrals, the original is supposed to be lost.[1] There are two transcripts of it: one in Trinity College Library, and the other under my own care in Primate Marsh's Library. In it we have an exact account of the churches in which Laurence O'Toole ministered, and some of which he may have helped to build. There we find the record of many churches whose very names and sites are now well-nigh forgotten, as St. Olave's, somewhere near the foot of Fishamble Street;[2] St. George's Church, in the modern South Great

---

[1] Mr. Mills of the Record Office informs me that the Archbishop of Dublin possesses three copies of the *Repertorium Viride*, one of which may be the original which the Christ Church Chapter certified to the Record Commissioner in the beginning of this century they possessed. I fear very much they knew nothing about it. At the beginning of this century our chapters had touched their lowest point. Dignities and offices were then conferred in virtue of political interest without regard either to religion or learning.

[2] St. Olave's must not be confounded with St. Owen's or Oudoen's. In the narrative of a tour in Ireland, in the time of Charles I., published in the second and third volumes of the *Christian Examiner* (1826-27), the writer mentions, t. ii., p. 219, that Archbishop Ussher when in Dublin preached every Sunday morning, at 8 a.m., in the Church of St. Owen, being his native parish. This tour has many curious details of Irish life at

George's Street; St. Stephen's Church, on the site of Mercer's Hospital; St. Martin's and St. Paul's Churches, within the Castle bounds; St. Michael-le-Pole, in Ship Street. All these, and others now unknown, were flourishing in the days of Laurence O'Toole.

The times of Strongbow and of the Fitz-Geralds and of Dermot MacMurrough's invasions must have been trying ones for the Archbishop.[1] He is said to have temporised, to have encouraged the people of Dublin to resist Strongbow and his allies when they attacked the city, and then to have submitted humbly and dutifully to Henry II. And yet there would have been no inconsistency in so doing. Let us strive to realize how matters then stood from Laurence O'Toole's point of view. In the end of 1170 Dublin was taken by King Dermot and Earl Strongbow. On that occasion Archbishop Laurence acted as mediator, to prevent effusion of blood. He recognised the broad fact that King Dermot was lord paramount of Dublin, and therefore used his sacred office to arrange terms of peace between Dermot the king and his men of Dublin. The next summer King Dermot was dead, and Roderic, King of Ireland, proclaimed a general crusade to drive the

---

that period. On p. 219 of the volume for 1826 we have a description of Ussher's studious life which I have never seen quoted. "Hee doth most industriously apply his studye, which hee hath placed at a good distance from his house to prevent distraction and diversion by the access of any companye to visit him, who are not admitted to disturb his studyes. This his course and order is so publique, as that few come to him att any time of the day save att the houres of relaxation, which is from 11 to 1 and soe about supper time. The rest of the day from 5 in the morning untill 6 in the evening is spent ordinariely in his study." I retain the quaint spelling.

[1] See his *Life* in Surius, t. vi., quoted above. This *Life* was written by a man who was practically a contemporary, Ralph of Bristol, Bishop of Kildare.

Welsh and Norman invaders out of Dublin. Strongbow and his partisans were the advance guard of the English invasion. But if we are to understand history aright we must throw ourselves back into the age we may be studying. We must strive to realize its circumstances, and view men and things as they were then viewed. Now to Laurence O'Toole, or to any Irishman of that age, what must Strongbow and Fitz-Stephen and Raymond le Gros[1] and their fellows have seemed? They must have simply been regarded on the same footing and in the same light as the Danes. They must have been viewed as freebooters. The fear of the Danes was then a real living terror. For a hundred years later a regular tax was paid to the kings of Man, a kind of black-mail, to secure the English and Irish coasts from plunder. Why even to the present time the memory and fear of Danish invasion has not quite died out on the eastern and northern coasts. Dr. Reeves tells an amusing story in the *Ulster Journal of Archæology*, how some fifty years ago, when the Ordnance Survey of Ireland was beginning, a party of sappers and miners landed early one morning on a small island, near Carlingford, off the coast of Mourne in the county Down. This was of old a favourite station for the northern invaders. A tremendous panic at once ensued as the report was spread far and wide that the Danes had come back once again to renew their old work of blood and fire and plunder.[2] If this has been the case in the

---

[1] I have already pointed out (p. 98) that Raymond le Gros was the ancestor of the family of Grace. I have not mentioned the steps by which the transformation of names was effected. They were Le Gros, Le Gras, Grace. He was a Fitz-Gerald however, being son of William Fitz-Gerald and grandson of Nesta, and so the Graces belong to the Geraldine faction.

[2] *Ulster Jour. of Archæology*, t. ii., p. 45, note *b*. Itinerary of Father E. MacCana. Edited by W. Reeves, D.D.

nineteenth century, how lively must have been the terror of Danish and other foreign invasions seven hundred years ago. It was only natural then that Laurence O'Toole should have urged his flock to active resistance against Strongbow and his free-lances as soon as King Dermot was dead and the acknowledged supreme King of Ireland had taken the field against the invaders. But then again, when Henry II. came he took good care to come fortified with ecclesiastical authority. He had a bull from a pope. He summoned, too, a council of the Irish bishops at Cashel. Thither he sent his legate, a clever Cistercian abbot, Ralph, Abbot of Buildewas in Shropshire, who managed his master's business with such skill that St. Laurence must have viewed it as his solemn duty as an obedient subject of Rome to submit to the authority of King Henry II.[1] And he did submit, and was honoured accordingly. We can trace, in Sweetman's *Calendar of Documents*, the attentions that were paid to the last Celtic archbishop. He travelled at the public expense, and thus introduced a practice which lasted to modern times. Let me here interpose a few words of explanation. If you are reading Primate Boulter's letters written in the last century, you will get a wondrous glimpse into the inner life of Ireland during the eighteenth century, both in Church and State. Or if you take up the autobiography of Mrs. Delany, wife of Dr. Daniel Delany, a senior fellow of Trinity College and Dean of Down, you will have a picture of the last century from behind the scenes which will help to explain much of modern history. Now in both these works you will find that the great

---

[1] Ralph was Abbot from 1150—1187. See Eyton's *Antiqq. of Shropshire*, vi. 317-35.

ecclesiastics of that day, and specially the Primates of Armagh and Archbishops of Dublin, always travelled at the public expense. Whenever an influential bishop or dean wanted to visit England he always requested the use of the Lord Lieutenant's yacht, and thus saved his fare. This custom had its origin in the earliest days of Norman dominion in this country. Thus the very first year that Henry II. reigned in Ireland we find in the public accounts for 1172-73, as given in Sweetman's *Calendar*, that Richard de Raelega rendered his bill for the passage of the Archbishop of Dublin, 8s. He travelled to the General Council of the Lateran in the same style. In the year 1178-79 we find one official rendering his accounts for the passage of the Archbishop of Connaught and the Irish bishop going to the Council, 35s. by the king's writ.[1] Another, the Sheriff of Kent, sends in his bill for the passage of Laurence, Archbishop of Dublin, and Bricteus, Bishop of Limerick, 15s.; while again the poor prelates seem to have travelled with a very slender banking account, as the Sheriffs of London and Middlesex send in their account for redeeming the pledges of the Archbishop

---

[1] The Lateran Council of 1179 held its sessions from March 5th to March 19th. It passed many useful disciplinary canons, some of which are still in force in the Church of England. They are given at length in Hoveden's *Chronica* (Rolls Series), t. ii., pp. 171-89. Hoveden notes that the Irish and Scotch bishops applied for licence before they went to Rome, and swore to defend the king's rights. His words are (p. 171): "Post Natale Domini venerunt de Hybernia in Angliam Laurentius Dublinensis, et Catholicus Tuamensis, Archiepiscopi, et quinque vel sex episcopi, Romam ad concilium ituri. Similiter de regno Scotiæ transierunt per Angliam episcopi et Abbates quam plures. Et illi omnes tam de Hybernia quam de Scotia et aliis insulis, per Angliam transeuntes, pro licentia transeundi juraverunt, quod neque regi neque regno ejus damnum quærerent."

of Dublin, 30s., and for the Bishop of Limerick 10s., by the king's writ.[1]

St. Laurence not merely travelled at the royal expense as archbishop, he also gave other proofs of his allegiance and good will towards the Anglo-Norman conquerors. He assisted at a Council held at Windsor about Michaelmas 1175, when a treaty was concluded with Roderic, King of Connaught, whereby the feudal supremacy of Henry II. was acknowledged by that prince, while King Henry, on the other hand, guaranteed Roderic in his hereditary possessions. St. Laurence secured, too, the possession of the rich abbey of Glendalough, once held by himself for his nephew Thomas. You can still see, in *Chartæ, Privilegia et Immunitates*, p. 1, the charter by which Strongbow and his wife Eva made over to their first cousin, as this Abbot Thomas was, the lands and estates pertaining to Glendalough, all of which were, by a subsequent charter, transferred to the See of Dublin and remained part of the endowment of the archbishops till the Act of Disestablishment deprived the Irish Church of its ancient landed property.[2]

I have referred in passing to the Council of Cashel which was held in the autumn of 1172. It has been a much contested point of history; let me then give you

---

[1] See Sweetman's *Calend. of Documents*, t. i., nos. 40, 52, 56, 57.

[2] See *Chartæ, Privilegia et Immunitates*, pp. 1, 4. Rev. J. O'Hanlon, in his interesting *Life of St. Laurence*, p. 36, strives to prove that Abbot Thomas was not St. Laurence's nephew. The lands of Glendalough, which were added to the endowment of the See of Dublin, carried with them the only trace of the ancient Celtic institution of Corbes and Herenachs, which survived in the southern districts of Ireland. A Corbe was appointed at Glendalough by the Archbishops of Dublin till 1476. See Ussher's *Works*, ed. Elrington, t. xi., pp. 428, 435.

a brief account of it drawn from original sources, and without any wish to decline in one direction or in the other from the strict line of historical truth and accuracy. The Council of Cashel assembled in the year 1172 by command of King Henry II. At it there attended, as Papal legate, Christian,[1] Bishop of Lismore, together with Donatus, Archbishop of Cashel; Laurence, of Dublin; and Catholicus, of Tuam: the Primate Gelasius being unable to attend through age and infirmities. There were present, in addition, the majority of the Irish bishops, together with many abbots, archdeacons, priors, and deans. The king was represented by Ralph, Abbot of Buildewas in Shropshire; Ralph, Archdeacon of Brecknock; Nicholas, a chaplain; and other chaplains; while the decrees of the council, when signed by the bishops, were confirmed by royal authority, so that the King's supremacy was then thoroughly recognised in the Irish Church. There were eight decrees or canons made, touching the following points.[2] The first forbade marriage within the degrees of consanguinity prohibited by the Roman canon law. The second ordered that children be catechised outside the church doors, and infants baptized at the fonts. The third canon ordered the payment of tithes. The fourth freed all ecclesiastical lands from secular exactions. The fifth forbade the exaction of the eric or composition for homicide from

---

[1] Christian was an Irishman by birth. He had originally been a monk of Clairvaux. About 1142 he was made first Abbot of Mellifont and then Bishop of Lismore. See Ussher's *Sylloge, epp.*, 43, 44; *opp.*, t. iv., pp. 539-42, and Colgan's *A A., SS. Hiberniæ*, p. 652, under March 18th, for the life of Christian.

[2] The decrees of Cashel will be found in Giraldus Cambrensis, *Expugnatio*, i., xxxiv., Bohn's ed., p. 232; or in Wilkins' *Concilia*.

the clerical members of a tribe or sept. The sixth dealt with testamentary jurisdiction and rules. The seventh related to the burial of the dead, concluding with the following important words: "That divine offices shall be henceforth celebrated in every part of Ireland according to the forms and usages of the Church of England. For it is right and just that, as by Divine Providence Ireland has received her lord and king from England, she should also submit to a reformation from the same source." Many misconceptions have arisen about this council. Some enthusiastic Protestants have thought that this council betrayed the liberties of the Irish Church, and that till its decrees were passed the Irish Church had been totally independent of Rome. This, you will easily see, is a mistake. Whatever else this council may have done, it did not say a word about Rome or the Pope. It recognises, indeed, the canon law of the West, and strives to conform the Irish Church thereto; but the same attempt had been made one hundred years earlier, when Lanfranc wrote to King Turlogh O'Brien complaining of the matrimonial irregularities of the Celts.[1] Council after council, synod after synod, had made similar attempts within the previous century, and yet the Irish held to their old customs, notwithstanding the very strong language used by the Pope, his legates, and his supporters among the Irish bishops. And this Council of Cashel was not much more successful, on some points at least. Thus, the fourth canon ordered that all lands and possessions of the Church be entirely free from all exactions of secular men, and especially that neither the reguli (princes) nor earls or other

---

[1] See Ussher's *Sylloge*, opp., ed. Elrington, t. iv., p. 492.

great men in Ireland, nor their sons, nor any of their household, shall exact provisions and lodgings on any ecclesiastical territories, as the custom is, nor under any pretence presume to plunder by violent means; and that "the detestable practice of extorting food four times a year from the vills belonging to the churches by neighbouring lords, shall henceforth be utterly abolished." This canon relates to the right claimed by the Irish chieftains of entering by force upon ecclesiastical property, and living there at free quarters four times a year; a right which, notwithstanding this canon of Cashel, they continued to exercise down to the reign of Queen Elizabeth. Thus, in a letter written from Athlone by Sir H. Wallop, the President of Connaught, in 1581, he tells how, on the 20th January, Mr. Thomas Le Strange had killed nineteen of the O'Melaghlins in a church seven miles from Athlone,—"All notorious thieves, and consorts of the O'Conors, *in which place they were taking meat*, as they term it;" or, in other words, they were exacting the vile custom reprobated by the Synod of Cashel more than four hundred years before—so little were the Celts inclined to surrender their ancient national customs at the dictation of any ecclesiastical body whatsoever.[1] So much for the Council of Cashel. Let us return from this digression.

St. Laurence O'Toole was closely connected with Christ Church, or the Cathedral of the Holy Trinity, as it should more properly be called. He lived as a bishop should live, beside his cathedral. He is said to have enlarged and beautified it. He certainly was eminently devout, as we are told in his *Life*, which appeared while

---

[1] *Calendar of State Papers*, 1574—1585, p. 282.

many were living who personally had known the Archbishop, that "he used to spend whole nights in the church prostrate before a crucifix, while before the morning's dawn he went forth into the cemetery adjoining the church to offer his prayer for the departed members of Christ's flock." He loved Glendalough, too, though it was apparently lapsing by degrees into an increasing barbarism, being infested by robbers who respected neither ecclesiastic nor layman, and even dared to mock and imitate the solemn ritual of excommunication. Notwithstanding the wild character of the inhabitants, St. Laurence delighted from time to time to retreat to the scenes of his youth, where he was wont to occupy that well-known and lofty spot, St. Kevin's bed, spending his time in meditation and prayer.[1] The Dublin cathedral of the Holy Trinity was dear to him; there is a chapel still used in the cathedral called after him, St. Laurence O'Toole's Chapel, and we owe much of our knowledge of the state and history of the cathedral prior to the English invasion to a charter granted to the cathedral by the same Archbishop. That ancient document, preserved in the Christ Church archives, will be found printed in *Chartæ, Privilegia et Immunitates*, p. 2, while an inspeximus of it, by King John, is printed in the same valuable work, p. 12.[2] From these documents we learn that the site of Christ Church was given by Sitric, Danish Earl of Dublin; that it was largely endowed by the MacTurkils, a

---

[1] St. Laurence's *Life* in Surii, *Vit. SS.*, t. vi., Nov. 14, cap. xxv.; O'Hanlon's *Life*, p. 68.
[2] An inspeximus, as the word implies, was a recital of an ancient grant in a later charter or document. In this manner the terms of many documents, the originals of which have perished, have been handed down to our time.

Danish family, which, as I have shown in a previous lecture, long possessed great estates in the north of the county, and whose descendants, so late as the last century, were still in existence; to whom must be added the Brodars, the O'Briens, and many others whose names can scarcely be recognised in King John's version. St. Laurence's own charter is intensely interesting. It dates from about 1178, and must have been issued soon after the change of the canons into monks of the reformed Augustinian order.[1] Probably the change in the organization caused the issue of the charter, so as to secure the due and legal devolution of the conventual property. The charter sets out the churches and estates pertaining to the cathedral, enumerating those we have ourselves known as Prebendal parishes, St. Michan's and St. John's. It mentions the church of St. Bridget as belonging to this cathedral, though afterwards transferred to St. Patrick's, and then gives a long list of churches in the north of the county, in Fingal and its neighbourhood, attached to the cathedral, concluding with the names of clerical witnesses, where we find Celtic, Danish, and Anglo-Norman clerics side by side. We have first four bishops, three at least of whom are Celts; then come five abbots, headed by Laurence's own nephew, Thomas of Glendalough, who is followed by Ralph of Buildewas, and Adam of St. Mary's Abbey. Then comes Torquil, evidently a Dane, who is Archdeacon of Dublin, to whom succeeds the earliest list of Dublin

---

[1] The change of secular canons into regulars was fashionable in England too at this epoch, though a reaction soon began. See Lect. XI., pp. 270-72, below; William of Newburgh, *Histeria Rer. Anglic.*, iv., 36, in *Chronn.* of Stephen (Rolls Series), i., 393; Stubbs's preface, *Epistt. Cantuar* (Rolls Series).

clergy we possess. They are evidently a mixed body, as their names show: Joseph, Presbyter of St. Brigid's; Godmund, Presbyter of St. Mary's; Edan, Presbyter of St. Patrick's; Cenninus, Presbyter of St. Michael's; Peter, Presbyter of St. Michan's; Richard, Presbyter of St. Columba's; Gillebert, Presbyter of St. Martin's, "et ceteris omnibus aliis Presbyteris Dublinii." The clerical signatures are then followed by the laymen, at the head of whom stands Hugo de Lacy, "Constabularius Dublinii."

I have called your attention to the fact that Celt, Norman, and Dane were thus ministering side by side. This is a most important fact to notice, as it shows conclusively that the Anglo-Normans made no clean sweep of the Celtic clergy, they retained the old organisation; while, on the other hand, English fashions in Divine worship were adopted by the ancient Celtic and Danish clergy. And now you may ask me what kind of worship was celebrated in Christ Church Cathedral by Laurence O'Toole. The answer is easy enough. The Synod of Cashel ordered the example of the English Church to be followed in Divine worship. The English ritual, the order of Sarum, was then introduced, and followed till the Reformation; after which the same Sarum Use—the same in substance, only translated into English—continues to be used to this day. Probably the Cathedral of the Holy Trinity, Dublin, was the first church in Ireland where the Sarum Use was officially adopted, just as the same church first saw the English Litany used under the direction and order of Archbishop Brown in the days of Henry VIII. But I am sure that if some among us could have seen the Cathedral of the Holy Trinity in the days of Laurence O'Toole, it would have cooled their zeal and love for the Celtic Church of the twelfth century. We have heard in our own time a great outcry about a screen in Christ Church and a representation of the Crucifixion in stained glass. I am somewhat afraid that the party who raised this cry, if they had their will, would abolish all cathedrals. They sometimes talk in laudatory language of the ancient Celtic Church and its arrangements, but had they gone into Christ Church seven hundred years ago they would have found much more to vex their souls than a screen and stained glass. In that cathedral was kept the miraculous staff of Jesus, which the English took away from Armagh. There, too, a miraculous crucifix was preserved, about which Giraldus Cambrensis tells some wonderful stories in his *Topography*. It was not introduced by the English. It stood in the cathedral in the years of independence, and Giraldus tells many marvellous tales of its performances even then; how, for instance, it spoke when solemnly adjured in a mercantile trial, how it became immovable when the Danish citizens desired to carry it off upon the conquest of Dublin by Strongbow, and how a penny sacrilegiously obtained thrice leaped back when offered before this wonder-working crucifix.[1]

Such was life and such was worship in the time of St. Laurence O'Toole. He seems to have been a thoroughly saintly and devout man. His lot, however, was cast in evil times, when men of action made more noise and exercised more influence than men of meditative piety. Statesmen, and not saints, were

---

[1] See Giraldus Cambrensis, *Topograph. Hib.*, Dist. ii., cap. xliv.-xlvi.

needed in high places then; and statesmen, and not saints, the Anglo-Norman kings of England provided as Archbishops of Dublin, as I shall show in my next lecture on Archbishop Comyn and St. Patrick's Cathedral.

[1] See my former volume, *Ireland and the Celtic Church*, ch. xvi., for more about St. Laurence O'Toole; and also Ussher's *Sylloge, opp.*, t. iv., p. 553; *Annals of Four Masters*, ed. J. O'Donovan, note to A.D. 1180. It may interest some travellers in Ireland to know that a cross in former times reputed miraculous, just like that of which I have spoken above, was found no later than last year (1888), built up into the wall of the chancel of Raphoe Cathedral, which is said to have been founded by St. Adamnan. It used to be called before the Reformation St. Adamnan's Cross, and must have been so treated about the time of the regal visitation of King James I., when the cathedral was repaired. The remains of Adamnan's Cross—for it crumbled into pieces when exposed to the air—are now carefully preserved by the vicar of the parish, the Rev. R. Bennett, A.M., who is making a bold effort to restore his ancient church in a style worthy of the memory of one of Ireland's noblest sons.

LECTURE IX.

JOHN COMYN AND THE ANGLO-NORMAN ARCHBISHOPS OF DUBLIN.

THE mediæval English Church was essentially a royal one. The royal supremacy was then acknowledged as fully and completely as ever under the Tudors. The monarchs used the organization of the Church for all the purposes of statecraft; its higher officers were checks and spies upon popular movements, while its ablest bishops, neglecting their spiritual offices, were wholly withdrawn to the affairs of temporal administration. The episcopate was thoroughly secularised under Henry II., and as the natural result the character of the bishops became sorely deteriorated. The pious mediæval and monkish chroniclers lament over this fact. They tell sad tales of the bishops of their time. William of Newburgh was a monk of northern England who lived through the long reign of Henry II., leaving us a chronicle, the *Historia Rerum Anglicarum*, which is most important for the history of that obscure period, and as such has been printed among the *Chronicles* of Stephen and Henry II. in the Rolls Series. He draws a very dark picture indeed of the bishops of his time, and tells us that Henry II. had much the same opinion of them. That monarch was a keen observer of character, and he saw very clearly the insincere and worldly motives which guided the men whose abilities he used. William of Newburgh in his History (iii., 26) tells us that King Henry justified himself in keeping sees vacant and appropriating their revenues to the purposes of state on this ground, "that it was much better that the money should be spent on the necessary business of the kingdom than consumed in episcopal gluttony; because the bishops are no longer like the ancients, but remiss and languid in their duty, and have become entirely immersed in the world." The description given us by the same pious and unsophisticated monk of some of the bishops of his time—of Longchamps, for instance, Bishop of Ely, Justiciary of England, and Papal Legate under Richard I.; of Hugh de Puiset, Bishop of Durham; and above all, of Wimund, Bishop of Man—amply confirms his testimony.[1] The account given us of Wimund reads more like a romance than a sober historical narrative. It is hard to imagine that such a prelate could have existed, only seven centuries ago, in our own immediate neighbourhood. Some of the Celtic bishops of Ireland, even of later times, were bad enough, as we shall hereafter notice, but none of them were quite as wicked and depraved as this Bishop of Man. Let us hear the story, and then we shall not be much astonished at any other tales of episcopal misdeeds which may come across our path.

Wimund was originally a poor boy—a peasant's child,

---

[1] See as concerning Longchamps, Bishop of Ely, the *Historia Rerum Anglicarum* in the *Chronicles* of Stephen, Henry II., and Richard I. (Rolls Series), ed. by R. Howlett, pp. 300—490; concerning Hugh de Puiset, pp. 78, 303, 304, 436-41; concerning Wimund, pp. 72-6. In lib. v., cap. 31, of the *Historia Rer. Anglic.* there is a curious story of a warlike Bishop of Beauvais captured at the head of his army by Richard I. in 1197.

in fact; and was educated as a chorister in Furness Abbey, a celebrated foundation on Morecambe Bay, whose ruins testify to its ancient greatness, and even still discharge a useful function in furnishing one of the great playgrounds for northern Lancashire. We have not as yet sufficiently recognised the important educational functions fulfilled by the abbeys of England and Ireland alike. The universities of England do not now supply much more than half the candidates for holy orders; the theological colleges make up the balance. In mediæval times the abbeys were the theological colleges of that period, and as such discharged a most beneficial office in affording room for the exercise of local talent. Many an intellectual flower would have been born to blush unseen had it not been for the abbeys of mediæval England; just as the Church of England has since the Reformation lost many a noble soul because the most expensive universities in Christendom have been the sole recognised channels of entrance upon her ministry. A Bede, an Alcuin, a Roger of Hoveden, a William of Newburgh, gained in the abbeys a wide intellectual training enabling them to transmit to posterity works of the greatest value; while as the tares ever grow among the wheat, so too men like Wimund gained in the same monasteries an intellectual training fitting them for an eminence of evil to which they otherwise could never have attained. Wimund in due course took holy orders; wherein he displayed such a keen intellect, such an unfailing memory, and such a ready eloquence, that in the earlier half of the twelfth century he was sent upon a mission to the Isle of Man, which lies within sight of Furness. He proved so pleasing to the barbarous inhabitants, half Scandinavian and half Celtic, his person being tall and athletic and his conduct free, jovial, and easy-going, that clergy and people united in electing him their bishop. The Manx Church seems in fact to have chosen its bishop on the same principle as that on which Saul was elected King of Israel,—because the candidate was head and shoulders taller than all the people.[1] Wimund soon revealed his true character. He was not contented with the episcopal office, but desired to emulate the Irish bishop-kings of Cashel, who were equal adepts with the weapons of temporal and of spiritual warfare.[2] He laid claims to the earldom of Moray, denying his real birth and asserting that he was the earl's son; and ravaged south-western Scotland with fire and sword. He married the daughter of the Thane of Argyle, and with his help brought the King of the Scots so low that he was fain to surrender to Wimund the southern portion of his kingdom, which then extended to Furness and the shores of Morecambe Bay. Success was fatal to him as to many another upstart pretender. He treated the monastery of Furness, which had been his earliest friend, with special severity, and ruthlessly plundered its tenantry. They were Celts, and possessed all the Celtic hatred of an oppressive landlord. The country people watched their opportunity, waylaid him when his escort was few in number, overpowered them, seized

---

[1] The original Latin of William of Newburgh, *Hist. Rer. Anglic.*, lib. i., cap. xxiv., is very telling. "Deinde apud Furnesium tonsoratus et regularem vitam professus, cum nactus esset scripturarum copiam cum otio competenti, adjutus triplici bono, scilicet acri ingenio, illabili memoria, apto eloquio, ita in brevi profecit, ut magnæ spei esse videretur. Evolutis diebus in insulam Man cum fratribus missus, suavitate eloquii et jocunditate faciei, cum esset etiam producto et robusto corpore, ita barbaris placuit ut ab eis in episcopum peteretur, et eorum quidem completum est desiderium."

[2] See *Ireland and the Celtic Church*, p. 268.

the piratical bishop, blinded and otherwise mutilated him, incarcerating him as a monk in the inland monastery of Byland, where William of Newburgh heard his romantic story from Wimund's own lips.[1] His monastic seclusion does not indeed seem to have worked a very deep repentance in the man, as the chronicler tells of Wimund's boast that if he could only recover his sight he would even still avenge his injuries sevenfold upon all his enemies. The episcopal character must have sunk very low when such a career could have been possible for a Bishop of Sodor and Man.

These general reflections upon episcopacy in the twelfth century will pave the way for the history of the first Anglo-Norman Archbishop of Dublin. They may seem at first sight derogatory to the system of Church government which we maintain and support; but, from another point of view, they may be regarded as an evidence of its Divine nature and authority, for surely no system that was not of God could have survived the wickedness of those who exercised it. At any rate this story will help you to understand the circumstances amid which John Comyn's lot was cast and his work was done.

---

[1] "Cum autem per subditam provinciam tanquam rex vallante exercitu gloriose ferretur, ipsique monasterio, cujus monachus fuerat, supra modum gravis exsisteret, de consensu nobilium insidiati sunt ei quidam provinciales, qui ejus vel potentiam vel insolentiam exosam habebant. Nactique tempus opportunum, cum præmissam ad hospitium multitudinem lento pede et raro stipatus satellite sequeretur, comprehensum vinxerunt, utrumque illi oculum, quia uterque nequam erat, eruerunt, causamque virulenti germinis amputantes, eum pro pace regni Scottorum, non propter regnum cœlorum, castraverunt."—*Hist. Rer. Anglic.*, i., 24, in *Chronicles* of Stephen, Henry II., t. i., p. 75 (Rolls Series).

St. Laurence O'Toole died on November 14th, 1180. Episcopal vacancies were not very quickly filled up by the Norman sovereigns, as they claimed the profits and rents arising from the estates attached to vacant Sees. The longer, therefore, they were kept unfilled, the more money accrued to the sovereign. The See of Dublin was not as yet, however, profitable enough to be long kept vacant. When its estates were enlarged, then we shall find that years might elapse before the English sovereigns would permit the election of a new archbishop. One point, however, Henry II. had already determined, and that was, no Irishman should again be Archbishop of Dublin; and his determination and example were followed, with a very few exceptions, down to the present century. There were twenty-three archbishops from the time of St. Laurence to the Reformation. Not one of these was an Irishman. One or two of them, like Archbishop Fitzsimons, from 1484 to 1511, may possibly have been born in Ireland, though even this is dubious, or at any rate were beneficed there prior to their elevation. But not one of them was otherwise than of pure English blood and extraction; a policy which was pursued down to the present century.[1] This was certainly most injurious to the spiritual interests of an important portion of the Church. I have often been surprised at the same time to see how exactly this precedent, with all its unfortunate

---

[1] From the Reformation to the Disestablishment there were twenty-three Archbishops of Dublin. Of these, seven alone were men of nominal Irish birth. Their names and dates were: Michael Boyle, 1663-78; John Parker, 1678-81; William King, 1703-29; Arthur Smyth, 1766-72; Charles Agar, 1801-09; J. G. Beresford, 1820-22; William Magee, 1822-31; and R. C. Trench, 1863-84. The connection of several of these with Ireland and the Irish Church was merely nominal, just sufficient to give a colour to the appointment.

results, is now followed by our colonists, who almost always send home for bishops for all their leading Sees. In Ireland in ancient times, in our colonies nowadays, this policy produced and produces the same result. Men are imported who are ignorant of the country, and whose interests all lie in another sphere. Such a course of action demoralises and degrades the local clergy. They feel themselves cut off from all prospect of attaining those higher rewards which lend a stimulus to hope and action, and as the natural result really first-class men avoid a field which implies and carries with it a stigma and a professional degradation. If I were a colonial Churchman I would prefer an inferior local man to a superior stranger, satisfied that though I might suffer a little at present, in the long run I was conferring a permanent benefit on my own Church by helping to raise its clerical tone and standard. A regiment which always imports its commanding officers from a strange corps will never develop courage, enterprise, or daring among its subordinates.

Let us return to the new Archbishop of Dublin. In September 1181—that is, ten months after St. Laurence's death—Henry II. issued his royal licence for election, and summoned the Chapter of the Convent of the Holy Trinity to perform their duty of election at the Benedictine Abbey of Evesham in Worcestershire, where through royal influence they selected a monk of that abbey, John Comyn, to fill the vacant episcopal office. He was only a deacon at the time, but had had large experience in State affairs, and had made himself very useful to the government of the time.

The story of John Comyn is indeed a most interesting illustration of Norman ideas about Church administration. He was but a deacon when chosen, or rather nominated, for the high and important position of archbishop—for the election was simply a farce. The kings of that period exercised a far more extended influence upon episcopal elections than they do now. The kings, or else their chief justices, presided at episcopal elections, and thus terrorised the bishops and chapters into choosing the royal nominees. Dean Hook tells us, in his *Lives of the Archbishops of Canterbury*, chap. ii., p. 387, that Henry II.'s chief justiciary, Richard de Luci, presided at the election of Becket, and compelled the reluctant prelates, who knew the man and his disposition right well, to elect the king's chancellor Primate of Canterbury. Becket's election offers an illustration of John Comyn's. Becket, like Comyn, was but a deacon when chosen archbishop. Gilbert Foliot, Bishop of Hereford, one of Becket's subsequent opponents, wittily remarked thereupon that the king had worked a miracle, for he had made an archbishop out of a soldier; so little was Becket's previous life in keeping with the episcopal character.

John Comyn, the new Archbishop of Dublin, was just the same. In early life he had taken clerical orders in the lowest degree. This step clothed him with privileges of the most valuable kind, but demanded no special restrictions and entailed no spiritual work. He became a statesman pure and simple, with a dash of the lawyer combined. Comyn was King Henry's most thorough-going supporter all through his quarrel with Becket. He was perpetually on the road between London and Rome. In 1167 and again in 1170 we find him at Rome, negotiating with the pope on behalf of the king and against the primate.[1] In 1167

---

[1] See *Roger de Hoveden*, Rolls Series, i., 276, and Giles' *Life and Letters of Becket*, ii., 369.

he bore a letter from the pope to the king, striving to bring matters to a compromise. In 1170 Comyn was sent back by the king, and reaching Rome at the moment when the news of Becket's murder arrived, found the pope so enraged that he refused to see any Englishman for eight days. But John Comyn had not visited Rome so often without learning the ways of the papal Court, and we hear therefore without surprise that a judicious douceur of 500 marks—that is, something more than £300— opened a way for him to the papal presence.

As Comyn's life began so it continued. There was not one atom of a clergyman about him, according to modern notions. He was one day an ambassador, the next day a judge, but never a priest or a pastor of souls. Comyn spent his life in state affairs. He went as ambassador to Spain in March 1177.[1] He was a lawyer too. King Henry was a great legislator as well as a great soldier. His reforms in our legal institutions and practices were many and practical. His name is held in honour for one special achievement,—he brought law and justice home to every man's door by the institution of assize courts. He dispersed, for this purpose, itinerant judges all through England. And in this great work John Comyn had his own share, as we find his name appearing in the list of justices appointed to dispense justice throughout the northern counties of England from the year 1160 to 1179.[2] Thus for twenty years at least before his election as bishop John Comyn was

---

[1] See Walter of Coventry, *Memoriale*, i., 286 (Rolls Series).
[2] See Benedict of Peterborough, *Gesta Regis Hen. II.*, t. i., p. 239 (Rolls Series); cf. the preface by Bishop Stubbs to t. ii. of the same writer, pp. lxv-lxxi; Madox, *Hist. of Exchequer*, pp. 84-96; Foss's *Judges*, i., 274.

active in the discharge of political and judicial functions, while his spiritual office and work seem to have been utterly forgotten. Yet, just as in the case of Thomas à Becket, he was judged the fittest man to hold a most important See, and like the same man he became in time the sturdiest champion of clerical rights and privileges.

Comyn forthwith departed to seek confirmation of his election, and also to consult with the pope concerning Irish affairs. He was ordained priest at Velletri on March 13th, 1182, and on the following Palm Sunday, March 21st, was consecrated Archbishop of Dublin by Pope Lucius III. So that the first Norman archbishop was just like the Danish Bishops of Dublin—he disdained an Irish or Celtic consecration and introduced a succession direct from Rome.

This pope, Lucius III., issued a bull on April 13th of the same year, confirming the archbishop in his possessions of the See of Dublin. He enumerates them, and thus incidentally gives us much precious information concerning the state of the diocese under Comyn's predecessor. We learn thence what the property of the See was when Laurence O'Toole died, and then from subsequent charters of King John and Henry III. and Pope Innocent III. we can easily trace how rapidly the Norman archbishops extended the estates attached to the See and the temporal powers exercised by its occupants. From the bull of Pope Lucius we find that St. Laurence possessed but little more than the manors or landed property attached to Swords, Lusk, and Finglas, with some other scattered possessions in the northern part of the county Dublin.[1] This bull, after enumerating

---

[1] See Bishop Reeves' *Analysis of the United Dioceses of Dublin and Glendalough*, where he gives a revised version and translation of the bull of Alexander III. to Laurence

and confirming his estates, then proceeds to direct the newly-consecrated prelate as to the festival days and occasions on which he is to wear the pallium; it places certain restrictions on the Celtic monks, who seem to have been asserting daring claims as to their exemption from episcopal supervision, and concludes by prohibiting the old Celtic abuse, which flourished, not only in Ireland but also in Wales, of the hereditary possession of benefices, handed down as of right from father to son. This bull is interesting to us as members of the diocese of Dublin, because it tells us of the Sees which were subject to its metropolitan jurisdiction. They were Wexford or Ferns, Ossory, Leighlin, Kildare, and the diocese of the Isles (Episcopatum Insularum), a title which has led some people to fancy that the Isle of Man was for a time subject to the See of Dublin, which is a great mistake. The bishopric of the Isles here referred to was that of Glendalough, so called because Glendalough itself is an island. The priory or abbey of St. Saviour's, a mile or so to the east, is also on another island, and several islands occur in the list of possessions belonging to the See and Abbey of Glendalough, as enumerated in various bulls and charters of that period.[1]

This bull of Pope Lucius laid the foundation of a prolonged controversy between Armagh and Dublin. It forbade any other prelate to hold synods, or to use any kind of jurisdiction within the diocese of Dublin, in virtue of which grant the two Archbishops of Armagh and Dublin waged a lengthened strife, the primate claiming the power of holding synods anywhere in Ireland and of

---

O'Toole, dated 1179, which should be compared with that granted to Comyn three years later.

[1] See *Register of All Hallows, Dublin*, ed. Butler, pp. 2, 106. See, however, for another view, note, p. 380.

raising his cross aloft within the Dublin diocese,; a claim which the Archbishop of Dublin as firmly resisted. Some persons will perhaps remark how very Irish that two archbishops should fight over such a paltry matter, and yet they will be surprised to hear that precisely the same contest was waged in England between the Sees of Canterbury and York. It went even farther in England than in Ireland. With us the Primate of Armagh used simply to abstain from attending Parliament or Convocation, assigning as his excuse the hostile action of the Archbishop of Dublin; but the matter was far worse in England. There we read of a national council held at Westminster March 14th, 1176, in presence of Hugh, Cardinal of St. Angelo, legate of the pope, when the controversy waxed so violent that the contending prelates with their retainers came to blows. The Archbishop of York arrived first and took the higher seat. The Archbishop of Canterbury followed with a crowd of attendants, who flung the York prelate out of the seat of honour, tore his vestments to pieces, and thus put an end to the Synod. Such were Church Synods in the Middle Ages![1]

Archbishop John Comyn obtained this bull conferring these privileges on the diocese of Dublin, and Archbishop Alan has preserved it for us in his *Register*. But Comyn was in no hurry to go and visit his diocese and avail himself of the privileges thus bestowed. He remained with the king for two years and a half at least after his consecration, leaving his diocese to the

---

[1] See *Chronicles* of Stephen, Henry II., and Richard I. (Rolls Series), t. i., pp. 203-4. For a narrative of the Irish quarrel and the many legal contests to which it gave rise see Harris' edition of Ware's *Bishops of Ireland*, pp. 71-80; cf. my *Ireland and the Celtic Church*, p. 330.

care of others. He spent the Christmas of 1182, the first Christmas after his consecration, at Caen in Normandy, where Henry II. then held his Court. The year 1183 and the first half of 1184 were spent by him in England, engaged doubtless in the business of the state, and it was only late in the autumn of 1184 that he proceeded to Dublin. But it was not spiritual work that brought him thither. He came simply to discharge purely secular business. John Comyn, Archbishop of Dublin, was very like some modern bishops. Primate Boulter, in the last century, was perhaps in modern times the best representative of this first Anglo-Norman archbishop. Boulter was noble in his generosity, profuse in giving, magnificent in his mode of life, but he had no higher idea of his spiritual office than Archbishop Comyn. Both looked on their secular and state functions as their great work, and neglected the Divine side of their mission. If you will take up Primate Boulter's letters covering a considerable portion of the first half of the last century, you will find them a very sad performance indeed. There is not one word in them which might not as well have been written by an Under-Secretary of State without any particular religious opinions. The archbishopric of Dublin, for instance, fell vacant in 1729 by the death of the celebrated, learned, and pious Dr. William King. The Primate at once writes off to London to secure the appointment of a bishop from England, as "the course most conducive to his Majesty's interest." His letters are all filled with the mere secular affairs of state and his devotion to them, utterly ignoring that higher work which rightly belonged to his office. What Boulter was in the eighteenth, that was John Comyn in the twelfth century, and even worse, for while Boulter constantly resided in Ireland, John Comyn seems to have lived there as little as he possibly could. He paid his first visit to his diocese in the autumn of 1184, and then came only for the purpose of preparing matters for the arrival of Prince John, who followed him the next year, when, by his levity, rashness, and want of common courtesy, that prince and his companions laid the foundation of much of the alienation which has since prevailed, not merely between the Celtic race and the Anglo-Normans, but also between the Anglo-Irish colonists and their brethren in England. But the Archbishop's heart and all his interest were in England and with the Court. We find him there at Christmas 1186. He spent the next two years in his diocese, and then King Henry II. seems to have invited him to the Christmas festival at Guildford, in Surrey, where he proved himself useful in dealing with the Papal Legate, Cardinal Octavian, who appeared at Court on St. Stephen's Day, and caused much trouble by his extravagant pretensions.[1] A year and a half later—in June, 1188—we find the Archbishop in Normandy, acting as ambassador between Prince Richard and his father, Henry II.; while fifteen months later still, in September, 1189, he was present assisting at the coronation[2] of the same prince when he ascended the throne as Richard I. upon the death of his father. And it was just the same as he

---

[1] Benedict of Peterborough, ii., 4, where it is specially noted that the legate went everywhere in his scarlet vestments and wearing a mitre, by papal command.

[2] Two Irish prelates, the Bishops of Ferns and of Annaghdown, assisted at this coronation. See Benedict of Peterborough (Rolls Series), ii., 79. Annaghdown is now united to Tuam. It was a small bishopric, extending over the district subject down to our own time to the Warden of Galway. Cf. Hardiman's *Hist. of Galway*, p. 68 ; Archdall's *Monasticon*, ed. Card. Moran, t. ii., p. 206.

grew older. He was present and assisting at the coronation of King John on May 27th, 1199. Eighteen months later we find him by the same monarch's side at Lincoln, in November, 1200, when King John received the homage of William of Scotland; while the next day the sovereign and archbishop alike assisted at the funeral of St. Hugh of Lincoln.[1] The first Norman Archbishop of Dublin, and, as we shall see, the second one too, were the devoted servants of Henry II., of his sons Richard and John, and of his grandson Henry III. The best portion, in fact, of the first ten years of Comyn's episcopate must have been spent in England.

How, you may ask me, in that case was the work of his diocese carried on? The reply is easy enough. He used the services of the neighbouring bishops. The Bishops of Meath, Kildare, and Glendalough were very convenient to Dublin, and they could perform all ordinary episcopal functions, while as for the diocese itself, a vicar-general or commissary, endowed with an episcopal commission, could discharge all the duties involved in the jurisdiction of his office as regards wills, charges of heresy, and matrimonial suits. Assistant-bishops, too, were sometimes used. Bishops, indeed, of the old Celtic consecrations were still plentiful in Ireland, and some of them may have been utilised.[2] But, further still, we catch glimpses, in the history of the Dublin archbishops, of coadjutor bishops, such as are now so much the fashion in England. The bishops of Glendalough were intended by one charter to have been thus utilised, though the design never seems to have

---

[1] See Walter of Coventry, *Memoriale*, t. ii., pp. 146, 171, 172; Girald. Camb., *Opp.*, t. vii., p. 114 (Rolls Series).
[2] See the sixteenth chapter of Ware's *Antiquities*, prefixed to Harris's edition of Ware's *Bishops of Ireland*.

been carried out; while in the time of Archbishop Fulk de Saundford, in the years 1266 and 1273, we find express mention of Robert, Bishop of Dublin, who must have been simply acting in the capacity of coadjutor to the Archbishop.[1]

But now a most interesting question arises,—Do we know anything of Archbishop Comyn's action when present here in Ireland? And to that question we can give a most satisfactory reply; for we know a great deal of what he did, much of which remains unto the present day. During the episcopate of John Comyn there may not have been much devotion to purely spiritual work, but he certainly attended carefully to the temporal welfare of the See.[2] He enlarged its estates, he increased its dignities, and by his personal liberality established one of our noblest cathedral churches. A notice of these various points will introduce you to the secret recesses of the Church history of the times.

Archbishop Comyn enlarged the estates and temporal

---

[1] See D'Alton's *History of the Archbishops of Dublin*, pp. 98, 103. See, however, for another view, note, p. 380.

[2] Archbishop John Comyn did not wholly neglect the spiritual affairs of his diocese. He held a synod, beginning on the 4th Sunday in Lent, 1186, where several canons were passed touching the celebration of the Sacraments and other practical questions. The decrees of this synod are printed in Ware's *Bishops*, p. 316, from the records of the Cathedral of the Holy Trinity, Dublin. Cf. Dalton's *Archbishops of Dublin*, p. 72. This synod decreed the use of stone altars in the Irish Church instead of the wooden tables previously in use. If a stone altar could not be provided, a slab of stone at least large enough to receive the sacred vessels should be inserted in the table. The altars were to be decently vested, eucharistic vessels of gold, silver, or, at least, pewter, and stone fonts, were to be purchased for every church. In fact, Archbishop Comyn's regulations show that the slovenliness still too often prevalent in Irish churches is an old national complaint.

possessions of the archbishopric. He found it a poor See, he left it a rich one; though in effecting his purpose his action was, I must confess, after a style and by means like those used by Ahab, King of Israel, when he possessed himself of the vineyard of Naboth the Jezreelite. Dublin, as I have already mentioned, had been originally part of the diocese of Glendalough. A bull of Alexander III., directed to St. Laurence, recognised the county of Dublin as far as Rathmichael as the diocese of Dublin, corresponding generally, I should say, to the territories under the rule of the Danes, together with those governed by the chieftain Mocholmoc, who seems to have owned all the districts of Dublin west and south-west of the city.[1] The diocese of Glendalough embraced the present county Wicklow, which was by grant from the same Pope confirmed to it. Glendalough, the city of St. Kevin, retained one clear trace of the old monastic organization of the Celtic Church,—it had an endowed bishopric and also an endowed abbey, but the abbacy was much richer and more valuable than the bishopric.[2] The abbey was at that time held by Thomas, nephew of St. Laurence.

---

[1] See *Chartæ, Privilegia*, etc., p. 3.
[2] For a list of the estates and possessions of the Abbey of Glendalough see the bull of Alexander III., A.D. 1179, in Dr. Reeves's *Analysis of Diocese of Dublin and Glendalough* already quoted, or in *Chartæ, Privilegia et Immunitates*, p. 3. A revised edition of this work would be a valuable help to Irish historians. The documents should be compared by an expert with the originals in the *Crede Mihi*, Alan's *Register*, etc., and annotated by a competent antiquarian. Dr. Reeves's revision of two charters in his *Analysis* shows what might be done in this direction. I suspect that the transcriber of fifty years ago made many mistakes, especially in the names of places. The Life of St. Laurence, as given in Surius and Messingham, describes the wealth of the Abbot of Glendalough as exceeding that of the bishop.

The bishopric was held by a man named Malchus, who had been Archdeacon of Dublin. The present occupants could not of course be disturbed, for vested interests have been always respected by all but the most revolutionary governments. But Archbishop Comyn determined to enrich his See by securing the reversion of those rich endowments. He therefore procured a charter from Prince John during his brief visit in 1185, uniting the See of Glendalough with that of Dublin, on account of the paucity of inhabitants in the former diocese and the poverty of the latter—a charter which was further confirmed by another issued by the same prince to the same archbishop some seven years later, in 1192, enacting that the Bishop of Glendalough should act as the Vicar and Chaplain of the Archbishopric of Dublin, and that the estates of the See should pass to Dublin.[1] But these charters affected the bishopric only, and the rich abbey remained behind. Some time, therefore, between 1190 and 1200 Archbishop Comyn procured a charter from the papal legate the Archbishop of Cashel, confirming a grant of the abbey to the Archbishops of Dublin made by Prince John.[2] The convent, indeed, struggled hard to avoid absorption into the archiepiscopal net, and appealed to the reigning pope, Innocent III., who by a bull, dated 1199, received the Abbey of St. Peter and St. Paul at Glendalough into his

---

[1] See *Chartæ*, etc., pp. 4, 7, 15, 16. On p. 15 there is an important bull of Innocent III., dated February 25th, 1215. Cardinal John Paparo is there described as legate sent to limit and shape the dioceses of Ireland—"ad informandas et limitandas Hibernienses Ecclesias." Paparo is said to have found Dublin included in the diocese of Glendalough, but to have made it a metropolitical See because it was a royal seat and the capital of Ireland.

[2] See an inspeximus of this grant by Richard II. in 1395, in *Chartæ, Privilegia et Immunitates*, p. 92.

special protection, threatening all assailants thereof with the wrath and indignation of Almighty God and of the blessed apostles SS. Peter and Paul.[1] All such threats were, however, in vain, for the Dublin prelates, regardless of papal bulls, absorbed the abbey as well as the bishopric, gaining estates which stretched over the whole county, from the sea to the very border of Kildare. The Abbot of Glendalough must have been one of the largest landholders in the whole district, and the transfer of his estates placed the Archbishop of Dublin in the same position. The archbishops were thus vested with great power, which they did not always use wisely. Archbishop Luke, the third Norman archbishop who beautified and extended Christ Church, was not equally careful of his estates. In 1230, just thirty years after the See obtained the property, he disafforested a large portion of the county Wicklow to pay the expenses of his episcopal election, which had been contested before the papal Court. None of us can now have a conception of the frightful tax upon the resources of this country implied in these frequent appeals to the papal tribunals, but we can all see a practical proof of their effects in the present state of the great central tract of Wicklow. Take the train to Bray, walk up the Long Hill and the Rocky Valley which lead to the top of the Great Sugar Loaf. Turn your gaze westwards towards Glendalough, and your eye will scarce rest on a single tree all over that central plain, including Calary Bog, Roundwood, and on to the waters of Clara Vale, Laragh and the Lugduff range. Here and there, as you drive, you will meet a plantation of modern growth. But, in general, the

---

[1] See *Chartæ, Privilegia*, etc., p. 11.

absence of trees lends a sense of desolation to what would otherwise be a splendid upland scene. And all this is due to the action of Archbishop Luke to gratify papal exactions in the year 1230.[1] The drain of wealth to satisfy absentees, whether foreigners in name or in reality, can never be anything but destructive to an agricultural country like Ireland.

Archbishop Comyn not only enriched the See of Dublin; he advanced it to the position of a great feudal dignity. The mere possession in fee of landed property, at this period, brought with it great power and dignities, the tradition of which still remains in the fancy prices rich traders and manufacturers were till lately willing to pay for landed estates. The owners of land in the twelfth century were entitled to hold Courts Leet and Courts Baron, in which all minor pleas could be tried, with a right of appeal, however, to the Courts of the Crown. But Archbishop Comyn was not content with a jurisdiction like that. He aspired to the position of a palatine lord, and to secure his purpose he was created, in April 1184, a baron, or rather, to use more technical language, was granted lands in barony near Ballymore in Kildare; while, some seven years subsequently, Prince John issued a charter conferring power upon the Archbishop of Dublin to hold courts and execute justice upon his tenants, whether in towns or in the country, totally irrespective of the local authorities; a provision which frequently brought the Dublin prelates into collision with the mayor and corporation, in which contests

---

[1] See Ware's *Bishops of Ireland*, ed. Harris, p. 320, and Sweetman's *Calendar of Documents*, t. i., p. 262, Nos. 1757, 1765, where a full account of this act of vandalism will be found.

the archbishops generally came off successful.[1] In virtue of this charter the Archbishop of Dublin became a terror to evil-doers. He had his seneschals, coroners, bailiffs, his prisons and his gallows, in abundance. It was no light matter in those times to be caught sheep-stealing, marauding, or moonlighting upon any of the extensive manors of the Archbishop. A long rope and a short shrift were the cure for such social pests. We have preserved for us a mass of documents giving us the particulars of this jurisdiction. The Archbishop held courts and exercised jurisdiction through his officers at Swords, St. Sepulchre, Ballymore, Shankhill, Castledermot, Clondalkin, Rathcoole, and Castle Kevin. At all these places he had gallows and gibbets. The episcopal gallows at Dublin was, of course, outside the city bounds. It stood somewhere near Harold's Cross, and we have on record a curious story of an unfortunate man named John Brekedent who about this time was acquitted of homicide and robbery in the King's Court. He went, however, to live at Rathcoole, upon the Archbishop's land, where he was charged with the same crime, and, notwithstanding his acquittal, was brought to Dublin, tried at St. Sepulchre, convicted, and duly hanged at Harold's Cross.[2] This brief notice will suffice to show you what a high and mighty prince the Archbishop of Dublin was in mediæval times, when Archbishop Comyn regulated all matters, from murder down to the weights and measures of bread, wine, and beer, over large portions of the present counties of Dublin, Wicklow, and Kildare.

---

[1] Cf. Sweetman's *Calendar*, t. i., p. 267, no. 1789, and *Chartæ, Privilegia et Immunitates*, p. 6.
[2] See J. T. Gilbert's *Municipal Documents* (Rolls Series), pp. 140-64.

Archbishop Comyn's See was elevated and enriched, but he could not rest, and his soul was not yet satisfied. His palace was, as I have told you, beside his cathedral of the Holy Trinity, on the site of the present Synod House. There he lived, though so powerful without the gates, yet subject to the jurisdiction of the provosts and corporation of Dublin, and overshadowed by the authority of the Constable, Justiciary, or Lord Lieutenant for the time being. He chafed under this subordination, and determined to get rid of it by erecting a residence and a great collegiate church outside the city gates and within his own immediate territory, which, fortunately for his purpose, ran close up to the city walls. This was the origin of St. Patrick's Cathedral, a subject on which I must say a few words.

St. Patrick's Cathedral was a parish church before it became a collegiate church, and it was a collegiate church before it became a cathedral church; a collegiate church, being a collegium or brotherhood of priests ruled over by a dean or warden, but having no necessary or actual connection with a bishop. St. Patrick's seems to have been an ancient church belonging to the purely Irish or Celtic population which gathered outside the walls of the Danish city of Dublin, and at a respectful distance therefrom. Such Celtic or Irish towns still exist, in name at least, in connection with many of our cities and towns. Thus we Dublin folk have our own Irishtown close to Ringsend. Irishtown was a portion of Kilkenny, and a separate and distinct borough returning two members to the Irish Parliament; Athlone to this day has a suburb called by this name, just outside the line of the ancient fortifications. St. Patrick's, St. Kevin's, St. Peter's, St.

Paul's, and St. Bride's, were the dedications of the churches which gathered round this Irish town outside the gates of St. Werburgh and St. Nicholas' Streets, and these were all Celtic favourites. Of St. Patrick, St. Bride, and St. Kevin of Glendalough we need say nothing; but sufficient proof of the popularity of SS. Peter and Paul among the Celts is offered by the fact that the great abbey or cathedral church of Glendalough was dedicated in their honour. St. Patrick's seems, however, to have had the pre-eminence over all the other suburban churches of the city. Possibly it was a larger church. Possibly it was the more difficult to get at, and required more self-denial and involved more danger in attendance, and therefore, from a Celtic point of view, brought more sanctity with it. It was originally situated on an island in the middle of a swamp or bog. It is called expressly "Ecclesia S. Patricii in Insula" by Pope Alexander III. writing to St. Laurence O'Toole. The keenest eyesight cannot now discover an island or water in this locality, but running underneath the streets is to this day a river which joins the Liffey below Grattan Bridge, and dividing at the cathedral into two streams rendered St. Patrick's an island seven hundred years ago. John Comyn considered the position, and saw that this spot offered the very advantages he desired. It was outside the city jurisdiction, it had a church, and a river always flowing and offering every convenience for mills,—a very necessary point in those times. In addition, it was a part of the estate of the See of Dublin, to which the Crown had granted large baronial rights. He, therefore, is said to have consecrated, on March 17th (St. Patrick's Day), in the year 1191, a new church in honour of St. Patrick on the site of the old church, which he threw down as doubtless too mean and poor according to his Norman notions. He made it a collegiate church, not attempting to interfere with the ancient conventual cathedral of the Holy Trinity; a church and community which seem to have behaved generously to the new foundation in transferring to it various endowments, and specially its ancient church of St. Bride's. In this collegiate church Archbishop Comyn placed thirteen prebendaries, whom he endowed out of the vast estates which had been conferred upon the See. He seems, at any rate, to have been a generous and lavish benefactor to his Dublin institution, though so often an absentee.[1] He made, too, another change. He removed the archiepiscopal residence outside the city walls, and planted it down beside the collegiate church. There he built a palace, the palace of St. Sepulchre, which still remains, though sadly fallen from its high estate, as the Archbishops of Dublin, about the beginning of this century, sold their ancient house of St. Sepulchre to the government, who turned it into a police barrack, in which condition it remains unto this day. The name of this palace has often puzzled people, and yet it is clear as daylight to any who will consider the circumstances and history of the times. The year 1887 will, I am sure, produce a crop of Jubilee designations and titles. How many Victorias, and Alberts, and Albert Edwards now figure in our family rolls, where they were totally unknown half a century ago. Every great public event, every historic crisis, every distinguished public man,

---

[1] All the original charters and bulls about the foundation of St. Patrick's Cathedral will be found printed in W. M. Mason's History of that church, App. I. Cf. the notices of the consecration of St. Patrick's in Dudley Loftus's *MS. Annals* in Marsh's Library.

leaves a mark, if nowhere else, at least in the nomenclature of the times. So was it in the twelfth century. The close of it was marked by a rage for crusades and the recovery of the Holy Sepulchre from infidel hands. In the year 1184 Heraclius, the Patriarch of Jerusalem, visited England, to induce Henry II. to undertake an expedition for its recovery. With this distinguished ecclesiastic John Comyn must often have consulted. The air of the times was thick with the Holy Sepulchre and its recovery, and therefore, when the Archbishop of Dublin wanted a name for his new home, he called it, in keeping with the spirit of the age, the Palace of the Holy Sepulchre. And now when you pass the horse-police barracks in Kevin Street, you will look upon it with more reverence, feeling that there you have a relic of the Middle Ages, the last remnant of the Crusades.[1] Archbishop Comyn went further. He not only removed himself outside the city jurisdiction, but he also set up a rival jurisdiction, and constituted the Manor of St. Sepulchre a liberty, as it was called, the Archbishop's liberty, with seneschals, coroners, courts, and bailiffs, which remained in active operation till fifty years ago, and of which you will find an elaborate statement in the Report of the Municipal Corporation Commission on the City of Dublin, in the Parliamentary Papers for 1835 and 1836. If you take up these reports and read them, you will be astonished to find

---

[1] See William of Newburgh's *Hist. Rer. Anglic.*, lib. iii., capp. x. and xxiii., in *Chron.* Stephen, etc. (Rolls Series), t. i., pp. 240, 272, about the Crusades and the visit of Heraclius. St. Sepulchre's parish in London, the Temple Church, and the Round Church of St. Sepulchre at Cambridge, all date back to the same period as St. Sepulchre's in Dublin, and witness to the same crusading movement. See *Archæologia*, t. vi., p. 172.

that within the lifetime of the present generation such traces and jurisdictions of the Middle Ages as ecclesiastical princes with prisons and magistrates of their own, still survived; Archbishop Whately, the great Whig prelate, being the last Archbishop of Dublin whose decrees consigned prisoners to an archiepiscopal prison for the common ordinary offences of everyday life. Perhaps it will be of special local interest to know that the liberty of St. Sepulchre, which was thus independent of the Lord Mayor and Corporation so lately as 1840, extended from Miltown to the south side of Stephen's Green, including Harcourt Street, Bishop Street, Bride Street, Bull Alley, Patrick Street, Harold's Cross, and a considerable portion of Rathmines township, which still doggedly maintains its ancient claims to independence as regards the jurisdiction of the city corporation.[1]

---

[1] The reference for the Municipal Corporation Commissioners' Report on St. Sepulchre's Manor and Liberty is *Parliamentary Papers*, 1836, vol. xxiv., pp. 289-98. They mention that the last exercise of the Archbishop's criminal jurisdiction was in 1803, when a case of forgery was tried before his seneschal. The prison of the liberty still exists, and is now a Female Reformatory School, rejoicing in the strange title of Rehoboth. I may throw out the suggestion that the liberty of St. Sepulchre is a remnant of ancient Celtic jurisdictions. The Municipal Commissioners report that it consisted of the ancient parishes of St. Kevin and St. Patrick. In a bull of Alexander III. to St. Laurence O'Toole, A.D. 1179, mention is made of the church of St. Kevin, "Cum suburbio et aliis pertinentiis" (see *Chartæ, Privilegia*, etc., p. 2). In a confirmation by Prince John to Archbishop Comyn (*l.c.*, p. 8), we notice the land of St. Kevin, "Quam antiquo jure possedit Ecclesia Dublinensis." In the charter founding St. Patrick's, issued by the same archbishop, we find among the endowments bestowed upon the new establishment, " Ecclesiam Sancti Kevini cum omnibus decimis et pertinentiis suis ; et omnes decimas de terra S. Kevini de dominico nostro ; cum omnibus decimis totius terræ Sancti Patricii; et de nemore ejusdem terræ quantum sufficit ad furnum Communiæ Suæ, et ad sepes illorum claudendas,

Institutions are very long-lived. They may be so antiquated as to have become mere mummies. Yet to the historian they are just as precious as the mummies of Egypt to the antiquarian. If gently opened up and carefully unrolled, their very abuses and decay may often reveal, as the manor and palace of St. Sepulchre do, the institutions, the social life, and the enthusiasms of ages long since buried in the gloom of a distant past.

---

et aream ad furnum faciendum; et communem pasturam terræ S. Kevini" (see Mason's *Hist. of St. Patrick's*, App. I.). It is evident from these extracts that there was a large extent of land, wood, and common pasture attached to the churches of St. Kevin and St. Patrick prior to the arrival of the English. Mr. Mills' paper on the Rental of the Liberty of St. Sepulchre, to which I have already referred, proves that St. Sepulchre's Manor extended over the same district in the fourteenth century, and the municipal commissioner found its extent precisely the same in the present century. The tenants on such church land were partly free, partly servile, according to Ussher's learned treatise on Corbes, Herenachs, etc., *Opp.*, ed. Elrington, t. xi., p. 421; and such the tenants of St. Sepulchre's were in the fourteenth century, according to Mr. Mills' paper and Alan's *Register*. We get even a glimpse of their origin, and that in a curious way. Since the foundation of St. Patrick's as a collegiate church in 1190, the archbishops of Dublin have always held the stall of Cualaun, or Cullen, as it is commonly called. It was formed by Archbishop Comyn, and endowed out of the demesne lands appertaining to St. Sepulchre, and then was connected with St. Kevin's Church, which was assigned to the Archbishop's vicar choral (*Repertorium Viride*, s.v. St. Kevin; and Mason's *St. Patrick's*, p. 48). It was evidently so called from the Cualanni, the primitive inhabitants of the eastern districts of Dublin and Wicklow. They had been reduced to servitude by subsequent invaders, but still formed the basis of the population, and were sufficiently numerous to impose their name even on ecclesiastical dignities. They have left their names stamped on the topography of the district from Dublin and Cullenswood far down into Wicklow. See *Ireland and the Celtic Church*, p. 52.

LECTURE X.

AN EPISCOPAL VICEROY AND THE BEGINNING OF ANGLO-NORMAN ANARCHY.

IN my last lecture I endeavoured to sketch the history of Archbishop John Comyn, who heads the list of Anglo-Norman archbishops. He was typical of all his successors. He set an example they all followed. They were English archbishops in Ireland, and every one of the pre-Reformation archbishops imitated their leader. They had no sympathy with the Celtic part of the population; nay, they thoroughly despised and disliked them; so much so that some three hundred years later, when Archbishop Fitz-Simons and Dean Alleyne were combining in 1497 to found an hospital near St. Patrick's Cathedral, they ordered that those only should be admissible who were proved Catholics, of honest conversation, of English nation, chiefly from the families of Allen, Barrett, Begg, Hill, Dillon, and Rogers, settlers in the dioceses of Dublin and Meath, above all, that no Irishman should ever be admitted; and this was fifty years before the Reformation.[1]

These early Anglo-Norman archbishops were all great courtiers, too, as my narrative has shown, very fond of hanging about the English Court, and figuring at Court ceremonials; while to crown the picture

---

[1] Mason's *History of St. Patrick's*, p. 142; cf. p. 144 and App. xiii.

Archbishop Comyn set an example which for hundreds of years was diligently followed by his successors. He seems to have imported numerous relations of his own, to whom he made leases of the property and lands of the See, granting a portion of the ancient palace grounds near Christ Church to one Gilbert Comyn, which the next archbishop handed over to the Chapter for the erection of a porter's lodge; while again about the middle of the thirteenth century we find notices of lawsuits between the Comyns and the Prior of the Holy Trinity touching lands held under that Corporation.[1]

Archbishop Comyn ruled the diocese of Dublin during part of the reign of Henry II., the whole of one son's reign (Richard I.), and during the greater part of King John's reign. That period was eventful for both Church and State in Ireland as in England. It was marked all through by ecclesiastical disputes. These Plantagenet sovereigns were perpetually at war with the Pope and his representatives. Becket's struggle with Henry II. was typical of many a similar struggle between the Crown and the Church, which went on throughout the sixty years covered by the reigns of Henry and his sons. Half of King John's

---

[1] Archbishop John Comyn introduced to Ireland his nephew Geoffrey de Marisco, endowing him, about 1200 A.D., out of the lands of the See. See Sweetman's *Calendar of Documents*, t. i., p. 42, No. 276. This Geoffrey became a great man in Ireland. He was Justiciary in February 1215 (*l.c.*, p. 84, No. 537), and continued for the following thirty years to play an important part in English and Irish political life, as this *Calendar* and the works of Matthew Paris abundantly prove. About the family of Comyn and their lawsuits see Dalton's *History of the Archbishops of Dublin*, p. 89, and the *Registrum Malmesburiense* (Rolls Series), t. i., pp. 250-57, where we have a notice of a trial between the Comyns and the Prior of Christ Church Cathedral.

reign was spent with the nation labouring under an interdict. From 1208 to 1214 the See of Exeter, for instance, was vacant because of this interdict. A conscientious priest or bishop had then a difficult time. On the one hand was the Pope forbidding the exercise of all his functions; on the other was the King threatening to hang, imprison, or exile those who refused to officiate as usual. Between the upper millstone of the Crown and the lower millstone of the Pope verily the clergy were in a bad case.[1] We are very apt indeed to allow our sympathies and feelings to run away with us in studying these ecclesiastical disputes, and to imagine that all the right and justice were with the Crown, and all the wrong and usurpation on the side of the Pope. Like many disputes, there was a certain amount of right and justice on each side; while each party was to a certain extent in the wrong. The true way to view these disputes is as follows. The Church then offered all through Europe the only channel by which the lower and the middle classes could rise to an equality with the nobility. Once the villein's son was clothed with even minor orders and had become a sub-deacon, the sacred mantle of clerical privileges surrounded him, and he was freed at once from the degrading and cruel laws to which his unclerkly kinsmen were subjected. The Church naturally strove, therefore, to extend its liberties, and the people sided with the Church. The Crown as naturally strove to restrict and narrow them, desiring complete supremacy

---

[1] See Prynne's *Records*, ii., 286. A priest once refused to perform divine service during an interdict. King John clad him in a complete suit of sacerdotal vestments made of lead, flung him into a dungeon, and left him there till hunger and thirst put an end to his existence. Many a man gained a reputation for martyrdom on slighter grounds.

over all persons and interests within its realm. Had the Crown completely succeeded, England might now be languishing under a despotism like that of Russia. Had the Pope completely succeeded, England might have been reduced to the condition of Naples, Spain, or the Papal States in days gone by. Happily for us, the struggles ended in a compromise which secured the due development of a manly, a temperate, and an orderly freedom.[1]

The ecclesiastical struggle, especially in the reign of King John, was marked in addition by civil struggles, fierce and bloody. In fact, the reigns of both kings, Richard I. and John, were years of civil war throughout England. Richard I. never attended to England at all. His whole heart was in war, specially in that against the Saracens. Richard I. was like William III.; neither cared one atom about England save for the money he could get out of it. A monkish chronicler tells us how King Richard sold everything to raise money for these wars. He even said that "it was a pity he could not get a buyer for London, else he would sell it."[2] The picture presented in the chronicles of England during this period of thirty years from 1190 to 1220 is something frightful.

Here I may refer to what perhaps for some will be a more accessible and pleasant source of information than the annals of monasteries, as this subject has been most accurately handled by Sir Walter Scott in his great novel of *Ivanhoe*, a work which, alas! seems now heavy reading to a generation fed upon the highly-spiced novels current at railway stations,

---

[1] See the preface to *Roger de Hoveden* (Rolls Series), t. i., pp. lxix-lxxi, ed. Stubbs.
[2] *Chronic.* Stephen, Richard I., etc., t. i., p. 306.

or the absurd fairy tales of a *She* and *Solomon's Mines*. Sir Walter Scott never displayed greater genius than when he discerned, as if by intuition,—for he had but few of the helps we now possess,—the state of England at the close of the twelfth century. Richard's reign, as depicted by the great novelist, was bad enough, but John's reign was much worse in point of civil dissensions. England was in a state of disorganization, and when that was the case we might anticipate beforehand that the government of Ireland would be completely neglected. And then, when we come to survey the facts of the case, we shall find our anticipations fully confirmed. The dissensions of England were merely temporary, and were crushed out in the long run by the royal authority. The dissensions were intensified in Ireland, and became chronic, for there the great English nobles found themselves unchecked by any superior power, and every man did whatsoever was right in his own eyes. Ireland thus lost the training and preparation for future national development which England gained from the Norman Conquest. Let me expand this point a little, for if ever you are to thread your way through the devious paths of Irish history, and to gain any solid useful lessons therefrom, you must have some general principles to afford you guidance.

For a century and a half after the Norman Conquest of 1066, the struggle between the Crown, the barons, and the people was unending. If you want to see a masterly *résumé* of that struggle and its effects, I would refer you to a document buried in the depths of the Rolls Series—Bishop Stubbs's preface to the second volume of the *Chronicle* of Benedict of Peterborough. In that preface that learned and philosophical historian shows how in God's providence the English constitution was developed. First, there was the foundation of Anglo-Saxon institutions, whose tendency was to self-reliance and individualism. Self-reliance is, however, very good only in moderation. When pushed to an extreme it becomes fatal to corporate cohesion and growth. Then came the feudal system to redress the balance. Listen to Dr. Stubbs' words, which express the matter much better than I can:—"The tendency of all the Anglo-Saxon institutions was to produce a spirit of self-dependence; that was the strength of the system. Its weakness was the want of cohesion, which is a necessary condition of particles incapable of self-restraint in the absence of any external force to compress them. For such a condition the feudal system was undoubtedly the fitting cure. There is much truth, though only half the truth, in Mr. Carlyle's observation that the pot-bellied equanimity of the Anglo-Saxons needed the drilling and discipline of a century of Norman tyranny. The guiding powers by which the machinery of feudalism forced into a common mass all the different interests, desires, and habits of the disunited race was, however, only one part of its operation. The feudal system was very far from being altogether bad. The essence of the system was mutual fidelity, and its proper consequence the creation of a corporate unity, and the recognition of it by every member, from the king to the villein. The bond was not a voluntary one, to be taken up and put aside at pleasure; the principle of cohesion was uniform throughout the mass. Self-reliance was proved not to be incompatible with order, mutual faith, and regard to law; and these are indispensable for national strength and national spirit." This extract sets forth the reasons why the feudal system succeeded in England and why it failed in Ireland. In England the feudal discipline lasted for a century, from the Conqueror to Henry II. The hour and the man then came. Henry II. fused all the opposing elements into one homogeneous mass. In Ireland the same feudal system was introduced, but there was no presiding genius in the shape of a monarch or a vigorous and permanent viceroy to seize the favourable moment and fuse the contending forces when the temporary discipline had done its work. The great nobles had it all their own way. The De Courcys, the De Burghs, the Geraldines, the Butlers, the De Lacys, quarrelled, fought, oppressed the people, defied the viceroys, despised the Crown, and never were crushed, as the iron hand of Henry crushed the Anglo-Norman feudatories in England. To the neglect of the Crown, to the weakness of the viceroys, to the selfish, foolish internecine struggles of the great feudatories of Ireland, its slow development and its subsequent sad history must historically be traced.

The quarrels of the Anglo-Norman nobles were, I repeat, the original cause of English failure in Ireland. You see I differ from Mr. Froude. He imputes all Irish troubles to the unfortunate Celts; I attribute them rather to the great Anglo-Norman nobles. But here someone may come forward, whose ideas are all modern, and who has not had sufficient historical training to recognise the fact that the twelfth was very different in every respect from the nineteenth century, and raise an objection. How could this have been? Surely if two great peers nowadays love to quarrel, raise forces, go to war with one another, besiege castles, and defy the Sovereign, the police and other forces of the Crown would make short work of them. They completely forget, however, the different circumstances of the age concerning which we are treating as compared with those of the times wherein we live. The great nobles of Ireland were simply feudatories claiming to exercise towards the Sovereign the same rights, and paying to him merely the same homage, as their Sovereign paid to the King of France for his continental dominions. The Anglo-Norman nobles of Ireland, such as De Lacy in Meath and De Courcy in Ulster, claimed to be independent princes, with right to levy war and make peace upon and with one another and with the Crown, not only in virtue of their grants from the Crown, but also in consequence of their succession to the ancient Celtic chiefs. And the Crown grants seem to sanction this view. Thus De Lacy was granted Meath, with all the rights and powers that the Melaghlins possessed previous to the Conquest; and these powers the De Lacys showed themselves noways backward in exercising. Let me give you a brief account of two or three of these struggles, as specimens of all the rest.

The De Lacys, as I have told you, were granted Meath as a Palatine kingdom, by Henry II. There they erected Trim Castle as the seat of their government. That castle is to this day as fine a specimen of Anglo-Norman architecture as exists anywhere within these islands, and ought to be repaired and maintained by the Board of Public Works as a national monument. And for this simple but most interesting reason, that it is a Crown or Royal castle. It was erected by the De Lacys, and was maintained by them as their seat of dominion till the Palatinate or Kingdom of Meath merged in the Crown by marriage, about the year

1470,[1] since which period the lordship of Meath has been part of the Crown possessions in Ireland, and in virtue of such lordship an annual quit-rent of some two or three pounds was paid by the Crown to the bishops of Meath until disestablishment. I have said this much about the Castle of Trim to stir you up to pay a visit thereto, and to enable you to realize, when standing there, how very real and modern was the lordship or kingdom of Meath and its authority. The De Lacys gained this lordship by virtue of a charter from Henry II. The first lord of Meath was Hugh de Lacy, concerning whom I have already spoken somewhat at large as the first lord lieutenant of Ireland. Hugh de Lacy left two sons, Walter and Hugh de Lacy, who became successively lords of Meath. But now turn your attention for a moment to another part of the county. The kingdom of Ulster was the one part of Ireland which obstinately refused to submit to Henry II. The Ulster men have ever been a stubborn generation. They were stubborn in their opposition to the Roman method of calculating Easter in the seventh and eighth centuries.[2] They were stubborn in their opposition to James II. They were stubborn as leaders of the Volunteer movement of 1782, and for a time as supporters of the rebellion of 1798; and they were stubborn in their opposition to the Anglo-Norman invasion of 1172. Henry II. could not himself attend to the conquest of Ulster. He adopted, therefore, the usual Norman policy as practised towards Wales. He made a grant of the earldom of Ulster to one of his courtiers, John de Courcy, and authorised him to hold

---

[1] See *Irish Statutes*, vol. i., p. 51; *Irish Arch. Miscell.*, vol. i., p. 30.
[2] See *Ireland and the Celtic Church*, p. 161.

as a palatine fief any lands he could conquer in Ulster. He acted on land as some civilised nations do still, and as our own did most effectively upon sea in the last great French war. He issued letters of marque authorising him to rob, plunder, and steal whatever he could, and to hold as of right whatever he could steal.[1] John de Courcy was just the man for this task. Giraldus Cambrensis describes his appearance and character in a few vigorous strokes. In person he was of fair complexion, tall, with very muscular limbs, of large size, very strongly made, of singular daring, and a bold and brave soldier from his youth. He had in the eyes of the Welsh archdeacon one virtue,—he was very reverential towards the clergy, and paid them their dues regularly; though in other respects he confesses that he was extremely parsimonious and inconstant.

The history of the De Courcys is intimately bound up with that of a family still amongst us. The Earl of Howth represents in the direct line one of the original Anglo-Norman invaders. John de Courcy was brother-in-law to Sir Almeric de St. Laurence, the founder of the Howth family, and first Anglo-Norman owner of that beautiful headland.

If you want to read Irish history of this period turned into romance, you should resort to Hanmer's *Chronicle*, where the adventures of De Courcy and of Sir Almeric, his brother-in-law, are told with all the minuteness of detail which special correspondents now bestow upon their descriptions of warlike operations.

---

[1] When Henry III. could not conquer his own brother-in-law, Llewellyn, Prince of North Wales, he wrote to Ireland inviting adventurers to enter Wales and possess themselves of any lands they were strong enough to hold. See Rymer's *Fœdera*, t. i., p. 200.

The orations which these commanders addressed to their troops on their expeditions into Ulster, the letters despatched to one another, the very speeches which Sir Almeric made in a battle when he and all his troops were annihilated, are set forth—though how the reporters got them the historian does not tell; for though reporters in our own day have sometimes posts of danger, and meet with some hard knocks, they never assuredly in modern times have been in such danger as they would have been in a battle between wild Irish kernes and Anglo-Norman soldiers. This much, however, we do know: John de Courcy with St. Laurence's help invaded and conquered Louth, passed thence by Newry into the county Down, and seized the sea coast towns of Carlingford and Ardglass,—where the castles he erected are still to be seen,—and thence advanced to Downpatrick, which he captured after a fierce battle. The north of Ireland as far as Carrickfergus and the county Antrim became thenceforth a regular Norman settlement, though beyond the limits of Down and Antrim the authority of the conquerors did not extend. The Earl of Ulster now set up great state. He made a royal alliance and married Affreca, a daughter of the King of Man.[1] He surrounded himself with a staff of officials, his constable, seneschal, chamberlain, chancellor. He coined money, and otherwise exercised all kingly rights. Now here in the De Lacys of Meath and the De Courcys of Ulster we have the elements of disunion ready to hand, and accordingly we find that during all the earlier years of John's reign, from the year 1200 onwards, Ireland was distracted by the fierce wars which raged between these two factions, till at last

---

[1] See *Chronicle of Man* in Camden's *Britannia*, p. 1053, ed. 1695.

De Courcy was seized by treachery at Downpatrick, carried captive to England, and lodged in the dungeons of the Tower of London.[1]

But dissensions were not confined to Ulster. They extended to the west and south, to Connaught and to Munster as well. William De Burgh was another of the lords lieutenant sent by Henry II. He was the founder of the peerage of Clanricarde, and the root whence sprang the numerous families rejoicing in the various names of De Burgh, Burke, and Bourke. William Fitz-Aldelm de Burgh—to give him the full name known to ancient historians—was distantly related to the royal family. He held the post of dapifer or steward of the household when appointed constable or chief justiciary of Ireland. While occupying that office he founded an institution, traces of which still remain with us. In describing Archbishop Comyn I told you about St. Sepulchre's Liberty, which endured till the year 1840. But the term "liberties" is still in common use, as applied to a large district of this city. And it is most exact, and embodies, as often current popular phrases do embody, a great historical fact. We still speak of the Liberties, and there were two liberties in the west of Dublin, the one adjoining the other. The archbishop's liberty was called St. Sepulchre's, or the Liberty of the Holy Sepulchre, and it was bounded on the north and west by the Liberty of St. Thomas's Abbey, alias Thomas-Court or the Liberty of Donore. That liberty also continued in active existence till 1840.

---

[1] See Gilbert's *History of the Viceroys of Ireland*, p. 60 and chap. xii. below, were I treat of the wars of Meath and Kildare.

The Abbot of Thomas-Court exercised jurisdiction there till the Reformation, and since the Reformation that jurisdiction continued in the family of the Earl of Meath, to whom it was granted upon the dissolution of the monasteries. St. Thomas's Abbey was one of the most magnificent monasteries round Dublin. Its Chartulary lies unprinted in the Bodleian Library, though it contains most valuable documents—unique of their kind—for early Anglo-Norman history; yet the English Treasury will not give money for printing a mere Irish document.[1] And yet the Abbey of St. Thomas had nothing to say to the mere Irish natives. It was a purely English or Norman institution. It was founded in honour of Thomas à Becket, after whom it was called in the year 1177, when Cardinal Vivian visited Ireland to confirm the English conquest by Papal authority. It was endowed with abundant privileges from time to time, till at last the lord abbot claimed exactly the same rights over the Liberty of Donore as the archbishop exercised in St. Sepulchre's.[2] But William De Burgh did something more than found St. Thomas's Abbey. Giraldus Cambrensis was very hostile to him, and painted his character in very dark colours, describing him as treacherous, crafty, hypocritical. "A braggart against the defenceless, a flatterer of the rebellious, he submitted to the powerful, he lorded over the humble, and, above all things else, was exceedingly covetous of gold," a metal in which, he adds, this country of

---

[1] Mr. Hardiman printed from it the famous *Statute of Kilkenny*, published in the Irish Archæological Series.
[2] The foundation charter of St. Thomas's Abbey can be seen in Leland's *History of Ireland*, t. i., p. 127; or in *Chartæ, Privilegia et Immunitates*, p. 2.

Ireland exceedingly abounds. William De Burgh was a failure as a Chief Governor of Ireland, but he had the art of ingratiating himself with princes, and as the result received large grants in the west of Ireland, including the city of Limerick, half of Connaught, excluding the royal fortress of Athlone and the five cantreds or baronies adjoining to that town.[1] As soon as De Burgh found himself in possession of these vast grants, the origin of the immense Clanricarde estates, of which we now hear so much, he assumed the rights and attitude of practical independence, and commenced a series of quarrels with his neighbours and with the viceroys, which involved the west in the same confusion as reigned in the north, through the jealousies of the De Courcys and the De Lacys.

Let us now hark back a little. Roderick O'Conor was King of Connaught and nominal King of all Ireland, when Henry II. and Strongbow conquered it. He reigned for twenty-eight years, and then his sons—following the example set them by the English princes, the sons of King Henry II.—rebelled against their father and improved upon their English models; for while King Henry conquered his rebellious sons, King Roderick's sons conquered their father, and in the year 1183 immured him as a monk in Cong Abbey, that beautiful building in which Lord Ardilaun has shown what taste and money, when combined, can effect in making a ruin beautiful without injuring its venerable and antiquated aspect. Cathal O'Conor, or O'Conor of the Red Hand—a very fitting name indeed for his whole race and generation at that time—

---

[1] See Reeves on the *Townland Distribution of Ireland* for an explanation of the term "cantred."

ascended his father's throne, and was duly acknowledged by the English Government, which claimed and received his homage. De Burgh now set an intrigue on foot against Cathal O'Conor, stirred up his brothers against him, lent them his active assistance, and expelled Cathal from his dominions. Cathal made treaties with the De Lacys and the De Courcys, invoking withal the help of the Viceroy, which was granted, and there in the early days of King John's reign we see the Viceroy and one party of the O'Conors fighting against De Burgh and another party of the O'Conors.[1] Could any colony have succeeded under such conditions? Could any country have been organized and civilized, when the parties who should have been the organizers were engaged in nothing else, save in showing an example of lawlessness, rapine, and murder, to chieftains only too ready to imitate their unhappy models? I have often remarked that it was not the feudal system that ruined Ireland. Have I not proved my case? Have I not fully proved that the failure of the feudal system in Ireland, and of the English government therein, arose, not from the system itself, but arose from the persons entrusted with the management and development of the system, which never once got the fair chance which was given to it in England? But now, you may say, what was the English Sovereign doing while Ireland was falling into this state of anarchy? The answer is easy enough. King Richard's reign saw the beginning of anarchy, simply because he never bestowed a thought on Ireland. His whole soul

---

[1] The origin and progress of this war, wherein the Viceroy, the De Burghs, and the two sections of the O'Conors took part, is fully depicted, from the Celtic side, in the *Annals of Lough Cé*, t. i., pp. 211, 223, 231, 239 (Rolls Series).

was in war either in Palestine or on the Continent, and we know that, even still, a great war abroad always diverts English attention from Irish troubles; while King John—even if he had not been such an utterly worthless fellow—was so fully occupied in his own quarrels with the Pope, and his bishops, and his English barons, that he had scarcely any time to think of the affairs of this country. Occasionally, indeed, he did bestow his attention upon Ireland. He sent in 1199, the first year of his reign, a vigorous Governor here, in the person of his illegitimate cousin, Meyler Fitz-Henry, who curbed and even conquered De Burgh. In the year 1210 he paid a visit in person to Ireland, and marched through the whole country, personally inspecting the fortresses from Carrickfergus in the north, all round by Hollywood, Carlingford, Trim, Dublin, to Waterford in the south; committing, on his departure, the government of Ireland to the strongest and most prudent viceroy she ever had in those early times, John de Gray, Bishop of Norwich, who ruled here for three or four years, from 1210 to 1213.[1] That man's handiwork is still to be seen amongst us. All previous viceroys had been mere soldiers. John de Gray was something more.

---

[1] King John is sometimes said to have introduced English laws into Ireland on the occasion of this visit. I have already shown that the English common law had been introduced long before by his father, Henry II. Still there is some historical foundation for this tradition, as will be seen by the following quotation from Sweetman's *Calendar*, t. i., p. 220, No. 1,458, wherein King Henry III., King John's son, thus expresses himself, in a writ, dated December 10th, 1226:—
"The King to the barons, knights, and free tenants of Leinster. When King John went to Ireland, he took with him men expert in the law, by whose counsel, at the instance of the Irish, he ordained that English laws should be in force in Ireland; and left these laws reduced to writing, under his seal, at the Exchequer, Dublin."

He was possessed of that knowledge of mankind which large literary training, combined with a practical knowledge of affairs, alone confers. He knew that the sword, and the gallows, and prison-houses alone, are measures of destruction, but not of civilization and prosperity. He believed in prevention rather than cure, and he, accordingly, erected strong fortresses in the most exposed spots, to prevent the incursions of the wild Connaughtmen upon the peaceful plains of Meath and central Ireland. He laid the foundations of Dublin Castle, he coined money and encouraged trade, and he built three great fortresses, two now in ruins, the third still in use, upon the most exposed spots of the English frontier. These castles were the fortresses of Clonmacnois, ten miles below Athlone; Randon or St. John's, ten miles above Athlone; and the Castle of Athlone itself. Let me say a few words about these castles, because they are genuine relics of this great episcopal viceroy. They have often vindicated his wisdom and his foresight by withstanding many a siege, and yet, owing to the narrow policy of our railway companies, they are utterly unknown to the crowds of our own city of Dublin, who yearly view with astonishment the ruins of Conway and Carnarvon Castles. Take Randon Castle, or St. John's as it is usually called. I saw a picture of it some two years ago in the ladies' newspaper, *The Queen*, yet how few Irishmen know one atom about it. It is situated on the broad island-studded waters of Lough Ree. If an English railway company had a lake twenty miles long and five miles broad, within two hours' ride of Dublin, what excursions they would organise thither all through the summer months, what commodious steamers they would have plying thereon. Yet we have two great companies running trains three parts empty to Athlone, and yet there is never an effort made by them to reveal the beauties of Lough Ree, and the many archæological and historical remains that cover its shores and islands. There you have Inis-Cleraun, or Quaker Island in modern phraseology, the seat of all the wondrous tales told of Queen Maebh, or Queen Mab of fairy renown, and of her tragical death. There you have, on the same island, a specimen of the real ancient Irish monasteries, with its cashel and its tiny square churches, founded by St. Dermot of Inis-Cleraun a thousand years ago. Time would indeed fail me to tell of all that is to be seen round Lough Ree in the way of ancient ecclesiastical ruins, because in the centuries which followed the introduction of Christianity Lough Ree was a favourite resort for the Irish hermits, who sought a solitary residence, like their Egyptian brethren, for the purposes of study and devotion. I can only mention a few of them, leaving you to go and explore them for yourselves, hampered though you may be by the stupid, ignorant neglect of our railway companies, who are, in very deed, their own worst enemies, so far as earning dividends is concerned. If you wish, then, to see the relics of Celtic Ireland round Lough Ree, spend two or three days there in a boat or yacht, camping on the uninhabited islands, wondrously redolent with wild flowers. Visit Nun's Island, Cashel Hill, Inis-bofin, Inchmore, All Saints' Island, and Inis-ainghin or Hare Island. Upon all of these you will find early Celtic churches. In some of them you will find beautiful windows, rare early crosses, wagon-roofed buildings, retaining even still the marks of the wattle centreings upon which they were raised, and Celtic inscriptions recalling the earliest days of Irish Christianity; and then you will feel that there is, even yet, unexplored and unknown ground, where holidays may be profitably spent, within our own island. As practical hints, I may add that a tent should be taken from Dublin, boats can be hired at Athlone, and that July, August, and early September are the best months for the exploration of the Shannon.

The Middle Ages, too, have left their mark upon Lough Ree. Randon is a point running far out into the lake about half way between Athlone and Lanesborough. It is admirably situated for offensive and defensive purposes, and as such was from the earliest ages used by the O'Conors, princes of Connaught, as the site of a strong dun, or fort, whence they could with safety issue forth at any moment to ravage the rich lands of Meath, which lay temptingly opposite to them. Many a hard battle between the men of Meath and the men of Connaught has Lough Ree seen. Many a weapon, spear, shield, sword, and many a coracle, the evidences and remains of these battles, lie now buried safe and silent in its translucent depths.[1]

The Bishop of Norwich, John de Gray, came to the West, surveying with a masterly eye the state of affairs. He saw the advantages of this ancient dun on the Rinn, or point, and he ordered at once the erection of a large castle on the lake edge.[2] He also built an elegant

---

[1] See, for instance, the story of a battle fought there in A.D. 1201, in *Annals of Lough Cé*, t. i., pp. 221-23.

[2] The name Randon or Randown, by which this fortress is known to the English chroniclers, is a corruption of the Celtic name Rinnduin, *i.e.*, the Rinn, or point, of the Dun, given to it in all the Irish authorities. See O'Donovan's edition of the *Annals of the Four Masters*, note on A.D. 1199, and his *Roscommon Letters* in the Royal Irish Academy, where he

Norman church a couple of hundred yards from the castle, and constructed a series of fortifications where the point joins the mainland, constituting the whole peninsula one vast fortress. He then handed it over to the great religious order of the Knights Hospitallers, who made it into a preceptory, where these priestly knights watched and prayed, and at the same time exercised stern control over the wild neighbouring tribes of the O'Kellys and the O'Conors. This fortress of Randon, or St. John's, continued to be one of the great English fortresses till the year 1600 or thereabouts, when it was handed over with some grants of land to a private family called Povey.[1]

---

gives all the traditions concerning Randown as he found them more than half a century ago, before the knowledge of the Irish tongue had vanished from the district as it has now. A couple of years ago I was wandering on the shore near Randon and Inis-Cleraun. I asked an old woman did she know the Irish name of the latter island. She replied in the negative, telling me she had no knowledge of Irish, though her father spoke it. Cf. also an interesting article by Dr. Petrie in the *Dublin Penny Journal* of 1840, No. 10, pp. 73-5.

[1] See *Patents of James I.*, p. 557, A.D. 1619. The ruins of Randon, or St. John, as it is popularly now called, are well worth investigation, as showing more completely than any others in Ireland the plan of a preceptory of the Hospitallers. O'Donovan has very fully described them in his letters, to which I have already referred. There is first a formidable wall a quarter of a mile long and twelve feet high, furnished with towers at short intervals and with a fine fortified gateway. This cuts off the peninsula from the mainland. Next comes the church, then the central fortress and keep encircled by a moat, while farther out, in the centre of a dense thicket, stands a curious lofty building, which may have formed a watch-tower whence a perpetual outlook was maintained. The fortified wall was probably built in the year 1251, when we find an order issued by Henry III. to enclose the vills of Athlone and Rendun, and repair their castles. See Sweetman's *Calendar*, t. i., p. 469, No. 3159. The name Randon is otherwise written by the Anglo-Norman scribes Randown,

But all through the intervening four centuries it was a great stronghold. In the Irish documents preserved in the Tower of London frequent mention is made of Randon, of money for its repairs, provisions for the garrison, and above all we find entries of numerous hogsheads of wine forwarded for their consumption, proving that in those halls, which now lie ruinous, with a peasant's cabin built beside and out of them, and pigs and cattle, cocks and hens running riot where wardens watched and knights ruled, the luxuries of life were not neglected, and the wines of Burgundy and of Gascony were matters of daily use.

The Bishop of Norwich erected two other castles, effectually cutting off the Connaught men from Meath, and compelling order far away amid the tribes of the distant West. Athlone Castle is still in daily use. After sustaining numberless sieges it has been modernized, and now Armstrong guns of the newest type frown from its walls; yet still we find in that castle abundant remains of our episcopal viceroy's work. The central keep and the eastern curtain,—where the ancient water-gate can still be traced,—and the whole main structure are due to him. While if we proceed ten miles lower down the Shannon you can still see the

---

Reindon, Reddon, Randoon, and Rawdon. See *l.c.*, Index. Near Randon, on the shores of the lake, there stand the extensive ruins of Kilmore, the mansion house of Sir James Shaen, showing what the residences of the ancient Celtic gentry of the seventeenth century were like. It was inhabited till the year 1731, as I find in Pue's *Occurrences* of that year an advertisement of the lands and mansion of Kilmore. There were twelve acres of gardens and orchards, stabling for forty horses, with large malthouse, brewhouse, pigeon-house, and barns. They are now in ruins. The Shaens were a leading Celtic family of Longford. The first Sir Arthur Shaen was made a knight by Queen Elizabeth.

ruins of the ancient Castle of Clonmacnois, which was built by him at the very same time.[1] That castle is a wonderful specimen of the strength, the massive and solid character of these mediæval buildings. Many of us have seen and wondered at the strength of the Castle of Heidelberg, where massive towers remain intact as French powder displaced but could not destroy them more than two centuries ago. You can see the same phenomenon at Clonmacnois. The Republican soldiers of Cromwell tried to blow up that castle and failed, as the French failed at Heidelberg. They merely split the massive structure, fractured the towers and drove them out of the perpendicular, in which position they stand to this day, after two centuries and a half of Western storm and rain; a testimony that the jerry-builder did not exist among the Anglo-Normans, or that if he did he did not attempt to palm off his work upon John de Gray, Bishop of Norwich and Justiciary of Ireland. It was a curious fact about both these castles of Athlone and Clonmacnois that they were built on ecclesiastical ground. In the Athlone case they were built upon the lands of the Benedictine Abbey of St. Peter; in the Clonmacnois case they were built upon the bishop's land; and in both cases the Crown and viceroy took scrupulous care to recompense the ecclesiastical potentates whose territories were invaded for the purposes of State. The Prior of Athlone was assigned four cantreds of land in the county Westmeath in exchange for the lands taken for the purposes of fortification; while in the case of the Bishop of Clonmacnois we have a writ still existing from the

---

[1] The precise date of its erection is fixed by the *Annals of Lough Cé*, ed. Hennessy, t. i., p. 251 (Rolls Series), at the year 1214.

King to his officials in Ireland, dated May 30th, 1216, ordering them to compensate the Bishop for his lands occupied in fortifying the Castle of Clonmacnois, for his fruit trees cut down, his cows, horses, oxen, and household utensils taken away; so careful was the State at that time in dealing with ecclesiastical property.[1]

John de Gray's rule in Ireland lasted less than four complete years, and left its mark on the secular far more than on the ecclesiastical side of our history.[2] He was a bishop, indeed, but he was a bishop such as that age and the Anglo-Norman system produced, and for ages continued to produce. He was far more of a statesman than of a divine or pastor of souls. In fact, years before this the Pope refused to make him Primate of England because his character was so extremely secular. The impartial historian must indeed acknowledge that the Pope had on his side as against the King all the really spiritual and religious minds of his time. The King wished to use bishoprics and Church livings as rewards for statesmen and for lawyers. The Church and the Pope claimed them as the provision for spiritual work and pastoral devotion. John de Gray took the King's side. He was an able ruler. He was a born statesman. He stood by the King all through his struggle with the Pope, braving all the terrors of the interdict and of excommunication; and though he may not have been a typical pastor of souls, he bestowed upon Ireland what she seldom enjoyed in those years

---

[1] See Sweetman's *Calendar*, t. i., p. 106, No. 693; p. 107, No. 694.

[2] John de Gray was Justiciary from 1210 (see Matthew Paris' *Historia Anglorum*, t. ii., p. 122, Rolls Series) to July 1213 (see Sweetman's *l.c.*, p. 75, No. 466), when he was succeeded by Archbishop Henry de Londres, who combined the two offices of Archbishop and Justiciary.

of John's troubled reign, a period of resolute and vigorous government, when the wild but proud feudal baron was duly restrained by the conjoint forces of civil and ecclesiastical authority, and peace and tranquillity shed a transient ray upon a land too seldom visited by their kindly and healing beams.

LECTURE XI.

ARCHBISHOP HENRY OF LONDON AND ST. PATRICK'S CATHEDRAL.

I HAVE in this lecture to introduce to your notice a typical Anglo-Norman archbishop, whose life sheds light on many a puzzling problem of the Middle Ages. John Comyn was the first Anglo-Norman Archbishop of Dublin. He was in deacon's orders merely when promoted to the Archbishopric of Dublin. He ruled this diocese for thirty years, and then ceased from his labours. He died October 25th, 1212, and the vacancy was soon filled, because we know from original State documents still in existence (*Rot. Litt. Pat.*, p. 97), that on March 5th of the year 1213, Henry of London, or, as he was then called, Henri de Londres, had been elected and confirmed in the archbishopric, but was not as yet consecrated.[1] His predecessor had been a deacon when elected to the archbishopric, Henri de Londres was an archdeacon when promoted to the same high office. But in all probability he was only in

---

[1] Episcopal and abbatial elections were then usually conducted at the King's Court, and under royal direction, by deputations from the chapters, who merely registered the royal will. Luke, Archbishop Henry's successor, was elected by two members of St. Patrick's Chapter present in London (Sweetman's *Calendar*, t. i., No. 1652), so complete was royal supremacy in the Middle Ages. See Bishop Stubbs's perface to *Roger de Hoveden*, t. i., pp. xix, xx (Rolls Series).

deacon's orders, as men with powerful interest were often appointed to the post of archdeacon when mere boys, and then went to the University of Paris to study canon and civil law, and thus qualify for the office held by them. This abuse lasted in Ireland till after the Reformation. In Elrington's *Life of Ussher*, p. 114, we find an account of Sir Adam Loftus, Lord Chancellor of Ireland, and the first Viscount Loftus of Ely. He obtained possession of the archdeaconry of Glendalough in 1594, though a layman. He never took holy orders, and yet, notwithstanding the opposition of Primate Laud, Lord Strafford, and the Archbishop of Dublin, he held that ecclesiastical office till his death in 1643. So persistent were mediæval abuses![1] I propose now to divide, for convenience' sake, this lecture into three portions. I shall first discuss the history of Henri de Londres prior to his consecration, because his story is typical of his times, and explains much of the religious failure of the Middle Ages. Then I shall treat of his career as an archbishop from an ecclesiastical point of view, and lastly describe him in his secular character as chief governor and ruler of Ireland at a very eventful period.

First then as to his career prior to his elevation to the episcopate. Henri de Londres was in his earlier days simply a statesman, a lawyer, and politician,—very like, indeed, to many of our own ablest bishops even within living memory. He was thoroughly secular. We can trace his career step by step for at least thirteen years prior to his elevation by the aid of the documents the English Treasury and English Record

---

[1] Cf. Brewer's Introduction to the first volume of the Works of Giraldus Cambrensis, in the Rolls Series.

Office have been publishing for more than half a century. He belonged to that school of statesmen whom Henry II. gathered round him and trained for their executive, their financial, and their judicial functions. If you wish to see a vivid and truthful picture of that school of statesmen, lawyers, and financiers you should turn to Bishop Stubbs' last volume, entitled *Lectures on Mediæval and Modern History*, and there you will find in Lectures VI. and VII. an account of the men whom Henry II. trained to carry out the measures which lie at the basis of our modern Constitution. John Comyn was an active member of Henry II.'s select civil servants, and according to some (Foss's *Judges of England*, for instance, ii., 90), Henry of London was another, as they identify him with a Henry of London whom the Chief Justiciary sent, about the year 1170, to collect the rents of the vacant See of Chichester, and lodge them in the King's Treasury. I do not think, however, that we can trace him so far back. The mere identity of name and title proves but little. Henry of London was a description which must have been common to many persons, even in the civil service. Then again reflect on the vast distance of time. A trusty agent to collect rents for the Treasury could scarcely have been under twenty-five at the time. Let us suppose him twenty-five in 1170. He was consecrated Archbishop of Dublin in 1213, that is forty-three years after. I can scarcely think that King John would have selected so old a man for such a troublesome post; while, in addition, the story I am about to tell you gives me the idea, in its incessant toil, labour, and travelling, of a much younger man.

We first distinctly come across Henry of London, the second Anglo-Norman Archbishop of Dublin, in the first

year of King John, which began with Ascension Day
1199, when he was acting as an itinerant justice in
Berkshire, in accordance with that wise system which
Henry II. established, and which still exists in the Assize
Courts, bringing justice home to every man's door, or at
least to every man's county town; while again in 1207-
1210 he appears as a regular Justice of the King's
Bench at Westminster.[1] He was, then, a lawyer, as all
archdeacons were at that period; for the Church has
this proud pre-eminence over our legal brethren, that
the legal profession has been developed out of the
clerical. The only lawyers originally were the clergy, as
the very dress of the judges, with their copes and other
ecclesiastical vestments, abundantly testifies.[2] From the
first year of King John, Henry, Archdeacon of Stafford—
for that was his archdeaconry—frequently appears in
the original records of the time. From them we get a
complete picture of our own Archbishop's life. He was
evidently one of King John's most trusted officials.
King John was an extraordinary character. He was
mean and depraved in his private tastes, and his familiar
friends and associates were of the lowest type; but he
knew how to pick out able and fit instruments for his

---

[1] See Foss's *Judges of England*, t. ii., p. 90. Since I wrote this lecture I have found the Archdeacon mentioned in a still earlier record, of 1194. Cf. *Rotuli Curiæ Regis*, ed. Palgrave, pp. 3, 55, which will again come before us.

[2] See Mr. Brewer's words in his preface to *Monumenta Franciscana* (Rolls Series), pp. xlix, 1 :—" Hitherto logic and law had absorbed the industry and genius of the age. From the accession of the Angevin dynasty the law formed the great passport to dignity and emolument. The great law officers of the Crown were entirely selected from the canonists. Bishops, deans, and abbots, beneficed and unbeneficed clergy, strove with might and main to obtain political appointments; where solicitation and court favour failed, bribery paved the way for the suitor's wishes."

public business. Thus the Archdeacon of Stafford appears in the most various capacities. He was frequently sent on important embassies. In November 1201 he was sent to Spain as ambassador to the King of Navarre;[1] in 1204 he was despatched into Ireland to negotiate with Cathal O'Conor, King of Connaught; and in 1209[2] he went to treat with the Emperor Otho and the magnates of Germany. King John paid him for his services in Church livings, which were simply heaped upon him. He was Archdeacon of Stafford when John came to the throne. In May 1202 he was rewarded for his services in Spain by his appointment to the living of Cheshunt in the diocese of London, together with another in the diocese of Norwich. In February 1204 he obtained an additional living in the diocese of Coventry; and yet, though he now possessed at least three livings and an archdeaconry, the King called him from his parochial work to act, the very next month, March 26th, 1204, as a judge in an Irish suit depending between Meyler Fitz-Henry, the Viceroy, and Walter de Lacy, the Lord of Meath. In December 1205 he received two more livings, one a prebendal stall in Bridgenorth Collegiate Church, and the other the rectory of Werfeld, in Chester diocese. But this was not all, or nearly all.

On the 4th of August, 1207, he got a prebend in Exeter Cathedral, followed, on December 27th of the same year, by another prebend in Lincoln. He seems to have acted out most thoroughly the principle of holding everything and resigning nothing, or next to nothing. He seems, indeed, never to have resigned

---

[1] *Rotuli Litterarum Patentium*, vol. i., p. 3, ed. T. D. Hardy (London, 1835).
[2] *Rot. Litt. Pat.*, p. 91.

anything he once obtained, save the stall at Bridgenorth, which he vacated in March 1208.[1] We must suppose that its emoluments did not cover the expenses which it entailed. But he soon made up the loss, for we find him appointed immediately afterwards to the deanery of the collegiate church of Stafford. The King next tried, in 1210, to have him consecrated as Bishop of Exeter, but the existence of the interdict prevented the accomplishment of his wishes.[2] John, however, did all he could for the Archdeacon, by committing to his custody the temporal possessions and estates of that See, on June 4th, A.D. 1212, at which period he must have held an enormous amount of Church patronage. There were rolled into his one personality one deanery if not two,—for he seems to have been Dean of Shrewsbury as well as of Stafford,—an archdeaconry, four or five cathedral stalls, and some five or six livings. What dreams of preferment must have dawned on expectant eyes when they heard of his higher promotion! And that higher promotion soon came, for we find him in the early months of 1213 Archbishop of Dublin. But here you may ask, If the bishopric of Exeter could not be filled up on account of the interdict, how could he have been consecrated to the archbishopric? The solution of this difficulty is easy enough. The interdict did not apply to the whole of John's dominions. It was purely local. Ireland was not included in it, and there or in France the Archdeacon of Stafford could easily obtain the consecration he required.[3]

---

[1] This pluralist archdeacon's *cursus honorum* can be accurately traced in the *Rot. Litt. Pat.*, ed. Hardy, already quoted.

[2] Matthew Paris, *Chronica Majora*, t. ii., p. 531 (Rolls Series).

[3] Hugh, Archdeacon of Wells, elected Bishop of Lincoln

Who his consecrators were we know not, nor where was the place of his consecration. Serious questions have been raised about the validity of English orders and the due transmission of the English succession, because no documents exist with reference to the consecration of one of Parker's consecrators. But if the non-existence or disappearance of documents be a valid ground of objection, it will be impossible to prove the validity of any orders at all in universal Christendom, for the records of the vast majority of episcopal consecrations have utterly disappeared.

The Archbishop may have been consecrated in Ireland. He was an old traveller, and a trip to Dublin would be little regarded by one who had a few years before penetrated the bogs and woods of Connaught. At any rate, he was well qualified by experience for the work cut out for him. The Anglo-Norman Archbishops were primarily intended to be the king's chief agents in ruling Ireland. When they were not actually viceroys, they were to be the viceroy's chief advisers and spies upon his conduct. Archbishop Henry had ample qualifications for his duties. He was a thorough lawyer, he was a trained diplomatist, he was an old treasury official,[1] and he knew Ireland and Irish affairs both practically and theoretically. Well would it have been for English rule in Ireland had English sovereigns always sent as experienced a statesman to

---

when Henry was chosen, three years before, for Exeter, obtained the royal leave to cross into Normandy for consecration by the Archbishop of Rouen; England being then under the interdict. See Matthew Paris' *Hist. Anglorum*, t. ii., p. 120, and *Chron. Maj.*, ii., 528 (Rolls Series). Hugh, though he had been the royal chancellor, played a trick on King John which may have prevented him sending the Archdeacon of Stafford to Normandy for consecration as Bishop of Exeter.

[1] *Rot. Pat. Litt.*, Pref., p. xxxvi.

manage her secular business as that prelate was to whom the ecclesiastical affairs of the diocese of Dublin were now committed.

The second part of this lecture deals with Archbishop Henry as he was an ecclesiastic, that is, as a bishop, because his career as an archdeacon was not ecclesiastical at all, but purely secular.

Archbishop Henry delayed some months after his consecration winding up his affairs in England, and then proceeded in the autumn of the same year, 1213, to Ireland, where he spent some eighteen months. During that period he was Justiciary and Chief Governor of Ireland. It is a curious fact that now, after more than six centuries have elapsed, we can trace his actions by the help of the original documents existing in our various record repositories. The English record system stands by itself in Europe in this respect. No other nation has such a copious store of original matter for history. The Vatican itself, where one would expect that a government of clerks or clergymen would have the richest store of documents, equals not the English and Irish records. The late Cardinal Cullen had experience of an interesting illustration of that fact. He thought he would establish the ancient rule of Rome over Ireland by the production of original documents out of the Vatican, proving its subjection to Papal authority from the earliest periods. The late Pope consented, and Theiner, the Vatican librarian, produced a volume some twenty-five years ago, which exists in our library; and what do we find ? It contains all the early Irish documents in the Vatican, and yet the earliest document now in the Vatican relating to Ireland or Irish affairs is dated 1218, or the beginning of the reign of Henry III., and is actually a bull commanding the kings, princes, barons, and people of Ireland to be subject to the King of England, on pain of excommunication if they were disobedient. Why! The records preserved in Christ Church Cathedral, in the Record Office, by the Archbishop of Dublin, and by myself in Marsh's Library, could supply many Papal bulls and documents of a much earlier date, not to speak of the documents preserved in the English Record Offices. Our early archives give us some interesting glimpses of Archbishop Henry. We get, for instance, a hint of his personal tastes and habits. He was evidently a sporting prelate, and devoted to hunting.[1] When, therefore, he was thinking of going over to his diocese he wished to improve the breed of deer which then coursed far and wide among the forests which covered his lands in the Dublin Mountains, up the beautiful valley of Glenasmoel, along the slopes of Kippure and Glencree, and round by Glencullen, Shankhill, and Shanganagh. Accordingly we find that at the end of July 1213 he obtained an order from King John to the guardians of the See of Coventry, then vacant, to supply our Archbishop with thirty fallow deer out of the park of Brewood, and to lend him their aid in catching them.[2] The worthy pre-

---

[1] The sporting clergy of the nineteenth century could plead high authority in their defence from later times than those of Archbishop Henry. Archbishop Abbot of Canterbury, in the time of James I., puritanical in doctrine though he was, used to hunt, and accidentally killed a man in the course of his amusement. Bishop Juxon kept a pack of hounds "which exceeded all other hounds in England for the pleasure and orderly hunting of them." Bishop Seth Ward, of Exeter, was devoted to the hunting field. See Overton's *Life in the English Church*, p. 313.

[2] The Dublin archbishops seem to have been very fond of crossing the breed of their deer. See examples of royal gifts of English deer to them in Sweetman's *Calendar*, t. i., Nos. 477, 2,124, 3,123.

late seems indeed to have been devoted to sport; at any rate, he was tenacious of his claims in this respect, for he was continually getting into trouble with the King and his servants about his hunting rights. There were great forests then all round Dublin, the memory of which is still kept up in the name of one of our suburbs, Cullenswood. Cullenswood Square and Cullenswood Avenue show to this day where the Archbishop's wood of Cullen existed, running up to the very fields, and gardens, and walls of his episcopal residence of St. Sepulchre. The King too had his own royal forests here in Ireland, where he could hunt whenever he or his officials wished to do so. There was no Phœnix Park then, or, at least, there was no royal residence in the Phœnix Park; for the Park then formed a part of the lands belonging to the Knights Templar of Kilmainham, where those military ecclesiastics hunted their own deer. But the King claimed a forest which stretched up the wild valley of Glencullen, and thus adjoined the episcopal forests, which extended over the mountains far down into Wicklow. The limits of forests are at all times very hard to define, and as the natural result the King's foresters and keepers often came into collision with the Archbishop's men. We have, a few years later, an interesting illustration of the quarrels arising out of these various jurisdictions. Let me tell you the story, for it is a most interesting and even amusing one. It happened some seven years after the Archbishop's consecration—that is, in January, 1220. The King had sent over a certain Thomas Fitz-Adam as keeper of the King's forest, with great magisterial power. The Archbishop had been now seven years or more ruling over his See. He had been to the great Lateran Council of 1215, had been made Papal Legate for

Ireland, and had consequently forgotten a good deal of his old zeal for the royal prerogative. He had now become very zealous for clerical privileges, because they were his own. He was like some that I have seen and noted in later years, who supported very sweeping and radical measures, even of confiscation, until the measures touched themselves, and then they became the most rabid and violent opponents of such legislation ; or like others who are the stoutest assertors of the rights of presbyters and the boldest opponents of prelatic authority—till they are made bishops. Then they become the greatest prelates of all.

So was it with Archbishop Henry when the royal claims and his own liberties and customs came into collision. We have the story told in two opposite versions. We have the version of Thomas Fitz-Adam, the chief forester, and that of the Archbishop, as both parties at once wrote to the King, and the letters have been published in the *Royal Letters* of Henry III. in the Rolls Series. The keeper tells how that at the season of Epiphany he had been perambulating the forests and seeing after the royal rights, when two foresters or gamekeepers had been brought before him shamefully beaten, and with their clothes torn to rags. They told how that they had been thinning out trees in the King's groves, when the Archbishop's men came upon them, and treated them thus. From these wounded bailiffs Fitz-Adam learned that near the spot where he was, but within the Archbishop's lands, there lived a noted poacher, who for years had been plundering the King's game. The keeper marched to the house, surrounded it, seized the poacher, and proceeded to search the house, when he discovered ample proofs of his poaching depredations. He found a bow and a bloody arrow, the antlers of a deer, its hide, and a portion of its flesh. He arrested the culprit, marched him off, and lodged him in gaol. Then arose a row. The Archbishop sent the Dean of Dublin and three priests to demand the surrender of the prisoner, as being one of his tenants, and subject therefore to his jurisdiction alone. The keeper refused, whereupon the Archbishop ordered all services to be suspended on the next day, the festival of the Epiphany, after which he excommunicated the keeper, who still, however, held on manfully to his prisoner, writing at the same time to the King to complain of the Archbishop's intolerable conduct. His letter is most interesting, for many reasons, and specially so at the present time, for we learn from it that boycotting was then practised, and that under all the forms of law. The keeper complains to the King that he had been excommunicated, though the King's servants were expressly excluded from the operation of such sentences without the royal assent.[1] Still, he was subject to all the penalties of excommunication. He was persecuted wherever he went; no one would speak to him, or supply him with food and lodging; he was shunned as a social leper, and he had been prevented holding the Hilary Assizes at Dublin.[2] It was a very serious matter to incur the wrath of the clergy in those times. So much as to the Archbishop and his sporting rights.

But let us now return to his earlier days, before he had become so intensely sacerdotal. He spent two years in Dublin immersed in the cares of Church and

---

[1] See a bull of Gregory IX. in Rymer's *Fœdera*, t. i., p. 200, on this point.
[2] See several letters bearing on this controversy in *Royal Letters*, Henry III., t. i., pp. 82-90 (Rolls Series).

State before he proceeded to the great Lateran Council which made Transubstantiation a formal dogma of the Christian faith. During that period he consummated the union of Dublin and Glendalough dioceses, which have ever since been ruled by the same prelate. The last bishop and the last abbot of Glendalough verified the old saying about waiting for dead men's shoes,— they lived till their expectant successors were well tired out. The last legal Bishop of Glendalough died in 1214. His name was William Piro; but still, though he was the last bishop recognised by the Pope and the King, the See of Glendalough maintained a secret and hidden existence in the Wicklow mountains, and a Celtic succession was preserved down to the year 1497, when, on May 30th, Denis White, the last occupant, made a formal surrender of the Glendalough See in the Chapter House of St. Patrick's. But you must observe that whatever shadowy rights the nominal bishops may have claimed, the real rights were possessed and enjoyed by the prelates recognised by the English Crown. The See and Abbey of Glendalough—for both were added to the See of Dublin—involved vast landed possessions, which continued to be episcopal property till twenty years ago.[1]

---

[1] The report of the Established Church (Ireland) Commission, 1868, gives the rental of the archiepiscopal estates then attached to Dublin. The Wicklow estates were identical with those which belonged to the Abbey and See of Glendalough from ancient Celtic times. The Archbishop held, for instance, the Manor of Glendalough, which alone contained 34,000 acres; and yet he derived from such an immense tract of country an income of but £237 9s. 3d., or not quite twopence per acre. Not an exorbitant rent, as the most determined tenant-righter will acknowledge. The Bishop of Glendalough exercised feudal powers over these estates, judging their tenants according to the Brehon system long before the Anglo-Norman invasion. See an inquisition held at Castle

Archbishop Henry marked his entry upon the See by a characteristic action. He was evidently not only tenacious of his rights, he was also very fond of money. When an archdeacon, he never resigned any of his various Church livings upon his appointment to a new one. He seems to have even retained when archbishop various secular appointments in England, and the same covetous tendency followed him to Ireland, where we are told that upon his arrival at St. Sepulchre, he summoned all his tenantry before him, called upon them to produce their titles, leases, and other grants received from his predecessors. The unsuspecting tenantry, anxious to gain their new landlord's goodwill, diligently produced every scrap of writing they possessed, which the Archbishop carefully collected, and then in his hall, where a large fire was burning, committed all the documents to the flames in view of the despairing and enraged tenantry, who thenceforth gave him the name of Scorch-Villein, by which designation the second Anglo-Norman archbishop has since been known.[1]

Kevin in the thirteenth century, printed in Gilbert's *Municipal Documents*, pp. 151-54. The estates of this See of Glendalough came in ancient times very close to Dublin. See a full description of them in the year 1229 in Sweetman's *Calendar*, t. i., p. 262, No. 1757; and an elaborate but very inexact rental of them some forty years later in the *Proceedings of the Royal Irish Academy*, t. v., pp. 145-62. This statement of the rents of the See in 1271 was made by Sir W. Betham from the great roll of the Pipe. Mr. James Mills, of the Irish Record Office, has compared it with the original, and corrected some of Betham's mistakes. Betham made out that the value of the See was then £2,500 per annum. It was in fact just about £1,250. At the death of Archbishop Henry the rental seems to have been about £600 per annum, a larger income than the justiciary then enjoyed, for he was only paid £580 a year. See Sweetman's *Calendar*, t. i., p. 214, No. 1413; Rymer's *Fœdera*, t. i., p. 182.

[1] See Ware's *Bishops*, ed. Harris, p. 319, where the story

Archbishop Henry marked, however, the early years of his episcopate by other measures. He enlarged and finished the Castle of Dublin, removing several churches—St. Martin's, St. Paul's, and perhaps St. Andrew's—in carrying out his design. The castle we now see gives but a small idea of the castle which our Archbishop erected. Within the last hundred and fifty years it has been to a great extent altered and modernized, but if you will look at Brooking's Map of Dublin, published early in the last century, you can see a picture of Dublin Castle as it appeared in the Middle Ages fresh from the hands of the episcopal builders.[1] Archbishop Henry was in those early days very zealous in the King's behalf. He pulled down churches to erect a royal castle; yea, he gave a greater proof of his devotion: he spent his own money in the royal service, and King John was not forgetful of his diligent servant. He rewarded him, therefore, not indeed out of his own pocket,—for King John was always very impecunious; but he gave him an English Church sinecure, and conferred upon him and upon the See of Dublin for ever an English title, which, as far as I can see, it still possesses. On September 13th, 1215,[2] King John bestowed on the See of Dublin the advowson and manor of Penkridge in Staffordshire, making the Archbishop of Dublin and his successors for ever deans of the collegiate church of Penkridge, a title and manor which the Archbishops of Dublin used and enjoyed down to the time of Archbishop King in the last century. You will perhaps be surprised to hear that, so lately as that prelate's time,

---

is told as set forth in the *Liber Niger* of the Archbishops of Dublin, fol. 437 (Marsh's Library copy). But see note, p. 380.
[1] There is a copy of Brooking's map in the National Libraiy, Kildare Street.
[2] Cf. Sweetman's *Cal. of Doc.*, t. i., p. 100, No. 652.

the Bishop of Lichfield did not attempt to visit that church without first applying to the Archbishop of Dublin for leave to visit and confirm within his peculiar jurisdiction of Penkridge. You must observe, however, one condition on which this grant of the deanery of Penkridge was made. It was expressly laid down in this grant, witnessed by the Pope's Legate, that it was made to the Archbishops of Dublin "not being Irishmen;" a limitation which received an additional illustration a year or two later, when the English court sent an order to all the bishops of Ireland that no Irishman should be admitted to any cathedral preferment whatsoever. From the time of this grant to the Archbishop Henry and his successors, the following long and portentous title, which is duly set forth in Archbishop Alan's *Liber Niger*, has been the correct archiepiscopal style and designation:—" Henry, by Divine mercy Regular Abbot of the Cathedral Church of the Holy Trinity, and Bishop of St. Patrick's, Archbishop and Primate of the Irish Church by grace of the Apostolic See, Dean of the free royal chapel of St. Mary's of Penkridge, Prince Palatine of Harold's Cross, Custos of the Suffragan Sees when vacant, and Custos of the spiritual jurisdiction, and of all the tithes in the same province;" in which title you will observe that the monastic origin and character of the early Irish episcopate are duly set forth.[1]

---

[1] See *Liber Niger Alani*, fol. 372 (Marsh's Library copy). The Archbishop is called, by Alan, Abbot of the Cathedral of the Holy Trinity. That cathedral was till the time of Henry VIII. governed by a prior. But a prior implies an abbot, to whom he is subordinate. The priors of Christ Church were subordinate to the archbishop, *quâ* abbot, but not *quâ* bishop, while the deans of St. Patrick's acknowledged the episcopal jurisdiction of the archbishop.

Archbishop Henry went to the Lateran Council of 1216 as the representative of King John as much as in his ecclesiastical character. He went charged to win the Pope over to the King's side. John had granted the Magna Charta under the joint compulsion of the Church and the barons. He wished now to retract and withdraw it. He had sworn to it, indeed, but no oaths could bind King John. He only desired to see his way sufficiently clearly, and then he would break any compact, and to this end he despatched the Archbishop to Pope Innocent. Many circumstances prove this. King John supported the Archbishop when at Rome, pledged his own credit and that of his Crown for money lent him, and paid his expenses when he came back. And Archbishop Henry did the King's work well. He manipulated the Pope for the King's purpose, and we therefore find that soon after his return the Pope excommunicated the rebellious English barons. Rome and its influences changed Archbishop Henry, however, and after his visit to the Council we find him much more of an ecclesiastic and much less a man of the world.[1] He held a synod a year or two after, in which he inculcated a much stricter life upon the Irish clergy, and made stringent regulations about their pastoral duties.[2] The higher ecclesiastical tone of the Archbishop is marked by a corresponding assertion of its rights on the

---

[1] Cf. Sweetman, *Calendar of Documents*, t. i., p. 120, Nos. 804, 805, 807.

[2] The canons of this synod are printed in Wilkins' *Concilia*, t. i., p. 548, from the *Crede Mihi*. They lay down stringent regulations concerning clerical celibacy and discipline, attendance at Church synods, and clerical conduct when going to and returning from these assemblies, the visitation of the sick on Sundays and holy days, with due celebration of the eucharist, the celebrant to be clad in a surplice and attended with a cross, lamp, and bell, carried by a clerk.

part of the Crown. A striking instance of this is found in the year 1223, when Henry III. uses language with respect to Papal jurisdiction quite worthy of Henry VIII. or Queen Elizabeth. The case is an interesting one. A certain Nicholas de la Feld sought to recover in the King's Bench, from the Abbot of St. Thomas's Abbey, some lands which, as he alleged, belonged to his family. The abbot disputed his claim by asserting that the said Nicholas was illegitimate. This assertion was referred, after the roundabout custom of the law, to the Ecclesiastical Courts for investigation. The Archbishop duly considered the case, and then some difficulties arising he transmitted the whole case to Rome for the Pope's determination. But Henry III., though a weak monarch, would not tolerate this appeal to a foreign jurisdiction. He wrote a very strong letter to the Archbishop, declared his own courts quite competent to settle all such questions, utterly rejected the transfer to what he calls "a foreign dignitary" of questions which ought to be determined in the national courts, and ordered him at once to dispose of the suit, notwithstanding the appeal to the Papal tribunals.[1]

The best known work of Henry of London still remains, however, amongst us, and was connected with St. Patrick's Cathedral. St. Patrick's was originally a simple parish church, as I have shown in a previous lecture. Archbishop Comyn made it a collegiate

---

They further ordain, in conformity with the Lateran decrees, that no one shall receive another priest's parishioners to confession or the eucharist without the special license of the said priest. They prescribe the due ornamentation of churches, the laws of tithe and many details concerning wills and testamentary jurisdiction, specially restraining the monks "cujuscunque fuit professionis" from interfering in such matters.

[1] See Sweetman's *Calendar*, t. i., No. 1,149.

church, dozens, yea, even hundreds of which then existed throughout England, Ireland, and Scotland; though at the present day scarcely a trace of such an institution remains save at Windsor, Westminster Abbey, and a few other places in England. Collegiate churches, indeed, disappeared in Ireland only in our own day. The collegiate church of St. Nicholas, Galway, ceased to hold this ancient position only since I was a boy, presided over, as it was so lately as 1860, by a warden, assisted by four priest vicars. You must remember that collegiate churches have nothing to say to colleges and college chapels, as we should be apt to imagine. They were called collegiate churches because a college, a collegium or corporation or brotherhood of clergy, went to live together and work together in association. You will, for instance, see the name used in its correct technical sense in the rubric about weekly celebrations following the office for the Holy Communion in the Book of Common Prayer. Collegiate churches were a mediæval institution, and yet it seems that we are inclined with one consent to return to a similar system in the Church of Ireland. Bishops in their charges, synodsmen in the synod, all seem to agree that the system of planting out solitary incumbents in miserable country parishes is a failure, leading to the appointment of men unfitted by age and experience for their position, and offering no chance for practical training in the work of the ministry. All seem more and more inclined to fall back upon the wisdom of the ancients which devised the system of collegiate churches, where were combined a common life, experienced guidance, dignified worship, together with that sense of sympathy and mutual support which are at present sadly wanting among us.

Now observe this. From 1190 to 1220 St. Patrick's was only a collegiate church, worked by a college of priests who held some thirteen prebendal stalls. About 1220 Archbishop Henry raised the collegiate church to the position of a cathedral, instituting four dignitaries, —dean, precentor, chancellor, and treasurer; ordaining that the dean should be elected out of the Chapter by the canons or prebendaries, and that the Use of Sarum and the statutes of that church should prevail in St. Patrick's. From that time we have the unique institution of two cathedrals in this diocese of Dublin. Sometimes, indeed, the example of London has been adduced as presenting the same phenomenon. There, indeed, we find a dean and chapter at Westminster as well as at St. Paul's. But Westminster is to this day merely a collegiate church and a Royal Peculiar. It is not a cathedral at all, and has no cathedral rights or dignitaries. But both our great churches of St. Patrick's and the Holy Trinity are cathedrals, and have been cathedrals—the church of the Holy Trinity since its foundation, St. Patrick's since its erection into a cathedral in 1220. The existence of two cathedrals in Dublin is indeed the only surviving evidence of a great struggle which was fought out far more bitterly in England than in Ireland. A few words of explanation will help to show the value of our peculiar institution in explaining mediæval history and life. Monastic chapters were a peculiar feature of Anglo-Saxon Christianity. The tenth century witnessed their introduction in order to secure a necessary reform. The secular canons had become hopelessly corrupt, and monastic chapters were introduced by St. Dunstan and other pious men desirous to see religious work done in a religious spirit. Two centuries elapsed, and then the bishops grew tired of monastic chapters. By the close of the twelfth century many of the bishops of England were engaged in a deadly struggle, striving to banish the monks from their chapters. We have in the *Rotuli Curiæ Regis,* the Records of the King's Bench of John's time, as edited by Palgrave, the story of a particular contest which exemplifies my statement. Hugh de Nonant was Bishop of Coventry about the year 1190. He determined to expel the monks from his chapter and to substitute secular canons. The monks determined upon resistance. They burst into the cathedral, assaulted the canons, and broke the bishop's head with their great processional cross. Thereupon arose a contest which was fought, with varying success, before the King's court, the Archbishop's court, and finally before the Papal tribunal. With that special struggle we have no more to do than just to note that Archdeacon Henry of Stafford, subsequently our Archbishop, was in 1194 the legal champion of the Coventry canons, against the monks before the courts at Westminster. The Archdeacon imbibed a hearty horror of monastic choirs, and when he came to Dublin and found one there as thoroughly monastic as that of Coventry, he resolved to found a new cathedral where secular canons should alone exist. He did not try to change the constitution of Christ Church Cathedral. Bitter experience had shown him what tough customers the monks could be. But a change he was determined to have. A monastic chapter was naturally obnoxious to a bishop. It was independent of him by virtue of its constitution. Archbishop Henry founded St. Patrick's Cathedral, or rather turned the Collegiate Church, with its organization of a dean and secular canons, into a Cathedral Chapter, and thus established beside his new Palace of St. Sepulchre a body which looked to himself, depended upon himself, and regarded him as their chief friend and patron. These observations will explain for you and bring into line with contemporary history what seems at first a mere Hibernian anomaly.[1] This somewhat curious constitution of our Dublin cathedrals has often led to serious quarrels between the two bodies. They carried on perpetual litigation before the King and the Pope, till at last, by a deed or composition of peace, made in the year 1300 between the two chapters, the cathedral of the Holy Trinity is recognized as the senior of the two corporations, the insignia of the archbishops as soon as they were dead were to be conveyed thither for safe custody, while their bodies were to be buried alternately in Christ Church and in St. Patrick's. This deed is well worth consulting, given as it is in full in the sixth appendix to Mason's *St. Patrick's*, for it shows that some of our modern arrangements found an exact parallel six centuries ago. The rule, for instance, there laid down that provincial synods are to be opened and closed at the Cathedral of the Holy

---

[1] See the history of this Coventry quarrel given at length in Sir Francis Palgrave's preface to the *Rotuli Curiæ Regis* (London: 1835), pp. xviii-xxviii; cf. Hoveden, iii., 168; Gervase, i., 550; Jocelin de Brakelond, p. 69; William of Newburgh, *Hist.*, iv., 36, in *Chronn. Steph.*, etc., i., 393-96 (Rolls Series), and p. 196 above. At the very same time the same kind of quarrel was going on at Canterbury between Archbishop Baldwin and the monastic chapter of his cathedral. He tried to adopt the same course as the Dublin archbishops. He endeavoured to remove his cathedral chapter from the convent of Christ Church, and establish it with secular canons at first at Hackington, half a mile from Canterbury, and then at Lambeth. Hence the origin of Lambeth Palace. See Hook's *Archbishops*, t. ii., pp. 549-55; and Stubbs's Preface *Epistl. Cantuar.* (Rolls Series).

Trinity, finds still an exact, but I fear unintentional and unconscious, obedience at the hands of the General Synod, which begins and ends its proceedings at the spot thus ordained by ecclesiastical authority, now well nigh six hundred years ago.[1]

I have wearied you out, doubtless, with these ecclesiastical details. To some, however, they may be of great interest, and to all they are necessary if they wish to understand the whole life and history of those mediæval times. The life of Archbishop Henry was not, as we might imagine, wholly taken up with these ecclesiastical cares. He became more of an ecclesiastic as he advanced in life, but he never wholly forgot his statesmanship and his skill in secular affairs. During the last ten years of his life, which ended in 1228, he was very often the actual as well as virtual ruler of Ireland, and, indeed, the country then needed a strong and determined hand. The reign of Henry III. was long and troublous in England, but as it was in his father's time so was it in the son's. The English rebels began their work in England, and then transferred the scene of their operations to Ireland, where they fought to such purpose as to render almost hopeless the prospects of Anglo-Norman dominion. The Celtic chiefs were rude enough in the thirteenth century, and rude enough in the seventeenth century

---

[1] Archbishop Alan, in his *Liber Niger* (fol. 391, Marsh's Library copy), tells us that the prebends of St. Patrick's were divided into sacerdotal, diaconal and sub-diaconal, and gives us the following as their order of precedence:—(1), Ten sacerdotal, viz., Colonia or Cullen, Kilmactalway, Swords, Iago, St. Audoen's, Clonmethan, Wicklow, Timothan, Castleknock, Mulhuddart. (2) Four diaconal, viz., Tipper, Tassagart, Dunlavin, Maynooth. (3) Eight sub-diaconal, viz., Howth, Rathmichael, Monmohenock, Stagonil, Tipperkevin (double prebend), Donaghmore (double prebend).

too; but the chief blame for Irish disturbance and anarchy at either period must be placed not on Celtic but on Anglo-Norman and English shoulders. Archbishop Henry did not indeed live to see the worst. He died about midsummer 1228, but he lived long enough to witness a struggle typical of countless others in the war of Meath, and to behold the foundations laid of the war of Kildare, which will engage our attention in the next lecture, and point a moral as necessary for the nineteenth as for the thirteenth century.

LECTURE XII.

THE WARS OF MEATH AND OF KILDARE, OR THE IRISH TROUBLES OF HENRY III.

I HAVE now endeavoured, in the course of several lectures, to set before you the transition period of Irish history, so far as the Church was concerned. I have described the steps by which the old Celtic order, represented by St. Laurence O'Toole, was merged into the newer style embodied in the persons and rule of the great Anglo-Norman episcopal princes. In a subsequent lecture I shall have more to say on this topic, and will then point out how comparatively local and partial was that change; but must now turn aside to consider the political and social forces which found play on the more secular side of Ireland's history, and largely helped to make this island's history the sad thing it has ever since been, a roll written, like the prophet's, within and without, with lamentation, mourning, and woe. I select for special treatment the first half of the thirteenth century, for two obvious reasons; first, because that period strikingly illustrates the fatal weakness of the feudal system in Ireland, as established by the Plantagenet princes. I have already shown you how they established here palatine nobles, endowed with enormous powers, and enjoying a kind of quasi-independence; a dangerous institution enough in England, where the power of the Crown was present to rule and to constrain, but a certain and fruitful source of mischief and of ruin in Ireland, where headstrong, passionate men were left to work out the devices and desires of their own wild wills, without trammel or restraint. A steam engine, working at the height of its power and under due guidance, is a magnificent machine; but a runaway engine, deprived of driver, stoker, and guard, ceases to be useful and becomes a most certain instrument of ruin and destruction. It will require neither a prophet nor a prophet's son to make due application of this modern parable to the circumstances of the thirteenth century, as I shall depict them. Then, again, I have another and most necessary reason for my choice of this period. It will conduce to brevity. During the three centuries from 1200 to 1500, Ireland's history simply repeats itself from year to year and from reign to reign, sometimes a little better, sometimes a little worse, but its story is always one of disorganization, war, and strife, the causes of which are to be sought in the state of England and of England's politics, as much as in that of Ireland. No historian's pen, no matter how skilful in depicting the past, could possibly make an interesting story out of the monotonous details of murders, raids, and rebellions—Anglo-Norman and Celtic alike—with which the annals of those times abound. Should I attempt the impossible task, you would be utterly sick of the dreary recital before two lectures were heard. I shall therefore, in the present lecture, tell you the story of the first half of the thirteenth century, as

---

[1] The best modern exposition of the nature of palatinate tenures will be found in the prefaces to the various volumes of the *Registrum Palatinum Dunelmense* in the Rolls Series, ed. by Sir T. D. Hardy.

typical of the political life of the whole period I am now seeking to cover; and then, in another lecture, I shall present you with a rapid survey, or a brief synopsis rather, of the leading events which stand out prominent amid the barren records of war and sedition. Let us then apply ourselves boldly to the difficult task of pourtraying the internecine struggles of the earliest Anglo-Norman invaders.

The leading interest of this period centres round three great families, the De Lacys, the De Courcys, and the Marshalls. The De Lacys, Walter, Hugh, and William, were the sons of the great viceroy who perished, in the early days of Anglo-Norman occupation, by the hand of young Fox.[1] They retained their father's property in England and Ireland, and his palatinate lordship of Meath. John de Courcy was made Earl of Ulster in the reign of Richard I., some short time before the year 1200; while William, Earl Mareschal or Marshall, by his marriage with Isabel, daughter of Strongbow and the Princess Eva, represented the great fiefs of Leinster, Striguil, and Pembroke.[2] Here were the elements of strife, confusion, and wars in abundance under one king, so worthless as John, and under another, so utterly weak and incapable as John's son, Henry III. It is hard to make an interesting story out of the materials we have in hand. They are abundant enough indeed, but they are wanting in any elements of patriotism, true nobility, high aim, or even striking gallantry and courage, save in the one case of the Marshall family. Plunder, treachery, perjury, hatred of peace and the things which make for peace,

---

[1] See p. 169 above.
[2] See a paper on the earldom of Ulster in *Ulster Journal of Archæology*, t. i., pp. 37-42.

utter disregard of duty and the obligations of high station and office, characterise all, or well nigh all, the leading actors.

De Courcy and the De Lacys were scarcely well settled in their possessions when they began to misuse their power. In the very first year of King John we read in a letter from that prince to Meyler Fitz-Henry, the justiciary of Ireland, instructions given to that official to enquire whether Henry Tyrrel, the Lord of Castleknock, had sided with John De Courcy and Walter De Lacy, and had aided in destroying the king's land in Ireland.[1] The tale is much the same whether we study the history of these families from the Irish documents or from the English. The *Annals of Lough Cé*, composed near Boyle, and under the auspices of the Macdermott tribe, tell precisely the same story as the English official records. One year De Courcy and De Lacy are united in waging war upon the O'Conors, the next year they are biting and devouring one another. The earldom of Ulster became the bone of contention between the De Courcys and the De Lacys. The De Lacys held Meath, which, on the east and north, marched side by side with Ulster. But Ulster possessed many advantages, from the Anglo-Norman point of view, which Meath had not. When Ireland was self-contained, and its princes were intent upon their own quarrels merely, Meath was the most desirable of possessions; but when England, Scotland, Normandy, and the other lands beyond the seas, became objects of intrigue and of interest, Meath, with its one port of Drogheda, and touching the sea nowhere else, seemed a far inferior principality

---

[1] Sweetman's *Calendar*, t. i., p. 14, No. 90.

to Ulster, with its harbours of Carlingford, Strangford, Ardglass, and Carrickfergus, which, even to this day, retain, in many a ruined castle, clear evidences of their flourishing commercial state in the earliest days of the thirteenth century. John de Courcy, in virtue of his extensive sea-coast, became a potentate whose alliance the Kings of Man, of Scotland, and even of Norway, counted worthy of their attention; while the De Lacys were, in the eyes of these foreign sovereigns, mere nobodies. John de Courcy, as Earl of Ulster, married Affreca, the daughter of the King of Man, coined money, and established such royal state that it was easy for Hugh de Lacy to insinuate suspicions of his loyalty into King John's mind.[1] He did so with such effect that De Lacy received orders to seize De Courcy as a rebel. This was, however, no easy task. De Courcy was a giant in size, and the mightiest warrior of his day. De Lacy made several attempts to carry out the king's command, and at last succeeded only through the treachery of De Courcy's servants, who betrayed their master, as tradition says, when engaged in his Good Friday devotions in the

---

John de Courcy during his rule at Downpatrick, which lasted during a period of well-nigh thirty years, from 1177 to 1205, made some progress in ecclesiastical organization, at least. He expelled the ancient Irish canons from the convent of the Holy Trinity, and introduced the Black Monks from Chester. They do not seem to have been very happy in their new situation, as we read in Rymer's *Fœdera*, t. i., p. 205, a doleful petition sent by the prior and monks of St. Patrick's (formerly the Holy Trinity), Downpatrick, telling of the repeated burnings of their buildings, and begging for a cell in England. I am sure they often wished themselves back in Chester. Among the monks introduced by De Courcy from England was Joceline, author of the *Life of St. Patrick*, who tells us that it was compiled at the solicitation of De Courcy, "the most illustrious prince of Ulidia." See Reeves' *Ecclesiastical Antiquities*, pp. 163, 229; Gilbert's *Viceroys*, p. 60.

monastery of the Holy Trinity, which now is the cathedral of Downpatrick. De Courcy was avenged upon his enemies, even in his capture. He seized a wooden cross, which stood at the head of a grave, and wielding it with all his gigantic strength, killed thirteen of De Lacy's attendants, before he could be disarmed.

Hugh de Lacy was now triumphant. De Courcy was compelled to take the cross and set out upon a crusade to Palestine,[1] while the earldom of Ulster was at once conferred upon the triumphant Hugh de Lacy.[2] But the troubles of the king with Ulster were only beginning when he installed De Lacy in the place of De Courcy. Within five years, that is, in the spring of 1210, King John was obliged personally to invade Ulster and chase Hugh de Lacy out of Ireland, seizing the possessions and principalities of the whole De Lacy faction in England and Ireland alike; while by a kind of poetic vengeance there stood by King John's side in that same invasion of Ulster the very John de Courcy whom De Lacy had defeated and deposed by King John's command in 1205; so tortuous, confused, and vacillating were Anglo-Norman policy and rulers in those times.

During the following twenty years, from 1210 to 1230, the De Lacys were the centre and source of Irish anarchy. Hugh de Lacy was a man of tremendous energy. He betook himself to foreign courts, and

---

[1] This fact we learn from the *Annals of Lough Cé*, ed. Hennessy, t. i., p. 235, A.D. 1204.

The tradition about the capture of De Courcy upon Good Friday has this much in its favour, that the official grants and records all attribute the capture of De Courcy and the appointment of De Lacy as Earl of Ulster to the months of April and May 1205. See Sweetman, *l.c.*, t. i., pp. 39 and 40, Nos. 259, 260, 263.

sought for support in Scotland, France, and Norway. Fifteen years after his expulsion from Ulster we find Queen Joanna of Scotland writing to her brother, Henry III. of England, in 1224, telling him of a rumour that the King of Norway would land in Ireland in the summer, in order to aid Hugh de Lacy.[1] The efforts of this latter were for a long time all in vain, till at last, in the spring of 1223, Hugh thought he saw his opportunity. The Archbishop of Dublin was justiciary of Ireland. He had been vigorous and courageous in his day, but he was now grown very old. Hugh de Lacy prepared to invade Ireland and reinstate himself in his Earldom of Ulster. But he was narrowly watched all the time by the king's advisers headed by William Marshall, Earl of Pembroke, the son of the old and trusted friend of King John.[2] Hugh had, too, a bitter enemy, who keenly noted his movements and quickly reported them to London, in his uncle Cathal O'Conor, King of Connaught, whose years, identical with those of

---

[1] The kings of Norway seem to have had designs on Ireland till late in the thirteenth century. The *Annals of Lough Cé*, ed. Hennessy (Rolls Series), A.D. 1263, cf. preface, pp. xlv-xlvii, the *Chronicle of Man*, and the *Annals of Clonmacnois*, under the same year, mention a projected invasion of Ireland by King Haco, who was lying with his ships at Lamlash on the Clyde. This fact, noticed in the briefest manner by the Irish chronicler, has been amply confirmed on independent grounds by the researches among the Sagas of modern Swedish historians; see Munch's *Norske Folks Historie* (Christiania, 1858), vol. i., part iv., p. 407. The Irish princes, forgetful of their old sufferings at Scandinavian hands, sent an embassy to solicit Haco's help against the Anglo-Normans, although there had been active diplomatic intercourse between the courts of Norway and of England for more than a century; an instance of which, in the case of this very Haco, can be seen in *Royal Letters of Henry III.*, t. i., p. 485. See Bishop Stubbs's *Lectures on Mediæval and Modern History*, p. 143.

[2] Sweetman's *Calendar*, t. i., Nos. 1,110, 1,126.

De Lacy's own, enabled him to recall many memories of raids and plundering expeditions made by the Palatine princes of Meath, the elder Hugh de Lacy and his sons, upon the wide-spreading and fertile plains of Connaught. It is most interesting, therefore, as a specimen of the fidelity with which some of the Celtic kings of the period served the English crown, to find Cathal O'Conor writing thus to Henry III. in March 1224. "Cathal, King of Connaught, to the King. Hugh de Lacy, enemy of the king, of the king's father, and of Cathal, whom King John, by Cathal's advice, expelled from Ireland, has, without consulting the king, come to that country to disturb it. Against Hugh's coming Cathal remains, as the Archbishop of Dublin knows, firm in his fidelity to the king. But the closer Cathal adheres to the king's service, the more he is harassed by those who pretend fealty to the king, and, as the justiciary knows, shamefully fail against his enemy; so that between Hugh de Lacy, on the one hand, and those who pretend to be faithful on the other, Cathal is placed in great difficulty;" not the only person, we may in passing remark, was the King of Connaught whom the weak, ever-changing policy of the English Court has placed in similar positions of difficulty in Ireland. Despite all his foes within or without Ireland, Hugh de Lacy landed in Ireland early in 1224, trusting that his name and extensive connection would speedily place him at the head of a force sufficient to extort favourable terms from the Crown. Thereupon arose what is called the war of Meath. The royal advisers adopted the best steps they could. The episcopal justiciary, Archbishop Henry, was at once superseded,[1]

---

[1] Sweetman's *Calendar*, t. i., p. 180, No. 1,185.

and William Marshall, Earl of Pembroke, the ablest soldier of the day, was appointed in his stead. William Marshall did his utmost with the means he possessed. We require no further explanations of the failure of English policy in Ireland during these early centuries, than those which a study of the official records of this rebellion supplies. The English government of that time trusted to volunteer help, to Papal mandates, to episcopal excommunications, to the mutual hatred and hostility of the nobles, but was utterly lacking in the first elements of a standing army or of a vigorous police. Rulers who pass laws, but have no force to back up these laws, will soon be despised in a semi-barbarous community, and so it was in Ireland in the year 1224.[1] The Earl of Pembroke was appointed justiciary, apparently because he could bring large forces of his own into the field; and then when Henry III. proceeded to assist him, he could only do so by committing Meath and its fortresses, including the all-important one of Trim Castle, to the custody of Hugh de Lacy's own brother, Walter de Lacy, who, of

---

[1] The state of utter unpreparedness for war in which the Anglo-Norman government then was, is best illustrated by an official statement of the stores in the three great royal castles of Athlone, Limerick, and Dublin about the year 1224, reported in Sweetman's *Calendar*, t. i., p. 187. In the castle of Athlone, the great frontier fortress of Connaught, was found, "4 coats of mail, 2 with and 2 without headpieces; 9 iron hats; 1 helmet; 2 mangonels, with 120 strings and slings; 1 cable; 1 crossbow with a wheel; 2,000 bolts: 1 small brazen pot; 5 broken tuns; 5 basins; 4 broken tubs; 2 anchors; ironwork of 2 mills; 1 chasuble; 1 consecrated altar; 1 figured cloth to put before the altar." In the castle of Limerick there were found stores amounting in value to eighteen pence, chiefly consisting of broken dishes. Dublin was not much better furnished than Athlone. The English government of that day had castles, but no arms; just as some now complain that we have abundant ships, but no guns.

course while pretending to oppose Earl Hugh, lent him all the assistance in his power. We have in the *Royal Letters of Henry III.* an interesting account of the struggle which ensued, set forth in a despatch from the Earl of Pembroke to his sovereign, detailing his operations from the middle of June till the end of August 1224. The letter is quite modern in its form, though drawn up in the Latin tongue. It enumerates the persons who have lent assistance, requests the Crown to express to them its gratitude by letter, details the operations of the army and notes its successes.[1] Earl William Marshall, according to this despatch, arrived in Waterford on the Wednesday before the festival of St. John the Baptist (June 24th), whence he marched to Dublin and was invested with the office of justiciary by the archbishop. The earl was a vigorous commander. He gathered such assistance as he could from the citizens of Dublin, —who naturally, as commercial men, were hostile to the plundering sway of the barons, and supported the Crown, —and then marched at once to Trim Castle, which he besieged for six weeks.[2] But he did not confine his attention to one place. Hugh de Lacy himself, far away

---

[1] *Royal Letters Henry III.* (Rolls Series), t. i., pp. 500-503.
[2] The financial resources of the Irish justiciary were of the scantiest kind. He seized three hundred marks lying in the Papal treasury at Dublin (*Royal Letters*, i., 325); six hundred cows and forty marks belonging to the Abbey of Mellifont (Sweetman's *Calendar*, t. i., p. 189); two hundred pounds belonging to St. Mary's Abbey (*l.c.*, t. i., p. 192). These ecclesiastical loans the king was compelled to repay. He borrowed £312 from some prominent citizens of Dublin. This loan was not repaid by the king. He compelled the city to repay it after a delay of five years, in return for permission to choose annually their own mayor (*Royal Letters*, i., 352; Sweetman's *Calendar*, i., 254). The Earl Marshall must have been hard pressed to make both ends meet, as in his despatch he reports to Henry III. that the expenses of the army were £16 a day.

in the north, was besieging the castle of Carrickfergus, which was holding out for the king. Marshall embarked a small force at Drogheda,[1] which, sailing straight from that port to the mouth of Belfast Lough, successfully relieved the assailed fortress, compelling Hugh de Lacy to retire. In quite the opposite direction Marshall's measures were equally successful. The county of Cavan was in those times called O'Reilly's country.[2] It is still a district celebrated for the vast number of its lakes, a feature of the landscape which made it, six centuries ago, a secure refuge for the native Irish against the Norman invaders, whose iron-clad warriors inevitably perished if they attempted to penetrate its bogs and morasses. The Celtic chiefs of this region lived in crannogs, or fortified islands,[3] many of which can still be identified. O'Reilly's country touches Meath on the north-west a few miles beyond the town of Kells, along a line where the diocese of Kilmore meets the diocese of Meath. Here the chief of the O'Reilly tribe had erected

---

[1] This Carrickfergus expedition was commanded by William le Gros, a famous commander in these Irish wars. His name often appears in the Irish *Annals*. He was one of the ancestors of the Grace family (Hennessy's *Annals of Lough Cé*, A.D. 1225, and *Annals of Four Masters*, A.D. 1225, ed. O'Donovan. Cf. pp. 98, 188, above).

[2] See *Irish Topographical Poems*, ed. by John O'Donovan, p. 57, in the Irish Archæological Series. It was acknowledged by the Crown as O'Reilly's country till Elizabeth's time (cf. *Ulster Journal of Archæology*, t. ii., p. 7).

[3] See *Ireland and the Celtic Church*, p. 292, for a note about crannogs and a list of authorities on that subject; to which I would now add Keller's *Lake Dwellings*, translated by John E. Lee, in two vols. (London, 1878), where it is stated (t. i., p. 654) that Ballynahuish Castle in West Galway, which was a crannog, was inhabited till the early years of this century. On the Cavan crannogs Sir W. Wilde wrote a paper printed in the *Proceedings* of the Royal Irish Academy, t. viii., p. 274.

a crannog at an advanced point to guard his boundaries.[1] William de Lacy, another brother of the earl, possessed himself of it, and placed in it, for security, his wife, the wife of his brother Thomas de Lacy, and his mother, Rose O'Conor, the second wife of the elder Hugh de Lacy, whose marriage, nearly fifty years before, had excited the wrath of Henry II., and caused the dismissal of that great chieftain from the position of chief governor of Ireland.

Here let me pause a little in the course of my narrative to note for you the tangled web of matrimonial connections which we already find woven among these earliest Anglo-Norman settlers. Many of them had already become in blood, if not in feeling and national sentiment, as much Celt as Norman. The elder Hugh de Lacy married Rose O'Conor, who survived her husband during more than forty years of widowhood, to find herself in her old age a fugitive amid the bogs, lakes, and crannogs of Cavan. Her eldest step-sons were Hugh and Walter, of whom Hugh, Earl of Ulster, was now the leading rebel in Ireland. Her own sons by De Lacy were William, Thomas, and Henry. Henry became a priest, but the soldier element in his composition was too strong for the clerical, and he was killed

---

[1] Mr. Hennessy, in his *Annals of Lough Cé*, t. i., p. 260, Note [8] (Rolls Series), identifies this crannog with the old Castle of Cloch-Oughter, in Lough Oughter, county Cavan. In Mr. E. P. Shirley's *Territory of Farney*, p. 93, he quotes a description of Monaghan in 1590, now preserved in the State Paper Office, which gives drawings of the residences of the Celtic chiefs in these crannogs. They were mere cabins built of wood, and in appearance like the dwellings of small farmers at the present day. Such as they were in 1590, such they were in A.D. 1224. The Celtic tribes changed nothing in the interval. The piles and flooring on which these cabins stood have been in many cases discovered intact.

fighting against the Earl Marshall at the Castle of Kilmore. William de Lacy,[1] the grandson of Roderic O'Conor, King of Connaught, married the daughter of William de Braose, a Norman noble; and her sister Maud was wife of Griffith, Prince of South Wales. But this was not all, or nearly all. Llewellyn, Prince of North Wales, and Hugh de Lacy's ally in rebellion, was married to the sister of Henry III., King of England; while, to crown the labyrinth of unions, the Earl Marshall was married to another sister of King Henry, and the King of Scotland to yet a third; and still, though thus connected together by matrimonial ties, they were all engaged in fighting and plotting one against another.[2]

Earl Marshall vigorously followed up the advantages which he had gained. Upon the same day he and his allies attacked the Castle of Kilmore in one direction and O'Reilly's crannog in another. William de Lacy was present in person at Kilmore, where he escaped with difficulty from the pursuit of his enemies, being so hard pressed indeed that he was obliged to kill his

---

[1] William de Lacy was the ancestor of Pierce Lacy, of the county Limerick, celebrated as a rebel in the time of Queen Elizabeth, and also of the Lynches of Galway (see O'Donovan's edition of the *Annals of the Four Masters*, A.D. 1186 and 1233). William de Lacy, called Blundus or Le Blund in the Anglo-Norman records, is styled William Górm, or Blue William, in the *Book of Fenagh*, ed. Hennessy, pp. 73 and 77, where his wars and ravages in Breifny (Leitrim and Cavan), and death in 1233, are celebrated; with which agree the *Annals of Clonmacnois* (cf. "Breifny Letters," *Ordn. Surv. Corres.*, Roy. Irish Acad., p. 194). William de Lacy died of wounds received at the hands of the O'Reillys. The *Book of Fenagh* enters into details, and names three weeks as the period during which he lingered sick of his wounds.

[2] See *Royal Letters of Henry III.* (Rolls Series), t. i., pp. 306, 502; Sweetman's *Calendar*, t. i., p. 183.

horse, fling away his armour, and take refuge in a morass, where his Celtic blood and training stood him in good stead, helping him to escape from the heavy-armed Norman soldiery.[1] At O'Reilly's crannog the Celtic tribes seem to have taken the initiative in the assault. The O'Reillys were ever the bitterest foes of the De Lacys. Nine years later they were the cause of the death of William de Lacy, and now they are the first to take advantage of his weakness and of the Earl Marshall's invasion. They attacked the crannog which he had wrested from them, and with the help of a detachment of the earl's knights and soldiers, captured the wife of William de Lacy, his sister-in-law, and his aged mother, the Connaught princess Rose O'Conor, together with an illegitimate daughter of Llewellyn, the Prince of North Wales, who seems to have been then visiting her Celtic relations in Ireland, or had perhaps fled thither for safety from the hostility of her own father.[2] The Earl Marshall was not a mere soldier, however. He knew how to unite diplomacy to war,

---

[1] The Celtic population have ever availed themselves of the bogs as their surest defence. Even so lately as the rebellion of 1798 it was so. I remember hearing as a boy of an attack by a large party of insurgents upon a gentleman's residence in the county Roscommon. Two mounted soldiers were sent to defend it. They were heard riding up the avenue, and believed to be the advanced guard of a large party. The insurgent commander immediately gave the order, "To the bogs, boys!" upon which the whole party sought security where the mounted yeomanry could not follow them. The soubriquet, "To the bogs, boys!" stuck to the man and his descendants ever after.

[2] The language of the Earl Marshall in his despatch to King Henry III. (*Royal Letters*, t. i., p. 502) is: "In dicto castro fuerunt uxor Willelmi de Lascy, filia Leulini soror Griffini de patre et matre." From Matthew Paris, *Historia Anglorum*, iii., 280 (Rolls Series), we learn that Llewellyn had two sons,

and was quick to avail himself of the advantages which the fortune of battle had placed in his hands. A new element of strife had lately entered into that seething devil's cauldron of violence and confusion which Ireland then was. The old King of Connaught, Cathal Crovderg, or Cathal of the Red Hand,[1] had died on May 27th of this very year 1224, as the chroniclers put it, "after triumphing over the world and the devil in the Abbey of Knockmoy, where he had assumed a monk's habit,"—that being the usual device of the age to secure heaven after a life of violence and crime.[2] Cathal of the Red Hand had been on the whole a true friend and ally of the Anglo-Norman sovereigns, who had in turn treated him honourably and supported him with vigour. His son and successor, Hugh O'Conor, seems, however, to have been inclined to

---

Griffin, illegitimate, and David, legitimate. In 1223 Hugh de Lacy joined with Llewellyn in a Welsh war against Henry III. and Earl Marshall. Cf. Matthew Paris, *Chronica Majora*, t. iii., p. 82, and the Welsh chronicle, *Brut-y-Tywysogion, passim.*

[1] Dr. O'Donovan has given us the explanation of this title in an interesting note in his edition of the *Annals of the Four Masters*, A.D. 1224. He gathered it from the traditions of the farmers and story-tellers in the counties of Galway and Mayo more than half a century ago. I must, however, refer the curious student to the note for further information, as the story will scarcely bear repetition in a book designed for general reading.

[2] The following extract from the Welsh chronicle *Brut-y-Tywysogion*, p. 327, about that double-dyed and blood-stained villain Llewellyn, Prince of North Wales, will show that the religious notions of Wales were no better than those of Ireland:—"A.D. 1240, Llywelyn, son of Jorwerth, Prince of Wales, died,—the man whose good works it would be difficult to enumerate, and was buried at Aberconway after taking the habit of religion. And after him David, his son by Joan, daughter of King John, reigned." A glance at the index of the work just quoted will show the character of his good works. He was excommunicated, immoral, a rebel, a treacherous and inhuman murderer.

a different course; and we cannot wonder at it. The traditions of his family told him that they had once reigned supreme over the whole country. He now saw the conquerors fatally divided among themselves, and the most active and vigorous of them bitterly hostile to the English sovereign. The ties of blood, too, ever powerful among the Celts, summoned him to the battle-field. The De Lacys were his own first cousins, and he had thus the double opportunity of aiding his own kith and kin and striking a blow in defence of his own ancient family rights and authority. Earl Marshall, however, availed himself of the capture of his aunt in O'Reilly's crannog, to compel the King of Connaught to follow his father's footsteps and remain an obedient subject of the English king; and thus it is that we find him writing in the despatch from which I have quoted, " Within fifteen days the mother of William, of Thomas, and of Henry de Lacy, will be a prisoner unless her nephew the King of Connaught return to the king's peace through her."

The justiciary's action seems to have been successful for a time. The entreaties of the elder Hugh de Lacy's aged widow weighed with King Hugh, and he united his forces with the earl's in the course of the autumn. The De Lacys' cause had now become hopeless in Meath. The King of Connaught was not the only Irish prince who assembled his forces to the assistance of the Earl Marshall. O'Brian, King of Munster, MacCarthy, Prince of Desmond, and many others, joined the royal army as soon as they saw which was the winning cause. Nothing succeeds, or ever has succeeded, in Ireland so well as success. Hugh de Lacy, Earl of Ulster, now fell back into his own dominions. He invoked the assistance of the O'Neills, ever hostile to the southern Irish, which was at once granted, and the combined forces took up a formidable position in what was called the Fews of Dundalk, a district which down to the wars of 1690 has often proved an effectual bar to the course of English conquest.[1] It is even still a wild though beautiful region. Slieve Gullion, its central mountain, situated midway between Newry and Dundalk, rises to the height of some two thousand feet, offering from its summit splendid views in every direction, and flinging off ranges of lofty hills, terminating on one side at the precipitous peak of Carlingford Mountain, well known to mariners as a conspicuous landmark, and extending in the north-westerly direction towards the city of Armagh. The Fews have been, as I have said, down to modern times a difficult country to invade. De Ginkle in 1690 had hard work to fight his way through it. About 1794 the same district was marked by a series of outrages and massacres in the parish of Forkhill, which led, in 1795, to a well-known incident called the Battle of the Diamond, between the Roman Catholics of the Fews and the Protestants of the north of the county Armagh. That fierce party fight originated, by way of reaction, the Orange Society, and largely contributed to impart the

---

[1] It may naturally be asked how could the O'Neills, Kings of Ulster, assist Hugh de Courcy, who claimed to be earl and palatine lord of Ulster. O'Donovan's note on the *Annals of the Four Masters*, A.D. 1173, explains the difficulty. Ulster has been since the fifth century the proper designation of Down and Antrim, which alone formed De Courcy's principality. The descendants of Niall of the Nine Hostages seized in the fifth century upon the western and northern portions of what we call Ulster, Donegal, Tyrone, Armagh, etc. The writers of Irish history call Down and Antrim Ulidia, while they apply the term Ultonia to the country of the O'Neills. The dominions of De Courcy and O'Neill did not interfere, therefore, the one with the other.

sectarian aspect which the rebellion of 1798 quickly assumed. As it has been down to our own times, so it was in the days of Henry III. and in the year 1224. The Fews of Dundalk and the Slieve Gullion range were then the southern barrier of Ulster, and of the dominions of the O'Neills and of the Earl of Ulster alike; and within its morasses, woods, and passes the combined forces of the Celtic and Anglo-Norman rebels entrenched themselves some time about the month of October 1224, when the rains of late autumn were rapidly helping to render the whole country impassable.[1] The Earl Marshall, with his southern allies, viewed the position, realized that it was an inaccessible one for Anglo-Norman soldiers, and therefore, like a wise man, made the best terms he could with the Earl of Ulster. O'Neill and De Lacy entered into a treaty without any confession of ill-doing or recognition of defeat. They declined to give any hostages, and simply made peace, reserving for future settlement with the king the terms on which they would consent to render allegiance and tribute to the Crown. Why need we pursue the story any further? The course of Hugh de Lacy's fortunes pursued henceforth the historic road ever followed by such careers in Ireland. The successful rebel became the king's bosom friend, his most trusted counsellor.

---

[1] See for a description of this pass between Dundalk and Newry in 1586, Marshal Bagenal's description of Ulster in *Ulster Journal of Archæology*, t. ii., pp. 150, 151 (cf. t. vi., p. 153), and Stuart's *History of Armagh*, 290-93. What it was in Queen Elizabeth's time such it was in the reign of Henry III., and for long after. In fact it is still a wild region. Twenty-five years ago, when voters were to be spirited away at contested elections in Newry, Dundalk, or Armagh, they were always taken to the Fews. Many a dubious Newry voter found himself, after a night's debauch, safe next morning among the spurs of Slieve Gullion.

In two years' time all his lands, castles, and dignities were restored to him. He had new grants of fairs and markets throughout his wide dominions, till at last, ten years after his rebellion, he stood by the king's side in opposition to his former conqueror's own brother, Richard, Earl Marshall; and then, after Marshall's defeat and death, was summoned into England as the king's wisest guide amid the tangled skein of Irish politics.[1] To understand, however, this latter portion of our story, and to perceive how curiously similar to modern Irish politics of the parliamentary kind were the more bloody sort of six centuries ago, I must now set before you in some detail the history of the great Marshall family, whose head was Earl Mareschal of England, of Pembroke, of Striguil, and of Leinster.

The Marshall family of the time of Henry III. had furnished for more than a century men of light and leading in England.[2] In the time of Henry I., and at the beginning of the twelfth century, we first find mention of them. The head of the family, Gilbert Marshall, was then impleaded in an action at law, and compelled to defend his claim to the great office of Earl Mareschal, whence his family subsequently derived their name. His son, John Marshall, succeeded him in his office, and after taking his due share in the civil turmoils of Stephen's troubled reign,[3] supported Henry II. in his great struggle against Thomas à Becket. John

---

[1] For the authorities as to these statements see Sweetman's *Calendar*, t. i., Nos. 1,498, 1,505, 1,544, 2,113, 2,285, 2,384; *Royal Letters of Henry III.*, t. i., pp. 437, 478.

[2] In spelling the name of this family I usually follow Mr. Sweetman's example and adopt the modern form of the word, viz., Marshall. Sir F. Madden in his edition of the *Historia Anglorum* spells it Mareschal.

[3] See *Chronicles* of Stephen, etc. (Rolls Series), t. iii., pp. 66, 67.

Marshall's son was the great hero of the family, and carried its glory to the highest point. It is but simple truth to say that during thirty years, from 1190 to 1220, the Great Earl, William Marshall, was the foremost figure in England and in English history next to the sovereigns themselves. He was the tried friend, the wisest, truest counsellor, of Richard I., of King John, and the guardian of the tender years of John's son, Henry III. William Marshall's life was a chequered one all the same. He was a member of what we might call the Young England party under Henry II. He was a young noble of great ability and great power. He chafed under the strong rule of Henry II., and sympathised with the king's sons in their opposition to their father. William Marshall took up arms as one of Prince Henry's partisans in 1173, adhered to him amid his various fortunes, and finally received the cross from his hands as he lay a-dying, a rebel against his father, June 11th, 1183.[1] Age and advancing years soon, however, exercised a chastening influence upon William Marshall. He laid aside the follies of youth. He eschewed the younger nobility and their designs, embraced the service of King Henry II., was trusted by him on some delicate missions, appointed to the earldom, and married by him to his young and richly-endowed ward, Isabella, daughter of Strongbow and Eva, and heir to all the vast possessions which Strongbow had gained by his marriage with the great Irish heiress of Dermot MacMurrough. William Marshall henceforth was the right-hand man and most trusty servant of the sovereign for the time being. He supported King John with all his vast influence in

---

[1] Hoveden's *Chron.*, ii., 279.

England and in Ireland against the pope and against the king's own rebellious vassals. William Marshall proved himself true at the greatest crisis of all, when King John, dying, left as his heir a young and helpless boy, with a French prince and army in possession of a good half of the kingdom. Marshall put aside all ambitious thoughts so far as he was himself concerned, took the young Henry III., placed him in the midst of the faithful barons, and made them swear allegiance to the child. Thenceforward, during the three or four years of life which remained, the great earl was the guide, tutor, and prime minister of the king; and when death claimed him as its own on May 16th, 1219, he confided the task of educating the king and watching over the interests of his country to his eldest son and namesake, William Marshall the younger. The chronicler Matthew Paris well expresses the universal feeling of loss and dismay at his departure in the few dignified words wherein he speaks of him as "one who, having been supreme governour of both the king and the kingdom, was justly called the Great on account of his magnanimity;" and then records the epitaph set up above his tomb in the Temple Church—

> "Sum quem Saturnum sibi sensit Hibernia, Solem
> Anglia, Mercurium Normannia, Gallia martem."

William Marshall the younger at once took up the reins of government which had fallen from his father's hands. In his earlier days he had followed his father's youthful example. He, too, had joined the Young England party of opposition. It would seem as if the earlier days of the thirteenth century were very like the times of Catiline of old, or those in which we now are living. The younger nobles generally flung in their lot with the opposition, only to become in their maturer years the strongest supporters of constituted authority. The younger Marshall supported Prince Louis, the French invaders, and the rebellious barons, just as his own father had allied himself with the sons of Henry II. in their treasonable designs. Recalled, however, to a sense of his duty by the old earl, his son proved himself the faithful minister of Henry III. He vigorously maintained the royal cause in France, on the Welsh border against Llewellyn, Prince of Wales; and, as I have already shown, was the only general to whom warlike operations could be entrusted when Hugh de Lacy strove to wrest Ireland from the feeble hands of the young king. An untimely death, however, overtook him also. He died in April 1231, without offspring, leaving his vast estates in England and Ireland to his brother, Richard Marshall. And now the troubles with the Marshall family began. King Henry had come to man's estate, and seems to have been disposed to resent the state of tutelage in which the Marshalls had kept him. He was intensely weak, and instead of feeling grateful for faithful service was keen to lend a ready ear to every sinister suggestion which interested flatterers were only too willing to pour into his mind. The young king had, in addition, yielded himself completely into the hands of Poitevin favourites headed by Peter des Roches, Bishop of Winchester. Against this fatal course Earl Richard Marshall protested as a true Englishman, in a spirit and tone worthy of his great father, the old earl. Matthew Paris, in his *Historia Anglorum*, tells us of the angry and insulting reply of the bishop to the earl's remonstrance. The bishop declared in the royal name, that the king would select any foreigners he pleased to defend his crown and kingdom, and that these foreign friends would know how to compel rebellious barons to do their duty.[1] Hence arose what is called the War of Kildare. Earl Richard and his friends at once withdrew from the Court and retired to his castles on the Welsh frontier, where he made an alliance with Prince Llewellyn, ever ready to engage in war against the English sovereign, and to utilise every malcontent who could assist him. The king and his Poitevin and Breton favourites met that move by a declaration of the forfeiture of Marshall's estates and their division among the foreigners. The year 1233 was marked by active operations along the Welsh border. The king marched from Worcester against the earl and his allies. The fortune of war was, as usual, somewhat diversified, but, on the whole, it went against the king and in favour of Earl Richard and the patriotic party. In the beginning of the next year, 1234, Henry III., changing his purpose after his manner, determined to dismiss his foreign advisers, and accordingly sent ambassadors to make peace with Earl Richard. Before their arrival, however, Earl Richard had passed over to Ireland, invited thither by false friends who, in union with the Bishop of Winchester, were compassing his destruction; foremost among whom was the earl's trusted friend and confidant Geoffrey de Marisco, the nephew of Archbishop John Comyn.

Geoffrey de Marisco, or Geoffrey Marsh, as we might modernise the name, had often been chief ruler of Ireland, was well skilled in all the arts of guile and statecraft, and thought he saw a chance open to

---

[1] Matthew Paris, *Hist. Anglor.*, ii., 354 (Rolls Series).

him of gaining a share in the spoil which the confiscation of the Marshall estates would produce. Marisco, though deep in the earl's confidences, was, indeed, all the while in secret league with Maurice Fitz-Gerald the justiciary, Hugh de Lacy, and Richard de Burgh, the bitter enemies of Richard Marshall. With their aid he concerted a plan to entice the earl to his destruction. To prevent Earl Richard making peace with the king, he sent messengers to the earl, telling him that the nobles of Ireland were plundering his lands by royal command; this led the earl to Ireland boiling with rage. Then, to secure the co-operation of the Irish barons, he, with the help of Peter des Roches, forged royal letters ordering the king's Irish vassals to arrest the earl for his treason, which letters Geoffrey de Marisco took good care the earl should behold as soon as he arrived in Ireland. Richard Marshall landed in Ireland in the February of 1234, accompanied by fifteen knights alone, trusting in the goodness of his cause, and in the resources of his Irish estates to furnish him with abundant help. He had, however, the most dangerous of enemies in Geoffrey de Marisco. He was most dangerous because he was a false friend, ever luring the earl on to destruction by counsel like that which Hushai the Archite gave to Absalom. Earl Marshall, when he arrived, found Maurice Fitz-Gerald the justiciary, Hugh de Lacy, Earl of Ulster, and Richard de Burgh arrayed against him, plundering his lands and capturing his castles. He wished to enter into negotiations with them; but De Marisco was at hand to stir up strife. "Why do you hesitate, or what do you fear?" was his artful suggestion. "We will not believe that you are the son of the victorious William, the old Marshal, who never once turned his back on his foes." Then, touching upon his family claims, he continued, "Lo! victory is at your doors. Consider, too, thy hereditary rights derived to thee from thy grandfather Strongbow, and show thyself not unworthy of them." Roused by this speech, he flung himself into the work of military preparations, and speedily gathering an army captured Limerick after a brief siege, and then, returning towards Dublin, recovered many of his castles which had fallen into the hands of the conspirators, who fled in every direction before him. They retired, indeed; but it was only to plot the earl's destruction the more securely. Hugh de Lacy and his friends first of all collected from every quarter the bravest and most powerful soldiers, English and Irish alike, to the number of one hundred and sixty knights and two thousand infantry. Then they sent the Templars to the Earl Marshall, demanding a truce. The Templars declared that they were the official military custodians of Ireland, and that they desired to consult the king, whether they should defend the country by force or quietly surrender it into the earl's hands. To these words of the Templars, Earl Richard made a dignified reply, which sheds much light upon the mediæval theory of feudal relationships between the Crown and the nobility. The Templars had accused him of treasonable practices against the sovereign; to which accusation the earl responded that he had in nowise acted treasonably against the sovereign, because the king had deprived him of his office of Earl Marshal and of his estates without the judgment of his peers, though he was always prepared to submit to it. "Whence," continued the earl, "I am no longer his man, but have been lawfully absolved from allegiance to him, not by myself, but by himself;"—showing us that Henry III. was simply regarded by his nobles as *primus inter pares*, and that the allegiance due to him was regarded as a conditional bond terminable, like a treaty between independent nations, upon any violation of its terms. The difference between the position of the nobility under Henry VIII. and under Henry III. can best be measured by this simple reply. If one of the great Tudor nobles rebelled, Henry VIII. entered into no treaty and accepted no excuse, but simply cut the rebel's head off. If one of the earlier Henry's vassals rebelled, he justified himself by the king's own conduct, and the king himself regarded the rebel as acting strictly within his legal rights. It is evident that the theory in vogue still taught that the sovereign was *Rex Anglorum* but not *Rex Angliæ*, and that the great nobles viewed themselves as subsidiary kings, clad with equal sovereign rights and privileges. The relation, indeed, between the kings of England and their great feudatories was scarcely different from that which existed between the kings of Tara and the subordinate princes of Ireland; and the king of Tara thought never a whit worse, but perhaps rather the better, of any of his subordinates who gave him the chance of a fight by declaring war against him. When the quarrel was fought out they were all the better friends afterwards, and so it was in England in the days of Henry III.

After Earl Marshall had thus cleared his own conduct, he dismissed the Templars, inviting Hugh de Lacy and his friends to a conference touching the conditions of the truce which they desired, and appointing a meeting for the next day upon the Curragh of Kildare. He then retired to consult with his friends. The earl was himself most anxious to agree to the terms proposed and grant a truce, but Geoffrey de Marisco again stepped forward with his treacherous suggestions. He reminded Marshall of the injuries he and his estate had suffered at the hands of his opponents, and pointed out that the possession of all Ireland lay within his grasp. It was the great object of De Marisco to lead the earl on to a fight, knowing right well not only that his adversaries were superior in numbers, but also that a large number of the earl's own followers would desert him in the fray. All the efforts of this wily and treacherous counsellor were therefore directed to the one end of rendering a compromise impossible. Earl Richard was again entrapped. Next day, April 1st, 1234, he advanced to the Curragh, followed by an army, every member of which—fifteen knights alone excepted, whom he had originally brought with him from England—was in the pay of his opponents; while Hugh de Lacy, Maurice Fitz-Gerald, and Richard de Burgh came to meet him from the opposite direction with one hundred and forty knights, gathered from every part of Ireland, and all thirsting for the rich spoils of the great house of Marshall. The colloquy which ensued was not very long. The allies demanded a truce. Marshall, acting on the counsel of De Marisco the night before, refused to grant one till De Lacy and his friends had surrendered his castles which they had seized. Thereupon Hugh de Lacy declared that there and then they would stake everything upon the issue of battle. Then it was that the earl perceived the toils amid which he was enclosed. The false and perjured Geoffrey now stepped forward when retreat was impossible, and, contrary to his own words the night before, proposed to the earl to accede to the demands of Hugh de Lacy; "for," said he, "my wife is sister of that great man Hugh de Lacy; wherefore I cannot follow thee into the battle as thy confederate "—a statement which first opened the eyes of the earl to the infamous plot against him. The words of the chronicler, Matthew Paris, as he dwells on the details of the scene, are very striking, and even picturesque. The treachery of De Marisco flashed at once upon the earl. To him, therefore, he thus addressed himself: "Wicked traitor, did I not just now refuse them a treaty by thy advice? It would be the part of a fickle man to grant that which I have just refused, and specially because I would then seem to do it from fear rather than affection. I know, I know that I have been this day betrayed to death, but it is better to die with honour for the sake of justice than to flee from the fight, and thus incur the reproach of cowardice." Then viewing his brother Walter riding after him, he ordered him to be sent back to his nearest castle, committing himself to the fortune of war. Matthew Paris enters at great length into the details of the fight, which seems to have largely centred round the person of the earl. He was a mighty warrior, and the conspirators feared to risk their own lives in a conflict with him. They left the battle with him entirely in the hands of mercenaries, whom they encouraged by the hope of large rewards. The fight was a long and tedious one, that first of April. It commenced very early in the morning, about five o'clock, and continued to rage till eleven. Followed by a few faithful friends, the earl wrought wonders. Before he joined battle he reminded his forces that he had taken up arms for the sake of justice, for the laws of the English people, and for the expulsion of the Poitevin and Breton favourites who were ruining the land : words which show that this Irish quarrel, so typical of many another, was fought upon English issues alone. Then he flung himself into the contest, supported merely by the faithful fifteen, while the traitorous remainder sought shelter in the neighbouring abbeys and churches. The battle was a prolonged one, but the result was not doubtful. Fifteen against one hundred and forty were odds too heavy for any band of heroes. A gigantic Irishman, most probably from Connaught, had been specially hired by Richard de Burgh to do battle with the earl, and for this purpose had been armed by him with his own armour. When the giant advanced to the combat Earl Richard thought from his insignia that he was Richard de Burgh, the nephew of his friend and ally, Hubert de Burgh, Earl of Kent. The earl did not wish to imbrue his hands in the blood of his friend's kinsman, but warned him off. "Fly, wicked traitor, lest I slay thee," said Marshall. "I will not fly," replied the giant, stretching forth his hands to pull the helmet off the earl's head; whereupon Marshall cut off both his hands with one blow of his sword. Another knight then rode forward to avenge his comrade; him the earl split in two from the head to the waist. A crowd of knights and soldiers now pressed round the earl on every side. His faithful steed was slain, and then, taking advantage of his position as he strove on foot to defend himself against overwhelming numbers, a foot soldier inserted a long Irish skene between the joints of his back armour, inflicting thereby a wound which rendered him helpless. The earl was carried captive to his own castle of Kilkenny, which Maurice Fitz-Gerald had captured a short time before. There he was detained and closely guarded. The strength of his constitution was such, however, that his wounds were rapidly healing, his appetite was restored, he was able to walk about his chamber, and even beguile the monotony of the sick-room by playing at dice. The recovery of Marshall was, however, the last thing the conspirators desired. They introduced a surgeon, therefore, who proceeded to cauterize his wounds in the rude method of those times. He plunged the hot iron so deep into his body that an acute fever rapidly ensued, of which the earl died on April 16th, and was immediately buried in the chapel of the Franciscans in his own town of Kilkenny.

Thus ended the war of Kildare. It was but an episode in the long struggle which went on between the barons and Henry III., and as such can only be fully understood in connection with the wider history of England. It is interesting for us, however, as showing how Irish conspirators could ally themselves for selfish purposes with foreign favourites whom all England detested, while the genuine patriot perished under the forms of law utilised by these conspirators and favourites for their own purposes. These Irish nobles —Anglo-Normans though they were—cared nothing and consulted nothing for the interests of England or of Ireland either.[1] They regarded not, as in De Burgh's

---

[1] These wars of Meath and Kildare seem to have taught the English government the importance of the Irish commercial towns. Well would it have been for this country had more attention been paid to their development; in that case many of our modern difficulties would have long since vanished. Henry III. with the help of the seaports established an Irish fleet between 1233 and 1241; Dublin and Waterford each provided two galleys, Cork, Limerick, and Drogheda one each. In 1252 the principal towns of Ireland formed a kind of Hanseatic league for mutual defence Representatives from

case, the interests even of their own kith and kin. They thought of nothing but the rich plunder of Strongbow's and Dermot MacMurrough's heir which lay within their grasp, and for the sake of that plunder Hugh de Lacy, Earl of Ulster, Maurice Fitz-Gerald the justiciary, and Geoffrey de Marisco, now an old and hoary-headed sinner, were willing to sacrifice truth and justice, the happiness and welfare of England and of Ireland alike. Can we wonder that Ireland did not prosper and that English rule did not flourish when administered by men so utterly selfish, so miserably short-sighted, so flagrantly treacherous and unjust?[1] It is with a genuine feeling of satisfaction and a sense of poetic justice, for once manifested in

---

Dublin, Drogheda, Limerick, Cork, Waterford, etc., agreed to meet at Kilkenny every three years. See Gilbert's *Municipal Documents*, pp. 100, 130. The dangers to which the commercial life of Ireland was exposed in the thirteenth century are clearly set forth in the Norman-French poem on the walling of the town of Ross or New Ross, in Wexford, which is very interesting, not only for the social life of the period, the occupations and trade organizations of a provincial Irish seaport, but also as showing the destructive influence on trade and commerce exercised by the early quarrels between the Geraldines and the Butlers. See the poem as printed in Gilbert's *Account of Facsimiles*, part iii., pp. 98-101.

[1] The original authorities for the story of this war of Kildare are Matthew Paris, *Chronica Majora*, t. iii., pp. 265-90; *Historia Anglorum*, t. ii., pp. 367-70; Roger of Wendover, *Chronica*, t. iii., pp. 72-86; Rymer's *Fœdera*, t. i., p. 213. The Irish *Annals* of the Four Masters, of Clonmacnois and of Lough Cé, all notice this war of Kildare. See also Gilbert's *Viceroys*, pp. 510-12. Mr. Gilbert, on p. 516 (cf. Richey's *Short History of the Irish People*, ed. Kane, p. 169), tells the strange story of the disappearance of the Marshall family. Isabel, granddaughter of Dermot MacMurrough, died in 1220, and was buried in Tintern in Wales. She is said to have predicted the extinction of her family in the male line, which happened in 1245, when her fifth and last son Anselm died without a son. The principality of Leinster with its great estates was

this life, that we read in the pages of Matthew Paris [1] that Geoffrey Marsh reaped nothing from his treachery, but died eleven years afterwards an outcast, a pauper, and an exile; a speaking and necessary example for his age, and for every age, that the ways of falsehood and wrong are not always the ways of success, but that in this imperfect world of ours the deeds of the evil-doer and the traitor are sometimes amply recompensed into their own bosoms.

---

then divided between Anselm's five sisters as follows. Matilda obtained Carlow, Jeanne or Joan Wexford, Isabella Kilkenny, Sibilla Kildare, Eva Dunamease and the territory of Leix, now called the Queen's County.

[1] *Hist. Anglor.*, ii., 494, 509.

LECTURE XIII.

TWO CENTURIES OF ANARCHY.

I PROPOSE in the present lecture and the next to take a rapid survey of the history of Ireland from the reign of Henry III. to the accession of Henry VII. I regard the triumph of the House of Tudor, represented by Henry VII., as marking the opening of the modern period of Ireland's history. I terminate my survey at that epoch, therefore, because the story of the manifold and stirring incidents of the sixteenth century, including the Reformation and its results, will require a far more minute study than we can now hope to bestow upon it. At some future time I hope to take up the history of Ireland during the sixteenth century. I shall then have to begin with the dawnings of the Reformation in Ireland, and shall be obliged to discuss its religious state in the period immediately preceding the Reformation in a more thorough manner than I can hope to do in the present course of lectures. And we shall have abundance of material for the purpose. The manuscript resources of Ussher's Library, preserved among the muniments of this University; the precious treasures of the Irish Record Office, never yet sufficiently utilised for this purpose; the manuscripts of Marsh's Library, and the various other collections in this city to which I have often referred, will abundantly help us in tracing the history of a period which has hitherto been only the chosen battlefield of rival controversialists. If ever I am enabled to deal with it, I hope to avoid the controversial attitude as much as possible, and shall strive to treat it impartially from the historian's standpoint alone; for undoubtedly controversy saps the springs of impartiality, and gives an unconscious bent to even the fairest mind.

There are two ways, very different the one from the other, which I might adopt in discussing the period of Ireland's history now under consideration. I might patiently follow out the details of rebellions, frays, and forays as given in the various authorities, English and Irish. These authorities—contemporary authorities, too—are numerous enough, so numerous, indeed, that one feels somewhat overweighted with the mass of material. Quite apart from the *Annals of the Four Masters*, which were compiled in the seventeenth century, out of much more ancient documents, we have on the Celtic side authorities, like the *Book of Fenagh*, written about A.D. 1300, the *Annals of Lough Cé*, the *Annals* of Dudley MacFirbis in the Irish Archæological Series, and the numerous other collections of annals, the origin and value of which Mr. O'Curry discusses in his lectures. Upon the English side we have the *Annals* of Friar Clyn, of Thady Dowling, Chancellor of Leighlin, and other fragments in the Irish Archæological Series, together with those of Pembridge and Henry of Marleburgh in Camden's *Britannia*. Perhaps, indeed, the best way to enable you to realize how copious are our resources, will be to refer you to Mr. Gilbert's *Fac-similes of the National MSS. of Ireland.* He has published a letterpress description of them; if you will turn to the Table, at the close of Part III., you will see that we want no kind of literature, poetical, romantic, or historical, to enable us to form a just estimate of these troublous ages. When we have added to them Rymer's *Fœdera*, Prynne's *Records*, Sweetman's *Calendars*, the various legal records printed by the Treasury, Mr. Gilbert's *Chartularies* and *Municipal Documents* in the Rolls Series, we shall feel ourselves embarrassed by the very abundance of the historical wealth set before us.

This fact has its own drawbacks, however. It seems to me that the reputation for dulness which Irish history has hitherto enjoyed, has largely arisen from the fact that conscientious workers like Leland have been bewildered in the thicket of details with which they found themselves surrounded. They have done their best to portray them, and have necessarily failed to interest their readers, while all the time they seldom tried to co-ordinate the history of Ireland with that of England, and thus arrive at the true solution of England's failure in this country. Just let me give you a few specimens of the *Annals*, from Celt and Anglo-Norman alike, and then you can easily judge of the difficulty of our task. I take first an extract from the Four Masters' account of the year 1250:—"In this year Felim O'Conor came from the north with a numerous force out of Tyrone.; he marched into Breifny, and thence into the Tuathas,[1] accompanied by Conor, son of Tiernan O'Conor, thence

---

[1] The Tuathas, or Districts, were an ancient Irish division in the east of the county Roscommon, which for the last three centuries has formed the rural deanery now called Tarmonbarry. It extended from the northern point of Lough Ree to Jamestown on the Shannon, thence to Elphin, including Strokestown, and thence again to Lough Ree. See O'Donovan's note, *Annals of Four Masters*, A.D. 1189; and the map prefixed to the *Tribes and Customs of Hy-Many*, Irish Archæological Society, 1843.

into Hy-Many, and they expelled Turlough out of Connaught, who again went over to the English. Felim then collected all the movable property of Connaught, and proceeded with it across the Curlieu Mountains, but the English sent messengers after him, and a peace being concluded between them, his kingdom was again restored to him. The hostages of Connaught were blinded by the English at Athlone. A great depredation was committed by Felim on Cathal O'Conor, and the latter was driven out of Connaught. A great army was led by Maurice Fitz-Gerald, Cathal O'Reilly, and other chiefs into Tyrone, and remained three nights at Tullyhoge, where they sustained much injury and hardship, but obtained no pledges or hostages from the O'Neills on this expedition. Florence MacCarthy was slain by the English of Desmond." This entry deals principally with the west and north-west. A century later the Anglo-Norman Franciscan friar, John Clyn, of Kilkenny, has just the same story to tell of the south-east. Thus, we read under the year 1345 in Clyn's *Annals*[1]: "About Easter there died Lord Maurice Fitz-Gerald and Gerald de Rocheford. Also the Powers burned, destroyed, and spoiled the whole country round Waterford, on which account certain of them were hanged, drawn, and quartered at Waterford.[2] On the Feast of the Baptist, Maurice, Count of Desmond, attacked the Castle of Menaht with a large army, but failed to capture it. There

---

[1] Irish Archæological Society, Dublin, 1849. p. 31.
[2] The Powers were an Anglo-Norman family named Poer, who after Strongbow's invasion dispossessed the O'Flanagans, the original Celts, in the barony of Upperthird, in the north-west of the co. Waterford. Two centuries had completely assimilated them to their ancient foes. See *Irish Topographical Poems*, ed. O'Donovan, notes, p. lxiii.

was war between Ralph de Ufford, Justiciary of Ireland, and Maurice Fitz-Thomas, Count of Desmond, and the justiciary deprived him of his estates, viz., Clonmel, Kerry, and Desmond, confiscating all his property for the king's use; and seized the Castle of Iniskysty, in Kerry, which was commonly reputed impregnable. Turlough O'Conor was slain by an arrow among his own people. Also, on Innocents' Day, the Irish of Slieve Bloom burned Bordwell and slew Robert Grace and other Englishmen, and on the same day Carvill MacGilpatrick, the prince of his country, is slain."

Again let us advance a century farther, and take the record of the learned Chancellor of Leighlin, Thady Dowling. Writing concerning 1462, he tells us "Thomas Fitz-John, of the Geraldines, died. He at first burdened the counties of Waterford, Cork, Kerry, and Limerick with Irish exactions. Others say that, on account of these exactions and outrages against the king's peace and the laws of Ireland, he was beheaded in Drogheda by the Viceroy and the Earl of Worcester. Thomas Fitz-John usurping upon his father and going to Drogheda, the latter gave him his curse, and said, 'Thou shalt have an ill end.'"

You can easily see that a lecture composed of details like these would be utterly devoid of life or interest. It would be as impossible to weld them into a continuous story, and as useless if possible, as it would be to compose history out of the details of backwoods warfare, or, to come nearer home, out of the wearisome story of Kerry moonlight outrages, to which the judges of the Parnell Commission have been doomed to listen. This method of writing the history of our period I shall steadily avoid, substituting for it what seems a more rational plan. I shall follow the main lines of historical development, tracing Irish troubles up to their true sources in English political and national quarrels, striving to co-ordinate the history of the two countries, and dwelling specially on certain leading events which mark the three centuries with which we deal. First, then, let us strive to gain a general notion of English history during this period. It may be divided into two great sections: from 1250 to 1400 forms one section, marked by external wars; from 1400 to 1500 forms another, marked by internal wars. During the century and a half from 1250 to 1400, the attention of the English sovereign, Parliament, and people, was fixed on the French war and on the wars with Scotland and Wales. Ireland during that period was simply looked upon as a good recruiting ground for soldiers and a very bad source of revenue. The thought of English statesmen was concentrated on two objects: defence of their continental dominions, and the internal unification of their own island of Great Britain. During the second period, comprising broadly the whole fifteenth century, the attention of England was centred at first upon the war with France, and then upon the Wars of the Roses, the struggle between the rival houses of York and Lancaster, which so largely modified the life of English society, and exercised influences traceable in our modern political divisions. These great movements —the Welsh, Scottish, and French wars, and the struggle of Yorkists with Lancastrians—were the real sources whence flowed Irish misrule and confusion.

Let us now begin with the time of Henry III. The long reign of that monarch was marked in England by perpetual struggles between the Crown and the barons, leading up to the development of parliamentary institutions, which took their final shape in England

and Ireland alike in the last quarter of the thirteenth century—that is, between the years 1275 and 1300. During the long and weak reign of Henry III. Ireland was comparatively peaceful. Throughout the whole of this thirteenth century the supremacy of the English Crown was acknowledged all over Ireland, even to the remotest corners of the west. The kings and chieftains of the Celtic race were regarded as English feudatories; they were summoned to help their liege lord in his wars, their counsel and advice were accepted; their succession and local jurisdictions were, indeed, respected, but the English Crown claimed and exercised supreme authority over all persons and things, secular and ecclesiastical alike, in every part of Ireland. Of this we have quite sufficient evidence from the ecclesiastical side. From the very beginning of Anglo-Norman rule in this country, the Crown of England claimed the disposal of all ecclesiastical dignities, and specially of the bishoprics. This power we find the Crown exercising in every part of Ireland, even in those counted the most Celtic. The four great archiepiscopal sees of Armagh, Dublin, Cashel, and Tuam, were of course always filled by the English sovereigns; but it si not till we actually inspect the documents which were issued on these occasions that we can realize how complete was Anglo-Norman supremacy in the time of King John and Henry III. Armagh was away in the neighbourhood of the O'Neills, the fiercest antagonists of the English in Ireland. The primacy fell vacant in 1203, but King John determines the occupant thereof as absolutely as if the see lay in Middlesex, and not in Ulster.[1] Tuam was away in the west of Connaught,

---

[1] Sweetman's *Calendar*, t. i., p. 31, No. 200. This may have happened in some measure, however, because the

at the very centre of the dominions of Phelim O'Conor, whose accession was duly notified to Henry III. in 1233,[1] and recognised by him. The archbishopric of Tuam fell vacant in 1235, whereupon the Dean and Chapter submissively report the vacancy, not to O'Conor, but to Henry III., and pray for the issue of a *congé d'élire;* and then King Henry, when granting the licence, directs them to choose a man able to rule the Church, faithful to the king, and useful to the kingdom.[2] But it was not merely the principal sees which the Crown thus claimed. The royal authority was omnipresent in Ireland. Killaloe is situated on the banks of the Shannon, and is even still, with all our railway system, a spot somewhat difficult of access. It was in the thirteenth century in the heart of the dominions claimed by the O'Briens, as it had been the favourite seat of their great ancestor, Brian Boru. The bishopric of Killaloe fell vacant in the last year of King John, and was filled up by him with a prelate rejoicing in the very English name of Robert Travers.[3] Kilmore, again, was in those times generally called Tirbrun. It was an ancient episcopal seat in the very

---

primate's principal residence was at or near Drogheda. The primates have lived at Armagh only since the last century. The pre-Reformation primates, and the post-Reformation primates, too, till a modern period, lived at the Castle of Termonfeckin, near Drogheda, and used St. Peter's Church in Drogheda as their Cathedral. See numerous proofs of this in a volume of Dudley Loftus' MSS. in Marsh's Library, styled *Precedents of Armagh*, being extracts from the fourteenth and fifteenth century registers of Armagh. Cotton, in his *Fasti*, notes that a pre-Reformation primate speaks with great contempt of the dean and chapter of Armagh as mere Irishmen, living, after the Irish fashion, "inter Hibernicos."

[1] Sweetman, *l.c.*, No. 2,114.
[2] Id., No. 2,296.
[3] Id., No. 738. Cf. Ware's *Bishops*, ed. Harris, p. 591.

midst of O'Reilly's country, but still, when there was an episcopal vacancy in 1250, the Chapter duly signified this fact to Henry III. by Patrick, their clerk, and received back from that monarch the necessary royal licence to proceed in the matter of their election.[1] The royal supremacy was better recognised in 1250 in the county Cavan than it was three centuries and a half later, when Queen Elizabeth was unable to fill the see of Kilmore during the last fourteen years of her reign, owing to the wars prevalent in that district.[2]

But there is no necessity for me to weary you with more details on this matter. A glance into Sweetman's *Calendar* will amply prove my contention, and show that no part of Ireland was exempt from the supreme dominion claimed by the English sovereigns. The most distant parts of Kerry, as Ardfert;[3] the wildest districts of Connaught, as Annaghdown, on Lough Corrib, in Galway; and Elphin, in Roscommon—all were as obedient in ecclesiastical matters to the royal licence

---

[1] Sweetman, *l.c.*, Nos. 3,046-47. Cf. Ware's *Bishops*, ed. Harris, pp. 226, 227.
[2] Mant's *Church History*, i., 284.
[3] The see of Ardfert and other distant Irish sees were often filled up by Englishmen, who soon grew tired of their episcopal duties in such wild regions, and resigned their sees, retiring upon English livings, where, like the returned colonial bishops of our own time, they acted as assistants to their English diocesans. The earliest instance of such resignation which I have noted is that of John, Bishop of Ardfert, a monk of St. Alban's, who died in 1245 (see Matthew Paris' *Hist. Anglor.*, ii., 398, 483, 511; iii., 274, 296). This abuse was flourishing till the Reformation. Two Irish bishops were in succession rectors of Laindon in Essex. John, Bishop of Ardfert, 1466-83, was the first. At his death James Hale, Bishop of Kildare, was appointed. They were both suffragans of the Bishop of London. James Hale was an English Franciscan friar. Ware's *Bishops*, ed. Harris, will supply many other examples.

as the great eastern ports of Dublin, Drogheda, and Waterford.

The English Crown exercised again, in conjunction with the Pope, the power of taxation all through the island. We have authentic records still existing which prove this. During the thirteenth century clergy and laity alike were frequently subjected to a tax called *Decimæ Saladinæ*, an impost which had its origin in the sensation experienced throughout Europe when the intelligence arrived that the Holy City had been captured by Saladin.[1] The laity soon escaped from their liability to pay this tax, but the Pope and king united to enforce it upon the clergy. This impost was the occasion of frequent taxations or enrolments of the value of the ecclesiastical livings of the Churches of England and Ireland, which have survived to our times. The kings of England soon learned to turn this ecclesiastical tax to their own purposes of statecraft. Edward I., son of Henry III., was a very strong sovereign, and, like most men of his type, did not at all relish the abstraction from his realms of large sums by papal officials. Sometimes, therefore, he seized the proceeds when they were collected. At other times he obtained a grant of these papal tithes for a long term of years by a little judicious pressure upon the Pope. By the year 1300 the taxation of the clergy was quite as much a source of royal as of papal revenue. In the year 1302 the Pope and the English Crown required money, and they both agreed to tax the Irish clergy. The Pope imposed the tax, and then, to ensure its collection, appointed the English sovereign its chief collector, granting him half the annual proceeds. A new taxation or enrolment was

---

[1] See Bishop Reeves' *Ecclesiastical Antiqq.*, Introd., p. 5.

made for that purpose, which was discovered in the year 1807 in the office of the Remembrancer of His Majesty's Exchequer at Westminster, whither it had been removed in the year 1323, nearly five hundred years before. These records were deposited in a leathern pouch, marked with the name "Hibernia," and there they had been consigned to oblivion. What an idea this simple incident gives you of the fixity, the continuity, of the English record system, and of the vast historical riches we may hope to gain from thence whenever that system is thoroughly explored! That taxation of 1302, thus providentially recovered, has become the basis of Dr. Reeves' great work called the *Ecclesiastical Antiquities of Down, Connor, and Dromore.* This taxation has within the last few years been published in a complete form in the series of *Calendars,* edited by Mr. Sweetman, to which I have so often referred; and it is useful for our special purpose, because it shows that the king's financial agents, Richard de Bereford, treasurer of Ireland, and William de Ryvere, canon of Sarum, exercised their powers in every part of the country, and collected taxes which were devoted to the support of Queen Margaret and the Prince of Wales as much as to the relief of the papal treasury in Clogher, in Tirbrun or O'Reilly's country, in Raphoe or O'Donnell's country, in Ardagh or O'Rourke's country, and even in the far distant diocese of Killala in the west of Mayo. These facts, which will be found set forth at greater length in the Introduction to the *Antiquities of Down and Connor* by Bishop Reeves, amply prove that about the year 1300 English dominion and authority were more widely respected in Ireland than they were two or even three centuries later.[1]

---

[1] See Dean Butler's notes to the treatise *De Concilio Hiber-*

Let us now take a rapid survey of the course of historical evolution in this country. Henry III. was weak and in continual conflict with his barons. He endeavoured, therefore, to throw the care of Ireland upon his eldest son. Ireland then played the same part, and served the same office, as Wales does now in the British Constitution. It was regarded as the natural inheritance and the birthright of the sovereign's eldest son; and, if Wales had not been so soon conquered, the sovereign's eldest son might still be called Lord of Ireland, and not Prince of Wales. Henry III. did not forget that his own father, the favourite son of Henry II., had been Lord of Ireland, and so we find that in 1249 Edward, the king's son, had a grant of the profits of Ireland, which, I fear, were not very large, to fortify Gascony,[1] and then in 1253 the same Prince Edward was appointed Lord of Ireland upon his marriage with the Infanta of Spain, all writs to run in the prince's name and his great seal to be formed after the model of the great seal of England.[2] Prince Edward, however, never seems to have cared for his Irish lordship, and we cannot wonder at his dislike. Gascony and France were far gayer and brighter places than Ireland, and it required a special mandate from the sovereign, ordering the prince to cross from Gascony in the year 1255, before he could drag himself to fulfil his Irish duties. A royal residence was, however, just as little fruitful of benefits for our distracted land in the days of Prince Edward as in those of his grandfather,

---

niæ, p. 25, in the *Irish Archæological Miscellany*, vol. i. Dublin, 1846.

[1] Sweetman's *Calend.*, t. i., Nos. 3,021, 3,022.

[2] Rymer's *Fœdera*, t. i., pp. 308, 327, 341 ; Leland's *History of Ireland*, t. i., p. 228. Dublin, 1773.

Prince John. Edward, like his grandfather, escaped to London, and then to France, as quickly as possible, leaving to justiciaries, as before, the care of his Irish dominions. Under these officials the development of Irish institutions followed closely upon the lines marked out in England. Ireland simply imitated England in such matters. Here now occurs one of the great landmarks of Irish history, upon which I would fain fix your attention.

The year 1295 saw the first really representative parliament in England, and Ireland soon followed suit. Ireland, at the close of the thirteenth century, was particularly happy in its viceroy, Sir John Wogan, to whom Edward I. entrusted the chief government of this island for a much longer period than was usual. Wogan came here in 1295, the very year when Parliament arrived at its full maturity in England. He surveyed the evils of the country and tried to find a remedy for them. For this purpose he summoned the first real Parliament which ever met in Ireland. It was modelled upon the English lines, and assembled about the year 1297. I say it was the first real parliament that met in Ireland; and yet you will often read of parliaments both in England and Ireland long before this period. They were not, however, parliaments in our sense of the word, meaning thereby representative assemblies. The parliaments prior to the year 1295, whether in England or Ireland, were merely meetings of the Great Council of the realm, where the great barons assembled to enact laws and give advice to the sovereign. The origin and growth of parliamentary institutions is, however, much too wide a subject to be discussed as part of a lecture; and there is the less necessity for doing so as Bishop Stubbs, in the sixteenth chapter of his *Constitutional*

History, and more succinctly in the introduction to his *Select Charters*, has treated the history of parliamentary development with a master's hand, tracing its course till it arrived at full maturity in the year 1295.[1]

Now let us fix our attention on Sir John Wogan's parliament of 1296 or 1297, the first really representative assembly which Ireland ever saw. We learn from its records, derived from the Black Book of Christ Church, Dublin, the objects of its meeting. The justiciary desired the establishment of peace and concord throughout Ireland, and with this end in view issued writs to the prelates and barons as usual, adding to them the new element of two knights, elected by each of the ten counties then known as such—Dublin, Louth, Kildare, Waterford, Tipperary, Cork, Limerick, Kerry, Connaught, and Roscommon; and two from each of the five liberties of Meath, Wexford, Carlow, Kilkenny, and Ulster. This assembly enacted many useful laws, and in particular dealt with two real evils which Wogan recognized as eminently dangerous to the State. One was the right claimed by the great nobles of waging private wars among themselves. This parliament enacted that no baron should dare to make war except by licence from the chief governor of Ireland, or by special mandate from the king. The other evil recognized by Wogan as a specially crying one was the gross neglect of their duties by the great barons, who had obtained their estates on condition of guarding the marches or boundaries of the English settlements. They neglected, in fact, their duties, and then Satan provided mischief

---

[1] See also about the history of the Irish Parliament, *Irish Legislative Systems*, by the Right Hon. J. T. Ball, LL.D., chap. i., and the authorities quoted by him on p. 217. Dublin: 1888.

in abundance for idle hands to do. This parliament peremptorily ordered the owners of the great estates to return to their posts, reminded them, in modern phraseology, that property had its duties as well as its rights, and threatened them with the confiscation of their lands and castles if they did not fulfil the conditions on which they were granted. But I must not be led aside from my fixed purpose to avoid overmuch of detail. If you wish to see more of the legislative effects of this earliest Irish parliament you should consult Dean Butler's reprint of its record,[1] or Leland's analysis thereof, as given in the first volume of his *History of Ireland*, pp. 252-58. Henceforth parliaments became frequent. Sir John Wogan was himself a great believer in parliamentary action. In 1310 he held one at Kildare, and in 1311 another at Kilkenny, where burgesses from the boroughs seem to have taken their seats for the first time side by side with the knights of the shires. This last parliament devised a method of carrying on parliamentary business which might well be commended to the present House of Commons; and, curiously enough, partook of none of that internecine spirit commonly associated with the name of Kilkenny. It ordered that all business should be referred to a committee of twenty-five persons, which said committee was then to be reduced by successive elections to one person who could not differ from himself, "qui a seipso dissentire non potest,"—a first-rate plan to secure unanimity and despatch in business.

But the story of Irish anarchy and English failure grows upon our hands, and will afford ample materials for another lecture.

[1] See his work *De Concilio Hiberniæ* in the *Irish Archæological Miscellany*, vol.i., Dublin, 1846.

LECTURE XIV.

THE WARS OF BRUCE AND OF THE ROSES.

SIR JOHN WOGAN was the nearest approach to a permanent English viceroy which Ireland ever had in those early ages. Edward I. was a strong and vigorous king, and supported a vigorous servant when he found him. And Wogan's lot was cast in stirring times, which have left their mark deep printed on Irish history. He not only inaugurated parliamentary institutions in Ireland, he also put a stop to the perpetual struggles between De Burgh, Earl of Ulster, and the Fitz-Geralds of Kildare and of Desmond. He advanced a step further, and effected what, in the eyes of a warlike monarch like Edward I., must have been specially meritorious: he made Ireland a source of strength instead of weakness to the English Crown. Edward I. was consumed with a thirst for the unification of Great Britain. He thoroughly subjugated Wales between the years 1276 and 1284. In 1294 he entered upon a war with Scotland, which lasted till his death and for years afterwards. That war was a fatal one for Ireland's prosperity. In the earlier years of it the barons and soldiery of Ireland lent effective help to Edward I. In the third year of the great Scottish war, that is in 1296, Sir John Wogan was able to lead a large Irish contingent into Scotland, headed by De Burgh, Earl of Ulster, Theobald Butler, and John Fitz-Thomas Fitz-

Gerald. We have fortunately still surviving some documents shedding light on this period. In the *Documents Illustrative of the History of Scotland*, edited by the Rev. Joseph Stevenson (Edinburgh: 1870), t. ii., p. 124, we find an enumeration of the various forces sent from Ireland for the conquest of Scotland, with the names of their captains, including De Burgh, Earl of Ulster, and members of other leading Anglo-Norman families, as Butler, Fitz-Gerald, Rochefort, Barry, and Cantoke, at that time Chancellor of Ireland. In this volume and at the same spot, we have an epistle addressed to Edward I., by the messenger whom he had despatched into Ireland to expedite the succour he had been promised from thence. It is a curious document, giving us a glimpse into the life of the Anglo-Normans then resident in Ireland. The messenger tells the king that he had been obedient to his commands, and had sought out the Irish barons. He had found De Burgh, the Earl of Ulster, in Connaught. The earl had many fair words for the king's ambassador, was ready to give his help, but when pressed for a definite date when his assistance might be expected, and for definite statistics as to the amount of such assistance the earl prudently declined to answer. And as it was with the Earl of Ulster, so was it with all the other barons. They too had fair words and fine speeches enough for the King's envoy, but they gave no satisfactory assurances such as a prudent general would rely on. During the lifetime of Edward I., the English were triumphant, and the Scotch were everywhere defeated notwithstanding the brilliant and heroic efforts of Sir William Wallace. But after the death of the king, and the appearance of Robert Bruce upon the scene, matters became quite changed for England, and infinitely more so for Ireland. The Bruces in Scotland were just like the De Lacys in Ireland, of whom I have spoken so much. They were Anglo-Norman nobles with a dash of Celtic blood, a most dangerous combination, as repeated bitter experience has taught the government of England.[1] Through their Celtic ancestors they had some shadowy claims upon the throne of Ireland, which the Scottish war with England led them to put in evidence. After the victory of Bannockburn, in 1314, Robert Bruce determined to invade Ireland. He effected several purposes thereby. He employed his brother Edward, who had begun to discover symptoms of dissatisfaction with his subordinate position, and had put forward claims to an equal share of authority over Scotland. He created an effective diversion against English military operations, and compelled a necessary division of the English forces. He prevented Irish troops from being sent over to Scotland, as had been the case in the campaigns against Wallace, securing, on the contrary, the co-operation as against England of the great Celtic chieftains of Ireland, especially of the O'Neills of the north, who were separated from him only by a few miles of sea, which they could cross in the course of a summer's morning. And Edward Bruce, too, did not come uninvited. Fifty years before, as I have already pointed out, the Irish princes did their best to induce the Scandinavians to renew their incursions.[2] And now again, as we learn from the petition of the Irish princes to Pope John XXII., the discontented Celtic chieftains forwarded an invitation to Edward Bruce to come and deliver the Hibernian

---

[1] See Dugdale's *Baronage*, under the name "Bruce," for the descent of that family.
[2] See p. 281 above.

Scots from Anglo-Norman dominion as his brother had delivered their Albanian cousins.[1] The invasion of Edward Bruce did not, however, benefit the Celtic party one whit, but merely involved them in one common ruin with their Anglo-Norman countrymen. Edward Bruce landed on the Antrim coast, as some say at Red Bay near Cushendun, or more probably at the fine, commodious, land-locked harbour of Larne, on May 25th, 1315. He came with three hundred ships and a large army. From that time till his death at the battle of Faughart, near Dundalk, on the 14th of October, 1318, a period of three years and a half, Ireland was simply a hell upon earth. Bruce marched triumphant throughout Ireland, penetrating to the most distant south and west, ravaging, destroying, burning the property and persons of clergy and laity alike; and then whatever the Scots spared, the armies of De Burgh, Earl of Ulster, or of the justiciary who followed upon his footsteps, took care to finish. It would be simply impossible to give you within my limits even the faintest conception of the terrible condition of Ireland during those years. Everything combined to intensify the confusion. The Anglo-Norman government, being in a state of collapse, was confined to Dublin and a few miles around. The army of Bruce came insultingly up to Castleknock, threatening the city of Dublin itself with capture. We have, as I have before noted, a monument of the near approach of Bruce to Dublin in the old city gate near St. Audoen's, the one relic of the Danish walls now remaining. The citizens were so terror-

---

[1] This complaint is contained in the *Scoti-Chronicon* of J. Fordun. It will be found in an English version in the Rev. R. King's *Church History of Ireland*, vol. iii., pp. 1119-35. It is well worth reading, as setting forth in a formal manner the indictment of the Celts against the Anglo-Normans.

struck at the approach of the Scots that they set fire to the old Ostman suburb on the north side of the Liffey; pulled down the Dominican Abbey, which then stood where the King's Inn now shelters our legal brethren; and with the stones extended the line of the city walls as far as Bridge Street, leaving St. Audoen's arch and gateway a solitary thing in the midst of a wilderness of surrounding houses. The Anglo-Norman rule at Dublin was weak; but, far worse still, the Anglo-Norman nobles throughout the country were as divided and as mutually hostile as ever, even in the presence of their foes. They could not unite even for the purposes of self-defence. Richard de Burgh, Earl of Ulster, when marching to meet Edward Bruce upon his landing in Antrim, met Butler, the Lord Deputy, marching from Dublin for the same purpose. De Burgh declined the Deputy's help, and soon found himself reduced to retreat before the united forces of Scotland and the northern O'Neills. The Celtic portion of the population were just as hopelessly at variance among themselves. Phelim O'Conor, King of Connaught, united his forces with De Burgh in the first instance, and marched with him as far as Coleraine. There Edward Bruce entered into negotiations with O'Conor, striving, and with success, to detach him from the side of De Burgh. While Phelim O'Conor was thus betraying his English allies to the Scotch invader, a cousin of his own, Roderick O'Conor, raised the standard of revolt in Connaught against King Phelim himself. Henceforth, all Ireland was aflame with war and violence. Every man's hand was against his fellow. Every kingdom, every petty principality, found a pretender to challenge the rule and ownership of its lawful chief, till at last the Celts who had invited Edward Bruce grew weary of their guest, and hated him with a perfect hatred. The Anglo-Normans were, as the Celts knew right well, bad enough, but the Scoto-Normans were ten times worse, and no one rejoiced more than the Celtic annalists when the battlefield of Dundalk put an end to the invasion of the Bruces. How bitterly must the Celtic princes have felt themselves deceived when the ancient documents embodied by the Four Masters, A.D. 1318, record with exultation the defeat of the champion they had themselves chosen in the following words: "Edward Bruce, the destroyer of the people of Ireland in general, both English and Irish, was slain by the English through dint of battle and bravery. And no achievement had been performed in Ireland for a long time before, from which greater benefits had occurred to the country than from this; for during the three-and-a-half years that this Edward spent in it, a universal famine prevailed to such a degree, that men were wont to devour one another."[1]

The internal disorganization resulting from the four-years' invasion of the Bruces was terrible, and left its mark deep upon the social state of Ireland. It relegated Ulster to barbarism. Under the Anglo-Norman Earls of Ulster, Down and Antrim had attained a certain degree of civilisation, and a large

[1] The *Annals of Lough Cé*, the *Annals of Clonmacnois*, together with those of Pembridge, Grace, Clyn, and Dowling, are rich in details of the Irish war with Bruce. The narrative of the Clonmacnois *Annals* is given by O'Donovan in his notes to the years 1315-18 in the *Four Masters*. Dean Butler's preface to Clyn's *Annals* draws a vigorous and impartial picture of the results of Bruce's invasion. I advisedly call it impartial, because he condemns his own ancestors, the Butlers, just as strongly as any others. Barbour in his poem of *The Bruce* gives a good account of it from the Scotch side. See the poem as published by the Spalding Club, 1856, pp. 321-49, 361-69, 416-24, and the notes on p. 523. Barbour's poem has also been published by the Early English Text Society.

English settlement had grown up there. The invasion of the Bruces ruined this colony, made all Ulster from sea to sea the dominion of the O'Neills, circumscribed English rule within the counties of the pale[1] bounded by Louth on the north, and by the re-introduction of Celtic tenures and land customs, gavelkind and repartition, destroyed all hopes of progress till the English Government took in hand the plantation of Ulster in the seventeenth century. The invasion of Edward Bruce flung back the development of Ireland's resources a good three hundred years. In the thirteenth century the O'Neills were confined to Mid-Ulster. In the year 1586 Shane O'Neill had one of his chief castles, far away in the south-east of Ulster, at Fathom, on Carlingford Bay.[2]

If there had been a wise and a strong king upon the throne, the very state of weakness, misery, and confusion produced by this Scottish invasion might have led to a social and political reformation. The Celtic chieftains, in their complaint to Pope John XXII., show that they possessed no small amount of political commonsense. They lay all the blame of the wretched state of Ireland upon the true cause. They do not blame the English sovereign, but they do blame the chiefs of the Anglo-Norman colony in Ireland, whom

---

[1] The term "pale" was not used to express the English dominion in Ireland till the fifteenth century. During the two first centuries of English dominion their sway extended, as I have already shown, over the greater part of Ireland. It was only the misrule of the fourteenth century led to its contraction within the four counties of Louth, Meath, Dublin, and Kildare, which, from about the year 1400, formed the March or Pale of the English. See a dissertation on this point in Hardiman's Introduction to the Statute of Kilkenny, pp. xxv-xxix, in *Tracts Relating to Ireland*, vol. ii., Irish Archæological Society, Dublin, 1842.

[2] See Bagnal's description of Ulster in 1586 in the *Ulster Journal of Archæology*, t. ii., p. 151.

they describe as the middle nation, neither English nor Irish, whose efforts were all devoted, not towards strengthening the kingdom, but towards aggrandizing themselves. The Irish princes had petitioned the Crown for measures which would have brought about a real fusion of races, and a thorough union amongst the people of Ireland. They had sought, some thirty years earlier, the abolition of the Brehon law system and the introduction of English law and justice throughout the whole country.[1] They had demanded that the distinction maintained between the English and Irish should cease, recognising it as fatal to any hope of progress in the country, and Edward I. was ready and willing to grant their demands, but his kindly intentions were defeated by his Irish advisers. Two or three years before, in the year 1314, they had sent a petition through John de Hothom, Bishop of Ely, whom Edward II. had sent to Ireland to report on its state. In that document they had demanded a settlement of the eternal land question, desiring to hold their estates direct from the Crown, and not from any feudal or palatine lords; or, to quote the words of the Irish princes: "About two years ago, a letter describing these

---

[1] Leland's *History of Ireland*, i., 243. The Irish offered 8,000 marks, or £5,333 6s. 8d., for the blessings of English law. The Celtic land tenures, pasture-lands held in common, and arable lands apportioned and re-applotted among the clansmen from time to time, were destructive of any improvements. Sir John Davis well notes, that no man will build or improve where his children have no right of inheritance. Tanistry was another Celtic custom sure to produce endless confusion. The Tanist was the successor of the actual chief, elected by the clansmen. The mode of election was not by votes. It was carried on in a more characteristic fashion, and the tribe's choice determined by the strong hand. In plain language, the best fighter of the chief's family, legitimate or illegitimate,—for they were not particular about such trifles,—carried the day.

outrages in a clear and simple way, with a view to obtaining a remedy, was addressed by several of the nobility of our nation to the king's council, and also to the king himself, through Lord John de Hothom, who is now, as we have been informed, Bishop of Ely; and we also made a courteous proposal to the same party, that, for his greater profit and our peace, we should hold our land, that land which is by right our own exclusively, immediately from himself; or that he should, with consent of both parties, himself divide our land, between us and them, for the sake of avoiding wholesale bloodshed. But never since have we obtained from himself or his council, any answer whatsoever to this application;" and thus again another lost opportunity was added to the sad and numerous list of similar incidents with which the tale of English rule in Ireland is only too thickly studded.

The long reign of Edward III., extending from 1327 to 1377, brought no change for the better as far as Ireland was concerned. We might, indeed, expect this beforehand, and without any study of the facts. England was too much engaged with her internal affairs, and her foreign policy, to think of the poor afflicted one that was laid at her very gates full of all kinds of political and social sores. Abroad, the attention of Edward III. was fixed on France, and the vain effort to retain England's continental dominions, to the neglect of her home development. The battles of Sluys in 1340, of Crecy in 1346, of Calais in 1347, of Poitiers in 1356, signalised his reign, and in many of them, as at Crecy and Calais, Irish soldiers maintained their traditional reputation. At home, too, there was quite enough, social and political, to engage the most vigorous sovereign. Scotland and Scottish affairs were an ever-pressing danger, separated, not by the sea, as Ireland was, but by a few mountains and heather-clad morasses. Ecclesiastical troubles, too, breeding social discontent were rife. Edward III. saw the rise and progress of movements religious and social, which affected Ireland as well as England. His reign beheld the great movement headed by Wickliffe, and the reaction against the mendicant friars, which was associated with it. A few words on this point will assist our story.

The introduction of the Dominican and Franciscan Orders into England and Ireland alike, had been in the thirteenth century the salvation of religion. The Franciscans especially came, like the Methodists of the eighteenth century, preaching to the poor and neglected classes. Here I can point you to a trustworthy and most impartial authority. I have made it my object throughout these lectures to call your attention to the great Rolls Series of historical works, where the prefaces contributed by eminent men have painted from original authorities the history of England during the times with which we are dealing. The late lamented and learned Professor Brewer edited, in that series, the *Monumenta Franciscana*, prefixing a preface where he portrays the strength and the weakness of the Franciscan movement in the thirteenth century. He heartily acknowledges the blessings it brought, and foremost among them he sets this fact: that they settled in the suburbs among the dregs of the population, and taught them practical Christianity. He notices that in England their rude, simple chapels were always placed in the poorest quarters. "In London, York, Warwick, Oxford, Bristol, Lynn, and elsewhere, their convents stood in the suburbs and abutted on the city walls.

They made choice of the low, swampy, and undrained spots in the large towns, among the poorest and most neglected quarters. Unlike the magnificent monasteries and abbeys, which create admiration to this day, their buildings to the very last retained their primitive squat, low, and meagre proportions. Their first house, at their settlement in London, stood in the neighbourhood of Cornhill, where they built cells, stuffing the party walls with dried grass. Near the Shambles in Newgate, and close upon the city gate of that name, on a spot appropriately called Stinking Lane, rose the chief house of the Order in England." Here, again, they resembled the early Methodists. Seek out either in England or Ireland the remaining specimens of the Methodist chapels of John Wesley's time. You will find them, not grand assertive Gothic buildings in the most fashionable quarters, but plain unpretentious structures in lanes and quiet streets where the humbler classes lived and worked. Thus it was with the Franciscans in England, and so, too, it was with the Franciscans in Ireland. Let me cite a few instances. Take our own city. The first Franciscan Friary was built in Francis Street about 1235, and Francis Street was in the Celtic suburbs outside the Newgate of Dublin, as the Franciscan house was outside the Newgate of London. In Athlone, the Franciscan house was built, at the same period, outside the north gate, on the low, swampy ground beside the Shannon, where the plain undecorated ruins still testify to the simple character of the earliest Franciscan teaching. In Kilkenny, the site of the Franciscan Abbey was just upon the city bounds, on the marshy banks of the river Nore.[1] So it

---

[1] See Clyn's *Annals*, Irish Archæological Society, A.D. 1849, p. 69.

was in Drogheda, Galway, and everywhere else throughout Ireland : the Friars came in the power of self-sacrificing love as missionaries to the masses, they settled among them and triumphed there, as Churches ever triumph when they trust not in the arm of flesh, but in the power of holy enthusiasm and of Divine love. Success, however, has always been fatal to the religious Orders. The Benedictines were superseded by the Cistercians, and Cistercians by reformed Augustinian monks, and they in turn, as they grew rich and slothful, by the Friars; and now in the fourteenth century the Irish and English Franciscans had begun to lose their first fervour.[1] One hundred years have ever been quite sufficient to change the spirit and radically alter the aspirations of such societies, ancient and modern alike. The complaint of the Irish to Pope John XXII. shows that the Minorites, as the Franciscans were usually called, had sadly fallen from the standard set before them by the gentle Francis of Assisi. Among the vexations and outrages there enumerated, they complain that the Anglo-Normans valued the life of an Irishman at nothing, placing it on the same level as that of a beast. This spirit of national hatred had even infected the religious Orders. The Cistercians in Armagh and Down publicly appeared in arms, and slew their Irish neighbours, yet celebrated Mass as usual. While, worst of all, they tell that Simon, a Franciscan, brother to the Bishop of Connor, whose mission and vows should specially have led him to preach peace to the outcast, publicly taught, in the very court and army of Edward Bruce, whom the Celts regarded as their

---

[1] An Anglo-Irish satirical poem ascribed to Friar Michael of Kildare, about A.D. 1308, witnesses to this decline. See Gilbert's *Account of Fac-similes of National MSS.*, p. 98.

champion, "that it is no sin to kill an Irishman, and that if he himself were to be the doer of the act, he would not for this be the one whit less ready to perform the celebration of the Mass."

The Franciscans and the other Mendicants were rapidly declining in the days of Edward III. Wickliffe in England denounced them, and Richard Fitz-Ralph of Dundalk, Archbishop of Armagh, proved himself an equally vigilant enemy of the Mendicants here in Ireland. The life of St. Richard of Dundalk, as he is sometimes called, favourably illustrates the history of the great primatial see of Armagh during our period. The succession of Armagh prelates was just like that of their Dublin brethren. From the year 1200, they were almost always Anglo-Normans. Now and then a Celtic divine might chance to obtain the primacy, but in the usual course of things the English sovereigns took good care to place prelates of English blood and training in that position. Luke Netterville, Albert of Cologne, John Taaf, Walter de Jorse, Roland Jorse, Stephen Segrave; all these at least, among the predecessors of Richard Fitz-Ralph, were certainly Anglo-Normans. And Richard Fitz-Ralph, who presided over the see of Armagh from 1347 to 1360, was just the same. He was born at Dundalk, trained at Oxford, where he became Chancellor of the University in 1333, whence he was made Archbishop of Armagh by the Pope, Clement VI., being consecrated at Exeter by the Bishop of Exeter and three other bishops on July 8th, 1347.[1] As soon as he obtained the chief position in the Church of his birth, he flung himself into the propagation of

---

[1] Exeter also claims to have been his birthplace. See Prince's *Worthies of Devon*, pp. 294-8, a reference which I owe to his Grace the Lord Primate.

the Oxford movement of his day. Wickliffe was then the hero of Oxford. He bitterly opposed the friars, he was the translator of the Bible into English, the patron and friend of the poor priests. And Primate Richard followed in his footsteps. He denounced the Irish friars, he maintained the sanctity and use of property. He is said to have translated the Bible into Irish; he was summoned, like Wickliffe, to answer for his views before papal tribunals, and though denounced by some as a heretic, the populace viewed him as a saint, and his bones when he died were carried back from Avignon and buried in the Church of St. Nicholas at Dundalk, where common report told that miracles were wrought by their power, and where, in fact, Primate Bramhall, in the days of Charles I., proposed to erect a monument to his memory.[1]

The period, indeed, during which St. Richard ruled at Armagh were terrible years, not only for Ireland, but for England, and for the whole of Europe, Asia, and Africa. The Black Death swept the towns and villages of England and of Ireland alike, clear of all inhabitants. Its ravages in England, changing as they did the whole face of English rural society, have been of late years the subject of much investigation. Its effects in Ireland were just as bad, but Ireland is more

---

[1] The Friars of Fitz-Ralph's day were not unlike some extreme teetotallers of the present time. They were not content to decline a lawful indulgence for Christ's sake, in refusing the use of property. They thought that all men should be even as they, if salvation was to be secured. Their favourite thesis was : Jesus Christ was a mendicant, therefore all Christians should be mendicant monks. In opposition to this view Fitz-Ralph maintained in his writings the Christian use of private property. See, for more about St. Richard of Dundalk, Ware's *Bishops*, ed. Harris, p. 81; Prince's *Worthies of Devon*, p. 294.

used to revolutionary changes, and its terrible results have, therefore, received the less notice amongst ourselves. Friar Clyn, the Kilkenny Franciscan, paints the progress of the plague of 1348 in a few vigorous strokes which we may here reproduce: "That pestilence deprived of human inhabitant villages and cities, castles and towns, so that there was scarcely found a man to dwell therein; the pestilence was so contagious that whosoever touched the sick or the dead was immediately infected and died; and the penitent and the confessor were carried together to the grave; through fear and dread men scarcely dared to perform the offices of piety and pity in visiting the sick and burying the dead; many died of boils and abscesses and pustules on their shins or under their armpits; others died frantic with the pain in their heads, and others spitting blood. The pestilence was rife in Kilkenny in Lent; from Christmas Day to the sixth day of March, eight friars-preachers died of it. Scarcely one alone ever died in a house. Commonly husband, wife, children, servants, went the one way, the way of death."

And now the cup of misery and woe was brimming over. War, pestilence, rebellion, misrule, neglect, had done their utmost, and English and Celt alike were overwhelmed in one common ruin. Why need I prolong the mournful tale, which becomes the dreariest of the dreary in its recital? Every attempt to remedy the state of Ireland only seems to have made the matter worse. A royal marriage with an Anglo-Irish heiress, instead of bringing a blessing marked the lowest point of English degradation. William de Burgh, Earl of Ulster and Lord of Connaught, was slain in Ulster in 1333, leaving an only daughter named

Elizabeth, to inherit his vast estates. Lionel, Duke of Clarence, second son of Edward III., married this young lady in 1352, and in virtue of the union claimed the honours and estates of her father.[1] He came as lord-lieutenant to Ireland, chiefly with a view to assert his titles and recover his estate in Connaught, which the other members of the house of De Burgh had seized, and at last successfully retained. The one enduring monument of his viceroyalty is the Statute of Kilkenny, which Mr. Hardiman edited, with conspicuous learning, some fifty years ago, for the Irish Archæological Society. Time would fail me to analyse the provisions of that Statute and point out its mischievous tendencies; and there is the less need to do so as Mr. Hardiman has achieved this task with admirable clearness in his Introduction. To that work I must refer those interested in the investigation of this sad period. Mr. Hardiman fixes, however, upon one point as the special vice of this legislative achievement. The Statute of Kilkenny strove in every possible way to accentuate the distinction between the English and

---

[1] The earldom of Ulster and lordship of Connaught were enjoyed by several successive members of the royal family, till at last in the person of Edward IV. they became the special inheritance and revenue of the English Crown. The Connaught estates were, however, never enjoyed by the Duke of Clarence or his successors. They were seized in 1333 by the most powerful of the junior branches of the family, Sir William de Burgh, ancestor of the Earls of Clanricarde, and Sir Edward Albanagh, progenitor of the Earls of Mayo. They renounced the English style and dress, adopting Irish names: Sir William that of MacWilliam Oughter, or the Upper, and Sir Edmund that of MacWilliam Eighter, or the Lower. Henceforth the De Burghs became the leaders of rebellion throughout Connaught till Cromwell's time. See O'Donovan's note on A.D. 1333, in *Annals of the Four Masters*, Hardiman's *History of Galway*, pp. 56, 57.

the Irish. It proclaimed the defeat of the English power in Ireland in doing so. It acknowledged that, beyond the south-eastern counties of Ireland, English power did not prevail. It strove, therefore, in the spirit of the old Mosaic legislation to raise a barrier between the inhabitants of the Pale, who were English, and those without the Pale, who were Irish. Just as Moses and Joshua endeavoured to cause the original inhabitants of Palestine to stink in the nostrils of the Jews, forbidding alliance or kinship with them, and ordering their utter extirpation, so did Duke Lionel and his Kilkenny Parliament. They prohibited alliance by marriage with the Celts, nurture of English infants by them, or the use of Irish names or dress by the English. They made it penal for the English to permit the Irish to graze on their land, to present them to ecclesiastical benefices, to receive them into monasteries, to entertain their minstrels, rhymers, and newstellers. Finally, they used the strongest language against the Brehon law,[1] proclaiming the English who submitted to it traitors against the Crown, without, however, substituting any effective code in its place. This Statute of Kilkenny has been well described as "no more than a peevish and revengeful expression of the resentment Duke Lionel felt from the opposition he had met with, and the loss of those lands he had come over to claim;" and as such it met with a deserved failure.[2] One great aim of this Statute was this: it desired to prevent Englishmen turning into Irishmen, and becoming, according to the old complaint,

---

[1] An unprinted Act of a Drogheda Parliament of 1476 calls the Brehon code "the wicked and damnable law called Brehon law." Cf. Hardiman's *Statute of Kilkenny*, p. 18.

[2] Cf. Hardiman's Introd., p. xi.

more Irish than the Irish themselves. But penal statutes not grounded on public opinion, and running counter to great natural forces, are sure to fail. Nothing could possibly hinder scattered Englishmen surrounded by overwhelming multitudes of Celts from conforming to their customs. The same process has ever gone on, and is still going on. You will find in your parishes no part of your parochial work more difficult than the effort to keep your scattered Protestant parishioners from assimilating themselves to the overwhelming Roman Catholic majority around. And so it was in the fourteenth and fifteenth centuries. The English Government passed highly penal statutes, but exercised no authority, enforced no law, established no effective police, and then were laughed at by English and by Irish alike. This Statute of Kilkenny was re-enacted by every parliament which sat in Ireland till the celebrated one which met at Drogheda under Sir Edward Poynings in 1495, and proved all through these dreary one hundred and thirty years a mere voice and nothing more.

Ireland's condition waxed worse and worse during the fifteenth century, as we might well expect. The Wars of the Roses ruined the English aristocracy of that age, and proved fatal to many of the Irish too. The usual fate of division and strife followed the Anglo-Irish during that prolonged struggle. The Earls of Ormond and the Butlers took the Lancastrian side. The Earls of Kildare and the Fitz-Geralds supported the Yorkists, till on the fatal field of Wakefield Green, December 31st, 1460, the Anglo-Irish soldiers perished in thousands fighting round the standard of Richard, Duke of York. War and strife in England intensified, of course, the internal confusions of Ireland. The houses of Butler and Fitz-Gerald had enough of bitter memories without this additional excuse for bloodshed which the dynastic struggle in England afforded; still, they only seemed to enjoy the fresh fuel thus added to the flame. But no matter what side won, the people of Ireland were the chief sufferers. When the Yorkists were in power, the Fitz-Geralds tyrannised. When the Lancastrians triumphed, the Butlers took a wild revenge, till at last the strong hand of Henry VII. intervened. Lambert Simnel, in 1487, and Perkin Warbeck, in 1492, each of them used Ireland as the weak point in England's armour, and with Geraldine help tried to restore the fortunes of the House of York. They landed in Ireland, and thence strove to overthrow the Lancastrian cause triumphant in the person of Henry VII. Their attempts failed, and that failure led the first Tudor monarch to turn his attention to this country, and send over a strong and determined viceroy. Henry was weary of Ireland and its perpetual troubles. He saw that it was a source of loss and weakness to England in its existing condition. Its Parliament represented a mere fraction of the whole island, and was simply the tool of one or other of two contending factions. He despatched, therefore, Sir Edward Poynings into Ireland, to investigate the condition of Irish affairs, and take his measures accordingly. Poynings chastised the Celtic rebels, restrained the quarrels of the Butlers and Geraldines,[1] and passed an Act at Drogheda in the Parliament of 1495, since known to fame as Poynings' Act. This statute, round which the controversies of the last century waxed fierce

---

[1] See Poynings' Act, abolishing the war-cries Cromabo and Butlerabo, in the *Irish Statutes*, vol. i., p. 55.

and furious, simply enacted that all acts, causes, and considerations submitted to the Irish Parliament should first be approved by the English Crown. Poynings' Act attained one useful purpose at any rate, for it effectually curbed the Anglo-Norman factions which then were ruling and ruining Ireland.[1]

I must stop, however; I have reached my limits, and were I to advance further, questions might be raised of burning interest, upon which I have no desire to touch. This much, however, I may say: Poynings' Act may have been, and doubtless was, sadly and selfishly misused in Williamite and Hanoverian times. But looking at it from the historian's standpoint, I am obliged to confess that Poynings' legislation was the only hope for Ireland if she was ever to be rescued from the anarchy in which the country then lay. Nothing good could be extracted from a mere Parliament of the Pale, the creature of Ormond one year, of Kildare the next. Poynings' Act was the turning-point of Irish history. It marked, indeed, the

---

[1] Poynings' Act will be found in the printed *Irish Statutes*, vol. i., p. 44. Edward III. sought to attain the same end by summoning a Union Parliament at Westminster. He endeavoured to anticipate Pitt's action by four hundred and twenty-five years. In 1376 he issued writs convoking the bishops, peers, and representatives of Ireland to meet in Parliament at London. This action provoked great opposition on the part of the Anglo-Normans both in Church and State. They attended the Parliament, but sent very vigorous protests against the convocation of such an assembly. The spirited and argumentative replies of the Archbishop of Armagh and of the County of Dublin are still on record. They can be read in the original Latin, together with the writs used on the occasion, in Leland's *History of Ireland*, vol. i., pp. 363-87, Appendix ii.; cf. Gale's *Corporate System of Ireland*, pp. cclix, cclxi, for another declaration of Anglo-Irish independence in 1460. Cromwell held the next Union Parliament at Westminster. Cf. Gale, *l.c.*, p. cclxiii.

lowest depth to which English rule descended since Henry II. landed, more than three hundred years before. Prior to it, however, the prospect ever grows darker and darker. Subsequent to it, the prospect ever grows brighter and brighter. The progress made by Ireland may at times seem to have been very slow, and at times appear to have been backwards rather than forwards. But the historian judges by centuries, not by years. The historic muse treads with a very majestic step, and marches with a giant's stride. Judging Ireland from a historic standpoint, surely even the most prejudiced must acknowledge that the Ireland of to-day, with its prosperity, its wealth, its trade, and its enlightenment, has steadily advanced century by century. The Ireland of 1600 was superior to that of 1500. The Ireland of 1700 surpassed that of 1600. The Ireland of 1800 was richer and more prosperous than that of 1700; and sure I am that the Ireland of to-day is a far pleasanter one to live in than the Ireland of our grandfathers' time. The whitewashing, refurbishing, and clearing of unpopular and misunderstood reputations is now a favourite occupation in some literary circles. I desire likewise to do somewhat in that same charitable direction, and I hope that these few words may in some slight degree help towards clearing the character and vindicating the measures of Sir Edward Poynings, the misunderstood and misrepresented Lord Deputy of King Henry the Seventh.

LECTURE XV.

THE CELTIC CHURCH IN ANGLO-NORMAN TIMES.

I MAY as well begin this lecture by telling you at once that I select this title, " The Celtic Church in Anglo-Norman Times," simply from reasons of convenience. I do not intend to convey that there were two Churches in Ireland then, as there are two Churches in Ireland now, with competing bishops in every see and competing incumbents in every parish. I intend something quite different, which, as I conceive, every honest inquirer will at once concede. Henry II. came to Ireland, and at the Council of Cashel ordered that there should be perfect conformity with the practice, rites, and discipline of the Church of England on the part of the Church of Ireland. Henceforth there were two parties in the Irish Church. There was the Celtic party and there was the Anglo-Norman party. They taught in the main the same doctrines, practised in the main the same rites, acknowledged the nominal supremacy of the same pope, and yet were as distinct from one another, and hated one another with as perfect a hatred, as if they rejoiced in the designation of Protestant and Papist, or the still more modern one of Orangemen and Nationalists. The basis of this distinction was already laid in the Anglo-Danish see of Dublin. In the long succession of the Dublin prelates, from the eleventh century downwards, Laurence O'Toole was the one genuine Celt, by birth, by training, and by consecration. With that one exception the bishops, clergy, and laity of Dublin were hostile to the Celtic Church and population. After the Synod of Cashel Anglo-Norman modes of worship, and Anglo-Norman bishops, clergy, and monks, and Anglo-Norman dedications of churches spread through Ireland wherever Anglo-Norman power and authority got a firm and lasting grip; while the Church in the native districts retained more of the ancient Celtic hue. I have arrived at this conclusion by a deduction from a large number of facts, a few of which I shall now proceed to lay before you. A full statement of them will enable you to determine for yourselves how far I am justified in speaking of the Celtic Church as still existing in Anglo-Norman times.

I make a broad division of the Irish Church for the purposes of this investigation. The Church of the eastern counties, from Coleraine in the north to Waterford in the south, was soon completely Anglicized, and with a few insignificant exceptions in the mountain districts, differed in no respect, in architecture, rites, and customs, from the Church in England. The same may be said of the leading towns in other parts of the country. Galway and Limerick, for instance, inside the walls, were as distinctly English in ecclesiastical matters as Carrickfergus, Dundalk, or Drogheda. Galway became a thoroughly Anglo-Norman town. Galway still rejoices in the title of the City of the Tribes, and people fondly imagine that there is something peculiarly Irish and peculiarly Celtic in this title. Why! it is quite the opposite. The tribes of Galway were simply a number of Anglo-Norman families who settled in that town and made it an exclusively English town in the midst of a Celtic district.[1] The dedications of the churches is one of the best evidences of the distribution of the population. The one great collegiate church of Galway, built in the most pronounced English fashion, is dedicated to St. Nicholas, and wherever the Anglo-Normans went they always dedicated the churches which they built in seaport towns to St. Nicholas of Myra, the patron saint of sailors. As it is in Galway, so it is in Cork, in Dublin, in Dundalk, in Carrickfergus: each of them has a church, and Dublin two churches, dedicated to this saint, the favourite of navigators.[2] Bearing in mind this limitation, however, we may broadly distinguish the Church of Ireland into the two great sections of the Church of Eastern Ireland, which was Anglo-Norman, and the Church of Western Ireland, which remained Celtic. Let us see, then, what we can learn concerning the life of each section.

What, then, are the facts which lead me to conclude that the Church of the western dioceses from Derry along by Kilmore, Ardagh, Elphin, Tuam, and down to Ardfert in Kerry and Ross in West Cork, remained true to its ancient character? An exposition of them

---

[1] See Hardiman's *Hist. of Galway*, pp. 6, 7. The names of the tribes speak for themselves. They were Athy, Blake, Bodkin, Browne, D'Arcy, Ffont, Ffrench, Joyce, Kirwan, Lynch, Martin, Morris, and Skerrett.

[2] A slight investigation will show that it is just the same in the seaport towns of England. Every ancient seaport has a church dedicated to St. Nicholas, and intended specially for the seafaring classes. The exceptions in Ireland can be easily explained. Waterford, Wexford, and Limerick were fully equipped with churches before the Anglo-Norman invasion. Sligo and Derry were Celtic towns in the middle ages, and Belfast did not exist.

will give you many a glimpse of the social and religious state of those early times. I pray you, therefore, to lend me your keenest attention, and to bear patiently if I seem to be very copious in detail. Appealing then to history as written by Celtic scribes, I find in the first place clear evidence in the *Annals of the Four Masters*, written two centuries and a half ago, that the north of Ireland retained its ancient Columban spirit for a century and more after the conquest. In my lectures published in *Ireland and the Celtic Church*, I called your attention to the fact that the Columban party in Ulster were the fiercest and most persistent opponents of the Roman view about Easter and the orthodox form of the tonsure.[1] That ancient spirit did not easily die out in Ulster, and specially in Derry, which as fondly cherished the memory of its founder, Columcille, in the thirteenth century as it did in the eighth, and reverenced his sanctuary, Iona, as it did of yore. The Derrymen, bishop, abbots, monks, and laity, were just as ready to show their love for Iona, and that in the real old Irish style, as Columba's own monastery, Durrow, was when she fought many a battle in the olden times with her neighbour Clonmacnois, the favourite foundation of Kieran the carpenter, in fancied defence of her patron's honour. The disciples of Columba were ever a fighting race. Columba was an O'Donnell, and the O'Donnells have ever dearly loved a fray. St. Columba himself in his earlier and wilder days followed the example of his forefathers, and his monasteries followed the example of their founder; and now, in the year 1200 A.D., we find that the traditional spirit has not died out in Derry. Derry regarded

---

[1] See p. 161 of that work.

herself as, next to Iona, the special church of St. Columba. The abbots of Derry were eminently the Coarbs or successors of Columcille in Ulster. The Four Masters tell us, for instance, that in 1150 Maelisa O'Branan, successor of St. Columba and "head of the happiness and prosperity of the north of Ireland," died. Flaherty O'Brollaghan was appointed his successor, and then the very next year we read that he made his visitation among the septs that owned his jurisdiction, and received his dues; for the reception of dues seems to have been the great object of episcopal or abbatial visitations in those times. The dues were, however, thoroughly in keeping with the Columban spirit, for the Four Masters tell us that the abbot received "a horse from every chieftain, a sheep from every hearth, and his horse, battle dues, and a ring of gold, in which were two ounces, from the lord of the country." Flaherty O'Brollaghan's rule at Derry lasted from 1150 to 1175, when we find his departure in peace chronicled after the following fashion:—"Flaherty O'Brollaghan, successor of St. Columbkille, a tower of wisdom and hospitality; a man to whom, on account of his goodness and wisdom, the clergy of Ireland had presented a bishop's chair,[1] and to whom the presidency of Hy (Iona) had been offered; died in righteousness, after exemplary sickness in the Duibhregles of Derry;[2]

---

[1] He seems to have been constituted the first Bishop of Derry at a synod held in 1158. He resigned the see after a time, and contented himself with the government of his abbey. Ware's *Bishops*, ed. Harris, p. 286. He was son of one of the married primates of Armagh who so excited St. Bernard's wrath.

[2] Duibhregles is composed of two words: *dubh*, black, and *regles*, the name for an abbey church in Irish, derived from the Latin *regula*, a rule. The Duibhregles of Derry was St. Columba's original abbey. It was probably called by this

and Gillamacliag O'Branan was appointed in his place in the abbacy." O'Branan lived till 1198, and then resigned the abbey, when we are told " Gilchrist O'Kearney was elected Coarb of St. Columbkille by the universal suffrages of the clergy and laity of the north of Ireland," and so the succession went on throughout the thirteenth century, just as if the Anglo-Normans had never set foot in Ireland and the Synod of Kells never had been heard of. In 1219 another O'Branan died, and another O'Brollaghan was elected Coarb of St. Columba, who exacted his dues and kept up the ancient traditions and the ancient warlike spirit, which was ready to burst forth if the slightest insult were offered to Columba's memory. The Four Masters themselves give an interesting instance of this under the year 1203. A Bishop of Sodor and Man, named Kellagh, or Nicholas, dared to erect a monastery in the very middle of Iona in despite of the monks of Iona, and did considerable damage to the town. He was claiming jurisdiction in fact over a monastery which had ever been exempt. The monastic community of Iona appealed to Derry and Ulster for help, which was at once granted, and, to quote the words of the *Annals*, "the clergy of the north of Ireland assembled together to pass over into Iona, namely, Florence O'Carolan, Bishop of Tyrone (*i.e.* Derry); Maelisa O'Deery, Bishop of Tirconnell (Raphoe) and Abbot of the Church of SS. Peter and Paul at Armagh; Awley O'Ferghail, or O'Freel, Abbot of the Regles of Derry, with many

---

name to distinguish it from the new Templemore, or cathedral church erected in 1164 by Flaherty O'Brollaghan, Bishop and Abbot of Derry. See Colby's *Ordnance Survey of Londonderry*, sec. ii.; *Annals of Four Masters*, ed. O'Donovan, A.D. 1173.

of the family of Derry, besides numbers of the clergy of the north of Ireland. They passed over into Iona; and, in accordance with the law of the Church, they pulled down the aforesaid monastery; and the aforesaid Awley was elected Abbot of Iona by the suffrages of the Galls and the Gaels."[1]

But the days of Columban supremacy were numbered at Iona. With the aid of the Columban bishops and clergy of Ulster, Awley O'Freel was established as the Columban Abbot of Iona, but he was the last of the long succession. That appointment is, however, an ample proof of the survival of ancient Celtic ecclesiastical customs in Ulster. The Irish were intensely clannish and tribal. The tribal chieftains were always selected from the same family; and the chiefs of their abbeys, the Abbots, were chosen, whenever at all possible, from the family of the first founder. Awley O'Freel, the last abbot of Iona, was an interesting example of this fact, for he was a lineal descendant from Eoghan, St. Columba's only brother.[2] Nothing could save Iona however, not even the blood of St. Columba's own family, because Norman ideas were advancing in Scotland and cutting off the estates which ancient piety had bestowed for the support of the island monastery. The Bishop of the Isles soon superseded the Columban abbot, and established a

---

[1] See Bishop Reeves's *Columba*, p. 411, for an explanation of this incident. Kellach was Celtic for Nicholas in 1203 made Bishop of Sodor and Man, who wished to establish episcopal jurisdiction in the island of Iona. Cf. *New Statistical Account of Scotland*, t. vii., pt. ii., p. 325, for an account of the relation of Iona to the bishops and style of Sodor and Man.

[2] See Bishop Reeves's *Columba*, pp. 342, 412; and his tract on abbatial succession in Ireland in the *Proceedings* of the Roy. Ir. Acad., January 12th, 1857.

cathedral, and that with Irish help, for one of the pillars still bears an inscription stating that a certain Donnel O'Brolcan, a member of a family noted in Ulster as stonemasons, had raised the edifice.[1] But now, mark my point: it was the Roman ideas working from the Scotch side, subtracting the estates of Iona in behalf of the new-fashioned canons of Holyrood, which put an end to the Columban institution at Iona. Ulster continued loyal to her ancient and her renowned saint. Derry took the place of Iona in the reverence of Columba's adherents, and if you will consult the *Annals of the Four Masters*, or the *Annals of Ulster*, you will find that every person who injured or attacked Derry till the year 1300 is said to have been punished through the instrumentality and power of Columcille.

The Columban Order was the most ancient and revered of Irish monastic societies, but it was not the only one which survived the great crisis of Anglo-Norman domination. All through the western half of Ireland we find monastic societies and institutions of the ancient type flourishing for centuries after that great change. The monasteries of Ireland, when viewed even in the most superficial manner, divide themselves into two classes, the Anglo-Norman and the Celtic. Contrast Glendalough with Tintern, Dunbrody and Jerpoint in the south, or Mellifont in the north. Compare Clonmacnois with St. John's, Newtown, near Trim; Innis-Cleraun in Lough Ree with Boyle, higher up the Shannon; or Innis-Murry with its neighbours Donegal and Sligo;

---

[1] Bishop Reeves in his learned essay on the Culdees, *Trans. Roy. Ir. Acad.*, t. xxiv., p. 28, says: "The reign of David I. (1124—1153) is celebrated by historians as the period when the Scotch dioceses became permanently defined." By the year 1203 the island of Iona had come within the influence of the new movement.

and a glance will show the vast distinction between the monasteries due to native Celtic influence and those due to Anglo-Norman and Roman ideas. The shape, constitution, architecture, of the Celtic monastery are as different from those of the Anglo-Norman as light is from darkness. The Celtic monastery is in every instance a collection of small, square, stone-roofed churches, without any architectural adornments, enclosed within a cashel or fortification, wherein were the stone or mud cells of the monks, and usually associated with a round tower. The Anglo-Norman monastery is a stately building, where the monks live the life of a community, sleeping in dormitories, dining in a common hall, and assembling themselves in one magnificent church, which witnesses by its style to the influence of the thirteenth and fourteenth centuries. The conquest of Ireland by Strongbow did not terminate the existence of the Irish type. Clonmacnois, Glendalough, Innis-Cleraun, maintained their existence and their ancient mode of life. Glendalough, indeed, was robbed of its estates by the see of Dublin, and lost its abbots. But the priory of St. Saviour still flourished as a dependent of the Celtic foundation of All Saints, or All Hallows Monastery, which once occupied the site of this college.[1] A number of these pure Celtic abbeys in the west never accepted any of the new-fashioned rules imported from England or the Continent. They were not submerged by the inundation of Cistercians, Augustinians, Dominicans, Franciscans, which overwhelmed their brethren in the east of the island. The original Celtic Orders or communities—followers of St. Kieran, St. Canice, St. Kevin,

---

[1] See Dean Butler's Introduction to the *Register of All Hallows*, p. ix, in the Irish Archæological Society's series.

and St. Columba—perpetuated in these rude and distant monasteries the customs of their forefathers.

Let me give you a few instances. Let us take first a well-known subject of controversy. No ecclesiastical question had caused fiercer contentions during the seventh and eighth centuries than the custom of the Celtic tonsure, which consisted in shaving all the hair in front of a line drawn from ear to ear, as distinguished from the Petrine or Roman tonsure, which was formed by shaving the top of the head alone. In England, Ireland, and Scotland alike, the Roman party had used every effort to extirpate it. They had tried that most effective of all controversial methods. They gave the Celtic tonsure a bad name, calling it the tonsure of Simon Magus. Yet the Celts would not abandon it.[1] The lay people, even in Ireland, adopted it, and it became a national symbol, indicating a man of Irish birth, race, and habit. We therefore find it prohibited by an Act of the Great Council of Ireland passed in the year 1295, which ordered that any Englishman conforming to this custom, having his head half-shaven, nourishing, and elongating his locks behind, after the Irish fashion, should be punished by fine and imprisonment.[2] The Easter question, again, seems at times to have shown symptoms that it was not yet dead. In the year 1444 the *Annals* of Duald MacFirbis tell us that

---

[1] This special mode of tonsure seems to have been universal among the Celtic race. It was found in Ireland, in England, and in Scotland (Bede, *Hist.*, iii., 26; iv., 1; v., 21); in Brittany (Greg. Tur., *Hist. Franc.*, x. 9), and in Spain (Conc. Tolet., iv., A.D. 633, can. xli.) See the article "Tonsure" in the *Dict. Christ. Antiqq.*, t. ii.; Harris's *Ware*, t. ii., pp. 238-40, and the references there given.

[2] This enactment will be found in the *Irish Archæological Miscellany*, t. i., p. 22.

at that late period "a Greate Controversie arose betwixt the Clergie of Ireland in this yeare touching Easterday."[1]

The ancient arrangements and officials of the Celts were preserved. The most interesting illustration of this fact is to be found in the celebrated case of the Culdees, who were regarded as a mythical kind of beings until the researches of Dr. Reeves brought together all the facts in an essay read by him before the Royal Irish Academy, and embodied in the twenty-fourth volume of the *Transactions* of that learned society. The name and office of the Culdees had previously formed a sort of romance round which all kinds of strange ideas gathered. Our Presbyterian friends even saw in them their own direct, though unacknowledged, ancestors; deposed, indeed, by intruding prelates, but still testifying to the antiquity of their modern organization[2]—a view which can only provoke a smile, for surely there is not much resemblance between the modern Puritanism, of which Irish Presbyterianism is one of the best representatives, and the ancient Celtic Church, with its asceticism and its sacramental doctrine, except in the shape of their churches, which in either case seem to have been square and ugly enough. And now a few words about the genuine history of the Culdees, as Dr. Reeves traces them in Armagh, Devenish, Clonmacnois, and elsewhere in Ireland; in St. Andrews, Dunkeld, Dunblane, and Iona, in Scotland; at York, in England; and at Bardsey Island, in Wales. He proves that they were simply the ancient Celtic monks in a state of corruption. One or two passages, which

---

[1] *Irish Arch. Miscell.*, t. i., p. 203.
[2] Reid's *History of the Presbyterian Church in Ireland*, t. i., p. 2.

I quote from his essay, will be a sufficient exposition of this theory. For its full proof I must refer you to the study of the Bishop's treatise. On page 30 of his essay the Bishop of Down writes: "In fact, the generality of monasteries, both in Scotland and Ireland, were in a state of decrepitude at the beginning of the twelfth century, and those which survived for any length of time owed the continuation of their existence either to the superaddition of a bishop and chapter or to their reconstruction on a new model. Most of the old religious communities were Keledei (or Culdees) till the changes last-mentioned took place, and then the name became limited for their brief future to those institutions which adhered to the original discipline, as contradistinguished from those which were remodelled or created in the new." Again, on the next page, Dr. Reeves proceeds: "John Pinkerton, whose sagacity and candour far outweighed any natural or religious bias, came to the conclusion that the Culdees were only Irish clergy. In the gradual corruption of the monastic order, they married, and left their culdeeships to their children, and after the havoc introduced by the Danes, usurped the rank of secular clergy. In short, they were merely corrupted monks, such as abounded in all the countries of Europe till the eleventh century, when the popes were forced to institute canons regular, which the princes gradually instituted into the chief monasteries, instead of the old depraved monks."

The theory of Pinkerton, in which Dr. Reeves agrees, is simply this: The monks of the Celtic Church were originally extreme ascetics. By degrees their discipline became relaxed. They married, and became mere secular clergy, till at last the entire religious character of a monastery vanished except in name, as we also find to have been the case in England with the ancient Celtic foundations, such as Glastonbury in Somerset, prior to the reforms of St. Dunstan in the tenth century.[1] Where this process of secularization was only partial, a shadow of the old society continued to exist under greater or less variety of discipline; the representatives of the original system being known as Kele-dei (servants of God), a title which, together with portions of Church property, in some cases descended from father to son, and in others was practically entailed upon members of certain families. The system, in fact, of the ancient Celtic monasticism was played out. It had done its work, and was now corrupt. The representatives of the old Order were living on the reputation of bygone ages, and were still styled Culdees, or God's servants; but they had only the name, and nothing of the reality. The title had become a mere empty form, witnessing, as titles do so often, to nothing else save to former greatness and to present degradation and vanity. In my previous course of lectures, published under the title of *Ireland and the Celtic Church*, I said that the work of the Church of Rome in Ireland during the twelfth century was that of a real reformation, and in no department was that reforming work more needed than in sweeping away, in Scotland and Ireland alike, that Culdee system which had lost its primitive power, and was good for nothing save for the purposes of ecclesiastical plunder and degradation.

So much of romance has, however, gathered round the idea and name of the Culdees that I must tell you

---

[1] See *Memorials of St. Dunstan*, preface by Bishop Stubbs (Rolls Series).

more about them, and point out some traces of their existence and system which have survived, I might say, even to our own times.

The Culdees, in Dr. Reeves' opinion, were then "the corrupt following" of the ancient Celtic monks, to whom was applied this name of Kele-dei or Culdees. Religion revived in the twelfth and thirteenth centuries, and then under the reforming influence practical work was found for these ancient corporations. At times they were entirely absorbed in new episcopal or monastic communities. At other times they were preserved and utilized under some other name, as at St. Andrews and at York. At St. Andrews the Culdees of the twelfth century shared, with the canons of the cathedral, the election of the bishop. They were gradually deprived of their privileges in this and other respects. The popes were ever specially hostile to the Culdees. Yet they survived at St. Andrews to the Reformation period, when their style was that of the "Provost and Chapter of St. Mary's, the chapel of the King of the Scots."[1] At York the Culdees were in possession of St. Peter's Church (now the cathedral) in the year 936. In the eleventh century they were displaced: canons, after the Continental fashion, took the place of the monks who represented the ancient Celtic foundation, and the Culdees established themselves in another quarter of the city, in a hospital at first called St. Peter's and then St. Leonard's.[2] As it

---

[1] See Theiner's *Vet. Monum.*, p. 67 (Rome : 1864).
[2] Dugdale, *Monasticon Anglicanum*, vol. vi., pt. ii., p. 607 (London : 1846). Dr. Reeves, on p. 59 of his Essay, says : "It would appear that these Colidei were the officiating clergy of the Cathedral Church of St. Peter's at York in 936, and that they discharged the double function of Divine service and eleemosynary entertainment; thus combining

was in St. Andrews and York, so was it in Ireland, only that here, as was most natural, Irishmen held more tenaciously to the ancient title. You have all heard the famous story of the Irishman rejoicing in all the electoral dignities of a newly enfranchised citizen of the United States, who was asked the question, "For whom will you vote?" "Against the Government, of course," replied he. Well, perhaps there is an element of truth in the satire. There is apparently a strain in the Celtic character which delights in opposition, political and ecclesiastical. When the Anglo-Norman Church and the Pope displayed their opposition to the Culdees, this only made the Celtic population the more determined in their adherence to them. Ireland is a great country for what is called the "ould stock," and the Culdees, useless, corrupt, lax and easy-going in discipline, were nevertheless "the ould stock" ecclesiastically, and therefore they survived the shock of the Conquest and the decrees of the Synod of Cashel in the monasteries of the west and north. Take Clonmacnois, for instance. The Culdees first appear there by name in the eleventh century, when a celebrated

---

the two leading characteristics of the old conventual system common to both the Irish and Benedictine rules. But when things assumed a new complexion, and a Norman archbishop was appointed, and the foundation of a new cathedral laid, and a more magnificent scale established for the celebration of Divine worship in this Metropolitan Church, the Colidei, or old Order of officiating clergy, were superseded; and, while they were excluded from their cathedral employment, they received an extension of their eleemosynary resources, and, in order to mark their severalty, they were removed to another quarter of the city, whither they took their endowments with them, and thus continued through several centuries, under an altered economy and title, till all memory of their origin had perished, save what was recorded in the preamble of their charter-book."

ecclesiastic, called, from his devotion to the poor, Conn of the Paupers, was head of the local Culdee hospital. The discipline of Clonmacnois cannot have been very strict in those times, according to modern ideas, for Conn's father, one Joseph, was soul friend or confessor to the monastery; while in the next century three generations of the same sept of O'Naghten, to which Conn and his father belonged, were chiefs of the Culdees and wardens of the hospital, transmitting the office from father to son, till at last we read in the *Four Masters*, under the date 1200, the following notice of the death of the third hereditary chief of the Culdees, rejoicing in a name very hard to pronounce: "Uareirghe, son of Mulmora, son of Uareirghe O'Naghten, one of the noble sages of Clonmacnois, a man full of the love of God, and of every virtue, and head of the Culdees of Clonmacnois, died on the tenth of March."[1] But I shall not delay you too long with the Culdees, for we have much of the same kind of ground to go over. I must, however, call your attention to one other place where some traces of the Culdee system remain to the present day. Ussher, writing in the fifteenth chapter of his *Antiquities of the British Churches*, tells us that within his own memory the presbyters who served in the choir and celebrated Divine offices in the churches of Armagh and Clones were called Culdees.[2] Acting upon this hint, Dr. Reeves, in his essay, traces the Culdees of Armagh all through the ages which elapsed from the Synod of Kells to the Reformation. In the thirteenth century

---

[1] The head of the O'Naghtens still occupies a respectable position among the landlords of Galway and Roscommon.
[2] de. *Works*, Elrington, vi., 174.

a dean and chapter were introduced at Armagh, according to the Anglo-Norman fashion, no such officials having been previously known in Ireland. But the Culdees of Armagh were continued in a modified shape. The chief, or prior, was made precentor of the cathedral, and the Culdees were constituted the vicars choral. In that shape they survived the Reformation, as Ussher testifies, and were incorporated by Charles I. as a body corporate, and had all their ancient estates confirmed to them.[1] As such they withstood even the shock of disestablishment; and I believe that in some way or other, thanks to the ancient Culdee endowments and charters, the vicars choral or Culdees of Armagh are still the best endowed musical corporation in Ireland.

But if the whole of this lecture which remains is not to be taken up with the one topic of the Culdees, I must direct your attention to some other subjects, which shed light on the survival of ancient Celtic ideas under the ecclesiastical rule of the Anglo-Normans and the Pope.

These original Irish monasteries in the west perpetuated their ancient customs in another direction. The literature produced in them is just the same, animated by the same ideas, marked by the same customs, before and after the English invasion. Fortunately we have ample means for making the comparison, and that in the works which have been published under the guidance of a great Celtic scholar, whom, alas! an untimely death has but lately removed from our midst. The *Chronicon Scotorum*, the *Annals*

---

[1] See Morrin's *Calendar of Patent Rolls of Charles I.*, pp. 125, 221; Reeves, *Culdees*, p. 18.

of *Lough Cé*, and the *Book of Fenagh*, constitute a monument which will ever keep fresh the memory of that generous and learned Irishman, William M. Hennessy, the Assistant Deputy Keeper of the Irish Records. Two of these works—the *Chronicon Scotorum* and the *Annals of Lough Cé*—have been published in the Rolls Series. The *Book of Fenagh* was published in conjunction with the late Mr. D. H. Kelly. The *Chronicon Scotorum* was originally compiled about the year 1150 by Christian Malone, Abbot of Clonmacnois, a member of one of the principal ancient families of Westmeath, which is not yet extinct even in the ranks of the landlords. It is simply a book of annals of that famous monastery by the Shannon side. The *Book of Fenagh* deals with a monastery some fifty or sixty miles higher up the same river, near the waters of Lough Allen, the first great expanse of the Shannon after it leaves the mountains of Cavan and Leitrim. The *Book of Fenagh* was composed about the year 1300. It depicts the history and asserts the claims of the monastery of Fenagh and its patron saint, St. Caillin.

The *Annals of Lough Cé* constitute a work which is perhaps the most effective for my purpose. It was the annals or chronicles of the Monastery of the Holy Trinity, which stands on an island in a lake of Rockingham demesne, some ten miles or so from Fenagh. It was begun before the English Conquest, and proceeds steadily for hundreds of years after that Conquest, and yet there is no change in the manners or customs of the community whose history it records. The state of Church discipline is just the same in 1300 as in 1100. Bishops, abbots, monks, parochial clergy, are married or not, just as they please. I have shown you that the office of Chief of the Culdees at Clonmacnois was handed from father to son for three generations all through the twelfth century. It was the same at Fenagh in Leitrim, where, as Mr. Hennessy in his preface shows, the office of Abbot of Fenagh was hereditary in the family of O'Roddy from the year 800 to 1516.[1] In the twelfth or thirteenth century a change seems to have been made, not only in Fenagh, but everywhere else throughout the Celtic system. The abbots of the monasteries were called coarbs, heirs, or successors of the original founders. No term is so common as coarb in the Irish annals. In the very beginning of the *Book of Fenagh* St. John is called the Coarb of the Blessed Virgin, in reference, doubtless, to our Lord's words to her, as recorded in John xix. 26, "Woman, behold thy son." The Pope is called the Coarb of St. Peter in the *Chronicon Scotorum*, A.D. 1148. The Abbot of Clonmacnois was the Coarb of St. Kieran, and the O'Roddys were the Coarbs of St. Caillin at Fenagh for nine hundred years. But, as I have said, the twelfth century saw a change. St. Malachy of Armagh, the friend of St. Bernard, was probably the author of it. He was scandalized at the marriage of abbots. "He restored the monastic and canonical rules of the Church of Erin," as the *Chronicon Scotorum* tells us when announcing his death in 1148. He seems to have divided the office of abbot into two parts. Henceforth we often find a clerical coarb who was clerical abbot, and a lay coarb who managed the temporal estates of the community and was lay abbot. This latter office the O'Roddys retained for themselves till long after

---

[1] On the hereditary succession in abbeys see Reeves's *Columba*, p. 335.

the Reformation, as in 1700 we find that Thaddeus O'Roddy still held the same office under the Bishops of Kilmore, for whose benefit he farmed the ancient estates of the monastery.[1] The *Annals of Lough Cé* witness to the same fact. The author quite naturally records, under the year 1070, the murder of St. Columba's successor at Iona by the son of the murdered abbot's predecessor, and is not scandalized when he tells us that the Bishop of Elphin, who died in 1246, had for his father the Abbot of St. Mochua's monastery at Balla, in Mayo. And the abbots of these Celtic monasteries did not easily surrender their privileges in this respect, as we learn from another source.

Among the many publications with which Dr. Reeves has enriched our historical literature, none has interested me more than *Primate Colton's Visitation*, for it has shown me conclusive evidence of this perpetuation of ancient Celtic Church life in Anglo-Norman times. The occasion of that visitation was as follows. In the year 1397 the diocese of Derry was vacant, and had been so for the previous two years. The primate had heard rumours of various irregularities in the see thus destitute of a chief pastor. He determined to go and investigate for himself the state of affairs, and the daily

---

[1] The family of O'Roddy preserved the insignia of their office, the *Book of Fenagh*, with the shrine and bell of the saint, till fifty years ago, when the last of the family was parish priest of Kilronan in Leitrim. The *Book of Fenagh* used to be lent out by him for a small gratuity. It was used by the peasantry in quarrels among themselves; an oath taken upon St. Caillin's book being esteemed as specially binding, and a breach of it as sure to be followed by terrible consequences. It is now safe in the Royal Irish Academy. O'Donovan's "Breifny Letters" in the *Ordnance Survey Correspondence* have much about Fenagh, its neighbourhood and its antiquities.

record of his work and journeyings now constitutes for us a trustworthy picture of the life of an Irish archbishop about the year 1400. It was a mighty and a perilous journey which the primate was undertaking. The Primates of Armagh usually then lived at Termonfeckin near Drogheda, and in Drogheda itself, as they did till the early part of the last century. He must have looked forward with somewhat of fear and trembling to a visit to Derry away in the dominions of the O'Neills. The records of that visit are full of interest. They show us the ancient Celtic officials the Herenachs and Corbes, flourishing and discharging their duties in every parish, and they prove, too, that the abbots of the old Columban foundation at Derry, the Black Chapel, as it was called, retained the ancient Celtic customs in one important respect. A certain abbot, named Odo O'Dogherty, a well-known name still about Derry, had taken to himself a wife called Katherine O'Dogherty. A few days before, this very Odo was elected abbot by his brethren in the presence of the primate, and solemnly instituted into his office, and yet, though they must have known right well of his marriage, they do not think him one whit the less fitted to bear rule over them. Primate John Colton has stricter notions, however, and he issues, therefore, a stern monition commanding the expulsion of poor Katherine from her home and husband.[1]

But it is not on points of discipline alone that we can trace the old Celtic spirit as still rife in ecclesiastical matters. It was universally prevalent. The monasteries in the thirteenth century were as completely tribal institutions, bound up with certain septs and

---

[1] Colton's *Visitation*, ed. Reeves, pp. 56, 57.

hated by other hostile septs, as they were in the seventh or eighth century. There was not the slightest reverence for a monastery as such. The tribes venerated—sometimes, but not always—the monasteries belonging to their own patron saint or their own tribe. But the monasteries of a hostile tribe, or of a different saint, were regarded as fair game for murder, plunder, and arson. The *Book of Fenagh* is an interesting instance of this mere tribal religion which the Church of Rome tried hard to abolish. There were two famous monasteries in contiguous districts, where the counties of Leitrim and Roscommon touch one another. One was called Cloone, the other was Fenagh, of which we have already spoken. Now we can have no conception, till we study the *Book of Fenagh*, of the bitter hatred, the deep-seated hostility, which existed between these two institutions. The *Book of Fenagh* shows us how little power the true spirit of Christianity had yet gained over the wild, passionate Celtic nature. It describes the visitations made by the Abbot of Fenagh when claiming the dues owing to him as successor of the famous St. Caillin. It is with the Fenagh abbot as with the Columban Abbot of Derry, of whom I have already spoken: the dues he most delights in are arms, battle dresses, war horses, and gold. And the Abbots of Fenagh needed those arms at times. They and their neighbours at Cloone hated one another. They belonged, indeed, to the same clan, but reverenced different saints as their founders. The *Book of Fenagh* indulges, therefore, in the most awful threats of hell and damnation against any member of their tribe who should da.e even to be buried in Cloone. It does not hesitate at anything to accomplish its purpose. It invades heaven itself, and records a conversation between St. Columba and St. Caillin on this subject.[1] St. Caillin is the first speaker. He asks Columba—

> "Say, O holy Colum, what
> On them shall the vengeance be,
> When they from me depart,
> That they may go to Cloone?"

To which Columba replies—

> "Each one that forsakes thee,
> Of thy own monks,
> Whilst we may be in heaven
> Shall in torment be.
> I pledge thee my hand,
> Whoever will thee oppose
> Shall get his evil reward
> After leaving the body."

But notwithstanding all the threats which the Abbot of Fenagh so liberally dealt out, the neighbouring tribes of the more distant west often plundered his fields and burned his buildings. In the *Annals of Lough Cé* we have a story told which gives us a vivid picture of monastic life and of tribal hatred in the year 1244. I shall tell the story as briefly as possible. Phelim O'Conor, King of Connaught, son of Cathal of the Red Hand, of whom we have heard so much in other lectures, was engaged in one of his annual plundering and murdering expeditions. He was marching on this occasion against the O'Reillys of Cavan; and Fenagh was and still is on the direct route from Croghan and the plains of Roscommon, where O'Conor lived, to Cavan and Leitrim. Phelim and his army encamped one night in the monastery of Fenagh. The church was quite roofless, and filled with a number of huts erected in the interior. These the army occupied by night, and then, in all the wantonness of mischief, set fire to them as they were departing in

---

Book of Fenagh, ed. Kelly and Hennessy, pp. 193, 203

the morning, smothering in the process the coarb's foster-son. Next day the coarb, O'Roddy, followed the army and in a rage demanded the eric[1] of his foster-son. O'Conor said he would give him his own award. "My award," said the vengeful coarb, "is, that the best man amongst you be burned by you as the eric of my foster-son"—a demand which, of course, O'Conor declined. The coarb was not satisfied, however. He declared his intention to follow O'Conor and his army till his eric was paid, which he did till the best hero in the army was accidentally killed by the falling of a beam, when the enraged coarb was bought off with a present of silver and of thirty horses. This fierce, passionate, bloodthirsty spirit was universal. No place was too sacred for attack. Innis-Cleraun in Lough Ree was a great sanctuary, and is still an object of reverence. St. Diarmid's memory still flings a halo round it, but in the twelfth and thirteenth centuries it was plundered and burned again and again. We do not wonder at the Anglo-Normans treating Clonmacnois thus in the very first years of the invasion, for they had the greatest contempt for St. Kieran and all the Celtic saints except St. Patrick. But when we find O'Conors, O'Donnells, O'Neills, and O'Briens treating in this manner spots so venerated as Clonmacnois, Innis-Cleraun, and Derry, we may be sure that religion was at a very low ebb indeed. And the fighting spirit of the ancient ecclesiastical kind, such as the bishop-kings of Cashel displayed, long survived even among the clergy. Let me illustrate this with a story, which will cast light upon other topics of which I have been speaking.

---

[1] Eric was a fine or compensation for bloodshed or injury according to Brehon law.

I must ask you to come with me to the neighbourhood of Birr, or Parsonstown, in the King's County. It is now famous for the possession of the largest telescope in the world; but it has also been noted for stirring events in the history of this country. And naturally enough, too, for it was on the borderland between the English and the Irish. It looked on the one side towards Galway; on the other side towards the palatinate of Tipperary, with its Norman castles manned by the Butlers and their retainers. In the neighbourhood of Birr the last genuine specimen of the ancient Irish chieftain lingered till the end of the last, or the beginning of the present, century. The MacCoghlan, or, as he is in the tradition of the country side still called, the Maw, was the last landlord who wore the ancient Irish dress and lived at home in the ancient Irish style. He was member of Parliament for the King's County, and dressed when in Dublin in the usual fashion, but once he set his feet back on his native heath, he cast Dublin and English fashions to the winds, and resumed the attire and customs of his ancestors. And he certainly had ancestors, not going back a mere wretched century or two like our mushroom families of to-day, but going back fourteen or fifteen centuries, all of whom had ruled the dominion which, in part at least, continued in his family till his own time, and now forms the Barony of Garrycastle, though in former times known as MacCoghlan's country.[1] Four hundred and fifty years ago there was a Bishop of Clonmacnois of that

---

[1] See, for a description of the dress, mode of living, etc., of the last MacCoghlan, the Irish *Penny Journal*, A.D. 1840, pp. 145-47; cf. *Irish Topographical Poems* in Arch. Soc. Series, notes, p. vii; O'Donovan's notes on Four Masters, A.D. 1178, 1572, 1601. About MacCoghlan's country in the

same family. It was natural that it should be so. Clonmacnois is but a few miles distant—six or seven at most—from the castle and territory of The MacCoghlan; and when Cormac MacCoghlan, a son of the family, took Holy Orders, it was but fitting, from a Celtic point of view, that the chief's son should rapidly rise through the various gradations till at last he was made Bishop of Clonmacnois about the year 1426. He ruled his diocese for eighteen years, and then died a most unclerical death. He must then have been at least fifty years of age; still the fire of youth and the love of fighting had not yet died out in the heart of a MacCoghlan, even though he was a bishop. Cormac MacCoghlan had been long at Clonmacnois, and, as bishop, was head of extensive estates and a numerous tenantry in King's County, Westmeath, and in Connaught. The Clonmacnois men, when headed by the monks, had often in ancient times proved themselves no mean warriors, and even still at a fair or market, and above all things at an election, till modern legislation tyrannically interfered with the amusement, were first-rate manipulators of their blackthorn sticks. Bishop MacCoghlan quarrelled with the head of his own family, The MacCoghlan, and both sides agreed to submit their complaints to the arbitration of a neighbouring chief named O'Madden. All the parties to the quarrel gathered in force to meet O'Madden, who seems, however, to have failed to keep his appointment. At any rate there was some delay, when the bishop,

---

year 1626, see Morrin's *Patents of Charles*, p. 96. It was then the seat of a Sir Matthew de Renzi, in whose memory a famous monument exists in St. Mary's Church, Athlone. He seems to have been an Irish scholar, though of German descent.

inflamed by the sight of such a number of armed men, and thinking it a pity that such a fine chance for a fight should be lost, would force the matter to a decision at once. He vigorously attacked the opposite party, but was utterly defeated; the bishop himself, his son James, Archdeacon of Clonmacnois, the bishop's two brothers, and the two sons of Archdeacon MacCoghlan, with more than twenty others, being slain on the Monday before the feast of St. John the Baptist.[1] How thoroughly Celtic the whole thing! How it reminds us of what we read seven or eight hundred years earlier, when the monasteries of Durrow and Clonmacnois, with their retainers, tenantry, and slaves, used to join in deadly battle! Yet this episcopal warrior died sixty years after Wickliffe, and but forty years before Luther was born. Mark, too, the traces of Celtic times in other respects. The bishop was just like the ancient abbots of Clonmacnois; he had his own son and placed him in a position of authority, while other members of the sept filled other positions of dignity and trust. I do not think you will need any further proof of the long survival of Celtic ideas in the Church of Ireland.

And yet we have much more evidence bearing on this very point. The threefold division of the tithes and other oblations and revenues of the clergy lasted, in the Celtic portion of the Irish Church, to a longer period than anywhere else in Europe. In the early Church, ecclesiastical revenues were sometimes divided into four portions, sometimes into three, one portion always going to the bishop for his support. This custom prevailed in France, Spain, and England, till

---

[1] See the whole story told in a paper in the *Journal* of the Kilk. Arch. Society, t. i., p. 380, by T. L. Cooke, Esq., on "A Wayside Ancient Monument at Drisoge in the King's County."

the sees were endowed with landed property, when the tithes and other oblations of the laity were wholly devoted to the parochial clergy, the monasteries, and the sustenance of the fabrics of the churches. This was in the time when the tithes were really a tenth of every kind of produce; when the tenth gallon of ale brewed in Dublin, and the tenth fish taken in the Bay of Dublin, belonged to the clergy. In the eastern dioceses, where the sees were at once endowed with ample estates by the Anglo-Norman conquerors, the bishops never seem to have enjoyed the "Episcopal Thirds," as this source of income was called. But in the west and north of Ireland it was quite otherwise. In the diocese of Clogher, which was thoroughly Celtic till the seventeenth century, the third part of the tithes was devoted to the support of the bishop, till the time of James I., when Bishop Montgomery obtained from the Crown a handsome endowment for the see. In the diocese of Tuam, this method of distributing the tithes lasted till the year 1717, when Archbishop Synge procured an Act of Parliament for the consolidation of the "Quarter Episcopals," as they were locally called, with the remainder of the tithes. In Killala we find a similar arrangement existing till 1663; in Elphin till 1633; in Derry and Raphoe till the plantation of Ulster in the times of James I. and Charles I. The most curious instance of survival of this ancient primitive custom remains, however, yet to be told, for it is a simple fact that the Quarter Episcopals continued to be a portion of the episcopal revenues of Clonfert and Kilmacduagh till the temporalities of these sees were vested in the Ecclesiastical Commissioners in the year 1833.[1]

---

[1] In the Isle of Man, which was thoroughly Celtic in its Church organization and discipline, we find the Episcopal

Again, the old literary life of the Celtic Church did not wholly die out in the west and north-west of Ireland. There was a far more active literary life in the Celtic parts of Ireland than in the Anglo-Norman districts—an activity which was perpetuated till the seventeenth century, when it produced such great epoch-marking works as the *Annals of the Four Masters*, and the great monumental collections of Colgan, for Colgan and the annalists called the Four Masters were all of them natives of the west and north-west of Ireland.[1]

The profession of poet, historian, and linguist continued to be a popular one in the west, down to the beginning of the last century. The history of the MacFirbis family amply shows how this literary life and the literary succession of the west were maintained. Sir James Ware gets credit for being a great Irish scholar. He was a diligent student and antiquarian, but his Irish scholarship was all due to Duald MacFirbis, an Irish scholar and historian from Mayo, whom he kept in his pay at his house in Castle Street, Dublin. Duald MacFirbis was a great Celtic scholar. He belonged to a family which can be traced backwards for at least four hundred years, following all the while the profession of poets and antiquarians to a Mayo chieftain. To his ancestors in the direct line we owe two of our greatest Celtic treasures: the *Book of Lecan*, written by a MacFirbis before the year 1416, which is

---

Thirds mentioned as a source of the bishop's revenue in a charter of the year 1505. Cf. Dugdale's *Monast. Anglic.*, vol. i., p. 718; and Dr. Reeves's exhaustive note in his edition of Colton's *Visitation*, p. 112 (Dublin: Irish Archæological Society, 1850).

[1] See O'Donovan's Preface to *Annals of Four Masters*, vol. iii.

now in the Royal Irish Academy; and the *Yellow Book of Lecan*, written about the same period, and in part by the same hand.[1] The wars and confusions of Ireland which I have already striven to depict never seem to have quenched the love of learning in the Celtic breast; and all through its darkest periods, Celtic schools existed after the ancient fashion, where Latin, Greek, history, and the Brehon law system were carefully studied, and the interpretations of the ancients transmitted by living tradition. Duald MacFirbis had no difficulty, even in Queen Elizabeth's reign, in finding such centres of Celtic study. He passed about 1590 into Munster, where he attended the school of law and history kept by the MacEgans of Lecan in Ormond, in Tipperary, whence after a time he transferred himself to the Academy of the O'Davorens of Burren in the county Clare.[2] After pursuing a lengthened course at these places, Duald MacFirbis then devoted a long life, terminated only by a sad and tragic death, to the subject of Celtic scholarship, wherein he not only rendered the most valued help to men like Sir James

---

[1] Lecan is in Mayo, on the left bank of the river Moy. The MacFirbises were settled there prior to the year 1397. Mr. Hennessy, in his Preface to the *Chronicon Scotorum*, gives much interesting information about the family. From his interesting narrative I have borrowed freely.

[2] The MacEgans, as Mr. Hennessy says, were hereditary Brehons and professors of the old Irish laws, and descendants of the men who compiled the splendid vellum MS. called the *Leabhar Breac*, or "Speckled Book," preserved in the library of the Royal Irish Academy. This MS., compiled in the year 1397, is the most valuable repertory now remaining of ancient Irish ecclesiastical affairs. It was composed in the county Galway. A lithographic fac-simile of it was published in 1876 by the Royal Irish Academy, under the direction of Mr. Gilbert. See his *Account of Fac-similes of the National MSS. of Ireland*, pp. 108-111.

Ware, Roderick O'Flaherty, and Dr. John Lynch, the author of *Cambrensis Eversus;* but also produced several independent works which are now of the greatest value. But if you are interested in the subject of Celtic literature, read O'Curry's *Manuscript Materials for Irish History*, or Hennessy's preface to the *Chronicon Scotorum*, and there you will see how deep are our obligations to Duald MacFirbis. I merely bring him forward as a notable instance proving that the traditions of ancient Irish scholarship were perpetuated in the Celtic portion of the Irish Church all through the ages of Anglo-Norman dominion.

Admitting, then, that there was a tone and colour and life peculiar to itself in the Celtic Church of Ireland, you may ask me what were the peculiar features of what I designate the Anglo-Norman Church. Its peculiarities were numerous. The Anglo-Norman Church built splendid churches and monasteries. Wherever there is a grand building or a magnificent ecclesiastical ruin in Ireland, from Limerick and Kerry in the south-west to Antrim in the north, it is due to the Anglo-Normans, or to Anglo-Norman influence acting upon the Celts. The Anglo-Norman Church had its controversies too, but they were concerning topics of interest in England. Transubstantiation and the nature of the Holy Communion were debated in England in the age of Wickliffe. Ussher tells us that about the same period Henry Crumpe, a monk of Baltinglass, wrote a treatise against that doctrine, to which William Andrew, Bishop of Meath from 1380 to 1385, replied.[1] The Anglo-Norman Church in Ireland was intolerant of opposition, and

---

[1] Ussher's *Religion of the Ancient Irish*, cap. iv., in Works, ed. Elrington, t. iv., p. 285. Crumpe was also an opponent of the Mendicants. Cf. Ussher, *l.c.*, pp. 302, 303.

used the temporal sword, as it did in England, to crush opposition. The opening years of the fourteenth century were rendered famous by the ecclesiastical and civil contests over the case of Dame Alice Kyteler of Kilkenny, accused of witchcraft and heresy, when a certain woman named Petronilla, of Meath, suffered death by fire at Kilkenny, in 1324—being the first person ever so punished in Ireland; while her high-born associates, William Outlaw and the Lady Alice Kyteler, narrowly escaped the same terrible fate by doing ample penance and covering with lead the roof of St. Canice's cathedral. The native Celts were soon after made to feel the stern arm of the same ecclesiastical discipline, when in 1327 a certain Adam Duff, a Leinster man, and of the tribe of the O'Tooles, was burned alive on College Green for denying the doctrines of the Holy Trinity and of the Incarnation, and rejecting the authority of the Holy See.[1] The Anglo-Norman Church was not content, however, with repressive measures. It strove to meet the rising tide of heresy and freethought which marked the fourteenth century by intellectual efforts as well. The Franciscan and Dominican friars were then the leaders of religious education. They must have known of the Celtic schools of Ireland and their teaching, but they scorned them because they knew nothing of the schoolmen and their methods. Under their inspiration, therefore, Archbishop Leech, of Dublin, obtained a bull from Pope Clement V., in 1311, establishing the

---

[1] The proceedings in these earliest cases of Irish heresy may be seen, those concerning Alice Kyteler in a volume published by the Camden Society (cf. Grace's *Annals*, pp. 100-2; Clyn's *Annals*, p. 16, Dublin Archæol. Scc.); and those in Adam Duff's case in Grace's *Annals*, pp. 107, 108, published in the same series. Cf. Pope Benedict's epistles on the subject in Theiner's *Vetera Monumenta*, p. 269 (Rome: 1864).

University of Dublin, a project which hung fire for a time, but was completed by his successor, Alexander de Bicknor, in 1320, when the Chapter of St. Patrick's Cathedral was endowed with university powers, a faint shadow of which was claimed so lately as the time of Dean Swift. A complete university organization was adopted, and continued in active operation, chiefly under Franciscan direction, all through the fourteenth century, but seems to have died from poverty and the confusion of the times, till revived in the days of Queen Elizabeth, when the College of the Holy and Undivided Trinity was founded for the same purpose, that Ireland might breed and teach a race of scholars from its own children and upon its own soil.[1] While again we can show that the same intellectual activity characterised the Dublin Franciscans of that period as animated their English brethren, for there still exists the diary of two members of the Dublin community, Simon Fitz-Simeon and Hugh the Illuminator, who about 1320 set out on a pilgrimage to Egypt and the Holy Land, leaving us a record of their travels which is still of importance, as illustrating the social and religious state of Egypt and the East when the enthusiasm of the Crusades had passed away.[2]

The feature, however, which chiefly strikes us in the Anglo-Norman Church, and confirms us in the

---

[1] For the history of this earliest University of Dublin, see Mason's *History of St. Patrick*, Appendix No. I.; Ware's *Antiquities*, ch. xv., in Harris's edition, pp. 242-5; Grace's *Annals*, p. 97, with Dean Butler's notes. During the reign of Edward IV. an Act was passed, in 1465, establishing a university in Drogheda; but this never came to anything. See Harris's Ware, ii., 245.

[2] This curious and little known Irish document was printed at Cambridge in 1778, by James Nasmith, and is in large part reprinted in the *Retrospective Review* for 1828, pp. 232-54.

distinction we have made between it and the Celtic Church, is the persistent and bitter hostility we can trace between these two sections of our Irish Christianity from the Conquest to the Reformation. That hostility burst forth, as I have already noted in an earlier lecture, in the very first days of Anglo-Norman rule. In 1186 a Council was held at Dublin by Archbishop Comyn, before which Giraldus Cambrensis preached a very cutting sermon, accusing the native Celtic clergy of all kinds of riot and ungodliness —the clergy of drunkenness, the bishops of carelessness—in reply to one preached by the Abbot of Baltinglass, the day before, in which he accused the Anglo-Norman clergy of corrupting their Irish brethren by their evil example.[1] The ball of mutual hostility when once set rolling, rapidly increased. Early in the thirteenth century the Anglo-Norman Church prohibited the admission of Irish clerks into monasteries, benefices, or cathedral dignities under English control, a statute which called forth the papal rebuke in 1220

---

[1] See Girald. Camb., *Opp.*, t. i., pp. 65-72 (Rolls Series). In his *Topograph*. Dist., iii., cap. xxxii., Giraldus shows that matters were very nearly becoming serious on that occasion. He tells us that he was speaking to Maurice, Archbishop of Cashel, concerning the sad state of the Irish Church, and throwing the blame upon the prelates. Giraldus, however, will tell his own tale best: " I drew a powerful argument from the fact that no one in that kingdom had ever obtained the crown of martyrdom. Upon this the archbishop replied sarcastically, answering it by a home-thrust: 'It is true,' he said, 'that although our nation may seem barbarous, uncivilised, and cruel, they have always shown great honour and reverence to their ecclesiastics, and never on any occasion raised their hands against God's saints. But there is now come into our land a people who know how to make martyrs, and have frequently done it. Henceforth Ireland will have its martyrs as well as other countries.'" Remembering the then recent murder of Thomas à Becket, we do not think the

and again in 1224.[1] Later in the same century the prelates of the Celtic portion of the Church replied by a similar prohibition, forbidding the admission of Englishmen to parishes or monasteries within their jurisdiction; a law which the Pope again annulled on the special ground that it was intended to secure the ancient Celtic abuse of hereditary succession to benefices. And so matters went on till the Statute of Kilkenny was passed, which again, as we have already noted, peremptorily forbade the admission of Irishmen to any benefice or other ecclesiastical preferment wherever English law or rule prevailed. The fourteenth differed in one important respect from the thirteenth century. The popes held the balance fairly in the earlier time. In the later period they became thorough partisans, and raised no protest against a legislation which was completely alien to the spirit of genuine Christianity. The Statute of Kilkenny was no longer protested against. The popes became the adherents of the Anglo-Norman party in the Irish Church, supporting their narrow exclusiveness till the lowest depths were reached, when Leo X. in the year 1515 issued a bull reorganizing St. Patrick's Cathedral. In that bull, dealing with the internal economy of a cathedral called after Ireland's patron saint,—over whose door, too, there then stood a statue

---

English archdeacon scored much off the Irish archbishop; though, as these pages have shown, the archbishop's history was somewhat inaccurate. But then, in an encounter of words and wits, point, not accuracy, always carries the day. In his treatise, *De Rebus a se Gestis*, in vol. i., quoted above, Giraldus tells us that the Bishop of Ossory told the archbishop, when supping with him the night of the archdeacon's sermon, that it was with difficulty he kept his episcopal hands off the preacher. Synods were lively in those days.

[1] Cf. Theiner's *Vet. Monum.*, pp. 16, 23.

of that saint, which now you will find in the baptistery or little chapel on the left of the south-western entrance,—there was inserted the following papal injunction: " Furthermore, that ancient custom, concerning Irishmen, by nation, manners, and blood, who should not be admitted in the said Cathedral Church of St. Patrick any royal dispensation notwithstanding; it is agreed that it shall flourish, grow strong, and prevail with a vigorous and perpetual care. Furthermore, let diligent examination be made as well by the Archbishop as by the Dean and Chapter, and if any person shall be found defective in these or in any other of the aforesaid matters, let him not be admitted, but rather let him be at once expelled."[1] Surely Church matters must have come to a dreadful pass in Ireland when the Pope, the Patriarch of Western Christendom, could, in the year 1515, thus lend himself to the ecclesiastical ostracism of the Celtic race, and avow himself the partisan of one section of the Church of Ireland.[2]

I have now come, however, to the limits which I have marked for myself. Were I to go farther I should

---

[1] See the original bull, as given in Mason's *History of St. Patrick's*, Appendix, p. xv; cf. pp. 142-44. This bull, I may remark, is not to be found in Theiner's *Vetera Monumenta Hibernorum*, published by papal authority in 1864.

[2] It is consoling, amid so much that was dark and un-Christian, to light upon some evidence of the existence of spiritual religion in those times of disorder of which we treat. In Marsh's Library I have under my care a manuscript once belonging to the learned Dudley Loftus. It is a transcript made in March 1688 for the benefit of the Roman Catholic Bishop of Clogher. It is of some interest in a political point of view, for it shows by its dedication to the " Right Rev. Father Patricke, Lord Bishop of Clogher, Chief Secretary for the King's Most Sacred and Excellent Majestie in the Kingdome of Ireland," that James II. had determined months before his deposition to overthrow the existing constitution. To the ecclesiastical historian it is of even still

tread upon the boundaries of the modern history of Ireland. At some other time, if God spares me health and strength, I hope to deal with that subject. I now close my lectures on the mediæval section of Ireland's history. They have not, like my previous course, dealt with characters and persons of world-wide reputation. St. Patrick, St. Columba, St. Columbanus, are much better known than John Comyn, Hugh de Lacy, or Richard Fitz-Ralph. But all the same, the period with which this course has dealt has more living interest for ourselves, for we are the recipients of its blessings and of its curse. I once heard an orator declare in one of our Synods, when speaking of Irish history, and the utility, or the opposite, of teaching it to young people: "In my opinion the less they know about it the better." I do not agree in that view, and I hope you do not agree in it either. It is an ignorant opinion; it is a narrow, a bigoted, and a dangerous opinion. What light, what guidance, what blessing for his country can one hope to gain from a man who thinks the less people know about the history of their own land the better? No man can be a true Irish statesman who knows not the past history of the land with which he deals. A physician might as well undertake to cure a patient without knowing the history

---

more interest. Its title is "The Pilgrim, or the Pilgrimage of Man in this World, wherein the Author plainly and truly sets forth the wretchedness of Man's life in this world without Grace, our sole protector. Written in the year of Christ 1331." It was given to the Bishop of Clogher by a man named O'Brien, who claimed descent from Brian Boru. He found it among his father's papers, and copied it for the bishop's use. It is evidently a translation of Guillaume de Deguildeville's celebrated allegory. I have not had time, however, to determine its relation to other versions.

of his life and disease, as a statesman undertake to legislate for a country of whose history he is ignorant. Every parochial clergyman has in his own limited sphere somewhat of a statesman's influence. He can promote love, joy, peace, social charity in his parish and neighbourhood, or he may be the minister of discord, hatred, and social disorganization. I can only hope that the effect of these lectures, to which you have been the listeners, may be the production of a healthy patriotic pride in your country's history, combined with a wider toleration, a broader sympathy, and a more kindly and loving charity towards every member of that highly composite race which now is called the Irish people.

NOTE.

Mr. James Mills, of the Dublin Record Office, has called my attention to three points in these lectures where his wide research leads him to differ from me. On p. 210 I have spoken of the bishopric of the Isles as undoubtedly the diocese of Glendalough, and not that of Sodor and Man. This is the idea of Ware and all subsequent writers, who could not see what Dublin had to do with the Isle of Man. Mr. Mills points out, however, that Theiner, in his *Documenta*, p. 14, has printed a bull which seems to show that in 1220 there was a connexion between Dublin and Man. The Archbishop of Dublin is there called "Metropolitanus loci" of the "Episcopus Insularum," who had just been elected by the "Conventus Furnesii" or Furness Abbey, which Society had a close connexion both with Man and Dublin; see pp. 201-2 above. On p. 215 I have spoken on Harris's authority of a Robert, Bishop of Dublin. Mr. Mills suggests, and I think most happily, that this was Robert de Prebenda, Bishop of Dunblane 1251 to 1280. In contracted Latin the difference between Dublin and Dunblane is extremely slight. See *Calend. of Documents relating to Scotland*, vol. i., no. 2395 and 2439; vol. ii., no. 65. On p. 264 Mr. Mills challenges the historical character of the story which attributes the nickname of Scorchvillein to Archbishop Henry; see a paper by Mr. Mills in *Journal of Royal Soc. of Antiquaries of Ireland*, 1890, p. 54, and Mr. Gilbert's *Chartularies of St. Mary's Abbey*, vol. ii., pref. p. cxxii., note.

INDEX.

ABBATIAL succession (*see* Reeves), 349.
Abbey of All Saints, 180, 351.
—— Athlone, 248.
—— Bective, 167.
—— Cong, 13, 240.
—— Furness, 202.
—— Glendalough (SS. Peter and Paul), 217, 222.
—— —— (St. Saviour), 351.
—— Holy Cross, 13.
—— Jerpoint, 84.
—— Knockmoy, 289.
—— Mellifont, 13, 167, 284.
—— St. Mary, 284.
—— Selsker, 78.
—— St. Thomas, 26, 167, 238, 239.
Abbot, Archbishop, 259.
Academy, Royal Irish, 2, 362.
—— *Proceedings of*, 285, 349.
—— *Transactions of*, 350, 353.
Adamnan's (St.) Cross, 199.
Admiralty, *Sailing Directions* of, 70, 78.
Adrian IV., Pope, 45-7, 61.
Affreca, 237, 279.
Alan, Archbishop, 185, 186.
Alexander III., Pope, 216, 226.
Alleyn, Dean, will of, 227.
Almonds, 128, 143.
Altars, stone, 215.
Andrew, Wm., Bishop of Meath, 373.
Anglo-Norman Church, character of, 373-78.
—— hostility to Celts of, 376, 378.
Anglo-Normans, cruelty of, 103.
Annaghdown diocese, 213.

Annals of Clonmacnois, 2, 9, 20, 281.
—— Dudley Loftus, 114, 223.
—— Dudley MacFirbis, 308, 352.
—— Four Masters, 2, 3, 6, 15, 114, 199, 371.
—— Friar Clyn, 308-10.
—— Lough Cé, 2, 6, 10, 241, 281, 360.
—— Pembridge, 308.
—— Thady Dowling, 308, 311.
—— Ulster, 2, 3, 6, 7.
Archæologia, 224.
Archdall's *Monasticon Hibernicum*, 66, 79, 84, 213.
Archdeacon, office of, 31, 252.
—— salvability of, 31.
Armagh, Primate of, 313, 334.
—— controversy with Dublin prelates, 210.
—— protest of, 341.
—— residence of, 314, 362.
Armagh city, Culdees at, 358, 359.
—— *Hist.* of, 292.
Assize courts, 208.
Athlone, 9, 11, 243, 245, 248.
—— abbey of, 248.
—— bridge of, 11.
—— castle of, 243, 247, 283.
—— church of, 368.
Atkinson, Prof., 2, 17, 77.
Atlantis, 79.
Audoen's (St.) Arch, 109.
Augustinians and Christ Church, Dublin, 59, 185.

BACON, 128, 140

Bag and Bun, 68, 102.
—— promontory of, 99.
Baldoyle, lands of, 118, 181.
Baldwin, Archbishop, 272.
Ball, Rt. Hon. J. T., 320.
Ballinloure, 100.
Ballymore, 219.
Baltinglass, Abbot of, 376.
Bannow, 68, 74.
Banquets, mediæval, 143, 144.
Bargy, barony of, 79.
Barnes, Rev. W., 79.
Barry, Robert, 76.
Basilia, 173.
Bassett's *Wex. Dir.*, 75, 78.
Bawn (Bo-dun), 9, 10.
Becket, 122.
Beg-Erin, 116.
Bells, sacred, 11, 362.
Benedict of Peterb., *Chron.* of, 231.
—— *Gesta* of, 208.
Benefices, hereditary, 33, 210.
Bennett, Rev. R., 199
Berengaria, Queen, 145.
Berkeley, peerage, 58.
Betham, Sir W., 264.
Bible in Irish, 335.
Bicknor, Archbishop of Dub., 375.
Birr, 367.
Bishops, Anglo-Norman in Wales, 40.
—— Irish, as English suffragans, 315.
—— mediæval, 200.
Black death, 334, 336.
Blackrock, 100.
Blinding, 8, 9, 21.
Bogs, 288.
Book of Fenagh, 360-65.
—— Glendalough, 2.
—— Kells, 13.
—— Lecan, 371.
—— Leinster, 2, 17, 19.
Boulter, Primate, 189, 212.
Boycotting, mediæval, 262.
Bramhall, Primate, 335.
Braose, W. de, 287.
Brawney, 169.
Brehon law, 329, 338, 366, 372.
Breifny, 13.
Brendan, St., 54, 74.
Brewer, Rev. J. S., 30, 36, 40, 43.

Brewer, Rev. J. S., *Mon. Francisc.*, 254, 331.
Bristol, cathedral of, 58, 59.
—— plan of, 58.
Brooking's Map of Dublin, 265.
Brown, Archbishop, 197.
Bruce, family of, 324.
—— wars of, Lecture XIV.
Brut-y-Tywysogion, 51, 61, 69, 96, 129, 141, 289.
Burgh, Richard de, 298, 303.
—— William de, 238, 336.
—— and St. Thomas's Abbey, 239.
Burke, family of, 238.
Butler, Dean, *De Conc. Hib.*, 317, 321.
—— *Hist. of Trim*, 166.
—— *Reg. of All Saints*, 351.
Butler, family of, 339, 340.
Butlerabo, 340.

CAERLEON, 9.
Cagework houses, 107.
Caillin, St., 361-65.
Camden's *Britannia*, 237.
Campbell, Ld., *Lives of Ch. Just.*, 154.
Canice, St. (Cainnech), 143.
Canons, secular, change of, 196, 270.
Canterbury, and monastic chapters, 272.
—— archbishops of, 211.
—— controversy with York, 211.
Cantred, 240, 248.
Carrickfergus, castle of, 285.
—— church of, 345.
Carrickshock, battle of, 86.
Carrig, castle of, 92, 116.
Carroll, Rev. W. G., *Succession of St. Bride's Clergy*, 100.
Cashel, bishop-kings of, 356.
—— Council of, 146, 189, 191-94, 343, 344.
Castledermot, 178.
Cé, Lough, Annals of (see Annals).
Celtic Church, Lect. II. and Lect. XV.
—— land tenures, 329.
—— school system, 372, 374.
Chartæ, Privilegia et Immunitates, 8, 109, 142.
Chester, parliament at, 157.
Ch. Ch. Cath. (Canterbury), 74.

Ch. Ch. Cath. (Dublin), 59.
—— and James II., 59.
Christian, Bishop of Lismore, 146, 192.
Christian Examiner, 186.
Chronicle, Hanmer's, 236.
—— Hoveden's, 106, 134, 137, 152, 190, 230.
—— of Man, 237, 281.
—— of Radulf de Diceto, 141.
—— Welsh, 4, 61, 96.
Chronicon Scotorum, 2, 3, 361.
Cistercians, description of, 42, 43.
—— in Ireland, 146.
Clanricarde, family of, 152, 238, 337.
—— estate of, 240, 337.
Clarence, Duke of, 337.
Clark, G. T., *Mediæv. Milit. Archit.*, 6, 30, 58, 63, 135.
Clement V., Pope, 374.
Clogrenan, 88.
Clonmacnois, 346, 350, 366.
—— *Annals* of (*see* Annals).
—— archdeacon of, 369.
—— bishop of, 248, 367-69.
—— castle of, 243, 248, 249.
Clyn, Friar, 308.
Coarbs of St. Columba (*see* Corbes), 347-50.
Cogan, Miles de, 113, 117, 119.
Coinage, Danish, 52.
Colby's *Ord. Surv. Mem. of Derry*, 348.
Colgan, John, 371.
—— *AA. SS. Hib.*, 145.
Collegiate churches, 268, 270.
Columba, St., 346-50, 364, 365.
Columban order, 346, 350.
Comyn, Archbishop John, 145, 184, 200-22, 227, 228, 251.
Congé d'élire in middle ages, 39.
Corbes and herenachs, 34, 226, 361, 362, 363.
Cotton's (Archd.) *Fasti*, 314.
Courcy, John de, 152, 236.
—— appearance of, 236, 279.
—— character of, 236.
—— Earl of Ulster, 277.
Courts, archiepiscopal, 220.
Cranes as food, 136, 137.
Crannog, 6, 285.
Crede Mihi, MS., 25, 26, 108, 267.

Cromabo, 340.
Crook, 105, 106, 130.
—— Wright's mistake about, 72, 106, 131, 132.
Crucifix, 198.
Crumpe, H., 373.
Cualaun (Cullen), prebend of, 113, 139, 226.
Culdees, 353-59.
—— at York, 356.
—— hereditary at Clonmacnois, 358.
—— in Scotland, 353.
—— in Wales, 33, 353.
Cullenswood, 113, 226.
Curragh, battle of, 300-03.

D'ALTON's *Archbs. of Dublin*, 215.
Dame's Gate, 119.
Danes, defeat of, 14, 15.
—— modern fear of, 188.
David's, St., see of, 38, 39.
Davis, Sir John, 329.
Decies, 98, 99.
Decima Saladinæ, 316.
Deer, episcopal, 259.
Delany, Mrs., 189.
Derry, abbots of, 346-50, 363.
—— bishops of, 347.
Dervorgil (of Breifny), 20, 21.
—— (of Dublin), 118.
Diamond, battle of, 291.
Diarmid, Mael-na-mbo, 19.
—— Saint, 366.
Dict. Christ. Antiqq., 352.
Dinin river, 88.
—— legends of, 88.
Dominus, title of, 136.
Donore, 238.
Downpatrick, cathedral of, 279.
Doyle's, Martin, *Notes and Gleanings*, 79.
Drogheda, 278.
—— Parliament at, 338, 340.
—— University of, 375.
Dublin, archbishops of, full title of, 266.
—— archdeacons of, 196, 217.
—— assistant-bishops of, 214.
—— capture of, 112-14.
—— castle of, 265, 283.
—— churches of: Christ Church or Holy Trinity, 59, 109.

Dublin, churches of: St. Andrew's, 135.
—— —— St. Audoen's or Owen's, 109, 186.
—— —— St. Bridget's (Bride), 196, 197.
—— —— St. Columba's, 197.
—— —— St. George's, 186.
—— —— St. John's, 196.
—— —— St. Kevin's, 226.
—— —— St. Martin's, 187, 197.
—— —— St. Mary's, 197.
—— —— St. Michael's, 178, 197.
—— —— St. Michael-le-pole, 187.
—— —— St. Michan's, 196, 197.
—— —— St. Nicholas, 345.
—— —— St. Olave's, 186.
—— —— St. Patrick's, 197, 226.
—— —— St. Paul's, 187.
—— —— St. Stephen's, 187.
—— —— St. Werburgh's, 59, 109.
—— Corporation of, contests with archbishop, 219, 220.
—— county of, protests of, 341.
—— *History of Co. Dublin*, by Dalton, 73.
—— —— —— of city of (Harris), 110.
—— —— —— (Gilbert), 8, 110.
—— map of, by Speed, 109.
—— materials for history of, 108.
—— *Penny Journal*, 13, 246.
—— plan, ancient, of, 109.
—— Strand, battle of, 119.
—— synod of, 86, 215, 376.
—— University, origin of, 374, 375.
—— winter climate of, 138.
Duff, Adam, 374.
Dugdale's *Baronage*, 324.
—— *Orig. Jurid.*, 147, 154.
Duibhregles of Derry, 347, 363.
Duncannon Fort, 105.
Dunstan, St., 270, 355.
Durham, palatinate of, 157.
Durrow, 87.
—— *Book of*, 168.
—— castle of, 168.
—— monastery of, 168, 346.
Dysentery, Irish, 141, 142.

EADMOTH, 53, 54, 55.
Easter, 346, 352.
Edan, Bishop, 181

Edward, the Confessor, 52.
—— I., 316, 318, 319, 322, 323.
—— II., 329.
—— III., 330, 331.
Egypt, 155, 156, 375.
Electuaries, 129.
Elizabeth de Burgh, Countess, 337.
Episcopal elections in middle ages, 39, 206, 251.
Eric, 366.
Eva, Princess, 107, 277.
Evans, Edward, 110.
Exeter, see of, 229, 256.
Eyton's *Antiqq. of Shrops.*, 189.

FAUGHART, battle of, 325.
Fenagh, Book of, 360, 361, 364, 365.
Ferns, abbey of, 66.
—— castle of, 65.
Ferrand, William, 100.
Feudal system in Ireland, 150-54, 233.
—— Stubbs, Bp., upon, 232.
Fews of Dundalk, 291, 292.
Finglas, battle of, 117.
—— manor of, 142.
Finnian, St., 51.
Fitz-Adam, Thomas, 260, 261, 262.
Fitz-Aldelm, William, 130.
Fitz-Geralds, origin of, 28, 95, 96.
—— strife with Butlers, 339, 340.
—— David, bishop, 31, 32, 38, 40, 129.
—— Maurice, 298.
Fitz-Henry, Meyler, 242, 255.
Fitz-Ralph, (of Dundalk,) Primate Richard, 334, 335.
Fitz-Simeon, Simon, 375.
Fitz-Simons, Archbishop, 227.
Fitz-Stephen, Robert, 64, 67.
—— invasion of, 74.
Fleet, Irish Channel, 304.
Flemings in Wales, 63.
Fordun, J., 325.
Forth, barony of, 79.
Forth, Dialect of, by Poole, 79.
Foss's *Judges*, 155, 253.
Four Masters, see *Annals of*, 2, 114.
Fox, family of, 169, 170, 277.
—— O'Caharny, 169.
Franciscans, 304.
—— as travellers, 375.
—— in Ireland, 331-34, 374, 375

Freeman's *Norman Conquest*, 15, 53, 121.
Froude, Mr., 233.

GALE'S *Corporate System of Ireland*, 341.
Gallows, episcopal, 220.
Galway, History of (Hardiman), 213.
—— tribes of, 344, 345.
—— warden of, 213.
Games of Middle Ages, 164.
Garrycastle, barony of, 367.
Gelasius, Primate, 10, 144, 145.
Gerald, of Windsor, 28, 96.
Gilbert (J. T.), *Acct. of Facsimiles Nat. MSS.*, 2, 13, 17, 372.
—— *Chartul. Mary's Abbey*, 8, 15, 85, 114, 118.
—— *Hist. of Dublin*, 8, 110, 135.
—— *Munic. Docc.*, 142.
—— *Viceroys*, 151.
Giles' *Life of Becket*, 207.
Gillamocholmogs, 85, 118,
Gillpatrick (Fitzpatrick), King of Ossory, 80, 83, 84.
Giraldus Cambrensis, Lect. II.
—— birth of, 27.
—— education of, 30, 31.
—— election to St. David's, 38-42.
—— excommunication of a bishop by, 36.
—— family of, 27, 28.
—— hostility to Cistercians, 42.
—— journey to Rome, 41.
—— sermons of, 145, 376.
—— works of: *Conquest of Ireland*, 45, 72, 100-6, 116, 123, 137, 151.
—— —— *De Rebus a se Gestis*, 34.
—— —— *Description of Wales*, 27, 34.
—— —— *Itinerary*, 30, 33.
—— —— *Topography*, 44, 142, 145.
Glanville, Barth. de, 127.
—— Ranulf de, 127, 147.
Glasscarrig, 65.
Glencullen, 85, 260.
Glendalough, 178, 184, 195, 350.
—— abbots of, 178, 216, 218.
—— archdeacons of, 252.
—— bishops of, 214, 263.
—— estates of, 264.

Glendalough, union with Dublin, 217, 263.
Glenmalure. 67.
Godwine, Earl, 52.
Gothred of Man, 115.
Grace, family of, 98, 188, 285.
Graigenemanagh, 13.
Graves, Rev. J., 14, 74, 130.
Greek at Glendalough, 178.
Gregory IX., Pope, 262.

HACO, King, 281.
Hall's *Picturesque Ireland*, 67, 70, 74, 75, 78.
Hanmer, J., 102, 236.
Hardiman's *Hist. of Galway*, 213
—— *Stat. of Kilk.*, 328, 337, 338.
Harding, Robert, 56.
—— descendants of, 56, 57, 58.
Hardy, Sir T. D., 255.
Harold, Earl, at Dublin, 52.
Harold's Cross, 220.
Harris's (W.) *Hibernica*, 79, 100, 116, 118.
—— *Hist. of Dublin*, 110.
Hennessy (W. M.), 2, 360.
Henry I., 28.
Henry II., 1, 74, 98.
—— arrival in Dublin of, 134-49.
—— character of reign, 121-26.
—— Church organization of, 144.
—— departure for Ireland, 129, 130.
—— —— from Ireland, 149.
—— dress of, 143.
—— edict of, 123.
—— estimate of bishops, 200, 201.
—— legal organization of, 147, 148.
—— motives for conquest of Ireland, 125.
—— palace at Dublin, 135, 136.
—— preparations for conquest, 126-29.
—— social improvements of, 148.
—— statute of, 148.
—— submission of Irish princes to, 134.
Henry III., 236.
—— favourites of, 296.
—— letters of, 261, 262.
—— Troubles of, Lect. XII.
Henry of London, Archbishop, Lect. XI., 249.

Henry as a judge, 254.
—— of London as a sportsman, 259-62.
—— as Archdeacon of Stafford, 254, 271.
—— career of, 252-74.
—— election of, 251.
—— title of Scorch-Villein, 264.
Heraclius, Patriarch, 224.
Heretics, Irish, 374.
Holy Cross Abbey (*see* Abbeys).
Hook's (Dean) *Archbishops of Cant.*, 207.
Hore, H. F., 86.
Horses, Irish, 133, 134.
Hospitallers, Knights, 246.
Hothom, 329.
Hounds, episcopal, 259.
Households, episcopal, 144.
Hoveden, Roger de, *Chronica* (*see* Chronicle).
Howard's *Hist. of Irish Excheq.*, 152.
Howth, Earl of, 236.
Hugh the Illuminator, 375.

INNIS-CLERAUN, 350, 366.
Innis-Loughlan, Fort of, 6.
Innis-Murry, 350.
Innocent III., Pope, 217.
Inspeximus, 195, 217.
Iona, 346, 348, 349, 350.
Irene, Empress, 8.
Irish Archæological Miscell., 6, 13, 14
Irishtown, 221.
Isabella, daughter of Princess Eva, 294, 305.
Isles, bishopric of (Glendalough), 210.

JESUS, staff of, 21.
Joanna, Queen, 281.
Joceline, 279.
John XXII., Pope, 324.
John de Gray, Bishop of Norwich, 9, 242-50.
John, King, in Ireland, 242.
John, Prince, charters to Dublin archbishop, 217, 219.
—— in Ireland, 163, 213, 217.
John of Salisbury, *Epp.*, 31.

Joly's (Rev. J. S.) *Bridge of Athlone*, 10.
—— *Our Church Bell*, 10.
Journal, Atlantis, 79.
—— *Dublin Penny*, 14, 74.
—— *Irish Penny*, 367.
—— *Kilk. Archæol.*, 14, 74, 79, 82, 86, 97, 99, 102, 130, 369.
—— *Roy. Arch. and Hist. Soc. of Ireland*, 113.
—— *Ulster Archæol.*, 277, 285, 292.
Judges, itinerant, 208, 254.
Justice, Lord Chief, office of, 154. 155.
Justiciaries, 152, 154.
—— origin of, 154.
Juxon, Bishop, 259.

KAVANAGH, Donall, 75-85, 113.
Keating's *Hist. of Ireland*, 4, 180.
Keller's *Lake Dwellings*, 285.
Kells, glebe land of, 84.
—— Synod of, 177, 180.
Kieran, St., 346, 366.
Kildare, war of, 297, 306.
—— authorities for, 305.
Kilkea Castle, 166.
Kilkenny Castle, records at, 171.
Kilkenny, Statute of, 337-39, 377.
Kilmore, castle of, 287.
—— diocese of, 285.
Kilronan, 362.
King-Harman, Col., 3.
King (W.), Archbishop, 212, 265.
King's (Rev. R.) *Ch. Hist.*, 325.
Kinsale, 72.
Kinsaley, parish of, 73.
Kinsellagh, mistake about, 72, 73.
—— tribe of, 73, 131.
Kyteler, Dame Alice, 374.

LACROIX'S *Manners of Middle Ages*, 137, 141, 143, 144.
Lacy, Hugh de, sen., 159-70.
—— appearance of, 165.
—— castle of, 166, 234.
—— charter to, 151.
—— death of, 169.
—— marriage of, 159, 161, 176, 168.
—— sons of, 235.
Lacy, Hugh de, jun., 277, 279.

INDEX. 387

Lacy, Hugh de, jun., rebellion of, 280-93.
—— triumph of, 292, 293.
Laindon, 315.
Lambeth Palace, origin of, 272.
Lamlash, 281.
Larne, 235.
Lateran Council, 190, 260.
La Touche (Dr. J. J.), *Report* of, 26, 39, 73.
Laurence (Sir Almeric de St.), 236.
Leabhar Breac (Speckled Book), 272.
Lecan, *Book* of, 371.
—— *Yellow Book* of, 372.
Leech, Archb. of Dublin, 374.
Leia, Peter de, Bishop, 32, 40.
Leighlin Bridge, 88, 161.
—— Black Castle of, 88.
Leighlin, Old, 88.
—— cathedral of, 88, 89.
Leinster, ancient extent of, 14.
—— *Book of*, 2, 178.
—— Mount, 65, 88.
Leland's *Hist. of Ireland*, 321, 329, 341.
Leo X., Pope, 378.
—— excludes Celtic clergy from St. Patrick's, 379.
Leperstown (Leopardstown), 100, 101.
Leprosy in Ireland, 100, 101.
Liber Albus of Christ Church, 25, 26.
Liber Niger Alani, 25, 26, 108, 142, 179.
—— of Christ Church, 25.
Liberties of Dublin, 238, 239.
Lindsay's *Coinage of Ireland*, 52.
Lionel, Duke of Clarence, 337, 338.
Llewellyn, Prince, 236, 287, 289, 297.
Loftus, Dudley, 114, 314, 378.
—— *Annals* of, 114, 153.
—— career of, 153.
—— edits Syriac liturgies, 153.
Loftus, Sir Adam, 252.
Lord Lieutenants, origin of, 152.
—— succession of, 162.
Louth, monastery of, 183.
Lucius III., Pope, 209.
—— bull of, 209.
Luke, Archbishop of Dublin, 8, 218, 251.

Lynch's *Legal Institutions*, 151.

MacCoghlan, Bishop of Clonmacnois, 367-69.
—— family of, 367-69.
MacFirbis, family of, 371-73.
MacGillamocholmog, 8, 85, 118.
MacMurrough, Dermot, 2.
—— ability of, 107.
—— birth of, 20.
—— character of, 20-3, 91.
—— charter of, 181.
—— death of, 114.
—— eldest son of, 84, 85, 182.
—— escape of, 48.
—— favourite son of, 75.
—— grave of, 66.
—— invades Ossory, 80-9.
—— letter to Strongbow, 94.
—— murder of father of, 112.
—— returns to Ireland, 65.
—— visits Henry II, 60-2.
Mado x, *Hist. of Exchq.*, 127, 154.
Magnus of Denmark, 96.
Malachy, St., 361.
Malone, family of, 360.
Manobeer, castle of, 29.
Mant' (Bishop) *Ch. Hist.*, 315.
Manx Church, 203, 370.
Marisco, Geoffrey de, 75, 228, 297-306.
Marquardt's *Röm. Staatsverwaltung*, 156.
Marquardt and Mommsen's *Röm. Alterth.*, 156.
Marriage of clergy, 32-4, 361-63.
Marsh's (Archbp.) Library, 179, 259, 314, 378.
Marshall (Mareschal) family, 293, 295.
—— property of, 306.
—— Richard, Earl of Pembroke, 296.
—— —— Welsh war of, 297.
—— —— his war of Kildare, 297-306.
—— Wm., sen., Earl of Pembroke, 150, 277, 294.
—— —— marriage of, 294.
—— Wm., jun., Earl of Pembroke, 281, 283, 284, 295.
—— —— campaign in Ireland, 284

Mason's *Hist. of St. Patrick's*, 223, 226, 272.
Matilda, Empress, 61.
Mayo, Earls of, 337.
Meath and Kildare, wars of, Lect. XII.
Meath, diocese of, 160.
—— palatinate of, 159, 160.
Mercer's Hospital, 100.
Michael of Kildare, Friar, 333.
Mills, Mr. J., 179, 186, 226, 264.
Minstrels, 338.
Mommsen's *Roman Provinces*, trans. by Dickson, 156.
Monasteries, Anglo-Saxon, 351.
—— Celtic, 350, 351.
Monastic chapters, 270, 272.
Monasticon Hibernicum (see Archdall).
Morison, Fynes, 6.
Morrin's *Cal. Pat. Rolls*, 359, 368.
Mountmaurice, Hervey de, 74.
Munch's *Norske Folks Historie*, 281.
Mynchin fields, 110.

NASMYTH, James, 375.
Nesta, 28.
Niall of the Nine Hostages, 4.
Nicholas, Saint, dedications to, 345.
Nicholas the chaplain, 145.
Nicholls and Taylor's *Bristol Past and Present*, 54, 55, 57, 59.
Nonant, Hugh de, 271.
Norbury, Earl of, 170.
Norway, King of, and Ireland, 281.

O'BRIAN, dynasty of, 5.
O'Brollaghan, Flaherty, Bishop of Derry, 347.
O'Conor, family of, 5.
—— Cathal, 240, 281.
—— Hugh, 289, 290.
—— Phelim, 365.
—— Roderick, 22, 82, 115, 194, 240.
—— —— attacks Dublin, 115.
—— —— invades Leinster, 90.
—— Rose, 286, 288.
—— Torlogh, 8, 10, 11, 13.
Octavian, Card., 213.
O'Curry, *Lectt.*, 2, 3, 17, 373.
O'Dogherty, Abbot Odo, 363.
—— Catherine, 363.

O'Donnel, family of, 346.
O'Donovan, Dr. John, 3, 14, 79, 289.
—— *Ord. Surv. Lett.*, 245, 362.
—— Pref. *Ann. Four Masters*, 371.
—— *Topog. Poems*, 285, 310.
O'Flaherty's *Ogygia*, 75.
O'Hanlon, Rev. J., 191.
O'Loughlin, Donnall, 3, 4.
O'Naghten, sept of, 358.
O'Neill, Shane, 328.
O'Neills, the, 134, 363.
—— and Ulster, 291.
O'Phelan, 99, 106.
Orange Society, 291.
Ord. Surv. Corresp. in *R. I. A.*, 65, 66, 89, 99.
O'Reilly, country of, 285.
—— tribe of, 285, 288.
Ormerod's *Cheshire*, 157.
Ormond, Earl of, 339, 341.
O'Roddy, family of, 361, 362, 366.
O'Rourke, Tiernan, 12, 20.
—— death of, 161.
O'Ryan, 99.
Ossory, bishop of, 377.
—— kingdom of, 82, 83.
O'Toole, St. Laurence, 113, 116.
—— attends Lat. Counc., 190.
—— career of, Lect. VIII.
—— charter of, 153.
—— *Lives* of, 177, 187.
—— palace of, 113, 114, 178, 179.
O'Tooles, 374.
Oughter, Lough, 286.
Outlaw, William, 374.
Overton's *Life in Eng. Ch.*, 259.

PALATINATES, 157, 276.
Pale, meaning of, 328.
Palgrave, Sir F., 136, 254, 271, 272.
Pallium, 210.
Parchment, 144.
Parliament, Irish, 312, 319-21.
—— of Wales, 157.
Parsonstown, 367.
Pass of Plumes, 87.
Patrick's, St., cathedral of, 221.
—— as a collegiate church, 222.
—— as a university, 375.
—— consecration of, 222.

Patrick's, St., precedence of canons in, 273.
—— —— origin of, 222.
Paris, Matthew, *Chron. Maj.*, 256, 257, 289.
—— *Hist. Angl.*, 249, 257, 288.
Peerages, palatine, 158, 167.
Penkridge, deanery of, 265.
Peter des Roches, Bishop of Winch., 296, 297, 298.
Petrie, Dr., 184.
—— *Life*, by W. Stokes, M.D., 6, 13, 51, 184.
Petronilla, 374.
Phœnix Park, 260.
Photius, 17.
Pilgrim, The, 379.
Pinkerton, John, 354.
Pipe Roll Society, 62.
—— accounts, 124.
Poaching, mediæval, 261.
Poddle, river, 110, 140.
Policy, Want of continuous Irish, 162, 164, 165.
Portionist rectors, 35.
Powers, family of, 310.
Poynings, Sir Edward, 339-42.
Precedents of Armagh, 314.
Prefects, Augustal, of Egypt, 155, 156.
Prendergast, Maurice de, 80, 88.
—— quarrel with Dermot, 91-3.
Princes, Irish, loyalty of, 282.
Princesses, Irish, and foreign nobles, 96, 161.
Prynne's *Records*, 229.
Pue's *Occurrences*, 247.

RANDON (Randown), castle of, 243, 245, 246.
—— description of, 246.
Raphoe Cathedral, 199.
Raymond le Gros, 98, 124, 173, 188.
Record Comm. *Report*, A.D. 1810-15, 26.
Record system, English, 258.
Ree, Lough, description of, 243-45.
Reeves, Bishop, 350, 353-59.
—— *Adamnan's Columba*, 349.
—— *Antiqq. of Down and Connor*, 101, 279, 316, 317.
—— *Colton's Visit.*, 362, 363.

Reeves, Bishop, *Diocese of Dublin and Glendalough*, 14, 180, 209.
—— on *Abbatial Succession*, 349.
—— on *the Culdees*, 350, 353-59.
—— on *Townland Distribution*, 240.
Refert Church, 177.
Regan, Maurice, 2, 21.
—— poem of, 25, 55, 72, 77, 98, 100, 102, 106, 113.
Reginald's Tower, 106.
Register of All Saints, ed. Butler, 118, 184.
—— of Malmesbury, 228.
—— of St. Thomas's Abbey, 25, 26.
Reid's *Hist. Presb. Church*, 353.
Renzi, Sir Matt. de, 368.
Repertorium Viride, 26, 100, 114, 185, 186, 226.
Report of Church (Irish) Comm., 1868, 263.
—— of Munic. Corp. Comm. of Dublin, 1835, 224.
—— Record Comm., 26.
Retrospective Review, 375.
Rhymers, 338.
Rhys, Prince of S. Wales, 141.
Ricart's *Kalendar*, 59.
Richey's *Short History*, 115, 137.
Robertson's (J. G.) *Antiqq. of Kilkenny*, 84.
Roche family, legend of, 78.
Rogers's (Thor.) *Six Cent. of Work*, 127.
Roses, Wars of, Lect. XIV., 312.
—— Irish nobles in, 339.
Ross, walling of, 305.
Rott. Chartt., 8.
—— *Curiæ Regis*, 136, 254, 271, 272.
—— *Litt. Patent.*, 255.
Royal supremacy, 200, 313, 317.
Ryan's *Carlow*, 166.
Rymer's *Fædera*, 136, 262.

SARUM, Use of, 197.
Saviour, St., Priory of, 351.
Schools, Celtic, 372, 374.
Scotland, *New Stat. Acct.* of, 349.
Scutage, 126, 127.
Seam, as a measure, 133.
Seebohm's *Village Communities*, 14
Selden's *Office of Chanc.*, 154.

INDEX.

Selden's *Titles of Honour*, 157.
Sepulchre, St., Church of (Cambridge), 224.
—— Manor of, 113, 139, 220, 224, 225, 238.
—— Palace of, 223, 224.
Seyer's *Memorials of Bristol*, 58.
Shaen, Sir J., 247.
Shane Castle, 4.
Shirley's *Territ. of Farney*, 286.
Simnel, Lambert, 340.
Sitric, of Dublin, 195.
—— of Man, 96.
—— of Waterford, 106.
Skelton, Rev. P., 15.
Slavery in Ireland, 181.
Slieve Gullion, 291.
—— Margy, 86, 88.
Smith, Robert, 88.
Smith's *Waterford* (*see* Waterford).
Sodor and Man, see of, 348, 349.
Staff of Jesus, 21, 33, 198.
—— of St. Cyric, 33.
Stillorgan, 100.
Stores in Ireland, military, 283.
Striguil, Castle of, 97.
Strongbow, birth of, 96.
—— burial of, 172.
—— capture of Dublin, 113.
—— character of, 62, 63.
—— charters of, 97, 114, 122, 123.
—— dominion of, 150.
—— invasion of, 105.
—— Lord Lieutenant, 170-74.
—— marriage of, 107.
Stuart's *Hist. of Armagh*, 292.
Stubbs, Bishop, *Constit. Hist.*, 20, 29, 38, 121, 127.
—— *Lectures on Med. Hist.*, 253.
—— *Mem. of St. Dunstan*, 355.
—— preface to *Benedict of Peterborough*, 232.
Sweetman's (H. S.) *Calendars*, 26, 124, 137, 140, 143, 152.
Swift, Dean, 375.
Swinfield, Bishop, *Household Roll* of, 133, 137, 141, 143.
Synods, mediæval, 211, 376, 377.
Systems, Irish Legislative, by Dr. Ball, 320.

TANISTRY, 115, 329.

Taxation, clerical, 316, 371.
Templars, Knights, 131, 299.
Temple Church, 224.
Templemore, 348.
Termonfeckin, 363.
Theiner's *Vet. Mon.*, 46, 258, 374, 377, 378.
Thomas-Court, 238.
Tintern Abbey, 74.
Tipperary, Palatinate of, 158.
Tirbrun, 314.
Tithes, division of, 369, 370.
—— introduction of, 146.
Tonsure, 346, 352.
Towns, Irish, 304.
—— League of, 304.
Transubstantiation, 373.
Travers, Robert, Bp. of Killaloe, 314.
Trees in churchyards, 142, 143.
Trench, Archbishop, 154.
Tricycling in Ireland, 81, 105.
Trim, *Hist.* of, ed. Butler, 166.
—— castle of, 234, 284.
Tuathas, 309.
Turkil, family of, 15, 16, 73, 113, 118, 195.

UAREIRGHE-O'NAGHTEN, 358.
Ulidia, 291.
Ulster, character of, 235.
—— conquest by De Courcy, 237.
—— description of in 1586, 292, 328.
—— earldom of, 237, 277, 337.
—— extent of, 291.
—— kingdom of, 235.
Ultonia, 291.
Uniat Greeks, 179.
Union parliament and Edward III., 341.
University of Dublin, 374, 375.
—— of Paris, 31.
Ussher, *Antiqq. of Brit. Ch.*, 358.
—— on *Corbes and Herenachs*, 34, 226.
—— *Rel. of Anc. Irish*, 179, 373.
—— studious life of, 187.
—— *Sylloge*, 192, 193, 199.

VALLANCY, General, 79.
Visitations, abbatial, 347, 364.

Visitations, episcopal, 347, 362, 363.

WALES, connexion with Ireland, 49-62.
—— Irish clergy in, 49.
Wallop, Sir H., 194.
Walsh, Rev. R., *Fingal and its Churches*, 49.
Walsh, Right Hon. J. E., *Ireland Sixty Years Ago*, 89.
Walter of Coventry, *Memorials of*, 208.
Warbeck, Perkin, 340.
Ward, Bishop Seth, 259.
Ware, Sir James, 371, 372.
—— *Antiqq.*, 214.
—— *Bishops*, 79.
Waterford, capture of, 106.
—— *Hist.* of, ed. Smith, 99, 101.
—— wine at, 133.
Wattle work, Irish, 135.
Wax, 128, 144.
Welsh Church, Lect. II.
—— resemblance to Irish, 33, 34, 51.
Welsh princes in Ireland, 51.
Wesley, John, 332.
Wexford, abbey of (Selsker), 78.

Wexford, castle of, 75.
—— *Directory* of (Bassett's), 75, 78, 79.
—— grant of, 64.
—— mediæval trade of, 78.
—— siege of, 75-80.
—— Stat. Survey of, 79.
—— topography of, 75.
—— walls of, 76.
Whately, Archbp., 225.
Wilde, Sir W., *Beauties of Boyne and Blackwater*, 166.
—— on *Crannogs*, 285.
—— *Report* on Irish Diseases and Deaths, 101, 141.
Wilkins' *Concilia*, 79, 143, 192, 267.
William of Newburgh, *Hist.* of, 196, 200-4, 224.
William the Conqueror, 52, 53.
Wimund, Bishop of Man, 201-4.
Winchester, see of, 128.
Wogan, Sir John, 319, 320, 322.
Woods in ancient Leinster, 86.
York, Cathedral of, 356.
—— St. Leonard's at, 356.
—— St. Peter's at, 356.

www.ingramcontent.com/pod-product-compliance
Lightning Source LLC
Chambersburg PA
CBHW051742300426
44115CB00007B/671